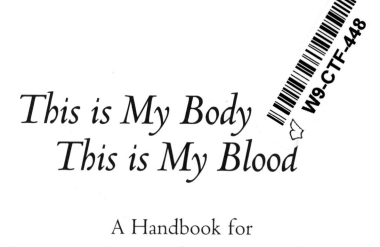

This is My Body
This is My Blood

A Handbook for
Getting to Know and Love the Holy Mass

Marie Diane Guay

(Jn 6:54) "Whoever eats my flesh and drinks my blood has eternal life, and I will raise him on the last day." NAB

THE ARTIST CHILD
MONTEREY, CALIFORNIA

Copyright © 2005 Marie Diane Guay, The Artist Child

ISBN:0-9749553-0-2

Published and Distributed by
The Artist Child
P.O.Box 2032
Monterey, CA,
93942-2032 U.S.A.

www.theartistchild.com

Printed in 2006 in Michigan, U.S.A.

ACKNOWLEDGMENT

This text is the fruit of my readings and the expression of my prayers and liturgical experience. Unless the text is marked as being a direct reference to Church teachings or a quotation taken from Church documents, it is in no way binding to the laws of the Church.

FORWARD

I want to express my gratitude to a few individuals for their help and support. They are: Father Felix J. Migliazzo of the Monterey diocese in California; Father Roland Bacon of the Sherbrooke diocese in Quebec province; Father Roger Tougas, Assumptionist from Sillery in Quebec province; Mr. Andre Couture, founder and driving force behind Saint-Raphael Publishing of Sherbrooke in Quebec province; and Christine Anne Mugridge, author and publisher from Hermitage Press, Santa Rosa, California, who encouraged me to publish this book.

I am grateful to my parents for raising me in the faith and taking me to Mass when I was a child. I am especially grateful to my husband for his precious support and encouragement.

I dedicate this book to our beloved Pope John Paul II who kept on showing us 'The Way' in today's jungle of religious and moral issues, and to the Holy Father, Pope Benedict XVI, who for many years has been a protector of the Truth, and of the treasures of the Catholic faith. Thank you Holy Fathers for continually reminding us and confirming to us the liturgical guidelines needed, so that the Holy Mass may be uniformly and reverently celebrated throughout the Catholic Church according to the tradition established by our Lord Jesus Christ.

Finally, I also dedicate this book to the youth, whom God loves and calls to be the living stones of the Church. In your life, may you be seduced by God's love and nothing else.

NOTES TO THE READER

1) The use of the masculine gender has been chosen for brevity.

2) Scripture quotations are preceded by their scriptural references to emphasize that the source of the quotation is the Word of God.

3) Scripture quotations are taken from *The Catholic Edition of the Revised Standard Version of the Bible*, and *The New Revised Standard Version of the Bible: Catholic Edition*, except when marked 'NAB', which indicates quotations taken from the *New American Bible*.

4) The use of this sign '✢' indicates excerpts taken from *The Roman Missal*, more specifically, except if otherwise noted, it refers to excerpts taken from the *General Instruction of the Roman Missal* (GIRM), third edition (2002). The associated footnotes at the bottom of the page give the reference from both the second and the third edition of the *GIRM.* They appear and are to be read as follows:
e.g. GIRM [259] 296;
    General Instruction of the Roman Missal;
    article no. 259 of the second edition of *The Roman Missal;*and
    article no. 296 of the third edition of *The Roman Missal.*

5) Excerpts taken from the *Order of Mass* found in 'Part Three, The Liturgy of the Mass,' are marked 'OM' and are taken from the second edition of *The Roman Missal,* published in 1974. The complete third edition of the *Roman Missal - GIRM and Order of the Mass -* issued in Latin in 2000, is yet to be issued in English. Thus, the reader might find some slight differences between the texts of the *Order of Mass* found in this book and those that will be found in the third edition of the *Roman Missal.*

iv

LETTERS OF APPRECIATION

Letter from Father Roland Bacon
of the diocese of Sherbrooke in Quebec
*A marvelous way to understand better and
better the liturgy of the Holy Mass*

We all know that the most important prayer of our Catholic religion is the Holy Mass. At the celebration of the Eucharist we join the Lord Jesus, we pray with Him to the Father, and we pray together as a community, a Church. We make present, we perpetuate till the end of time, the death and resurrection of Jesus Christ, our Savior.

We have surely noticed that during the Holy Mass there are multitudes of signs we don't even understand. How can a sign talk to us, if we are not aware of its significance? A sign is useless if we don't know what it means. We easily admit that to give life to a sign, a symbol, we must be able to read it correctly.

We so often have a lot of questions about the liturgy of the Mass, but we don't know where to find the answers to them.

What is the meaning of the altar?
Why should the faithful be able to clearly see the altar?
Why is there a special pulpit to proclaim the Word of God?
Why does the priest wear a special vestment to celebrate the Holy Mass?
What are the origins of the vestments and the meaning of their colors?
Why do we kneel, stand and sit?
Why do we begin the Eucharist and all our prayers with the sign of the Cross?

We could add so many other questions about the liturgy, but still don't know where to find the answers.

In her book *This is My Body, This is My Blood,* Mrs. Marie Diane Guay answers clearly many of our questions and she does it so pertinently and so justly because she took the answers out of the explanations given by the Holy Church in the *General Instruction* of the new *Roman Missal* and other Church documents.

I read the manuscript of Mrs. Guay, and I recommend the reading of her book, without reservation, to all those who want to know more about the liturgy, and most of all who want to understand more and more the liturgy of the Holy Mass.

We appreciate what we know and understand...
... but we remain so indifferent to what we ignore.

Let us make an end to our ignorance or misunderstanding of so many signs of the Holy Mass, the most important liturgical action of our Catholic faith. We'll surely find out that the Holy Mass can become more and more interesting, and, most of all, more and more profitable to our spiritual life.

Mrs. Guay deserves our thanks and congratulations for her so practical work. May the Lord Bless her and all the readers of her book.

Roland Bacon, priest
Sherbrooke, Quebec

Letter from Rev. Felix J. Migliazzo
Chaplain Ave Maria Convalescent Hospital
Monterey, CA.

Marie Diane,

I deeply appreciated the opportunity to have read your magnificent treatise, *This is My Body, This is My Blood.*

I have read once, and sometimes twice, this extraordinary masterpiece. What a perfect tool for those in the R.C.I.A. Program!

Actually, I have been reeducated and refreshed on so many facets of the Mass, its History, its Liturgy and so many elements for *Catechesis on the Mass.*

The *Holy Rosary,* my favorite prayer, as a summary of the Gospel, is just perfect.

I treasure this copy of *This is My Body, This is My Blood* and in all humility, I feel so incompetent to evaluate it, as it should be. I admire you for the tireless effort and time you have spent to produce a book that hopefully will be in the hands of our Christian community.

Prayerfully,

Father Felix
Rev. Felix J. Migliazzo,
Monterey diocese, California.

TABLE OF CONTENTS

PART THREE

Let Us Rediscover the Holy Mass... step by step

INTRODUCTORY RITES (sequel)

Liturgy of the Eucharist AΩ

PART FIVE
Elements for Catechesis on the Holy Mass
Let Us Test our Knowledge

QUESTIONS & ANSWERS ABOUT...

QUESTIONS & ANSWERS...

... FOR LAY MINISTERS ABOUT LITURGICAL MINISTRIES

ILLUSTRATIONS

PREFACE

Why does one choose to attend Mass? Even though we might have been blessed with a Catholic upbringing, in today's world attending Mass is really a personal choice. These days one who does not practice his faith will not suffer social detriments as he would have in times past. On the contrary, today's society often mocks or even despises one who mentions his faith or religious practice.

We attend Mass because we love the Lord and want to render unto Him due worship. We attend Mass to acknowledge our need for salvation and to celebrate our hope for resurrection. We attend Mass to gather and pray with people with whom we share the same faith, the same creed, which makes us feel connected in God. We attend Mass because we like to go into the house of God, and to fill our soul and heart with holy thoughts. We enjoy singing with the music and praising God. We like the liturgy and the rituals of the Holy Mass. They have become for us familiar references that we use to direct our praises and prayers to God. We anticipate answers from the Lord through the scripture readings and the homily, and from our heart to heart with the Lord, especially at the time of Communion. We attend Mass so that we may lift up our lives to the Father, offering Him our joys and sorrows, trusting that Christ will make our load lighter as He offered to do. *(Mt 11:28)"Come to me, all you that are weary and are carrying heavy burdens, and I will give you rest."* We attend Mass because we want to give thanks to the Father Who provides all things for us. We attend Mass because God calls us. *(Jn 10:27)"My sheep hear my voice, and I know them, and they follow me."* We attend Mass because it is an essential part of our relationship with God, Whose love for us is pure and will last eternally. We attend Mass because we believe that it pleases the Father and that He gives us His love most especially by means of the Body and Blood of Christ. We attend Mass because we believe that God is there really present.

According to who we are and where we are in our relationship with the Lord, we might have high expectations towards the Church and the Holy Mass. If that is your case, then you should be involved in serving God in your parish or elsewhere in the Church. *(Mt 9:37)"The harvest is plentiful but the laborers are few."* If there is a fire in your heart burning with love for God... *(Lk 12:49)"I came to bring fire to the earth, and how I wish it were already kindled!"* ... know that you are blessed and be thankful. How can one be so blessed and not say 'yes' to the Lord's request? *(Lk 1:38)"Let it be with me according to your word."* Maybe that is why I was pleased to say 'yes' when the Lord asked me to write this book, *This is My Body, This is My Blood.*

Marie Diane Guay
a.m.d.g. - *Ad Majorem Dei Gloriam*
For the Greater Glory of God

Part One

Judaic Heritage

Let Us Discover Our Liturgical Roots

The Origins of the Holy Mass
&
The True Priestly Heritage

The Judaic Origins of the Church

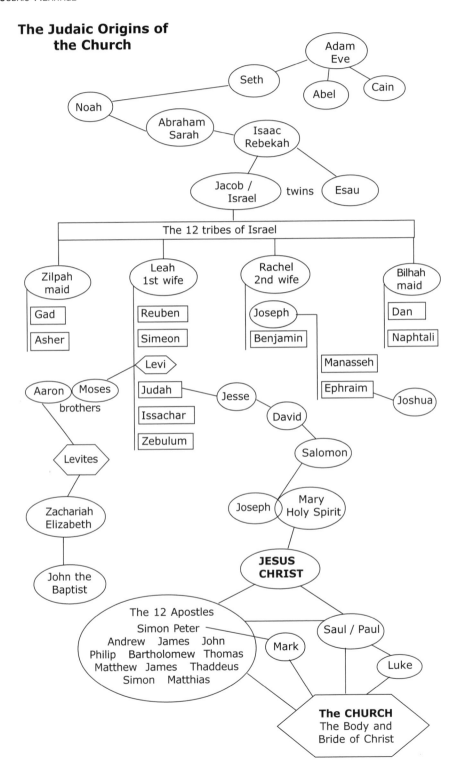

Judaic Heritage
Introduction

When God created man, He did not abandon him on Earth like an orphan. On the contrary, throughout the ages, God the Father has faithfully kept on trying to establish and to maintain a relationship with man. When God created us, He put His seal of love on our heart, thus establishing in us the immutable desire to find perfect love, that is, the desire to find Him, our God and Creator. *(2Co 1:21-22)"[He] has anointed us, by putting his seal on us and giving us his Spirit in our hearts as a first installment."*

According to the Bible, in the time of Enoch, Adam and Eve's grand-child, people were already praying to the Lord. *(Gen 4:26)"At that time men began to call upon the name of the LORD."* Down through the generations, from Adam and Eve to Jesus and Mary, and now to us, the Lord has mercifully and faithfully reached out to us, the fallen ones, whom He loves so much because we are His creation.

God had chosen the Israelites to be His people, and He made a covenant with them through Abraham their Patriarch. He promised them His protection if they would stay faithful to His commandments, which He taught them through His prophets. *(2Kg 17:13)"Yet the LORD warned Israel and Judah by every prophet and every seer, saying; Turn from your evil ways and keep my commandments and my statutes, in accordance with all the law that I commanded your ancestors and that I sent to you by my servants the prophets."* But as the bible reveals, many among the people of God turned away from the Lord and His covenant to serve pagan gods. And when the people of God started to suffer, they turned to the Lord again. Sound familiar?

Through His prophets, God promised to send the Israelites the Messiah, the Anointed One, One who would be born among them and be their Savior. Christ, the Messiah, did come and was born among the Israelites. But since Israel rejected Him as their Savior, Christ then offered salvation to all of humanity. Christ instituted the new covenant promised by the Father; a covenant written on our hearts through which the Father reveals Himself and His mercy. *(Heb 8:6-13)"[Jesus] is the mediator of **a better covenant**, which has been **enacted through better promises**. For if that first covenant had been faultless, there would have been no need to look for a second one. God finds fault with them when he says:*
"The days are surely coming, says the Lord, when I will establish a new covenant with the house of Israel and with the house of Judah; not like the covenant that I made with their ancestors, on the day when I took them by the hand to lead them out of the

land of Egypt; for they did not continue in my covenant, and so I had no concern for them, says the Lord. **This is the covenant that I will make** *with the house of Israel after those days, says the Lord:* **I will put my laws in their minds, and write them on their hearts**, *and* **I will be their God, and they shall be my people**. *And they shall not teach one another or say to each other, 'Know the Lord,' for they shall all know me, from the least of them to the greatest. For I will be merciful toward their iniquities, and I will remember their sins no more."* [1]
In speaking of 'a new covenant,' he has made the first one obsolete. And what is obsolete and growing old will soon disappear." [bfa]

By the means of the institution of the Eucharist and of His Holy sacrifice on the Cross, Jesus Christ brought us, the new people of God, from the Passover to Easter, from the old covenant to the new covenant. *(Lk 22:20)"This cup which is poured out for you is the new covenant in my blood."*

The origins of the Holy Mass start many centuries before the night of the Last Supper when Jesus instituted the Eucharist. To find the origins of the Mass we need to look to Judaism and to the history of the Israelites. We need to go back to Moses, to Abraham, Isaac and Jacob, even to Adam and Eve, whose children, Cain and Abel, were already offering sacrifices to the Creator. *(Gen 4:3-4)"In the course of time Cain brought to the LORD an offering of the fruit of the ground, and Abel brought of the firstlings of his flock and of their fat portions. And the LORD had regard for Abel and his offering."*

So before we start studying the liturgy of the Holy Mass, let us look into the Judaic heritage of the Mass and of the Priesthood, the Priesthood through which the celebration of the Holy Sacrifice of the Mass is made possible and without which we would not have the Holy Mass.

(Ps 110:4) "You are a priest for ever after the order of Melchiz'edek."

---

1. Jer 31:31-34

The Origins of the Holy Mass

In 1997 I had the privilege to visit the basilica of Saint Peter of Rome. I was very impressed by the signs of history and of holiness of the Catholic Church. I was especially moved when I found myself standing by the tomb of Saint Peter, above which the construction of the basilica was begun in 323. Here I was, standing by the sepulcher of Saint Peter, the apostle that Jesus Christ Himself had entrusted as the first pope of His Church two thousand years ago. As I continued my visit, I realized that the magnificent altar of the basilica had been erected right over Saint Peter's sepulcher on the floor above. Thus, throughout the centuries, popes, one after the other, have continually celebrated the Holy Mass over the tomb of the first pope, and this tradition continues today during the reign of Pope Benedict XVI, the 264th successor of Saint Peter. Among all the great feelings and emotions that I experienced that day, I felt especially proud to be part of the Catholic Church that has protected, glorified and celebrated the sanctity of the Sacrifice of Jesus Christ for the past two thousand years. Indeed, as a faithful bride who keeps alive the memory of her beloved departed bridegroom, the Church has kept on offering to God the Father the memorial of the Sacrifice of His beloved Son, as Jesus Christ himself commanded: *(Lk 22:19)"Do this in remembrance of me."*

Throughout the centuries, the memorial of the Sacrifice of Jesus Christ was gradually organized into the liturgy of the Mass as it is practiced today. Although there was already considerable liturgical uniformity in the two first centuries, it was not absolute. The liturgy of the Roman rite of the Mass, which is used today, results from the liturgical reform attributed to Pope Saint Gregory I, the Great (590-604).[2] Then, in 786, Pope Adrian I, the 95th pope, issued the first Sacramentary,[3] named the 'Gregorian Sacramentary' after Pope Saint Gregory I, the Great. A uniform liturgy of the Mass was thus introduced and eventually universally adopted throughout the Catholic world.

Other modifications were made to the liturgy of the Mass during the history of the Church. The current liturgy, the new *Order of Mass*, is the fruit of a major liturgical reform initiated by the Second Vatican Ecumenical Council[4] (1962-1965). In 1969, Pope Paul VI approved a revised second edition of the *Roman Missal*. The publication of the first edition was authorized by the Council of Trent, and implemented by St. Pius V[5] in 1570. The second edition of the *Roman Missal* will soon be replaced by the third edition, which was issued in 2000 by Pope John Paul II, and still awaits its translation and publication into the many languages of the people of the Church.

2. Pope St. Gregory I, the Great (64th pope), see Part Five, Catholic Glossary.
3. Sacramentary: Missal, see Part Five, Catholic Glossary.
4. Ecumenical Councils, see Part Five, Catholic Glossary.
5. Pope St. Pius V, see Part Five, Catholic Glossary.

For centuries now, priests and faithful all over the world gather to celebrate the Eucharist together at every moment and every hour of the day, thus unceasingly making present 'the Sacrifice of the Cross' through the Holy Mass. In other words, the sacrifice of Jesus on the cross that took place two thousand years ago has never come to an end. It has kept on washing away the debts caused by our sins, and buying us eternal life, saving us from the power of darkness and from eternal death. Because of this unending Mass the Precious Blood of Christ never stops flowing on earth, thus constantly renewing Christ's victory over death and over the evil one. This unending Mass is also a continuous prayer of thanksgiving[6] to God the Father for giving us the life of His only begotten Son, Jesus Christ.

The Catholic faith and its liturgy contain many elements that have their origins in the Judaic faith and liturgy of the Old Testament; that is, the religion known for its long tradition of worshiping the One Who Is, the True God, God the Creator. When Jesus founded His Church, He did not reject the Jewish faith. On the contrary; *(Mt 5:17)"Do not think that I have come to abolish the law or the prophets; I have come not to abolish but to fulfill."* Since Jesus was raised in the Judaic faith, His teaching and His religious practices came from Judaism. Indeed, the Gospel often testifies to the fact that Jesus and His disciples honored the Jewish faith. *(Jn 18:20)"I have always taught in synagogues and in the temple, where all Jews come together."* Moreover, Jesus chose to institute the Sacrament of the Eucharist and the Sacrament of Holy Orders while celebrating with His apostles one of the most meaningful traditional Judaic feasts, the meal of the Passover. Jesus' last Passover meal has come to be commonly known as the Last Supper.

After Jesus ascended into Heaven, not only did His apostles and disciples maintain their practice of the Jewish faith—*(Acts 3:1)"Now Peter and John were going up to the temple at the hour of prayer."*—moreover, filled with the Holy Spirit they also kept on proclaiming the Good News in the synagogues as Jesus had done. *(Acts 13:5)"They proclaimed the word of God in the Jewish synagogues."* NAB After Pentecost and the evangelic missions of the apostles and disciples of Jesus Christ, the number of Christians started growing in a significant way.[7] Jesus came to bring salvation first to the Jewish people, the people of the covenant. *(Mt 10:5-6)"Go nowhere among the Gentiles, and enter no town of the Samaritans, but go rather to the lost sheep of the house of Israel."* When the Jewish authorities rejected Jesus, they rejected 'The Way' to salvation, which was then offered to all men. *(Acts 13:46.47)"It was necessary that the word of God be spoken to you first, but since you reject it and condemn yourselves as unworthy*

---

6. The word 'Eucharist' means 'thanksgiving'.
7. See the Acts of the Apostles and the Letters of Saint Paul to the early Christian communities.

of eternal life, we now turn to the Gentiles. For so the Lord has commanded us, 'I have made you a light to the Gentiles, that you may be an instrument of salvation to the ends of the earth.'" NAB *(Rom 1:16) "[The gospel] is the power of God for salvation to every one who has faith, to the Jew first and also to the Greek."*

The religious practice of the early Christian communities of the first century included both the traditional Judaic rituals as well as the new Christian rituals. *(Acts 2:46)"And day by day, attending the temple together and breaking bread in their homes, they partook of food with glad and generous hearts."* Since the temple was reserved for Judaic practices, the first Christian communities celebrated the Eucharist at home. In those days, the celebration of the Eucharist was defined as 'the breaking of the bread'.[8] The early Christian communities practiced the baptism in the water in conformity to the baptism of repentance and conversion initiated by Saint John the Baptist, the same baptism that Jesus Christ received[8a] and during which the Heavens opened and the voice of the Heavenly Father was heard. *(Mt 3:17)"This is my beloved Son, with whom I am well pleased."* NAB It is only at the end of the first century that disciples of Christ were called Christians. *(Acts 11:26)"In Antioch the disciples were for the first time called Christians."*

Already in the first century, the Roman empire felt threatened by the Christians because they kept on increasing in number. Therefore, from the first to the third century the Christians suffered great persecutions by the Romans.[9] The Jews who regarded the Christians as heretics did not hesitate to expel them from their synagogues and their communities. *(Acts 13:50)"The Jews incited the devout women of high standing and the leading men of the city, and stirred up persecution against Paul and Barnabas, and drove them out of their district."* There was a time when Saint Paul (Saul) was among those Jews who persecuted the Christians. *(Acts 8:3)"Saul was ravaging the church, and entering house after house, he dragged off men and women and committed them to prison."* Saint Paul himself says: *(Acts 22:19-20)"Lord, they themselves know that in every synagogue I imprisoned and beat those who believed in thee. And when the blood of Stephen thy witness was shed, I also was standing by and approving, and keeping the garments of those who killed him."* But then Paul had his encounter with Christ. *(Acts 22:7-8)"And I fell to the ground and heard a voice saying to me, 'Saul, Saul, why do you persecute me?' And I answered, 'Who are you, Lord?' And he said to me, 'I am Jesus of Nazareth whom you are persecuting.'"*

---

8. The breaking of the bread; celebration of the Eucharist by early Christian communities: Part Five, Church Norms, Arrangement and Furnishing of Churches, The Altar.

8a. Jesus was baptized but He Himself did not baptize: *(Jn 4:2)"It was not Jesus himself but his disciples who baptized."*

9. In 313, the emperor Constantine ended the persecutions by the Edict of Milan.

Due to the persecutions of Christians during the second and third centuries, Christianity was completely set apart from Judaism. The following text gives us a description of the Christian liturgy of the second century. *"As early as the second century we have the witness of St-Justin Martyr for the basic lines of the order of the Eucharistic celebration. They have stayed the same until our own day for all the great liturgical families. St. Justin wrote to the pagan emperor Antoninus Pius (138-161) around the year 155, explaining what Christians did:*

> *On the day we call the day of the sun [Sunday], all who dwell in the city or country gather in the same place.*
>
> *The memoirs of the apostles and the writings of the prophets are read, as much as time permits.*
>
> *When the reader has finished, he who presides over those gathered admonishes and challenges them to imitate these beautiful things.*
>
> *Then we all rise together and offer prayers* for ourselves... and for all others, wherever they may be, so that we may be found righteous by our life and actions, and faithful to the commandments, so as to obtain eternal salvation.*
>
> *When the prayers are concluded we exchange the kiss.*
>
> *Then someone brings bread and a cup of water and wine mixed together to him who presides over the brethren.*
>
> *He takes them and offers praise and glory to the Father of the universe, through the name of the Son and of the Holy Spirit and for a considerable time he gives thanks (in Greek: eucharistian) that we have been judged worthy of these gifts.*
>
> *When he has concluded the prayers and thanksgiving, all present give voice to an acclamation by saying:'Amen.'*
>
> *When he who presides has given thanks and the people have responded, those whom we call deacons give to those present the 'eucharisted' bread, wine and water and take them to those who are absent."* [10]

Isn't it remarkable how the Eucharistic celebrations of the second century resemble our celebration of the Holy Mass today?

---

10. CCC 1345, quoting St. Justin, *Apol.* 1, 65-67: *PG* 6, 428-429; the text before the asterisk (*) is from chap. 67.

Even though it was mainly the horrible persecutions of Christians that brought a final separation between Christianity and Judaism, differences in beliefs of each faith also supported the separation. Indeed, the Jews who became Christians believed that Jesus Christ was the Messiah announced by the prophets of the Old Testament. Thus, they adapted their practices of worship and prayer to reflect Christ's life and teaching; they ceased partaking in animal sacrifices and also changed the day on which they worshiped the Lord. Since Jesus Christ resurrected on a Sunday, Sunday became the Christian day to worship the Lord rather than the traditional Jewish Sabbath, which was and still is celebrated on Saturday.

Moreover, as the passion, the death, and the resurrection of Our Lord Jesus Christ took place during the feast of the Passover, then, instead of celebrating the Passover, Christians started to celebrate Holy Week and Easter during Passover, and Easter became the most important Christian feast. Because Our Lord's passion, death, and resurrection took place during the celebrations of the Passover feast, the time of the year to celebrate Easter was set, and still is, by the same tradition observed by the Jews that sets the date for the celebration of Passover. So while the Jewish Passover is celebrated on the first Saturday following the full moon of the spring equinox,[11] Easter is celebrated on the first Sunday following that same full moon (cf. CCC 1170).

So when did men start worshiping God? Throughout time and history, in all civilizations, men have always had the instinct to worship God —or whatever they understood to be God—and to make offerings and sacrifices to Him. Worshiping is such a universal and ancient tradition that it is impossible to clearly identify and date its origin. However, the only worship that is valuable and holy is the one given with a contrite heart to the true God, the Living God, God the Creator, the Triune God. And there dwells the essence of worship found in the Judaic and Christian heritage.

Let us look further into the Judaic heritage of the Catholic faith and liturgy. In the Pentateuch,[12] we find several stories about the early people of God making animal sacrifices as offerings to the living God. In the book of Genesis, the first book of the Bible, there is the famous story of Cain and Abel,[13] whose main theme revolves around their making offerings to God. *(Gen 4:4-5)"And the LORD had regard for Abel and his offering, but for Cain and his offering he had no regard."*

---

11. Equinox: day of the year when the hours of day light are equal to the hours of night. This happens twice a year, at the beginning of spring and fall.
12. Pentateuch: the first five books of the Old Testament: Genesis, Exodus, Leviticus, Numbers and Deuteronomy. It contains the history of the Israelites and their ancestors, their faith in God's Revelation and His covenant with them, His chosen people. However since Jesus Christ came to establish a New Covenant, the people of God, who were first exclusively the Israelites, extends to and also includes Christians.
13. Cain and Abel were children of Adam and Eve.

This story has become famous because of its tragic end. Indeed, Cain killed his brother Abel out of jealousy, for the Lord God preferred Abel's offering to his. Cain was banned from his home and from God's presence, he became a fugitive and a wanderer on the earth (cf. Gen 4:12). Fortunately for us, Adam and Eve gave life to other descendants, one of whom we know to be Seth. Then, several generations later, we find Seth's descendant, Noah, perpetuating this traditional ritual of making sacrificial offerings to the Lord. *(Gen 8:20)"Then Noah built an altar to the LORD, and took of every clean animal and of every clean bird, and offered burnt offerings on the altar."*

Another famous story about a sacrificial offering to God in the Old Testament takes place some two thousand years before Christ. This story tells us how Abraham, descendant of Noah, was prepared to make the greatest sacrificial offering of his life. *(Gen 22:2-3.11-12) "[God] said, "Take your son, your only son Isaac, whom you love, and go to the land of Mori'ah, and offer him there as a burnt offering upon one of the mountains of which I shall tell you." So Abraham rose early in the morning, saddled his ass, and took two of his young men with him, and his son Isaac; and he cut the wood for the burnt offering, and arose and went to the place of which God had told him. But the angel of the LORD called to him from heaven, and said, "Abraham, Abraham!" And he said, "Here am I." He said, "Do not lay your hand on the lad or do anything to him; for now I know that you fear God, seeing you have not withheld your son, your only son, from me.""*

How striking is the love of Abraham for God. Abraham was already an old man when God promised him a great offspring. *(Gen 15:5)""Look toward heaven, and number the stars, if you are able to number them." Then He said to him, "So shall your descendants be.""* And despite the fact that his wife Sarah had been barren, she gave birth to Isaac in her old age, according to God's promise.[13a] And now, Abraham was ready to give God the life of his beloved son Isaac. *(Heb 11:19)"He reasoned that God was able to raise even from the dead, and he received Isaac back as a symbol."* NAB It is as though God wanted to see if Abraham loved and trusted Him enough to give Him the life of his beloved son, as God would give to Abraham's descendants, God's people to be, the life of His only begotten Son, Jesus, so that they might receive salvation. Thus, how even more striking is the love of God the Father for us.

The Bible tells us that Isaac begot Jacob, and that God told Jacob: *(Gen 32:28)"You shall no longer be called Jacob, but Israel."* Then, according to God's promise, Abraham had a great offspring. Israel begot twelve sons from whom was born the nation of Israel, the twelve tribes, whom God called His people. And according to God's promise ... *(Isa 11:1.2.10)*

13a. God's promise that Sarah would give birth (Gen 17:16.18:10).

"A shoot shall come out from the stump of Jesse,... . The spirit of the LORD shall rest on him,... the nations shall inquire of him, and his dwelling shall be glorious."; Jesus Christ, our Lord and Redeemer, came out of the root of Jesse, one of Abraham's offspring.

From the book of Exodus, let us now look at the story of a sacrificial offering that took place some twelve hundred years before Christ. This time, it is Moses, a descendant of Abraham through Jacob and Levi, who according to the tradition of his ancestors offers an animal sacrifice to the Lord on an altar. *(Ex 24:4-8)"Moses then wrote down all the words of the LORD and, rising early the next day, he erected at the foot of the mountain an **altar** and twelve pillars for the twelve tribes of Israel. Then, having sent certain young men of the Israelites to **offer holocausts** and **sacrifice** young bulls as peace offerings to the LORD, Moses took half of the blood and put it in large bowls; the other half he splashed on the altar. Taking the **book of the covenant**, he read it aloud to the people, who answered, 'All that the LORD has said, we will heed and do.' Then he took the blood and sprinkled it on the people, saying, '**This is the blood of the covenant**[14] which the LORD has made with you in accordance with all these words of his.'"* NAB/ bfa It is interesting to note that in the midst of this holocaust ritual, Moses reads aloud for the people from the book of the covenant. As a matter of fact, since Moses had just received the laws of God and had just written them down in the book of the covenant, then, this was problably the very first time that the Word of God was ever read aloud for a gathered assembly of the people of God. This might have been the first liturgy of the Word. Eventually, proclaiming and scrutinizing the holy scriptures became a very important part of Judaism.

Most of the sacrifices that were offered to God by the Israelites at the time of the Old Testament involved the holocaust of animals. Indeed animals such as calves, **lambs**, rams, and doves were slaughtered and burned on the altar.[15] The book of Leviticus discusses different kinds of sacrificial offerings. *(Lev 7:37)"This is the law of the burnt offering, of the cereal offering, of the sin offering, of the guilt offering, of the consecration, and of the peace offerings."* This book also reveals that the purpose for making a sacrificial offering was to seek **cleansing from sin**—*(Lev 14:19)"The **priest** shall offer the sin offering, to make atonement for him who is to be cleansed from his uncleanness."* bfa—or to **give thanks** to the Lord. *(Lev 7:13)"With the sacrifice of his peace offerings for thanksgiving he shall bring his offering with cakes of leavened bread."*

---

14. The same words are used during the Mass at the time of consecration: ◆ᴼᴹ "...This is the cup of my Blood, the Blood of a new and everlasting covenant... (cf. Mk 14:24)." These are the words that consecrate the wine so it becomes the Blood of Christ.
15. The Hebrew word for altar comes from a word meaning to slaughter for sacrifice.

These sacrifices were acceptable only when performed in **compliance with the prescriptions** of the Mosaic law.[16] *(Lev 7:37.38)"This is the law of the burnt offering…, which the LORD commanded Moses on Mount Sinai."* At the time of Moses, the people of God already understood that the offering that was pleasing to God, was the one made with a **contrite heart**. *(Ex 25:1-2)"The LORD said to Moses; Speak to the people of Israel, that they take for me an offering; from every man whose **heart makes him willing** you shall receive the offering for me."* bfa

So, according to the prior quotes from the book of Leviticus, in Moses' time, two of the purposes for a **priest** to offer a **sacrifice** were **thanksgiving** and **atonement for sins.** The offerings made in thanksgiving were considered to be **peace offerings**, and required a **bread offering** as well as an animal offering, such as **lambs**, which were then sacrificed at the **altar**. *(Lev 23:19)"One male goat shall be sacrificed as a sin offering, and two yearling **lambs** as a peace offering."* NAB/ bfa The **blood** of these animals was at the center of the sacrificial ritual, and for offerings to be pleasing to God, they had to be made with a **willing heart** and in **compliance with the prescriptions** of the Mosaic law.

All of these elements are present in the liturgy of the Holy Mass. Indeed, the Eucharistic celebration is a prayer of **thanksgiving** to God the Father, during which the **priest**, in the name of the gathered assembly of the faithful, presents with a **contrite heart** an **offering of bread** and wine to God the Father at the **altar**. Then, in **atonement for sins** and in **compliance with the prescriptions** for the Rite of Holy Mass, the priest consecrates the offerings of **bread** and wine to become the Body and **Blood** of Jesus Christ, thus making present, in an **unbloody** manner, the **sacrifice** of the **Lamb** of God. Once the sacrifice is accomplished the people pray to the Lamb of God to grant them **peace**. As you see, through Jesus Christ's institution of the Eucharist until the Sacrifice of the Cross, and with the Holy Spirit guiding the Church, the essential elements of the liturgy of the Old Testament have evolved to become the liturgy of the Holy Mass.

The ritual of incensing the offerings on the altar during the Holy Mass is also a practice that originated in the Judaic liturgy of the Old Testament. The Church has even kept the same manner of incensing. *(Lev 16:12-13)"He shall take a censer full of coals of fire from the altar before the LORD, and two handfuls of crushed sweet incense, and he shall bring it inside the curtain and put the incense on the fire before the LORD, that the cloud of the incense may cover the mercy seat that is upon the covenant."*

---

16. The Mosaic Law recorded in the Pentateuch includes the civil, moral and religious laws of the Israelites.

In the Mosaic law, the prescribed ritual for reconciling with God involved the priest putting the people's sins on the head of a goat, which would then become their scapegoat. *(Lev 16:21)"Laying both hands on its head, he shall* **confess** *over it all the sinful faults and transgressions of the Israelites, and so put them on the goat's head. He shall then have it led into the desert by an attendant."* NAB/bfa As the **scapegoat** was **sent to die in the desert**, so the people's sins would also die, thus purifying their flesh but not their conscience.[16a] When Jesus, as the Priest of His own sacrifice, took upon Himself the sins of the world and let people put Him to death, He became the Victim offered in sacrifice for the sins of all. He fulfilled the Mosaic law and became the ultimate scapegoat. But so many could not, and still cannot, understand that only Jesus, the Lamb of God, can really take away sins and bring peace and reconciliation with God.

The Father chose the feast of the Passover for Jesus to fulfill the Mosaic law. This is the most significant feast for the Israelites, since it was, and still is, the celebration of their liberation from slavery and bondage in Egypt. However, Jesus' passing over to His Father brought humanity much more than liberation from human bondage. It brought us liberation from sin and evil, and saved us from eternal death.

To accomplish His plan to liberate the Israelites from the Egyptians, God gave Moses instructions that Moses was to transmit to the Israelites who were then in bondage in Egypt. These instructions explain the meaning of the feast of the Passover. *(Ex 12:3.5-8.11-13)"Every one of your families must procure for itself a lamb, one apiece for each household. The* **lamb** *must be a year-old male and* **without blemish***. Then, with the whole assembly of Israel present, it* **shall be slaughtered** *during the evening twilight. They shall* **take some of its blood** *and apply it to the two doorposts and the lintel of every house in which they partake of the lamb. That same night they shall eat its roasted flesh with* **unleavened bread** *and bitter herbs. You shall* **eat like those who are in flight***. It is the Passover of the LORD. For on this same night I will go through Egypt, striking down every first-born of the land, both man and beast, and executing judgment on all the gods of Egypt - I, the LORD! But the blood will mark the houses where you are.* **Seeing the blood, I will pass over** *you."* NAB/bfa With the blood of a lamb on their doorposts, the angels of the Lord recognized the people of God and **passed over**; thus they were spared from God's wrath, which was not so for the Egyptians.

Here are some excerpts that further describe the **feast of the Passover** as it was still celebrated in Jesus' time. *(2Ch 30:5)"They issued a decree... that everyone should come to Jerusalem to celebrate the*

16a. That which brought purification of the flesh but not of the conscience (cf. Heb 9:13-14). Only the Blood of Jesus can take away sin.

Passover in honor of the LORD, the God of Israel." *NAB* Jesus was well accustomed to this feast. *(Lk 2:41-43)"Each year his parents [Joseph and Mary] went to Jerusalem for the feast of Passover, and when he was twelve years old, they went up according to festival custom. ...Jesus remained behind in Jerusalem, but his parents did not know it."* *NAB* This is the time when Joseph and Mary had lost Jesus and after looking for Him for three days, *(Lk 2:46)"they found Him in the temple, sitting among the teachers, listening to them and asking them questions."*

In the midst of the feast of the Passover, the Jewish people celebrated the feast of **Unleavened Bread** which "*...commemorates the **haste of the departure** that liberated them from Egypt... "(CCC 1334 bfa).* It was a time to rejoice. *(2Ch 30:21)"The people of Israel who were present at Jerusalem kept the festival of unleavened bread seven days with great gladness."* On the first day of the Passover, the feast started by throwing out the leavened bread. *(Ex 12:15.16)"Seven days you shall eat unleavened bread; on the first day you shall put away leaven out of your houses. On the first day you shall hold a holy assembly, and on the seventh day a holy assembly."*

The Passover and the feast of Unleavened Bread also commemorates how **God miraculously fed His people** during their forty years exile in the desert. *(Ex 16:14-15.31.35)"When the layer of dew lifted, there on the surface of the wilderness was a fine flaky substance, as fine as frost on the ground. ... Moses said to them, "It is the bread that the LORD has given you to eat." The house of Israel called it **manna**; it was like coriander seed, white, and the taste of it was like wafers made with honey. The Israelites ate manna forty years, until they came to a habitable land; ... until they came to the border of the land of Canaan."* bfa "*...the remembrance of the manna in the desert will always recall to Israel that it lives by the bread of the Word of God (cf. Deut 8:3); their daily bread is the fruit of the promised land, the pledge of **God's faithfulness to his promises**.... "(CCC 1334 bfa).* The Lord used the exile to make His people worthy of the promised land. *(Deut 8:2.3)"...the LORD your God has led you these forty years in the wilderness, in order to **humble you, testing you to know what was in your heart**, whether or not you would keep his commandments. He humbled you by letting you hunger, then by feeding you with manna, ... in order to make you understand that one does not live by bread alone, but by every word that comes from the mouth of the LORD."* bfa

Jesus, God's Word made flesh (cf. Jn 1:14), is the bread that comes down from heaven to feed and sanctify all of us souls. *(Jn 6:32-33.35) "Amen, amen, I say to you, it was not Moses who gave the bread from heaven; my Father gives you the true bread from heaven. For the bread of God is that which comes down from heaven and gives life to the world. **I am the bread of life**."* NAB/bfa

Daily offerings were presented during the Passover. *(Lev 23:8)"On each of the seven days you shall offer an oblation to the LORD."* [NAB] Yet, a special sacrifice offering was made on the first day. *(Mk 14:12)"On the first day of the Feast of Unleavened Bread,... they sacrificed the Passover lamb."* [NAB] The sacrifice of the **Passover lambs** was not only to commemorate the night they fled from Egypt, but also an opportunity for the Israelites to be made worthy, **to be cleansed of their sins**. *(2Ch 30:17)"The Levites had to kill the Passover lamb for every one who was not clean, to make it holy to the LORD."* The slaughtered lambs were eaten on the first day of the Passover as an evening family meal, which was served with a few drinks of wine. *"The 'cup of blessing' (cf. 1 Cor 10:16) at the end of the Jewish Passover meal adds to the festive joy of wine an eschatological dimension: the messianic expectation of the rebuilding of Jerusalem. When Jesus instituted the Eucharist, he gave a new and definitive meaning to the blessing of the bread and the cup"* (CCC 1334 [bfa]).

It was not a coincidence that Jesus Christ instituted the Eucharist and was sacrificed as the **Lamb of God** [17] during the days that the traditional Passover lambs were sacrificed for the cleansing of sins. It was all part of the Father's perfect plan that Christ would offer His sacrifice amidst these meaningful Judaic settings, so that His people, Israel, would realize that Jesus was the foretold messiah, Who came to fulfill the law and the prophets (cf. Mt 5:17). Jesus' mission and teaching are the accomplishment of God's revelation and covenant with Israel. With Jesus' institution of the Eucharist, His Sacrifice, and His glorious resurrection, God transformed the feast of the Passover into the celebration of a new covenant, one that offers salvation to all men. It was also part of God's perfect plan that because of the feast of the Passover, a great number of the Jewish people would be present in Jerusalem, and thus witness the sacrifice of Jesus Christ.

In his letter to the Corinthians, Saint Paul explains the Christian meaning of the feast of the Passover and of the Unleavened Bread.[18] *(1Co 5:7-8)"Clean out the old yeast so that you may be a new batch, as you really are unleavened. For our paschal lamb, Christ, has been sacrificed. Therefore, let us celebrate the festival, not with the old yeast, the yeast of malice and evil, but with the unleavened bread of sincerity and truth."*

---

17. (1Pt 1:18.19)"You know that you were ransomed from the futile ways inherited from your ancestors, not with perishable things like silver or gold, but with the precious Blood of Christ, like that of a lamb without defect or blemish."
18. Since Jesus used unleavened bread to institute the Sacrament of the Eucharist, the Church has established that the bread to be used for the Eucharist shall be unleavened. See the bread of the Eucharist: Part Five, Church Norms, Requisites for the Celebration of the Mass, Matter of the Sacraments, The Eucharist.

Although Jesus knew that He was about to give His life in sacrifice—
*(Mt 26:2)"You know that after two days the Passover is coming, and
the Son of Man will be handed over to be crucified."*—Jesus still
chose to celebrate the Passover with His disciples. *(Lk 22:8)"Jesus
sent Peter and John, saying, "Go and prepare the Passover meal for
us that we may eat it."* Jesus chose that night, the night of His Last
Supper, to institute the memorial of the sacrifice of His own life,
offered for our salvation.

The following excerpt from the Gospel according to Saint Matthew, who
was present at the Last Supper, relates **the institution of the Eucharist**
by Jesus Christ. *(Mt 26:26-28)"While they were eating, Jesus took a
loaf of bread, and after blessing it he broke it, gave it to the disciples,
and said, "Take, eat; this is my body." Then he took a cup, and after
giving thanks he gave it to them, saying, "Drink from it, all of you; for
this is my blood of the covenant, which is poured out for many for the
forgiveness of sins.""* Such was Jesus' will and testament so that we
could inherit eternal life. Since then, in memory of Jesus' sacrifice, the
sharing of the bread and of the cup, which is communion with the Body
and Blood of Jesus, has been the center of the Church's faith.

The offerings that Jesus chose for the celebration of the Eucharist, the
bread and wine, were already present in the Jewish liturgy and had
been so for a long time. Indeed, in the first book of the bible, we find
Melchizedek presenting such an offering to God. *(Gen 14:18) "And
Mel-chiz'edek king of Salem brought out* **bread and wine**; *he was
priest of God Most High."* bfa And here is another example from the
Pentateuch. *(Num 15:8-10)"...for peace offerings to the LORD, then
one shall offer with the bull a* **cereal offering** *of three tenths of an
ephah of fine flour, mixed with half a hin of oil, and you shall offer for
the drink offering half a hin of* **wine**,... ."* bfa With Jesus Christ's new
sacrificial offering ritual, the bread and wine offerings became much
more valuable. During the celebration of the Eucharist, **by the grace
of the Father and the power of the Holy Spirit**, the bread and
wine are **changed into the Body and Blood of the Son**, Jesus
Christ. However, this miracle could not take place until the Lamb of
God had accomplished the greatest act of love by giving His life for us
on the cross. *(Heb 9:17)"For a will takes effect only at death, since it
is not in force as long as the one who made it is alive."*

The night of the Last Supper is filled with events that changed the
fate of humanity. The most important Jewish feast, the Passover,
became the scene of the institution of the Eucharist, the ritual of the
New Covenant. *(Mk 14:24)"This is my blood of the covenant, which
is poured out for many."* This New Covenant was soon inherited by a
new and extended people of God, to whom was given the promise of

eternal life. *(Jn 6:54)"He who eats my flesh and drinks my blood has eternal life."* When He instituted the Eucharist, Jesus also instituted a new priesthood to perpetuate the sacrificial ritual of the New Covenant. *(Lk 22:19)"Do this in memory of me."* NAB Then, after the Last Supper, that same night at Gethsemane, Jesus laid down His life for us—*(Mt 26:53)"Do you think that I cannot appeal to my Father, and he will at once send me more than twelve legions of angels?"* —so that the Father's will be done. *(Mt 26:39)"Yet not what I want but what you want [Father]."* Animated by the desire to do His Father's will and by the love He has for all human souls, Jesus takes on Himself all the sins of the world and becomes the ultimate scapegoat and the ultimate Passover lamb, and lets Himself be slain in sacrifice for the sins of humanity. *(Isa 53:7)"Like a lamb that is led to the slaughter, and like a sheep that before its shearers is silent, so he did not open his mouth."*

With the sacrifice of the Eucharist, Jesus Christ brought humanity into a whole new era where animal sacrifices did not have a place anymore. Animal sacrifices could never take away the sins of anyone. The sacrificial ritual of the Lamb of God is the only sacrifice acceptable at the Father's altar for washing away sins. *(Jn 1:29)"Behold, the Lamb of God, who takes away the sin of the world."* After the sacrifice of the cross, animal sacrifices could not be justified anymore. *(Heb 10:10) "And it is by God's will that we have been sanctified through the offering of the body of Jesus Christ once for all."*

Although the Jewish people were offering sacrifices in accordance with the Mosaic law, their offerings could never be valuable enough to meet the price required to free their souls. No sacrifice could, except the sacrifice of the Lamb of God. *(Heb 9:13-14)"For if the sprinkling of defiled persons with the blood of goats and bulls and with the ashes of a heifer sanctifies for the purification of the flesh, how much more shall the blood of Christ, who through the eternal Spirit offered himself without blemish to God, purify your conscience from dead works to serve the living God."* While the original sacrifice of the Passover lambs brought freedom to the Israelites from the Egyptian bondage, the sacrifice of The Lamb of God brought much more to all of humanity. Christ's holy sacrifice delivered us from the bondage of sin and eternal death. *(Rom 6:23)"For the wages of sin is death, but the gift of God is eternal life in Christ Jesus our Lord."* NAB *(Rom 10:13)"Every one who calls upon the name of the Lord will be saved."*

Where are we two thousand years later? Do we understand that by offering His life in sacrifice Christ Jesus really bought freedom for us human souls? Do we even understand that we need to be saved? Do we understand that this world is not our home, but that we are in exile on earth? Do we understand that Christ opened the gates of Heaven for us? Do we know that Jesus made it possible for us to go home and live free and joyful with Him and the Father for Eternity? *(Jn 14:3)"And when I go and prepare a place for you, I will come again and will take you to myself, that where I am you may be also."* Moreover, do we believe that Christ is truly present in the Eucharist? *(Mt 26:26.28)"This is my body... this is my blood."* [19]

We need to let Christ take care of our souls. As long as we are on earth, we are engaged in a constant battle with evil. We can all relate to times when we feel pulled in every direction, as Saint Paul did: *(Rom 7:15)"I do not understand my own actions. For I do not do what I want, but I do the very thing I hate."* Although man has become scientifically and technologically advanced, he still can not control the invisible world and the forces of darkness, which are constantly working to keep man in bondage and away from God. It is only by entering into God's grace that one can be protected against evil. *(Jn 4:10)"...If you knew the gift of God... ."*

When Christ's Blood was shed, human souls gained access to Heaven, starting with the repentant thief—*(Lk 23:43)"Truly I tell you, today you will be with me in Paradise."* The bodies of departed saints were even awakened while Jesus was still on the cross. *(Mt 27:50.52-53)"Jesus cried again with a loud voice and yielded up his spirit. The tombs also were opened, and many bodies of the saints who had fallen asleep were raised, and coming out of the tombs after his resurrection they went into the holy city and appeared to many."*

When we celebrate the Eucharist, we give thanks to the Father for Jesus Christ's sacrifice, and we celebrate Christ's victory of life over death, of good over evil. When we celebrate Mass, we celebrate the victorious sacrifice by which we were delivered from sin and inherited eternal life. *(Jn 6:53)"Truly, truly, I say to you, unless you eat the flesh of the Son of man and drink his blood, you have no life in you."* When we celebrate the Mass, the Father receives our offerings of bread and wine, and changes them into the Body and Blood of Christ. Each time we receive the Body and Blood of Christ Jesus, each time our souls are fed with this heavenly food, we break away a little more from the powers of this world that have been keeping humanity in bondage for ages. The Holy Mass, which the Catholic Church has perpetuated and protected for two thousand years, allows us to receive the victorious fruits of the sacrifice of Jesus Christ.

---

19. Real Presence of Jesus Christ in the Eucharist: Part Five, Appendix 'B', Eucharistic Miracles.

Jesus Christ clearly stated that He did not come to abolish the covenant of the Old Testament, but rather to accomplish it. The fact that the Church has adopted many elements from Judaism indicates that, just as Jesus Christ did, She acknowledges her Judaic origins. This is especially true of the Old Testament, which the Church has incorporated in the bible and adopted as part of the fundamentals of faith, because She acknowledges the divine nature of this revelation. It is not a coincidence that the most important Catholic feasts are celebrated at the same time of the year as important Jewish feasts.[20]

Many elements of Judism have found their way into Catholic tradition. For example, the tabernacles of our churches—and even their interior veils—, remind us of the tabernacle that Moses built to house the Ark of the Covenant:[21] *(Ex 40:21)"[Moses] brought the ark into the tabernacle, and set up the curtain for screening, and screened the ark of the covenant;... ."* As God was present in the Ark, which was kept in the tabernacle, Jesus is truly present in every tabernacle[22] of the world where the Eucharist is reserved. The Eucharistic bread, the Host, somewhat fits the description of manna. *(Ex 16:31)"...manna; it was like coriander seed, white, and the taste of it was like wafers made with honey."* The *candelabrum*[22a] is a reminder of the *menorah*, and the *zucchetto*[22b] is a reminder of the *yarmulka*. The norms for ordination of priests, liturgical vestments, liturgical colors, ritual of anointing, incensing of offerings, the altar, the sanctuary and its furnishing, holy scripture readings, prayers and hymns of the Mass, all of these find their origins in Judaism.

However, not all Judaic customs found their way into Catholic tradition. For example, while the day of the Lord in Judaism is Saturday, Catholics celebrate the day of the Lord on Sunday, because that is the day on which Jesus Christ rose from the dead. Although Catholics must attend Mass on Sundays, since every day belongs to the Lord and daily reception of the Eucharist further sanctifies the soul, priests and faithful gather daily to celebrate the Mass. *(Mk 2:27)"The sabbath was made for man, not man for the sabbath."* NAB

20. See Part Five, Appendix 'A', Comparative Calendar of Catholic and Judaic Feasts.
21. The Ark of the Covenant contained the two tables of the Law (the ten commandments), a gold jar containing manna, and Aaron's rod (cf. Heb 9:4). Construction of the Ark and the tabernacle: see Ex 25-27.
22. Since Jesus Christ is truly present in the Eucharist, then He is present in all the tabernacles of the world where the Eucharist is reserved. Also see Part Five: Appendix 'F', Essential Catholic Prayers, Prayers for Communion and Private Eucharistic Adoration, Eucharistic Prayers from Fatima; and Appendix 'B', Eucharistic Miracles.
22a. As for the *menorah*, the *candelabrum* is a seven branched candleholder used to grace the sanctuary. Seven candles should be used when Mass is celebrated by the Bishop (cf. GIRM [79] 117). The menorah was a prominent furnishing of the Temple (Ex 25:31-32). It became an emblem of Judaism and of the State of Israel.
22b. Zucchetto: skullcap worn by the pope and other Church prelates.

*(Ps 110:4) "You are a priest forever
according to the order of Melchizedek"*

*(Heb 8:1)"We have such a high priest, one who is seated at
the right hand of the throne of the Majesty in the heavens, a
minister in the sanctuary that the Lord has set up."*

The True Priestly Heritage

The true priesthood is the one that is at the service of God the creator. Its origins are found in the Bible, starting with Melchizedek, known as king of righteousness, king of peace, and one who worshiped the God of Abraham: *(Gen 14:18-19)"Melchizedek, king of Salem, brought out bread and wine, and being a priest of God Most High, he blessed Abram with these words: "Blessed be Abram by God Most High, the creator of heaven and earth.""* NAB It is interesting to note that Melchizedek brought offerings of bread and wine, the same kind of offerings that Jesus Christ used when He instituted the Eucharist.

After Moses took the Israelites out of Egypt, he led them into the desert and to Mount Sinai. There, God gave Moses the tables of the law, which contained the social, moral, and religious laws to be observed by His people (cf. Ex 19-31). Following the Lord's command, Moses appointed his brother Aaron and his sons of the tribe of Levi to be God's priests: *(Ex 28:1)"Bring near to you your brother Aaron, and his sons with him, ...to serve me as priests."* Thus was instituted the priesthood of the Levites,[23] which from that time and until the coming of Jesus was considered the only legitimate priesthood. *(Num 3:7.10) "[The Levites] shall perform duties for [Aaron] and for the whole congregation in front of the tent of meeting, doing service at the tabernacle; ...it is they who shall attend to the priesthood, and any outsider who comes near shall be put to death."*

While the Levites were appointed by God to be His priests according to the order of Aaron, Jesus Christ was appointed by God to be the high priest of a different order. *(Heb 5:10)"Declared by God high priest according to the order of Melchizedek."* NAB This declaration had been foretold in the Old Testament. *(Ps 110:4)"The LORD has sworn and will not change his mind, 'You are a priest forever according to the order of Melchizedek.'"* This leads one to believe that the priesthood according to the order of Melchizedek holds the highest status in the eyes of the Lord. The Levites were priests of the old covenant, and Christ is the high priest and the victim of the new covenant. While the Levites' claim to the priesthood was based on genealogy, Christ's priesthood is based on His perfection, sanctity, and divinity. *(Heb 5:9)"...when he was made perfect, he became the source of eternal salvation for all who obey him... ."* NAB Since not even Christ appointed Himself priest, no one may do so. *(Heb 5:4-5)"No one takes this honor upon himself but only when called by God, just as Aaron was. In the same way, it was not Christ who glorified himself in becoming high priest, but rather the one who said to him: "You are my son; this day I have begotten you".*NAB

---

23. The levites receiving office of priesthood: see *Ex* 32:26-29; *Num* 18:21-26. The books of *Leviticus, Numbers,* and *Deuteronomy* provide a significant amount of information about the priesthood and its office. Priesthood also see: *Heb* 4:14-7:28.

Before the coming of Jesus Christ, the offerings made to God by the Levitical priests could only purify the flesh, but they could not take away sins. *(Heb 10:11)"And every priest stands daily at his service, offering repeatedly the same sacrifices, which can never take away sins."* But through Jesus Christ, Son of God and high priest according to the order of Melchizedek Who offered Himself in sacrifice, all souls can be cleansed from sin. *(Heb 10:12.14)"When Christ had offered for all time a single sacrifice for sins, he sat down at the right hand of God. For by a single offering he has perfected for all time those who are sanctified."* Not only did Jesus Christ make the only worthwhile sacrifice that could take away the sins of humanity, but by doing so he opened for us the gates of Heaven— *(Heb 4:14)"We have a great high priest who has passed through the heavens, Jesus, the Son of God."* NAB—and made it possible for us to go home to Him and the Father. *(Jn 14:3)"I go and prepare a place for you."*

Under the first covenant, the breads of offering were reserved to the Levite priests.[23a] *(Mk 2:26)"[David] went into the house of God... and ate the bread of offering that only the priests could lawfully eat, and shared it with his companions."* NAB But when Jesus Christ, the priest above all priests, instituted the Eucharist, He commanded that the offerings of bread and wine, His Body and Blood, be received by all of his disciples (cf. Mt 26:26-28). With the celebration of the Eucharist, the holiest of all rituals, the priesthood of the new covenant presents the offerings of bread and wine to the Father, so that through consecration God is made present for His people to receive Him. The institution of the Eucharist was made complete and received all of its might only after Jesus Christ, the Priest of the Most High, had offered Himself as the Victim of the holiest sacrifice, and had resurrected from the dead. Through the sacrament of the Eucharist, Christ, in the person of His priests, celebrates His Resurrection, His victory over sin, evil, and death. *(Rom 6:9)"We know that Christ, raised from the dead, dies no more; death no longer has power over him."* NAB With the Eucharist, it becomes possible for all human souls to receive Life and endless graces. One who receives the Eucharist, receives the victory of the Body and Blood of Jesus Christ and partakes in Christ's promise. *(Jn 6:54)"He who eats my flesh and drinks my blood has eternal life, and I will raise him up at the last day."*

Even though Jesus Christ is the Son of God and the highest of priests, He is not foreign to human pain and sin. But contrary to Levite priests, Jesus had never sinned. *(Heb 4:15)"For we have not a high priest who*

23a. Bread of offering, bread of the Presence, see (Lev 24:5-9; 1Sam 21:4). Twelve cakes of leavened bread, representing the twelve tribes of Israel, were placed on a table set before the Ark of the Covenant. On each Sabbath day, the priests would eat the bread of the Presence in the holy place, and replace it with fresh bread.

is unable to sympathize with our weaknesses, but one who in every respect has been tempted as we are, yet without sin." That is why Jesus Christ, our high priest and shepherd, is The way to God's mercy. *(Heb 4:16)"Let us therefore approach the throne of grace with boldness, so that we may receive mercy and find grace to help in time of need."*

Jesus Christ, the anointed One, chief of the highest priesthood, and Head of the Church, passed His authority and the responsibility of the Church on to Saint Peter. *(Mt 16:18-19)"And I tell you, you are Peter, and on this rock I will build my church, and the powers of death shall not prevail against it. I will give you the keys of the kingdom of heaven, and whatever you bind on earth shall be bound in heaven, and whatever you loose on earth shall be loosed in heaven." (Jn 20:21-23) "'Peace be with you. As the Father has sent me, so I send you.' And when he had said this, he breathed on them and said to them, 'Receive the holy Spirit. Whose sins you forgive are forgiven them, and whose sins you retain are retained.' "* NAB

By these words Jesus Christ founded His Church, and, as the twelve Apostles and many disciples were gathered around the Mother of God at Pentecost, by the power of the Holy Spirit the Father breathed life into His Church. *(Acts 2:1-4)"When the time for Pentecost was fulfilled, they were all in one place together. And suddenly there came from the sky a noise like a strong driving wind, and it filled the entire house in which they were. Then there appeared to them tongues as of fire, which parted and came to rest on each one of them. And they were all filled with the holy Spirit and began to speak in different tongues, as the Spirit enabled them to proclaim."* NAB

The Judaic feast of Pentecost celebrates the day that Moses received the table of the law written by God on Mount Sinai. The Christian feast of Pentecost celebrates the day that the Church was born, the day that God sent His Holy Spirit who manifested Himself as tongues of fire, anointing all those who were present, and writing His law in their hearts (cf. Jer 31:33).[24]

Christ's Church was established on a new order of priesthood, the same order that Christ was priest of, the order of Melchisedech. *(Heb 7:12) "For when there is a change in the priesthood, there is necessarily a change in the law as well."* Indeed, Christ brought changes on issues of the law such as access to the priesthood, the ministering of God's mercy, and the forgiveness of sins. At the hour Jesus died on the cross, the Father gave His people a dramatic sign indicating that His relationship with them was about to change. *(Mk 15:37.38)"Jesus gave a loud cry and breathed his last. The curtain of the temple was torn in two, from top to bottom."* This curtain hid the Holy of Holies where the Ark of the Covenant had dwelt. This part of the temple was accessible to the priests only. But suddenly the Holy of Holies was exposed for everyone to see. It is as though the Father was saying that forevermore everyone would have access to Him. Through Christ's new priesthood, God is made present in the Eucharist and all have access to Him and to His promise of Eternal life. *(Jn 6:54)"He who eats my flesh and drinks my blood has eternal life, and I will raise him up at the last day."*

When priests gather around the altar to concelebrate a Mass, it manifests the unity of the priesthood[25] which Jesus instituted during the Last Supper within His institution of the sacrament of the Eucharist. Jesus instituted the Holy Orders so that He may be made present to us in the sacraments, especially in the Eucharist. The Apostles were consecrated priests in Christ when, at the Last Supper, Jesus taught them how to offer the Eucharist—*(Mk 14:22-23)"While they were eating, he took bread, said the blessing, broke it, and gave it to them... . Then he took a cup, gave thanks, and gave it to them, and they all drank from it."* [NAB] —and commanded them to perpetuate this holy ritual. *(Lk 22:19)"Do this in memory of me."* [NAB] At more than one occasion Christ spoke about the importance to celebrate this new covenant. *(Jn 6:53)"Unless you eat the flesh of the Son of Man and drink his blood, you do not have life within you."* [NAB] After Jesus went to the Father, His apostles continued to teach about the importance of the celebration of the Eucharist. *(1Co 11:26)"For as often as you eat this bread and drink the cup, you proclaim the Lord's death until he comes."*

---

24. See Part Five, Appendix 'A', Comparative Calendar of Catholic & Judaic Feasts.
25. The Holy Orders is the Sacrament that ordains men to the Priesthood. They become representatives of Christ, especially at the administration of sacraments. The institution of the sacrament of Holy Orders is celebrated by the Church on Holy Thursday.

After His resurrection, Jesus gave Saint Peter instructions on how to care for His living Church. *(Jn 21:15.16.17)"Do you love me more than these? ... Feed my lambs. ... Tend my sheep. ... Feed my sheep,"* [with the Word and the Eucharist]. Jesus told the Apostles: *(Mk 16:15) "Go into all the world and preach the gospel to the whole creation."* Also... *(Mt 28:18-20)"All power in heaven and on earth has been given to me. Go, therefore, and make disciples of all nations, baptizing them in the name of the Father, and of the Son, and of the Holy Spirit, teaching them to observe all that I have commanded you; and behold, I am with you all days, even unto the consummation of the world."* [DR]

In this following excerpt from the New Testament, Saint Peter expresses his vision and understanding of the Christian priesthood, and of Christ's spiritual living Church and its destiny. *(1Pt 2:4-8)"Come to him, to that living stone, rejected by men but in God's sight chosen and precious; and like living stones be yourselves built into a spiritual house, to be a holy priesthood, to offer spiritual sacrifices acceptable to God through Jesus Christ. For it stands in scripture: "Behold, I am laying in Zion a stone, a cornerstone chosen and precious, and he who believes in him will not be put to shame." To you therefore who believe, he is precious, but for those who do not believe, "The very stone which the builders rejected has become the head of the corner," and "A stone that will make men stumble, a rock that will make them fall.""*

This book is a tribute to the Holy Mass as well as a tribute to the sacrament of Holy Orders, which is essential to the sacrament of the Eucharist. Indeed, without a properly ordained priest there can not be Eucharistic consecration. Thus we, the faithful, could not receive the Body and Blood of Christ as Christ intended. The priestly consecration is a legacy that the Church received from the Apostles, Christ's chosen ones, that has been passed directly from the hands of the Apostles to their successors, the bishops. Then, through an unbroken line passed down the centuries, bishops consecrate priests by imposition of the hands, giving them the power to consecrate the Eucharist and to administer the other sacraments, which are the sources of God's graces. This unbroken transmission of the priestly consecration retains its authenticity under the authority of the successor of Saint Peter, the Pope, to whom all bishops and priests owe obedience.

"Thus the risen Christ, by giving the Holy Spirit to the apostles, entrusted to them his power of sanctifying: they became sacramental signs of Christ. By the power of the same Holy Spirit they entrusted this power to their successors [the bishops]. This "apostolic succession" structures the whole liturgical life of the Church and is itself sacramental, handed on by the sacrament of Holy Orders." [25a]

25a. CCC 1087, cf. *Jn* 20:21-23.

The Holy Spirit has witnessed and intervened in each and every one of these priestly consecrations as He also witnesses and intervenes in each and every consecration of the Eucharist. Christ has entrusted His priests, those who have received Holy Orders, with maintaining God's covenant with humanity. *(Lk 22:19)"Do this in memory of me."* NAB *(Mt 26:28)"For this is my blood of the covenant, which will be shed on behalf of many for the forgiveness of sins."* NAB

Each time a priest exerts his sacerdotal powers during a sacrament, Christ uses him to manifest Himself to us, to manifest His divine mercy. Each time a priest offers and consecrates the Eucharist, Christ is present as Priest and Victim of His own Sacrifice, and then the consecrated bread and wine become Christ's Body and Blood. That is why only legitimate priests of Christ can offer this holy sacrifice. *"Let only that Eucharist be regarded as legitimate, which is celebrated under [the presidency of] the bishop or him to whom he has entrusted it."* [26] *"Only validly ordained priests can preside at the Eucharist and consecrate the bread and the wine so that they become the Body and Blood of the Lord."* [27] *"Christ is the source of all priesthood: the priest of the old law was a figure of Christ, and the priest of the new law acts in the person of Christ."* [28]

"The celebration of the Eucharist is the action of both Christ and His Church. "For in it Christ perpetuates in an unbloody manner the sacrifice offered on the cross, offering himself to the Father for the world's salvation through the ministry of priests. The Church, the spouse and minister of Christ, performs together with [Christ] the role of priest and victim, offers [Christ] to the Father and at the same time makes a total offering of herself together with him."'' [29]

A priest is one that consecrates his life to mediate between man and God, yet knowing that *"Only Christ is the true priest, the others being only his ministers."* [30] More specifically, priests have been *"...consecrated in order to preach the Gospel and shepherd the faithful as well as to celebrate divine worship [the Holy Mass],* as true priests of the New Testament." [31] When the priest offers the Lamb of God to the Father, he offers Him on behalf of all the faithful that are present. *"'It is in... the Eucharistic assembly of the faithful (synaxis) that [**the priests**] exercise in a supreme degree their sacred office; there,*

---

26. CCC 1369, quoting St. Ignatius of Antioch, *Ad Smyrn*, 8:1; SCh 10, 138.
27. CCC 1411.
28. CCC 1548, quoting St-Thomas Aquinas, *STh* III, 22, 4c.
29. Eucharist, CE, quoting *Eucharisticum Mysterium*.
30. CCC 1545, quoting St-Thomas Aquinas, *Hebr.* 8,4.
31. CCC 1564, quoting *LG* 28; cf. *Heb* 5:1-10; 7:24; 9:11-28; Innocent I, *Epist. ad Decentium*: PL 20, 554 A; St. Gregory of Nazianzus, *Oratio* 2, 22: PG 35, 432B.

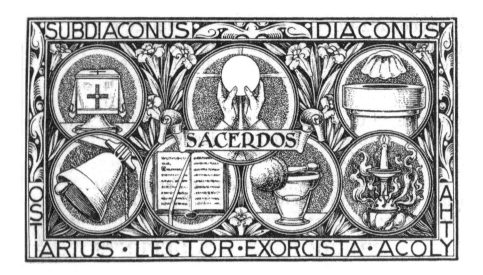

acting in the person of Christ *and proclaiming his mystery, they unite the votive offerings of the faithful to the sacrifice of Christ their head, and in the sacrifice of the Mass they make present again and apply, until the coming of the Lord, the unique sacrifice of the New Testament, that namely of Christ offering himself once for all a spotless victim to the Father.' From this unique sacrifice their whole priestly ministry draws its strength."* [32]

God the Father is the One who chooses and calls the priests to be ordained. However, those who are called have to accept with their own free will to answer the call to this holy mission. *(Heb 5:1)"For every high priest chosen from among men is appointed to act on behalf of men in relation to God, to offer gifts and sacrifices for sins."* Even though priests have been chosen for their ministry, they are still human beings whom, like us, make mistakes and are subject to weaknesses. *"This presence of Christ in the minister is not to be understood as if the [priests] were preserved from all human weaknesses, the spirit of domination, error, even sin. The power of the Holy Spirit does not guarantee all acts of ministers in the same way. While this guarantee extends to the sacraments, so that even the minister's sin cannot impede the fruit of grace, ..."* [33] In other words, knowing human nature, out of love for us, His children and His priests, the Father made sure that even though if at times a **priest may lack faith** or may not be in the state of grace, **God would still be totally present** in His sacraments to pour His graces and mercy on to the faithful.

---

32. CCC 1566, quoting *LG* 28; cf. 1 *Cor* 11:26; cf. *PO 2* (bold face added).
33. CCC 1550.

By means of our baptism in Jesus Christ, we became part of a chosen race, and a royal priesthood. ✛*"Through his cross and resurrection he freed us from sin and death and called us to the glory that has made us a chosen race, a royal priesthood, a holy nation, a people set apart. Everywhere we proclaim your mighty works, for you have called us out of darkness into your own wonderful light."* [34] This 'Eucharistic Prayer Preface' is probably inspired by the following excerpt from a letter of Saint Peter to early Christians, a letter in which he tells them that they are the people of God. *(1Pt 2:9)"But you are a chosen race, a royal priesthood, a holy nation, God's own people, in order that you may proclaim the mighty acts of him who called you out of darkness into his marvelous light."*

Our baptism in Christ made us citizens of heaven, people of God; a people God founded on the Old Covenant and built up with the New Covenant. *(Ep 2:19-22)"You are no longer strangers and aliens, but you are citizens with the saints and also members of the household of God, built upon the foundation of the apostles and prophets, with Christ Jesus himself as the cornerstone. In him the whole structure is joined together and grows into a holy temple in the Lord; in whom you also are built together spiritually into a dwelling place for God."*

To be baptized is so important for salvation that the Church teaches that if there is no priest available, anyone, baptized or not,[35] can baptize a person facing a life threatening situation, if that person has never received this initial sacrament. *"In case of necessity, **any person can baptize** provided that he have the intention of doing that which the Church does and provided that he pours water on the candidate's head while saying:'I baptize you in the name of the Father, and of the Son, and of the Holy Spirit.' "* [35a]

Although we become part of the royal priesthood of Christ by our baptism, it is understood that our function and status in the Church differs from the ordained priest who consecrates his life to serve Christ's Church and to bring the sacraments to His people. *"While the common priesthood of the faithful is exercised by the unfolding of baptismal grace - a life of faith, hope, and charity, a life according to the Spirit -, the ministerial priesthood is at the service of the common priesthood It... is a means by which Christ unceasingly builds up and leads his Church".*[36]

Nonetheless, the non-ordained faithful have an important function in the priesthood of Christ and in the effort to foster the growth of God's kingdom. *"The baptismal seal enables and commits Christians to serve*

---

34. The Order of Mass, Eucharistic Prayer Preface no. 29, Sundays in Ordinary Time I.
35. Anyone, baptized or not, can baptize: cf. CCC 1256.
35a. CCC 1284 (bold face added).
36. CCC 1547.

God by a vital participation in the holy liturgy of the Church and to exercise their baptismal priesthood by the witness of holy lives and practical charity".[37]

We, the faithful, who are the non-ordained royal priesthood, may and shall join spiritually with the celebrating priest in offering to the Father the Sacrifice of the Eucharist when attending the Holy Mass. We the non-ordained royal priesthood may and shall also offer our Mass on the altar of our souls not only for our sake but also for the good of other souls. *"Not only do the priests offer the sacrifice, but also all the faithful: for what the priest does personally by virtue of his ministry, the faithful do collectively by virtue of their intention."* [38]

For times when we, the non-ordained and the ordained, think that Jesus Christ, our big brother, savior and high priest, does not understand our trials, does not care about us or can not help us, we should meditate upon the following. *(Heb 2:17-18)"Therefore he had to become like his brothers and sisters in every respect, so that he might be a merciful and faithful high priest in the service of God, to make a sacrifice of atonement for the sins of the people. Because he himself was tested by what he suffered, he is able to help those who are being tested."*

Then let us think of what Jesus Christ endured when He took our sins on Himself so that we may have access to Eternal Life: *(Isa 53:2-12) "He had no form or majesty that we should look at him, nothing in his appearance that we should desire him. He was despised and rejected by others; a man of suffering and acquainted with infirmity; and as one from whom others hide their faces he was despised. Surely he has borne our infirmities and carried our diseases; But he was wounded for our transgressions, crushed for our iniquities; upon him was the punishment that made us whole, and by his bruises we are healed. All we like sheep have gone astray; we have all turned to our own way, and the LORD has laid on him the iniquity of us all. He was oppressed, and he was afflicted, yet he did not open his mouth; like a lamb that is led to the slaughter, and like a sheep that before its shearers is silent, so he did not open his mouth. By a perversion of justice he was taken away. Who could have imagined his future? For he was cut off from the land of the living, stricken for the transgression of my people. They made his grave with the wicked and his tomb with the rich, although he had done no violence, and there was no deceit in his mouth. Yet it was the will of the LORD to crush him with pain. He shall bear their iniquities. He poured out himself to death, and was numbered with the transgressors; yet he bore the sin of many, and made intercession for the transgressors."*

---

37. CCC 1273, cf. *LG* 10.
38. The Sacred Liturgy, Encyclical Letter by Pope Pius XII, *Mediator Dei,* no. 86, quoting Pope Innocent III, *De Sacro Altaris Mysterio,* 3:6 (13th century).

The Unity of the Church is in
One Lord,
One Faith,
One Baptism,
One Body in Christ,
One Magisterium, and
One Liturgy of the Mass
uniformly celebrated
throughout the Church.

Part Two

Preparing Ourselves and the Temple

Let Us Prepare to Celebrate the Sacred Mystery.

The Day of the Lord

(Ex 20:8-11)"Remember the sabbath day, and keep it holy. Six days you shall labor and do all your work. But the seventh day is a sabbath to the LORD your God; you shall not do any work.... For in six days the LORD made heaven and earth, the sea, and all that is in them, but rested the seventh day; therefore the LORD blessed the sabbath day and consecrated it." Therefore, Sundays and holy days are to be saved for worship, leisure and rest.

"On Sundays and other holy days of obligation the faithful are bound to participate in the Mass" (CCC 2192, cf. CIC, c. 1247). To fulfill the obligation to worship, one must participate in a complete Mass (*cf. SC* 56) with joyful spirit and pay attention to the celebration. Someone who comes late and/or leaves early does not completely fulfill his obligation. Full participation includes receiving Holy Communion. Missing Mass without a good excuse is a grave matter. However, one may be excused or dispensed from his obligation for matters such as: health, care of infant, travel, weather... .

✝ Let Us Prepare to Celebrate the Sacred Mystery ΑΩ

Mass is not a show for an assembly of spectators, but rather, it is a gathering of souls who have been personally called by God to worship Him. While the simple fact of showing up makes us guests of God, our personal preparation and participation in the liturgy turns us into better hosts for God when the time comes to receive the Body of Christ at communion. There are simple things that we can do for our souls, our churches and our celebrations, which will provide a more holy and prayerful atmosphere. *The Roman Missal*, the *Sacramentary*, contains instructions to that effect, especially in the first part called the '*General Instruction of the Roman Missal*'.

Here are some of the guidelines taken from *The Roman Missal*, along with ideas inspired by my own experiences attending Mass and as a lay minister. The purpose of these guidelines is to make our celebrations more prayerful and to show due reverence for the sacred mystery, and to prevent disrespectful behavior and improvisation.

a) **Hymns:** Chosen pieces should promote the participation of the faithful, but also recollection and a spirit of praise. They should be known well enough by the assembly, and be easy enough so that all are able to sing. Chosen hymns should foster the participation of all the faithful.[1] They should also reflect the theme of the Mass. Sacred music such as Gregorian chant and polyphony are the most appropriate for the Liturgy of the Mass. ♪

b) **Decorations:** We like our church to look nice, and also to display the pastoral activities of the parish. But beware of too many decorations. They might become a distraction. Make sure that Christ stays the center of attention. For example, I know of a banner for the Jubilee year 2000 that spent the year hanging in front of the main crucifix in the sanctuary, thus hiding the crucifix from all! Let us make sure that Our Lord and the altar are always at the center of our liturgical celebrations.

c) **Preparing ourselves**: There are simple things that we can do to nurture inner peace and predispose our heart and soul while we are home preparing or driving to church. We can pray the rosary, listen to sacred music, or just sit in silence. Preparing ourselves for Mass means that we should make a point of adopting the appropriate frame of mind. *(Col 3:2)"Set your minds on things that are above, not on things that are on earth."*

---

1. Cf. GIRM [19] 41.

33

As we **dress for church** let us keep in mind that we are getting dressed for the Lord, the King of all kings. So let us dress nicely yet modestly in order to be reverent to the house of God, and without becoming a distraction that may take the attention of others away from the main attraction, Jesus Christ. [2]

Then, in order to respect the **Eucharistic fast** let us remember that, except for water and medicine, we should not have any thing to eat or drink within one hour of receiving communion. [2]

Since we must be in a **state of grace** to receive communion, there are times when, to prepare ourselves, we need to first confess our sins and receive absolution in the **sacrament of penance**. [3]

In order to honor a request of the Mother of God as well as to prepare themselves for Mass personally and as a community, in some parishes before Mass, mainly before weekday Masses, the faithful pray **the rosary** together. [4] The **Way of the Cross** [5] is another devotion that one may practice to prepare for Holy Mass or at any time when visiting a church.

d) Church behavior: *(Jn 2:17)"Zeal for thy house will consume me."*
With respect for all, and also to predispose ourselves to commune with God, let us remember the following:

1. arrive before the Mass starts to **prepare** your heart;
2. when entering the church, **sign yourself** from the holy water font and mentally recall what it means; [6]
3. as you enter your pew make a **genuflection** (on one knee), or bow, to Christ your King who is present in the tabernacle; [7]
4. by reverence for the Lord's real presence and by respect for those who are praying, one should **keep a sacred silence** in church or, only when necessary, speak with a low voice. Restrain from talking before, during, and after the Mass;
5. **follow Mass** in your missal, participate in answering to the liturgy and singing the hymns;

---

2. Cf. CCC 1387, cf. CIC, can. 919.
3. Sacrament of Penance / Reconciliation: see Part Three, Liturgy of the Word, Penitential Rite. State of grace: free from sins, at peace with God. Confession: see CCC, nos 1422-1424, 1440-1460, 1485-1498; Part Five, Appendix 'E', The Commandments.
4. Rosary, see Part Five, Appendix 'G', The Rosary.
5. The Way of the Cross: see Part Five, Appendix 'F', Essential Catholic Prayers; and Questions & Answers, About Holy Objects present in a Church, Questions 11, 12.
6. This action calls to mind three important aspects of the Christian life: the Holy Trinity, the Cross and the Sacrament of Baptism, our Baptism. Water Font: also see Part Five, Catholic Glossary.
7. A genuflection is also made when coming out of a pew, and whenever passing in front of the Blessed Sacrament.

6. *(Mt 5:23.24)"If you are offering your gift at the altar, and there remember that your brother has something against you, leave your gift there before the altar and go; first be reconciled to your brother."* This call to reconcile with our brother can often be met in sacramental **confession**; and

7. Just as the priest is the last one to enter the church at the begining of the Mass (be on time), the priest and ministers should be the first ones to leave the church at the end of the Mass (stay until the end). It is a matter of respect for the office of Christ's ministers.

8. It is important to **seek unity** and to act together as one body when the time comes to stand, kneel, pray, and sing. ✚ [8] *"A common posture, to be observed by all participants, is a sign of the unity of the members of the Christian community gathered for the sacred liturgy: it both expresses and fosters the intention and spiritual attitude of the participants. ...the faithful should follow the directions which the deacon, lay minister, or priest gives according to whatever is indicated in the Missal."* [9] Of course, one who is incapacitated may stay seated during Mass. During common prayer and singing, all should seek vocal unity and follow the assembly's rhythm and tone, so we are as one voice.

e) **Preparing the Sanctuary**: the requisites (necessaries) for the celebration of the Mass are usually kept in the sacristy. At an appropriate time before the Mass starts, the **sacristan** prepares the altar and the sanctuary. The altar shall be dressed according to Church Norms: ✚*"The altar is to be covered with at least one **white cloth**. In addition, on or next to the altar are to be placed candlesticks with **lighted candles**: at least two in any celebration, or even four or six, especially for a Sunday Mass or a holy day of obligation. ... Also on or close to the altar, there is to be a cross with **a figure of Christ crucified**. The candles and the cross adorned with a figure of Christ crucified may also be carried in the Entrance Procession."* [10]

Nothing else but what is listed above may be placed on the altar before the Mass. Flowers may be placed near or around the altar, but not on its mensa. [11]

---

8. In this book, this sign ✚ indicates quotations taken from *The Roman Missal*, the *Sacramentary*: see Notes to the Reader, p. iv.
9. GIRM [20] 42, [21] 43. Part Three, Let Us Rediscover the Holy Mass... step by step, gives the appropriate postures to follow during Mass as instructed by the Holy See.
10. GIRM [79] 117 (bold face added).
11. Cf. GIRM [268] 305, 306. The mensa is the top of the altar.

Before the Mass, the *Sacramentary*—which is the book that contains the prayer texts for the priest to celebrate Mass—is set near the celebrating priest's chair, and the *Lectionary* is placed on the ambo.

On a side table called the **credence table**—which sits near the wall on the left side of the sanctuary as seen from the nave—the sacristan sets the following vessels, linens, and articles needed for the Mass:[12]
- the chalice, and the paten with a large host for the Communion of the celebrating priest,
- a ciborium (ciboria) of small hosts for the Communion of the people;
- a corporal, a purificator and, if needed, the pall;[13]
- two cruets containing the wine and the water;
- the vessel of water for the blessing of the people, if needed;
- the Communion-plate for the Communion of the faithful;
- vessels and linens needed for the washing and cleansing of hands.
- the Missal stand for the altar, and the little bell.

"A vessel of water and a [purificator] for cleansing the fingers of ministers who distribute [Hosts at Communion], may also be placed on the credence table or at some other convenient place." [14]

The number of hosts needed for Mass depends upon how many faithful are expected and also on the quantity of consecrated Hosts already present in the Eucharistic reserve. However, *The Roman Missal* states that: ✝*"It is most desirable that **the faithful**, just as the priest himself is bound to do, **receive the Lord's Body from hosts consecrated at the same Mass.**"*[15] *"The bread used in the celebration of the Most Holy Eucharistic Sacrifice must be unleavened, purely of wheat, and recently made so that there is no danger of decomposition."* [15a]

If the gifts of bread and wine are to be presented by the faithful, the vessels containing the gifts - the ciboria with the bread and the wine cruet or the decanter - should be placed on the table of the gifts, that is a suitable and secure side table covered with a white cloth. The **table of the gifts** is to be placed in a convenient place in the nave, such as near the front pews.

The **crucifix** and its bracket, **the candles**, the ***Book of the Gospels***, and sometimes the thurible (censor), are to be set out for the entrance procession.

---

12. Cf. GIRM [80] 118. Sacred vessels & accessories: see picture in Part Three, Liturgy of the Eucharist, Offertory Rites, Procession of the Gifts.

13. A second corporal is needed when the purification of the vessels is to take place at the credence. If communion under both kinds is distributed to all, additional chalices, each with a purificator, are to be placed on the credence before the Mass.

14. CMRR, Chapter 5, no. 239.

15. GIRM [56h] 85 (bold face added).

15a. *Redemptionis Sacramentum*, no.48: see Part Five, Church Norms, Requisites for the Celebration of the Mass, Matter of the Sacraments, The Eucharist.

The sacred vessels used for containing the Body and Blood of Christ shall be worthy of Him: *"Reprobated, is any practice of using for the celebration of Mass* **common vessels**, *as... vessels made from glass, earthenware, clay, or other materials that break easily. This norm is to be applied even as regards metals and other materials that easily rust or deteriorate."* [15b]

If **incense** is to be used during the Mass, the thurible (censor) is prepared ahead of time by the sacristan in the sacristy. The thurible may be carried in the entrance procession or brought into the sanctuary at the appropriate time of the Mass. Incense may be used during the Entrance procession, the veneration of the altar, the procession of the *Book of the Gospels*, the Offertory, and the Elevation of the Eucharist.

St. Michel church, Sillery, Quebec

15b. *Redemptionis Sacramentum*, no. 117 (bold face added).

f) Liturgy team: The Liturgy team oversees all of the liturgical ministries and functions related to the liturgical celebrations. Although the bishop is the chief priest of his diocese, it is the responsibility of the pastor to see that the liturgy is properly carried out in his parish. To encourage and sustain apostolic action of his parishioners, the pastor usually surrounds himself with a few parishioners to form the liturgy team along with the deacon - if one is appointed - and the designated pastoral assistant. Together they plan the Eucharistic celebrations, which includes choosing and supporting lay faithful for different liturgical ministries.

Lay persons may be entrusted with liturgical duties if they have been properly trained, and as long as these duties are not reserved to the priest. [16] Thus, the liturgy team should make sure that cantors, commentators, readers, servers, and extraordinary ministers of Holy Communion have received proper assistance and training for their function, and that they understand well their assignment.

All those who are involved in serving at the liturgy of the Mass should work together in harmony at preparing efficiently the celebration of the Mass. All should follow instructions from the *Roman Missal* and Church documents. Lay ministers should keep in mind that the celebration of the Mass is the responsibility of the **celebrating priest**, thus, the priest is the one who has the last word and the right to decide what is suitable for the celebration. [17]

The *Roman Missal* provides helpful instructions concerning liturgical ministries. For example, here are some guidelines concerning masters of ceremony and commentators. ✦*"The **commentator**, ... provides the faithful, when appropriate, with brief explanations and commentaries with the purpose of introducing them to the celebration and preparing them to understand it better. The commentator's remarks must be meticulously prepared and clear though brief. ...It is appropriate, at least in cathedrals and in larger churches, to have some competent minister, that is to say a **master of ceremonies**, to oversee the proper planning of sacred actions and their being carried out by the sacred ministers and the lay faithful with decorum, order, and devotion."* [18]

Regarding **lectors**, the *Roman Missal* says that laypersons may be commissioned to proclaim the readings from Sacred Scripture as long as they are well suited to perform this function, have a correct pronunciation and diction, and that they have received proper

---

16. Cf. GIRM [70] 107.
17. Cf. GIRM [73] 111.
18. GIRM [68] 105, [69] 106 (bold face added).

preparation. ✝*"So that the faithful by listening to the readings from the sacred texts may develop in their hearts a warm and living love for Sacred Scripture."*[19]

Let us consider the following about scripture reading: ✝*"By tradition, the function of **proclaiming the readings is ministerial, not presidential**. The readings, therefore, should be proclaimed by a lector, and the Gospel by a deacon or, in his absence, a priest other than the celebrant. If, however, a deacon or another priest is not present, the priest celebrant himself should read the Gospel. Further, if another suitable lector is also not present, then the priest celebrant should also proclaim the other readings."* [20]

Regarding the support that can be given to lay people involved in ministries, let us look, for example, at the support that can be given to readers. Not everyone has a natural talent to read aloud in front of a crowd. Yet, this does not mean that we should put aside people who do not have the talent. To the contrary, let us use this opportunity to improve the knowledge and skills of lay ministers in our parish, especially the youth. For example, we can have a workshop for readers given by a parishioner who has a talent for speaking in public. Besides improving the effect of the readings during our liturgical celebrations, it gives the readers more self-confidence, which is rewarding for those who help them.

The General Instruction of the Roman Missal provides instructions regarding the use of **the ambo**, the place from which readers exercise their function. ✝*"...From the ambo only the readings, the responsorial Psalm, and the Easter Proclamation* (Exsultet) *are to be proclaimed; it may be used also for giving the homily and for announcing the intentions of the Prayer of the Faithful."*[21]

In the same manner that the altar is reserved for the consecration of the bread and wine into the Body and Blood of Christ, the ambo is reserved for proclaiming the Word of God, giving the homily, and presenting our petitions to God. Therefore, the ambo should not be used by the commentator, cantor, and/or choir director.

---

19. GIRM [66] 101, cf. Second Vatican Ecumenical Council, Constitution on the Sacred Liturgy. *Sacrosanctum Concilium,* no.24.
20. GIRM [34] 59 (bold face added).
21. GIRM [272] 309. Norms for the Ambo: also see Part Five, Church Norms, Arrangement and Furnishing for Churches, the Ambo.

Among all the liturgical ministries practiced by the laity, being an **extraordinary minister of Holy Communion** especially requires spiritual preparation and practical training. The Church gives clear instructions on this matter:

> *"Extraordinary ministers of Holy Communion should receive sufficient spiritual, theological, and practical preparation to fulfill their role with knowledge and reverence."* [22]

Liturgy teams should make sure that their extraordinary ministers have a great reverence for the Body and Blood of Christ, so that their reverence is apparent, especially when they distribute communion. Becoming an extraordinary minister should be an opportunity to raise one's spiritual consciousness about Christ's holy sacrifice while learning more about the rituals of the liturgy. It is a responsibility that goes beyond the service itself.

It is not mandatory to have extraordinary ministers of Holy Communion to distribute communion at every Mass. This ministry is only meant to help the priest(s) when the number of faithful to receive communion is especially great. It is primarily the role of the priest(s), and then the deacon, to distribute communion and to carry ciboria from or to the tabernacle.

> ✦*"In the first place, it is the office of the priest and the deacon to minister holy communion to the faithful who ask to receive. ... In addition, it is the office of an **acolyte** [23] who has been lawfully instituted to distribute holy communion ... in the absence of a priest or deacon or... whenever the number of faithful who come to communion is so great that the celebration of Mass... would be too lengthy."* [23a]

When planning liturgical celebrations for events or important feasts such as Christmas or Easter, liturgy teams righfully tend to introduce artistic elements to give a special character to the celebrations: for example, having a live nativity scene at Christmas Mass. However, when doing so, let us make sure that we are following the Norms of the Church as found in the *General Instruction of the Roman Missal,* and in other documents approved by the Holy See.

Both parts of the Mass, the liturgy of the Word and the liturgy of the Eucharist, form a single act of worship during which the faithful are instructed and nourished.[24] Here is an excerpt from *The Roman Missal*

---

22. NCUBK, Part II, No.28.
23. Since all seminarians and candidates for the permanent diaconate receive the office of instituted acolyte before ordination, then this ministry is reserved to laymen.
23a. The *Sacramentary,* second edition, Foreword, p.16; cf. *CIC,* can. 910 §1.
24. Cf. GIRM [8] 28.

that well defines the essence of the celebration of the Mass, an excerpt that all faithful - but especially those serving in a liturgical ministry - should be familiar with.

> ✟ *"At Mass—that is, the Lord's Supper—the People of God is called together, with a priest presiding and acting in the person of Christ, to celebrate the memorial of the Lord, the Eucharistic Sacrifice... For in the celebration of Mass, in which the Sacrifice of the Cross is perpetuated,* **Christ is really present in** *the very liturgical* **assembly** *gathered in his name, in the person of the* **minister***, in* **his word***, and indeed* **substantially** *and continuously under the* **eucharistic species.***"* [24a]

That is to say, that while Christ is **spiritually** present in the assembly, in His word, and in the person of the priest, He is **substantially** present in the Blessed Sacrament. Thus, His Eucharistic presence is superior and requires the appropriate reverence.

The liturgy team should insist that everyone scheduled to serve in a liturgical ministry arrive early enough before the Mass. Not only as a sign of respect, but it helps create a spirit of unity among those serving, which results in the proper carrying out of the celebration. The more experienced ministers can support the newer recruits, especially **altar servers**, among whom, we should keep in mind, many priests first found their **vocation**. Servers and extraordinary ministers of Holy Communion should always wash their hands before the Mass, and abstain from serving if they are sick.

It goes without saying that **being a Catholic** is an essential condition to serve in any liturgical ministry, as well as being **in good standing with the Church** in our marital or celibate life. Each time before serving in a ministry, each individual should make sure that, to the best of his knowledge, he is in a **state of grace**.

A person does not become a minister simply by performing a liturgical task. It is only through ordination that the priest and the deacon become ministers with a particular participation in the office of Christ.

24a. GIRM [7] 27, cf. SVEC, Decree on the Ministry and Life of Priests, *Presbyterorum ordinis*, no. 5; Constitution on the Sacred Liturgy, *Sacrosanctum Concilium*, no. 33. - Ecumenical Council of Trent, Session 22, *Doctrina de ss. Missae sacrificio*, 17 September 1562, chapter 1: Denz-Schön, 1740; Paul VI, Solemn Profession of Faith, 30 June 1968, no. 24: AAS 60 (1968), p. 442. - SVEC, Constitution on the Sacred Liturgy, *Sacrosanctum Concilium*, no. 7; Paul VI, Encyclical Letter *Mysterium fidei*, On the doctrine and worship of the Eucharist, 3 September 1965: AAS 57 (1965), p. 764; Sacred Congregation of Rites, Instruction *Eucharisticum mysterium*, On the worship of the Eucharist, 25 May 1967, no. 9: AAS 59 (1967), p. 547 (bold face added).

g) **Vesting for the Mass:** Part of the **priest's preparation** for the Mass is to dress with the liturgical vestments, a ritual that usually takes place in the vesting room or in the sacristy, wherever the vestments are kept. As a sign of respect and appreciation for the priest who brings us Jesus in the Eucharist, it is customary to provide assistance to the priest when vesting for the Mass; a practice usually appreciated by the priests. The person designated to prepare the vestments, usually the sacristan, lays the liturgical vestments out ahead of time in the appropriate order.[25] This person may also assist the priest by handing him the liturgical vestments as he dresses for Mass, and after the Mass, by putting the vestments away as the priest removes them. This role may be assumed by a religious or lay sacristan, or by any designated person.

h) **Choir director/Cantor:** Since the choice of hymns and their key often determine the level of participation of the faithful, choir directors/cantors should consider all of the following:
- choose a key that is accessible to most people;
- have a fairly constant and easy repertory so that everyone knows the hymns and may participate;
- avoid secular hymns and hymns that change the words of the prayers of the Mass (e.g. Kyrie, Gloria, Sanctus...)
- take note of hymns that generate the most participation; and
- never play background music while the priest, or a lector, is speaking. [25a]

Here is a helpful guideline on the role of the choir and music during Mass: *"A choir is primarily a service to the congregation. Its role, and only reason to be, is to allow the congregation to sing, to dialogue. Its role is not to assume by itself all sung parts of the celebration..., singing together establishes a congregation and situates it as such in its relationship with God, ...it must be heard and seen, without giving a recital."* [26]

✢ On the importance of singing, the *Sacramentary* says:*"The Christian faithful who gather together as one to await the Lord's coming are instructed by the Apostle Paul to sing together psalms, hymns, and spiritual songs (cf. Col 3:16). Singing is the sign of the heart's joy (cf. Acts 2:46). Thus Saint Augustine says rightly, "Singing is for one who loves." There is also the ancient proverb: "One who sings well prays twice.""* [27] ♪ 𝄐

---

25. Appropriate order: see Part Five, Church Norms, Sacred Vestments & Vesting Prayer.
25a. See Part Three, Liturgy of the Eucharist, The Eucharistic Prayer, footnote 32.
26. Translated from the *Prions en Église* (Living with Christ), October 1996.
27. GIRM [19] 39, quoting St. Augustine of Hippo, *Sermo* 336, 1: *Patrologiae cursus completus: Series latina*, J. P. Migne, editor, Paris, 1844-1855, (hereafter PL) 38, 1472.

The sanctuary is the place where the altar stands and where the memorial of the Sacrifice of the Cross is offered. Therefore, to preserve the sacredness of our celebrations, the sanctuary should be reserved only for those who directly serve in the liturgy of the Word and in the liturgy of the Eucharist. Thus, unless the choir is clergy, except for the cantor, **the choir and the musicians should not be in the sanctuary**, but either in the nave with the congregation or in the choir loft.[28]

i) **Spiritual gathering:** In many parishes, there is a new tradition of greeting people before Mass as they come into the church. Since the priest needs to make himself available at the confessional before Mass, the greeting should be done by lay ministers such as greeters or ushers. However, the greeting should not disturb those who are already there praying in preparation for the Mass.

Although it is pleasant and acceptable to discreetly say hello to one another as we arrive in church, we should keep in mind that **Mass is not a social gathering**, but a spiritual one, which calls for recollection. ✝ *"Even before the celebration itself, it is commendable that silence to be observed in the church, in the sacristy, in the vesting room, and in adjacent areas, so that all may dispose themselves to carry out the sacred action in a devout and fitting manner."* [29]

Since it is important for the members of a congregation to gather and talk with each other, parishes often provide an area for socializing after the Mass. It has become popular in many parishes to make the **church's hall** available after Mass for people to gather around coffee and donuts or for an occasional pancake breakfast, and according to the response it is greatly appreciated. Gathering after Mass is a great opportunity for parishioners to get to know one another, and for the pastor to get to know his parishioners better. Moreover, it leaves the church free and silent for those who wish to pray, to make their personal 'Act of Thanksgiving,' or to simply spend some quiet time alone with the Lord. After all, and first of all, the church is the **house of God**, a house of prayer, where God dwells, and where one comes to worship Him. Since Jesus is always substantially present in the tabernacle, observing sacred **silence** shows our reverence for Christ present in the Blessed Sacrament.

---

28. Cf. GIRM [258] 295, [274] 312, [275] 313.
29. GIRM [23] 45.

In conclusion

It is not only up to the pastor and a few lay ministers to make the Eucharistic celebrations more prayerful and alive. Everyone must get involved starting with preparing ourselves for the Mass and participating actively in the liturgy. You may also get involved in one of the liturgical ministries. Ask your pastor. Your parish may need servers, readers, extraordinary ministers of Holy Communion, choir members, or ushers. You may also help with the care of the sacred linens or with decorating the church. Although the actions of liturgical committees set the general atmosphere for Mass, only you can, and must, prepare your heart, mind, and soul, so that Mass becomes a more holy experience.

Although we are bound to attend Mass on Sundays and on other 'holy days of obligation', we may be excused for a serious reason such as: illness, the care of infants or family members, work... . However, you should speak to your pastor in order to be dispensed.

How much time do you set aside for Mass? Some people prefer a Mass that lasts an hour and a half, while others prefer a twenty minute Mass. Is it possible to find a middle ground without compromising the sacredness of the Mass? Since we take the time to come to Church and attend Mass, we should take the time to celebrate every part of the liturgy, which otherwise would make our liturgical celebration incomplete. We should invest ourselves in each celebration of the Mass, so that we are not just going through the motions. If at times you become distracted and find it difficult to follow the Mass and to participate as well as you would like, then try praying and asking God to help you become more absorbed in the Mass, and less absorbed in your own thoughts. But no matter how we feel, attending the Holy Mass always sanctifies our soul a little more. Mass is truly a delight for the soul, even though our senses fail to perceive it.

♪ Let us take the time to congratulate the choir and even to make requests for our favorite hymns. Show support to your pastor. Let him know when you liked his homily and tell him what you would like him to speak about. Do not underestimate the importance of showing your interest and support.

🔔 And let us ring the church bells at least fifteen minutes before Mass starts, so that everyone in the parish will know that God is calling His people to come and celebrate Mass. Who knows, maybe some people will make a last minute decision to join the celebration.

a.m.d.g.
Ad Majorem Dei Gloriam
For God's Greater Glory   ♪   🔔   ✝   📖

Part Three

The Liturgy of the Mass

Let Us Rediscover the Holy Mass
... Step by Step

The Liturgy of the Word
&
The Liturgy of the Eucharist

📖 Introduction to the Liturgy of the Mass

The liturgy of the Mass is composed of two parts, the liturgy of the Word and the liturgy of the Eucharist. While the Gospel reading is the summit of the liturgy of the Word, the consecration of the bread and wine into the Body and Blood of Christ is the summit of the liturgy of the Eucharist, and the summit of the Mass. The liturgy is structured into the form of a dialogue between God and His people. For example, in the liturgy of the Word God speaks to His people through the scripture readings, and between the Readings, we, His people, respond to God through either the Responsorial Psalm or the Gospel Acclamation. At times during the Mass God speaks to us through the priest, as in the proclamation of the Gospel, and at other times the priest speaks to God on our behalf, as in the Eucharistic prayer. Then, when we join together to speak to God by the means of one of the common prayers, such as the General Intercessions, much power is given to our prayer. *(Mt 18:19)* *"If two of you agree on earth about anything for which they are to pray, it shall be granted to them by my heavenly Father."* NAB

The liturgy of the Mass is a well-designed psychological process that provides us with familiar mental references. People who attend Mass regularly know well that these references make it easier for them to recollect and focus on worshiping God. Trying to do so without familiar references can be more challenging. The more comfortable we become with the liturgy and its rituals, the easier it is to be made aware of God's presence, to open up to Him, and to receive His graces.

As Christians, we are called to holiness, which is a necessary condition to enter heaven. Following the call to holiness is a journey that takes us home to the Father in heaven, and during which our soul is gradually sanctified by the grace of God. This journey takes us across many new and uncharted frontiers deep within our souls and minds, which at times might appear to be like a jungle. The obstacles that we encounter during our journey - and that tend to keep us from getting closer to God - are often those of our fear of the unknown and of having to amend our lives. Although we know that only good things can come to us when we turn to God, we tend to believe the lies and the fears that the evil one sets in our minds as traps to keep us away from our Lord.

Hence, throughout our journey it is imperative to follow trustworthy guidance. Jesus Christ, the Son of God, came and showed us 'The Way'; and after giving His life to save us from eternal condemnation, Jesus gave us the Eucharist as our inheritance so that we may have Life, and be strengthened to walk 'The Way'. Through the 'apostolic succession,' Jesus has entrusted the forgiveness of sins, the teaching authority, and the celebration of the sacrifice of the Mass to the Church.

Thus the teachings of the Church together with the sacraments, and especially the Eucharist, form the only and sure path to an eternal blissful life in heaven.

The liturgy of the Mass contains rituals that enhance the sacredness of the Mass and address the faithful spiritually, mentally, and emotionally. The rituals of the Mass address us through our five senses. Here are some examples. Before the Mass, we **hear** the sound of the church's bells calling us from a distance. Then the moment we walk into the church, our **sight** is taken by the arrangement and the decoration of the church and of the sanctuary; the center aisle, the height of the ceiling, the stained-glass windows, the votive candles, and the lighted sanctuary lamp, which bears witness to the presence of Our Lord in the tabernacle. As we enter the church, we **touch** the holy water in the water font and bless ourselves. As the entrance procession starts, our **sight** is taken by the shape and the colors of the liturgical vestments, and by the crucifix, the lighted candles and the *Book of the Gospels* being carried and held up high. We **hear** the Word of God, the prayers and the hymns. We hold our missal throughout the Mass, **touching** and turning the pages that contain the holy liturgy. At the time of the consecration, the burning incense calls upon our senses of **smell** and **sight**, while helping us realize that our prayers and singing are rising up to the Father, as the smoke from the incense rises in the sanctuary. At the time of the elevation, the **sound** of the little bell helps us realize the holiness of the moment. Then when the time comes to receive communion, we **taste** the eucharisted bread and wine.

The liturgy of the Word prepares us for the liturgy of the Eucharist, and especially for the Holy Sacrifice of the Mass and for Communion. Every part of the liturgy is important and none of it should be left out. For example, we may not discard a reading or the profession of faith. ✠*"These readings should be followed strictly"; "Moreover, it is unlawful to substitute other, non-biblical texts for the readings and responsorial Psalm, which contain the word of God."* [1]

It is a good idea for us, the faithful, to look in our missals/missalets at the readings and the liturgical texts of the day before the Mass starts. It allows us to better participate in the liturgy of the Mass and to be more spiritually involved in our worship. The choice of Mass and of Eucharistic Prayer for Sundays could be published in the bulletin. When we understand how the priest chooses the prayers in the *Roman Missal,* we can follow them in our own missal. Attending Mass becomes a more fulfilling experience the more we participate in offering spiritually the sacrifice of the Mass with the priest. We become more aware of the blessings that God has in store for those who come to worship Him.

---

1. GIRM [318] 357, [34] 57, cf. John Paul II, Apostolic Letter *Vicesimus quintus annus*, 4 December 1988 , no. 13: AAS 81 (1989), p. 910.

(Mt 4:4) "Man shall not live by bread alone,
but by every word that proceeds / from the mouth of God."
(Lk 10:27) "You shall love the Lord your God with all your heart,
and with all your soul, and with all your strength,
and with all your mind; and your neighbor as yourself."
(Lk 6:31) "Do to others as you would have them do to you." [NAB]

The Liturgy of the Word 📖
Introductory Rites

(Jn 1:14)"The Word became flesh and lived among us".
*(1Tim 2:3.4)"God our savior who desires everyone to be saved
and to come to the knowledge of the truth."*
(Jn 8:32) "The truth will set you free." NAB

The Mass usually begins with the entrance procession while the assembly sings the entrance hymn. However, during weekday Masses, the priest usually enters the sanctuary alone and directly from the sacristy while the assembly recites the entrance antiphon. When there is an entrance procession and when it is ready to start, the commentator /cantor invites the community to stand. The signal to stand might also be given by the choir starting to sing the entrance hymn, or by the ringing of a bell near the sanctuary. The **congregation stands** from the entrance of the priest until before the first reading.

ENTRANCE ANTIPHON (Opening Hymn) :
✠ *"The purpose of this chant is to open the celebration, foster the unity of those who have been gathered, introduce their thoughts to the mystery of the liturgical season or festivity, and accompany the procession of the priest and ministers."* 2 ♪

The Mass can be a great spiritual experience, especially when we invest ourselves in the liturgy right from the beginning. Singing together the opening hymn reduces the differences among us and raises the level of unity to which God calls us. *(Jn 17:11)"That they may be one just as we are."* NAB So to help setting a pace of unity right from the start, let us stand and sing the opening hymn. If unfortunately there is no singing, let us make sure to recite together the entrance antiphon. The entrance antiphon is an excerpt taken from either the Old or the New Testament and usually presents the theme of the Mass.

As the congregation joins in singing, those in the **entrance procession** adopt a solemn attitude as they walk up the center aisle from the back of the church towards the sanctuary, while maintaining a uniform distance between each other. The order of the procession is usually as follows: the **cross bearer**, a server, leads the procession carrying the crucifix held high; followed by two other servers acting as **candle bearers** walking side by side; the deacon, or a reader, follows carrying the ***Book of the Gospels*** slightly elevated; behind him, the other reader(s), then the concelebrant(s), if any. Those who are not carrying anything walk with joined hands. The position of honor at the end of the procession is reserved for the celebrating **priest**.

---

2. GIRM [25] 47.

According to local customs and the solemnity of the celebration, the entrance procession may also include a **thurifer**, [3] extraordinary ministers of Holy Communion, many clerics, and even the bishop.

Upon entering the sanctuary, those who are not carrying anything make a deep bow in front of the altar, or genuflect if the tabernacle with the Blessed Sacrament is in the sanctuary. The servers deposit the thurible, the cross, and the candles at their appropriate places before taking their positions in the sanctuary. The readers proceed as follows: ✦"If [the lector] is carrying the Book of the Gospels, he approaches the altar and places the Book of the Gospels upon it. Then the lector takes his own place in the sanctuary with the other ministers." [4] The Lectionary is never carried in the procession. [5]

VENERATION OF THE ALTAR:
As the priest enters the sanctuary, he makes a profound bow in front of the altar. Then after taking his position behind the altar, at the center, he puts his hands flat on the altar. [6] And—✦"As an expression of veneration,... the priest and deacon then kiss the altar itself; ... the priest [may then] also incenses the cross and the altar." [7] As we, the faithful, join spiritually in the veneration of the altar, we begin to prepare our inner altar for the moment when, in our name, the priest offers the sacrifice of the Mass on the altar to the Father.

THE SIGN OF THE CROSS:
The entrance hymn is sung through the procession and the veneration of the altar. ✦"When the Entrance chant is concluded, the priest stands at the chair and, together with the whole gathering, makes the Sign of the Cross." [8] The priest alone says aloud:
✦OM "In the name of the Father, and of the Son, and of the
    Holy Spirit!
    [The people answer:] **Amen**"

As for all Christian activities, the Mass starts with the Sign of the Cross, which dedicates the celebration to God the Trinity. When we make the Sign of the Cross, we show that we are Christians, and we also profess our belief in the chief mysteries of our faith. Indeed, when we recite the Sign of the Cross, we profess our faith in the unity of God and in

---

3. When a thurifer is present he is the one to open the entrance procession. Thurifer: the one who attends to the thurible (censor), see Part Five, Catholic Glossary.
4. GIRM [149] 195.
5. Cf. GIRM [82] 120; Lectionary: see Part Five, Catholic Glossary.
6. Altar: Part Five, Church Norms, Arrangment and Furnishing of Churches, The Altar.
7. GIRM [27] 49.
8. GIRM [28] 50.

God the Trinity. And as we sign ourselves, we profess our faith in the Incarnation and Death of Christ on the cross. Starting Mass with the Sign of the Cross is to call upon the Lord, greeting Him and acknowledging His presence among us. *(Mt 18:20)"For where two or three are gathered together in my name, there am I in the midst of them."* NAB Praying is like talking with God on a heavenly telephone; and making the Sign of the Cross is like dialling His telephone number. The Church grants an indulgence to those who bless themselves - make the Sign of the Cross - properly. Unfortunately, sometimes we do it mechanically. So let us sign ourselves consciously.

GREETING:
Facing the people, the celebrating priest opens his hands and welcomes the assembly with a greeting such as:
✛ OM *"The grace of our Lord Jesus Christ, and the love of God and the fellowship of the Holy Spirit be with you all.* [9]*
[The people answer:]* **And also with you.***"

What a beautiful greeting this is. I love hearing these words and meditating on them. They warm my heart; they make me feel that I am truly being greeted in the house of God as a member of Christ's family. ✛ *"[The priest] signifies the presence of the Lord to the community gathered there by means of the Greeting. By this Greeting and the people's response, the mystery of the Church gathered together is made manifest."* [10] *"The priest does not say "Good morning", etc.,* as the **sacred greeting** obviously **includes all human sentiments of goodwill***. He introduces the Mass briefly."* [11]

---

9. This greeting is taken from 2Co 13:13.
10. GIRM [28] 50.
11. CMRR, Chapter 5, no. 251.

The greeting imparts the true spiritual dimension of the gathering. It contains words that raise our spirits, making us receptive to what we are about to hear during the Mass. Then as the priest briefly introduces the Mass, he may remind us of the importance of our participation; as we sing and follow closely the liturgy in our missals, we open the way to our souls to the Lord. As part of preparing our hearts to meet with the Lord we may remind ourselves that:

- we are God's children,
- we are part of a mystery called the Body of Christ,
- Christ is alive, dwelling within us,
- we can trust Christ's love for us, and
- Christ is about to feed our souls with His Word and Holy Sacrifice.

(Mt 4:4)"One does not live by bread alone, / but by every word that comes forth / from the mouth of God." NAB

Purification Rite

As an introduction to the Mass, the liturgy invites us to become conscious of ungodly influences and sins[11a] that we might be carrying, and to pray for purification. Just as we make a point of cleaning our house and of looking our best when we are expecting company, we should also make sure that our souls are as clean as possible before hosting the Lord our God. To do so, the liturgy offers the choice of two rites: **a) Rite of Blessing and Sprinkling of Holy Water** and Blessing of salt (optional), or **b) Penitential Rite**. Although the Father grants His forgiveness to the repentant who ask, it is the Blood of Christ, made present during the eucharistic sacrifice, that washes away our sins. *(Ps 51:9)"Wash me, make me whiter than snow."* NAB

Most Catholics are familiar with holy water because we usually sign ourselves with Holy Water when entering the church. Then at certain Masses during the year we witness the 'Rite of the Blessing of Water', more especially at the Easter Mass, when we renew the promise of our baptism. Once the water has been blessed, the priest walks around the church with the vessel of holy water and sprinkles the faithful, who then sign themselves. Maybe you recall how being sprinkled with holy water tends to make everyone smile with joy. It is a good practice to keep holy water at home for private use.

Even though we might not be as familiar with the rite of blessing of salt and the use of blessed salt, it is also part of the Church's tradition. Both the blessed salt and the holy water are sacramentals[12] that are consecrated to be used as a medium to protect us against evil, or to chase evil out of our churches, homes, souls, and surroundings. Let us look at both rites, the blessing of water and the blessing of salt.

11a. Venial sin versus grave sin: see p. 56, footnote 16.
12. Sacramentals: see Part Five, Catholic Glossary.

A) RITE OF BLESSING & SPRINKLING OF HOLY WATER :

✙OM [*"The rite of blessing and sprinkling holy water may be celebrated in all churches and chapels at all Sunday Masses celebrated on Sunday or on Saturday evening.... . After greeting the people the priest remains standing at his chair. A vessel containing the water to be blessed is placed before him. Facing the people, he invites them to pray, using these or similar words*:]

> 'Dear friends,
> this water will be used
> to remind us of our baptism.
> Let us ask God to bless it,
> and to keep us faithful
> to the Spirit he has given us.'

[After a brief silence, he joins his hands and continues:]

> 'God our Father,
> your gift of water
> brings life and freshness to the earth;
> it washes away our sins
> and brings us eternal life.
> We ask you now
> to bless ✠ [13] this water,
> and to give us your protection on this day
> which you have made your own.
> Renew the living spring of your life within us
> and protect us in spirit and body
> that we may be free from sin
> and come into your presence
> to receive your gift of salvation.
> We ask this through Christ our Lord.' "

Or:

BLESSING OF SALT (optional):

✙ OM[*"Where it is customary, salt may be mixed with the holy water. The priest blesses the salt, saying*:]

> 'Almighty God,
> we ask you to bless ✠[13] this salt
> as once you blessed the salt scattered over the water
> by the prophet Elisha.
> Wherever this salt and water is sprinkled,
> drive away the power of evil,
> and protect us always
> by the presence of your Holy Spirit.
> Grant this through Christ our Lord.'

[*Then he pours the salt into the water in silence.*"]

---

13. This sign represents the moment when the priest blesses the water and salt by making the sign of the cross over it.

(2Kg 2:21-22)"Then [Elisha] went to the spring of water and threw the salt into it, and said, "Thus says the LORD, I have made this water wholesome; from now on neither death nor miscarriage shall come from it." So the water has been wholesome to this day, according to the word that Elisha spoke."

As an antiphon is sung, the priest sprinkles himself with holy water as well as all those present in the sanctuary, and then walks through the church sprinkling the people with holy water. *(Ezek 36:25-26)"I will sprinkle clean water upon you to cleanse you from all your impurities, and from all your idols I will cleanse you. I will give you a new heart and place a new spirit within you, taking from your bodies your stony hearts and giving you natural hearts."* NAB

The priest returns to stand at his chair, joins his hands and says:
✛OM"*"May almighty God cleanse us of our sins,*
and through the Eucharist we celebrate
make us worthy to sit at his table
in his heavenly kingdom."'
[To which the congregation answers with one voice:] **R. Amen.**

The blessing and sprinkling of holy water at the beginning of Mass recalls our baptism, but also, as light chases darkness, holy water chases away any evil that might be present, and protects us against it. The sprinkling of holy water tends to bring on good thoughts and a **devotional attitude**, which allows the remission of venial sins. It disposes the faithful to receive graces during the Mass; it opens for us the way to the Father's arms where we come for mercy and comfort. Sprinkling holy water in the church before Mass is like cleaning house out of reverence for the Lord.

Holy water is a symbol of baptism, the initial sacrament that we receive only once. **Our baptism** washes away the sins from our souls, activates the spring of inner life, and allows spiritual life to start gushing forth within our souls. *(Jn 4:14)"The water that I will give will become in them a spring of water gushing up to eternal life."* Even though invisible to us, this spring is very real, especially for those who know to keep on drawing on its water. This very concept is embodied in the blessing of water as the priest asks God to 'renew the living spring of His life in us.' Holy water is a symbol of the mystery of spiritual life.

Christians are called to be like salt. *(Mt 5:13)"You are the salt of the earth; but if salt has lost its taste, how can its saltiness be restored?" (Mk 9:50)"Have salt in yourselves, and be at peace with one another"* and, *(Col 4:6)"Let your speech always be gracious, seasoned with salt, so that you know how you should respond to each one."* NAB "Salt represents Christian wisdom and integrity of life... Salt was used during the scrutinies of catechumens (examination of catechism students) and the Baptism of infants, [it is used] in the blessing of holy water and the rite of consecration of a church and of an altar." [14]

Although the blessing of salt is seldom practiced in our liturgical celebrations, the use of blessed salt as a means to chase evil has been practiced since the beginning of the Church. With its sacraments and sacramentals, the Catholic Church has a rich tradition of efficacious ways to fight evil. The concept of cultivating good and fighting evil, of winning the battle against the enemy, is common to many faiths. Although we human souls belong to different faiths, we were all created by the same God for the purpose of loving Him and serving Him. And since there is only one God, in the end *(Jn 10:16)"So there will be one flock, one shepherd,"* the Christ.

Some people think that evil goes away by simply denying its presence and power. Others think that evil just does not exist, that it is pure fabrication. Should we trust our limited knowledge... or the Church's teachings and the Word of God? There is a real battle taking place in the invisible world. *(Rev 12:17)"the dragon... went off to make war on... those who keep the commandments of God and hold the testimony of Jesus."* Knowing that the evil one loves to torture souls, and especially those who love God, you might want to choose to make regular use of sacramentals to fight evil and to keep it out of your life.

B) PENITENTIAL RITE:
Do you resent having to say that you are a sinner? Well you shouldn't. How can we receive God's help if we act as though we do not need Him? How can we improve ourselves and our lives if we do not acknowledge our weaknesses? How can you fix something, if you do not acknowledge it is broken? Can anyone say that they are always doing God's will; that they never offend Him? Let us not be in denial. Most of the work we have to do while on earth is on ourselves. The Penitential Rite leads us to our inner temple, where we may reconcile with God. *(1Co 3:16)"Do you not know that you are God's temple and that God's Spirit dwells in you?"*

✢*"Then the priest invites those present to take part in the Act of Penitence, which, after a brief pause for silence, the entire community carries out through a formula of general confession. The rite concludes with the priest's absolution [of venial sins], which, however, lacks the efficacy of the Sacrament of Penance".* [15]

---

14. CE, Salt.
15. GIRM [29] 51.

In the penitential rite, the priest leads us, the faithful, to acknowledge our state of sinfulness and to repent by saying a formula such as:

✠ OM *"As we prepare to celebrate the mystery of Christ's love,*
let us acknowledge our failures
and ask the Lord for pardon and strength."

Then to bring us, the faithful, to ask for God's forgiveness the priest leads us in reciting aloud the:

ACT OF PENITENCE

✠OM *"I confess to almighty God,*
and to you, my brothers and sisters,
that I have sinned through my own fault,
in my thoughts and in my words,
in what I have done,
and in what I have failed to do:
and I ask blessed Mary, ever virgin,
all the angels and saints,
and you, my brothers and sisters,
to pray for me to the Lord our God."

When we say the 'Act of Penitence' and humble ourselves by admitting that we are not perfect, something magnificent happens. Our heart opens to God's love and mercy! *(Jn 14:23)"Whoever loves me will keep my word, and my Father will love him, and we will come to him and make our dwelling with him."* NAB Asking Mother Mary, the angels and saints, and our brothers to pray to God for us raises our individual consciousness to a more universal one. It helps us realize that we are all part of the same body, the CHRIST! You will surely agree that Mother Mary, the angels, and the saints have a closer relationship with God than we do. That is why their intercession is so efficient and precious to us. As we ask for their intercession, we might receive the grace to realize that all the heavenly hosts are present at the Mass.

After this common confession—which does not replace a sacramental confession—, we may sign ourselves as the priest concludes by praying for the forgiveness of our **venial** (minor) **sins:** [16]

---

16. Venial (minor) sins as opposed to mortal (grave, deadly sins: CCC 1857: "For a *sin* to be *mortal*, three conditions must together be met: 'Mortal sin is sin whose object is **grave matter** and which is also committed with **full knowledge** and **deliberate consent**.'" *RP* 17§12; CCC 1858:"*Grave matter* is specified by the Ten Commandments, corresponding to the answer of Jesus to the rich young man: 'Do not kill, Do not commit adultery, Do not steal, Do not bear false witness, Do not defraud, Honor your father and your mother' *(Mk* 10:19). The gravity of sins is more or less great: murder is graver than theft. One must also take into account who is wronged: violence against parents is in itself graver than violence against a stranger." Gravity of sins: also see CCC 1854-1864. Since mortal sins can only be absolved when the sinner is repentent, and through the sacrament of penance, one repenting from mortal sins needs to see a priest.

✝OM *"May almighty God have mercy on us,*
   forgive us our sins,
   and bring us to everlasting life.
[To which we answer:] ***Amen.***"

We continue our 'Act of Penitence' by asking for God's mercy as we respond to the priest, or cantor, in the Kyrie Eleison.

KYRIE ELEISON ♫

✝ OM *"V. Lord, have mercy.*   **R. Lord, have mercy.**
   V. Christ, have mercy.   **R. Christ, have mercy.**
   V. Lord, have mercy.   **R. Lord, have mercy.**"

After the 'Act of Penitence', instead of using the 'Kyrie Eleison', the priest may choose to lead the faithful to pray for God's mercy by having them respond to one of the four other penitential prayers found in the missal. Here is one of the other penitential prayers:

✝OM *"Lord, we have sinned against you:*
   Lord, have mercy,
[The people]   **R. Lord, have mercy.**
   Lord, show us your mercy and love,
[The people]   **R. And grant us your salvation.**
[The priest then blesses us while praying for forgiveness:]
   May almighty God have mercy on us,
   forgive us our sins,
   and bring us to everlasting life.
[The people]   **R. Amen.**"

Oh how good it feels to be reconciled with God! *(Ps 27:4)"One thing I ask of the LORD; / this I seek: / To dwell in the LORD's house / all the days of my life, / To gaze on the LORD's beauty, / to visit his temple."* NAB

How do I know if I need to receive the sacrament of reconciliation? If I have transgressed any of the Ten Commandments,[17] or if I just do not feel at peace with God, then I am not in a state of grace and I need to receive absolution in the **sacrament of reconciliation**[18] before I can receive communion. But no matter what I might have done, I can be absolved of my sins and reconciled with God if I am repentant and confess my sins, and truly want to amend my life. It is an act of love towards God to trust in His mercy and forgiveness.

---

17. The Ten Commandments & other guidelines to do our examination of conscience to prepare for our confession: see Part Five, Appendix 'E'. The Church requires that we confess our sins at least once a year. Cf. CCC 2042; CIC, can. 989, CCEO, can 719.
18. Sacrament of reconciliation: if you have any doubt about needing God's forgiveness, go see a priest for personal confession. First, make an examination of conscience (CCC 1454-1455), then go confess your sins with the firm desire to amend yourselves, and do your penance (CCC 1459-1460). Reparation is needed for sins even when they have been forgiven: see Part Five, Catholic Glossary, Plenary Indulgence.

The Holy Mass is a process of sanctification that starts with the penitential rite. By the means of this rite, we go inside ourselves and **examine our conscience**; we acknowledge our weaknesses and transgressions, and ask for God's forgiveness and help. We seek to be cleansed from our venial sins so that we may reach a state of grace, that is, being in a state to receive God's graces: His mercy, His forgiveness, and other heavenly blessings such as the granting of our prayers. Foremost, being in a state of grace means being in the required state of holiness to receive holy communion and to benefit from its fruits.

Through the sacrament of Holy Orders, Christ gives authority to priests to act in His name, and uses them to bring His people the grace of the sacraments. *(Jn 20:22-23)"Receive the Holy Spirit. If you forgive the sins of any, they are forgiven them."* When, in sacramental confession, we **confess** our sins **repentantly**, the priest can **absolve** us, which **reconciles** us with God while removing our **guilt**. Absolution can set us free from our worldly chains, giving us the mental disposition to start fresh and leave our sorrows behind. Confession brings us **healing**. *(Ps 103:12)"As far as the east is from the west, / so far does he remove our transgressions from us."* Also *(Heb 10:16-17)""I will put my laws in their hearts, / and I will write them upon their minds,... ."' / 'Their sins and their evildoing / I will remember no more.'"* [NAB]

At the moment that we regret our sin, God forgives us. But, actually asking God for forgiveness brings us to admit to ourselves that because of our human nature we are limited in our capacity, and even our desire, to remain united to God twenty four hours a day. *(Rom 7:19-20)"For I do not do the good I want, but I do the evil I do not want. Now if [I] do what I do not want, it is no longer I who do it, but sin that dwells in me."* [NAB] Nonetheless, God grants his forgiveness according to the following: *(Mk 11:25)"Whenever you stand praying, forgive, if you have anything against anyone; so that your Father in heaven may also forgive you your trespasses."*

RECONCILIATION WITH GOD

So why do we need reconciliation with God? Each time we choose to ignore God, we separate ourselves from Him, provoking a rupture in our relationship with God. That is called sin. That is when we start following our will instead of His. Our thoughts, words, and actions become of this world, instead of God's. Then we lose sight of God, of His Love and of His plans, and we lose our way.

(Jn 8:34) "Everyone who commits sin is a slave of sin." NAB
(Jn 8:32) "The truth will make you free."
(Jn 14:6) "I am the way and the truth and the life." NAB

When by the grace of God we come to realize that we have distanced ourselves from Him and that His plans are much better than ours, then we find the Lord reaching out for us with his faithful love. As we acknowledge our sin, we turn to the living Christ who dwells in us, and renew our relationship with Him. That is called reconciliation through repentance. Blessed is the one who acknowledges his sinful nature, he becomes available to receive God's graces.

(Lk 15:21)"Father, I have sinned against heaven and against you." NAB
(Lk 15:7)"There will be more joy in heaven over one sinner who repents than over ninety-nine righteous persons who need no repentance."
(Ps 19:8)"The law of the LORD is perfect, / refreshing the soul. / The decree of the LORD is trustworthy, / giving wisdom to the simple." NAB

Now, let us rejoice in our reconciliation and sing **Glory to God**!

🔔 GLORIA ♫

✠ OM *"Glory to God in the Highest,*
and Peace to his people on earth. [cf. Lk 2:14]
Lord God, heavenly King,
almighty God and Father, [cf. Gen 35:11]
we worship you, we give you thanks,
we praise you for your glory.
Lord Jesus Christ, only Son of the Father,
Lord God, Lamb of God,
you take away the sin of the world:
have mercy on us:
you are seated at the right hand of the Father:
receive our prayer.
For you alone are the Holy One, [cf. Rev 15:4]
you alone are the Lord,
you alone are the Most High,
Jesus Christ,
with the Holy Spirit,
in the glory of God the Father, Amen!"

These words of praise to God the Trinity were inspired from the song the angels sang to the shepherds of Bethlehem to tell them that Immanuel, the Son of God, was born. *(Lk 2:13.14)"And suddenly there was with the angel a multitude of the heavenly host praising God and saying, "Glory to God in the highest, / and on earth peace among men with whom he is pleased!"* Let us give praise to God the Father, the Son, and the Holy Spirit, Who dwells among us and Whose faithful love we can trust. *(Ps 106:1)"Praise the LORD! / O give thanks to the LORD, for he is good; / for his steadfast love endures for ever!"* Let us glorify Christ's victory over evil and death. *(Rev 12:10)"Now have come the salvation and the power / and the kingdom of our God / and the authority of his Messiah."*

Let us glorify the love and the peace that God the Father gives us, His children. Let us celebrate our reconciliation with Him. Let us tell God the Trinity that we are back in His camp with Mother Mary, the angels, and the saints, who never cease praising Him.

OPENING PRAYER: (Collect)
This first prayer of the eucharistic celebration completes the introductory rite. ✦*"The priest then invites the people to pray, saying, with hands joined, Oremus (Let us pray). All pray silently with the priest for a brief time. Then the priest, with hands extended, says the Collect [opening prayer], at the end of which the people make the acclamation, Amen."* [19] The brief moment of silent prayer allows the faithful to **become conscious of God's presence**, and to mentally prepare to present their petitions to God during the opening prayer.

---

19. GIRM [88] 127.

The opening prayer, or collect, usually expresses the character of the celebration. Traditionally, the collect is addressed to God the Father, through Christ, in the Holy Spirit.[20] The petitions presented in the 'Opening Prayer' always include either promises of God taken from the Scriptures or recall blessings that God has bestowed on us His people. Here is an example of an 'Opening Prayer', in which we recall and petition for the blessing to be renewed in Christ:

♰ *"Father of love, you made a new creation through Jesus Christ your Son. May his coming free us from sin and renew his life within us, for he lives and reigns with you and the Holy Spirit one God, for ever and ever."*[21] Then the people respond: ***"Amen."***

📖 Liturgy of the Word

The Word of God teaches us who God is and what are His laws and His plan. So let us ask the Holy Spirit to open our hearts and to help us understand what God wants to tell us through His scriptures today. *(Jn 14:26)"The holy Spirit that the Father will send in my name —he will teach you everything and remind you of all that [I] told you."* [NAB] *(Heb 4:12)"The word of God is living and active, sharper than any two-edged sword, piercing until it divides soul from spirit, joints from marrow; it is able to judge the thoughts and intentions of the heart."* The holy scriptures are God's Will and Testament to us His people.

Three readings are assigned for Sundays and solemnities:[21a] the first one from the **Prophets**, the second one from the **Apostles**, and the third one from the **Gospel**.[21b] Besides the fact that these readings are related by a common theme, often the first reading is a prophecy about Christ that the accompanying Gospel shows as accomplished, with the epistle emphasizing the accomplishment of the prophecy, and exhorting us to follow Christ. In most cases, the three readings show the continuity of God's work of salvation from Adam and Eve through Jesus and Mary. The first reading, the responsorial psalm, the second reading, and the Gospel acclamation are usually read by a lay reader. To enhance the greater sacredness of the words of Jesus Christ, Our King and Savior, the celebrating priest, or deacon, is reserved for the reading of the Gospel. **Everyone now sits to listen** to the two first readings, which the celebrating priest briefly introduces.

---

20. Cf. GIRM [32] 54.
21. Sacramentary, Tuesday of the Third Week of Advent.
21a. A solemnity is a major feast: Christmas, Easter,... see the liturgical calendar.
21b. Norms for the choice of Mass readings: see GIRM [318-320] 357-362.

FIRST READING:

The First Reading is taken from the Old Testament, except during Easter season when it is taken from the 'Acts of the Apostles.' The reader stands at the ambo and reads the sacred text from the *Lectionary*. He introduces the reading by mentioning from which book of the bible it is taken. For example: a reading from the Book of the Prophet Isaiah.

I use to think that the Old Testament could not carry messages for us because it was too ancient. Eventually, I understood that truth does not change, only our way to look at it does. These texts are not only rich in the history and customs of the Hebrew people, they also contain the story of great signs, such as the parting of the Red Sea, teachings of wisdom and hope, and God's plan for our redemption. *(Isa 7:14)"The Lord himself will give you this sign: the virgin shall be with child, and bear a son, and shall name him Immanuel."* NAB

In the Old Testament, we discover how prophets like Daniel were blessed with mystical visions, encounters with angels, and other supernatural experiences. We read about generations of the Hebrew people praying and praising the Lord for they knew Him to be almighty and trustworthy. We learn that God tests His people, but keeps His promises and grants His children mercy, protection, and life.

Readings from books such as *Ecclesiasticus* (Sirach) or *Wisdom* always impress me because their content is still so relevant. Although essential rules of life might have now been forgotten, their truths have not changed. Here is an example among many: *(Sir 37:10)"Seek no advice from one who regards you with hostility; / from those who envy you, keep your intentions hidden."*NAB God kept sending His prophets to teach us 'the way' that leads to Him and that protects us from the traps of this world. These texts nourish our faith and bring us wisdom. They remind us of God's love for His children, for those who do His will.

Through the Old Testament, we get a bigger picture of the story of God's love for humankind. *(Prov 8:22-23)"The LORD created me at the beginning of his work, / the first of his acts of long ago./ Ages ago I was set up, / at the first, before the beginning of the earth."* These readings invite us to stretch our minds and imagine the events of an era for which the Old Testament is the best, if not the only, reliable source of reference. The Old Testament helps us to better appreciate the present moment, to understand that eternity is now, on a common thread with the past and the future.

To conclude the first reading, the reader says:
♦OM *"The word of the Lord.*
[All respond:]   ***Thanks be to God.***"

As mentioned earlier, the liturgy of the Mass has been designed in the form of a dialogue. Have you noticed how we just went from being greeted by God through the priest, to asking God for mercy and forgiveness, which the priest gave us in the name of the Lord? Then after standing and singing the 'Glory to God' to Him, we sat to listen to the First Reading of His Word. And now (as we **remain seated**) the 'Responsorial Psalm' allows us to speak to God collectively.

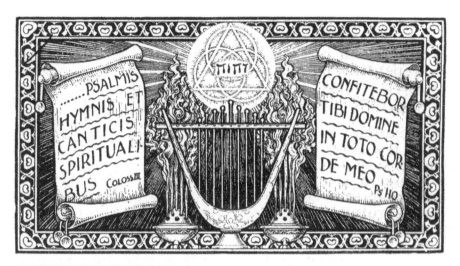

RESPONSORIAL PSALM:
✝"The responsorial Psalm should correspond to each reading and should, as a rule, be taken from the Lectionary." [22] The Psalm is sung or recited from the ambo by the reader or cantor. After each verse of the Psalm, the congregation participates by reciting or singing the designated responsorial refrain, as indicated in their missals.

The book of Psalms preserves the bulk of the religious poetry of Israel. In the 'Introduction to the Psalms' in 'the Bible of Jerusalem', we find the following statement: *God inspired the feeling that his children ought to have towards Him and words they ought to use when speaking to Him.*[22a] As we read this religious poetry, we discover the various sentiments that the people of Israel of the Old Testament had towards God. Some of the Psalms celebrate God's glory, and praise Him for granting the prayers of His people. Others express the suffering, the repentance, or yet the complaint of the people of God. We also find passages expressing confidence that God will deliver His people from their enemies. In other words, the Psalms depict the perception that the Hebrews had of God centuries ago and how they addressed God during their spiritual and emotional trials, as well as while worshiping Him.

---

22. GIRM [36] 61.
22a. Translated from *La Bible de Jérusalem,* Éditions du Cerf, Paris, 1961.

When reading the Psalms, it becomes obvious that human sentiments towards God today are not that different from what they were in the time of King David, the author of the Psalms. We might find comfort in the Psalms, in the fact that we are not the first, nor the only ones, whose sentiments towards God, and relationship with Him, change according to how our life is going. Our ever-changing states of mind and soul are nothing new to the Lord, Who knows the human nature.

Even though most of the texts chosen for the Responsorial Psalm are taken from the book of Psalms, for example: *(cf. Ps 23:1-6)"The LORD is my shepherd; / there is nothing I shall want...",* it might also be a hymn taken from another book of the bible. Such is the case, for example, with the Magnificat: *(cf. Lk 1:46-55)"My soul proclaims the greatness of the Lord; / my spirit rejoices in God my savior... ",* [NAB] which may be chosen for liturgical feasts in honor of Mother Mary.

SECOND READING:

The Second Reading is usually taken from letters written by the Apostles, or St. Paul. These texts, known as the '**apostolic letters**' or '**Epistles**' are inspired by Christ's teachings and addressed to the early Christian communities. The congregation **remains seated** while the reader stands at the ambo and reads from the *Lectionary*. First, he mentions from which book of the bible the reading is taken, for example: 'A reading from the first letter of Saint Paul to the Thessalonians.'

Throughout history, the apostolic teachings have guided the lives of Christian families and communities. The 'apostolic letters' reveal that early Christians had questions very similar to ours on matters like spiritual quests, social behavior, and family issues. What did Christ say about marriage, divorce, religious practice, legal issues, and about sin, forgiveness, and resurrection? They wanted to know how to live according to the Gospel of Jesus Christ. Through these letters, we learn that the early Christians discussed fundamentals of the faith in the same light that today's Catholics discuss the interpretation of the scriptures in the light of the Church's teachings.

However, due to their differences, the early Christian communities grew apart, to the point where Christ's Church split into different factions. Sound familiar? We should learn from history and strive to implement Unity in us and among us, Christians, just as God is One. We should strive to implement in our lives the teachings of Christ that the Apostles taught the first Christian communities. *(1Pt 5:5)"You who are younger must accept the authority of the elders. And all of you must clothe yourselves with humility in your dealings with one another, for 'God opposes the proud, but gives grace to the humble.'"*

(Rom 12:9)"Let love be sincere; hate what is evil, hold on to what is good." NAB Or yet: *(Jas 1:12)"Blessed is the man who perseveres in temptation, for when he has been proved he will receive the crown of life that he promised to those who love him."* NAB These exhortations, which are quite simple, can be very demanding to live by. Although we may want to follow Christ, between our personal goals and the world's continuous solicitations, we tend to lose sight of Christ's teachings.

That is why not only do we need to listen to the Word of God and worship as a community regularly, but we also need to take the time on our own, with the Holy Spirit and in the light of the Church's teachings, to read and meditate regularly upon the Scriptures. We could share the fruits of our readings and meditations with family and friends, and in our prayer groups. We need to read the Scriptures because we need to be reminded again and again what the essential rules and goals of a Christian life are so that they become part of our way to think and live. *(Mt 4:4)"...'One does not live by bread alone, but by every word that comes forth from the mouth of God.'"* NAB

To conclude the Second Reading, the reader says:
⊕OM *"The word of the Lord!*
[All answer:] **Thanks be to God***"*

GOSPEL ACCLAMATION:

In our liturgical dialogue with God, we His people, just went from listening to God in the First Reading, to responding to Him in the Psalm. Now, after listening to God's Word in the Second Reading, our participation in this dialogue continues with our singing *Alleluia*, before and after the reader sings or recites the acclamation verse that announces the Gospel Reading. Let us now **stand to sing.** ♪

⊕*"...An acclamation of this kind constitutes a rite or act in itself, by which the assembly of the faithful **welcomes and greets the Lord** who is about to speak to [them] in the Gospel and professes [their] faith by means of the chant. [The Alleluia] is sung by all while standing and is led by the choir or a cantor, being repeated if this is appropriate. The verse, however, is sung either by the choir or by the cantor."* 23
⊕OM " V. Alleluia. ♪ **R. Alleluia.**
  V. [Verse]   **R. Alleluia.**"

---

23. GIRM [37] 62 (bold face added).

The **Alleluia** is sung except during Lent when it is omitted, and replaced by a verse of praise, usually: 'Praise to You Lord Jesus Christ, King of endless glory.' The **acclamation verse** may be taken from either the Old or the New Testament, and is usually directly related to the readings. The verse usually contains inspiring, uplifting, or exhorting thoughts, which tend to make us more receptive to the words of life that Christ is about to proclaim to us in the Gospel reading. *(Mt 5:16)* *"Your light must shine before others, that they may see your good deeds and glorify your heavenly Father."* [NAB]

PROCESSION OF THE BOOK OF THE GOSPELS

During the singing of the acclamation of the Gospel, the priest or deacon carries the *Book of the Gospels* slightly elevated in a reverent procession from the altar to the ambo.

To further enhance the **sacred character** of the message of Jesus Christ, the procession may include two **candle bearers** and the incensing of the *Book of the Gospels*. ✠*"During the singing of the Alleluia ..., the priest puts some [incense] into the thurible and blesses it. Then, with hands joined, he bows profoundly before the altar and quietly says,* Munda cor meum (Almighty God, cleanse my heart)." [24] While the servers come to stand facing one another on each side of the ambo, where they will remain during the proclamation of the Gospel, the priest, or deacon, carries the *Book of the Gospels* to the ambo, and the thurifer stands near by to assist with the **incensing**.

If the **deacon is to proclaim the Gospel**, before the processsion of the *Book of the Gospels*, the deacon goes and stands before the priest to receive the following blessing:

✠OM *"May the Lord be in your heart and on your lips that you may worthily proclaim his Gospel. In the name of the Father, and of the Son, ✠[24a] and of the Holy Spirit."* The deacon answers: *"Amen."*

The words of this blessing seem to be inspired by the following excerpt taken from the book of Isaiah: *(Isa 6:5-7)*""*I am a man of unclean lips,... ; for my eyes have seen the King, the LORD of hosts!" Then flew one of the seraphim to me, having in his hand a burning coal which he had taken with tongs from the altar. And he touched my mouth, and said: "Behold, this has touched your lips; your guilt is taken away, and your sin forgiven."*"" It is remarkable how loving and wise God is. God needed Isaiah to prophesy, but Isaiah thought of himself as being unworthy. So God took Isaiah as he was and did what was necessary for him to be made worthy to accept his mission.

---

24. GIRM [93] 132.
24a. ✠ The priest makes the sign of the cross over the deacon.

GOSPEL:

✢*"When the Sacred Scriptures are read in the Church, God himself speaks to his people, and Christ, present in his own word, proclaims the Gospel."*[25] *(Jn 13:35)"This is how all will know that you are my disciples, if you have love for one another."* [NAB] Since the Gospel is the teaching of Jesus Christ, the summit of the Liturgy of the Word, **all keep on standing to listen to the Gospel**.

Standing at the ambo with hands joined, the priest or deacon announces the reading of the Gospel as follows:

✢^{OM} "The Lord be with you.

[The people answer:]   ***And also with you.***
[The priest or deacon says:
e.g.: *A reading from the Holy Gospel according to Saint Mark*.]
[All respond:]   ***Glory to you, Lord.****"*

As he announces the Gospel reading, the priest makes the **sign of the cross** with his thumb on the opened *Book of the Gospels*, and then on his forehead, lips, and heart. If incense is used, before proclaiming the Gospel, the priest **incenses the *Book of the Gospels*** at the ambo. The people also sign themselves with the thumb on the **forehead, lips, and heart**; a gesture that reminds us of the great commandment: *(Mt 22:37)"You shall love the Lord, your God, with all your heart, with all your soul, and with all your mind."* [NAB] As we sign ourselves, we may ask God to purify our thoughts, which originate from our hearts and that are expressed through our lips, and we may also ask God that His word may take root in our souls.

In Catholic editions of the Bible, the canon, the Old Testament contains **46** books and the New Testament contains **27** books, for a **total of 73** books. Only 4 of these books constitute the Gospel of Jesus Christ. They are accounts of the life and teaching of Jesus Christ written by the four evangelists: St. Matthew and St. John, whom were among the twelve Apostles of Christ, and lived with Him during His public life; and Saint Mark and Saint Luke, whom are known to have been taught by Saint Peter and Saint Paul, respectively, and some of the other Apostles.

According to St. Jerome, the four evangelists are prefigured as follows in a vision of Ezechiel (Ezek 1:10): Saint Matthew is symbolized by the 'man', because his Gospel starts with Christ's genealogy, and he stresses His human and kingly character; Saint Mark is represented by the 'lion', because his Gospel starts with Saint John the Baptist, 'the voice of one crying in the desert', and emphasizes the miraculous powers of our Lord; Saint Luke is represented by the 'ox', the animal of the sacrifice, because he starts his Gospel with the history of Zechariah the priest,

---

25. GIRM [9] 29.

offering sacrifice to God, and accentuates the universal priesthood of Christ. Saint John is represented by the 'eagle', because from the beginning of his Gospel he soars above the things of the earth and time, and dwells upon the divine origin and nature of Jesus.[26]

The most precious parts of the Gospel are those reporting Christ's teachings in Christ's own words: *(cf. Mt 24:35, Mk 13:31, Lk 21:33) "Heaven and earth will pass away, but my words will not pass away."* Not only are Christ's words still alive today, but Christ Himself is alive and He lives forever, resurrected and victorious over death. Since our big brother Jesus made it back home to heaven, blessed are those who believe in and act upon His words—*(Jn 14:6) "I am the way and the truth and the life. No one comes to the Father except through me."* NAB—they shall make it home to heaven too! Jesus promised His Spirit to guide us during our journey: *(Jn 14:26)"The Holy Spirit, whom the Father will send in my name, will teach you everything and remind you of all I have said to you."* As promised, God sent us the Holy Spirit, and that holy event, which marks the foundation of the Church, first took place on the feast of Pentecost, fifty days after Christ's resurrection and nine days after His ascension. The Holy Spirit has been with the Church ever since, and each time we call upon Him, He is there for us.

When Christ gave His life out of love for us, His lost brothers and sisters, He paved the Way and built the first and only bridge that can take us home to heaven. But to reach our home, we still have to choose to follow the path of Christ, and we have to walk the way. The Gospel of Jesus Christ is a map that helps us find our way back home. Christ taught us that the way to heaven is paved with good behavior and sincere commitment: *(Mt 7:21)"Not everyone who says to me, 'Lord,*

26. Cf. *The New Testament*, Revision of Challoner-Rheims version, Preface, The Four Gospels (see bibliography).

Lord,' will enter the kingdom of heaven, but only the one who does the will of my Father in heaven."* What is the Father's will? His commandments. *(Mt 22:37.39-40)"You shall love the Lord your God with all your heart, and with all your soul, and with all your mind... You shall love your neighbor as yourself. On these two commandments depend all the law and the prophets."* And by doing God's will, we become part of Christ's manifestation on earth.

However, Jesus never pretended that going back home was going to be an easy journey. *(Mt 16:24)"If any man would come after me, let him deny himself and take up his cross and follow me."* And he also said: *(Mt 10:16)"Behold, I send you out as sheep in the midst of wolves; so be wise as serpents and innocent as doves."* However, Christ, Mother Mary, and our heavenly family are watching and helping us every step of the way. Consider this. Do you think that God the Father Almighty, Creator of heaven and earth, would have sacrificed His only son Jesus Christ to save us if He didn't think that we could make it back home? Our heavenly Father is awaiting us at the end of our journey, where He already plans to give us, His children, our inheritance: *(Rev 2:10)"Remain faithful until death, and I will give you the crown of life."* ᴺᴬᴮ By our baptism we become God's children (cf. CCC 1279; Jn 1:12), but when we decide to go back home, we become prodigal sons of God: *(Lk 15:23.24)"Let us celebrate with a feast, because this son of mine was dead, and has come to life again; he was lost, and has been found."* ᴺᴬᴮ

Every soul is a potential heir, but only those who claim their inheritance and work for it can inherit Eternal life. As much as we need God's grace to enter Eternal Life, God needs our consent to bestow His graces upon us, to free us from death, and to give us Eternal Life.

The Gospel, Christ's teaching, is so rich that a lifetime on earth is not enough to understand it all. The evangelist Saint John says: *(Jn 21:25) "There are also many other things that Jesus did, but if these were to be described individually, I do not think the whole world would contain the books that would be written."* ᴺᴬᴮ Praise be Jesus!

To conclude the proclamation of the Gospel, the priest or deacon raises the *Book of the Gospels* in front of himself and says:
✠ ᴼᴹ *"This is the Gospel of the Lord!*
[All respond:]   ***Praise to you Lord Jesus Christ.***

Then [the priest] **kisses** the book [of the Gospels], saying quietly:
    May the words of the Gospel wipe away our sins."

The congregation now **sits to listen to the homily**.

HOMILY:

The preaching of homilies during the Holy Mass is a function that is exclusively **reserved to the ordained**, the priest or deacon, and to the exclusion of the nonordained religious and lay faithful. This norm can not be dispensed with because it touches the closely related functions of teaching and sanctifying. The faithful, especially members of institutes of consecrated life, can participate in the ministry of the word at Mass as readers, or at other times as catechists.[27] ✠"*The homily is necessary for the nurturing of the Christian life. It should be an exposition of some aspect of the readings from Sacred Scripture or of another text from the Ordinary or from the Proper of the Mass of the day.*"[28] Homilies are a time for a pastor to educate his faithful on the teachings of Christ in the light of the tradition of the Church. Pay attention! God often uses His priest's homilies to give us personal messages and guidance.

There are many levels of teaching found in the Scriptures, and the same text can be approached in many different ways. Priests and pastors often invest a lot of time preparing their Sunday homily. It is not an easy job. Not only do our priests and pastors have to preach within the boundaries of the Church's teachings, but people expect them to have all the answers about God, while being entertaining and inspiring. Let us be reasonable!

The Church promotes a pastoral teaching that actualizes the Word of God. Thus the priest might preach, for example, about how the call to holiness applies to all of us today. Or he might exhort us to take God at His word by following His commandments and watching our prayers being granted. The priest might also choose to speak about success stories that acknowledge today's miracles, prophets, and saints. These stories usually act as positive reinforcements that strengthen our faith while showing us its value.

In today's world, we are constantly being solicited and exposed to all sorts of social and moral issues, and at times we become confused. We need our pastors to give us clear and **proper Christian guidelines** to help us follow the Lord's Way in our everyday life. We need to hear from our priests that our local clergy and bishop support the Pope and his position on religious, moral, and secular issues. Besides being a tremendous witness of faith and hope, our late Pontiff, Pope John Paul II, provided us with an incredible amount of written material, in which we find proper guidance concerning today's social and moral issues.

---

27. Cf. *Collaboration of the Non-Ordained Faithful in the Sacred Ministry of Priest*, Theolgical Principles, 2; Practical Provisions, art. 2 §2.
28. GIRM [41] 65, cf. Sacred Congregation of Rites, Instruction *Inter Oecumenici*, On the orderly carrying out of the Constitution on the Sacred Liturgy, 26 September 1964, no. 54: AAS 56 (1964), p. 890.

For example, Pope John Paul II loudly and clearly denounced the 'culture of death', which is responsible for abortions, sterilizations, suicides, euthanasia, and all sorts of deadly addictions; and promoted the 'culture of life' as a remedy and only choice for Christians. He repeatedly reminded us that the call to holiness can only be answered by joyfully carrying our cross through repentance, prayer, and sacrifice, and through a sincere devotion to the Lord's real presence in the Eucharist. Pope John Paul II also kept on prophesying about a 'new spring' that the Holy Spirit is about to bring into the Church.

I have had the pleasure to experience **homiletic dialogs**, which is a style of homily where the priest answers **a *couple* of spontaneous questions** asked by members of the congregation relating to the scripture readings of the day. This form of homily reminds us of how Jesus answered people's questions while teaching in synagogues and by the lake of Galilee. Since homiletic dialogs require a special preparation and an assembly that is willing to participate, this form of homily is more appropriate for pastoral activities such as spiritual retreats or prayer meetings during which the Holy Mass is celebrated. Homiletic dialogs tend to bring the faithful to greater participation in the Mass and to deepen their reflection on the holy scriptures.

However, when agreeable to the pastor and parishioners, homiletic dialogs may also take place during a regular Mass. It is an opportunity for the pastor, and for the congregation, to take the pulse of the congregation's spiritual awareness. As parishioners openly ask their questions, they tend to express their understanding of the scriptures and of the faith. Using this question and answer format sends an important message to the congregation. That is, understanding the holy scriptures is not a gift that the Holy Spirit reserves for the clergy, but rather a gift that He offers to the whole Church, which includes the lay people. It confirms to the people of God that enlightened by the Holy Spirit and the Church's tradition, the Word of God is for everyone to study, understand, and share. *(1Tim 2:3.4)"God our savior, who wills everyone to be saved and to come to knowledge of the truth."* [NAB] *(Lk 24:45)"Then he opened their minds to understand the scriptures."* Homiletic dialogs might produce a new dynamic in the congregation while helping the pastor to establish a pastoral orientation that better serves his parishioners.

When we are committed to a Christian life, we understand that our spiritual growth often requires making leaps of faith towards intangible realities. *(Jn 20:29)"Blessed are those who have not seen and have believed."* [NAB] *(Heb 11:1.3)"Now faith is the assurance of things hoped for, the conviction of things not seen. By faith we understand that the world was created by the word of God, so that what is seen was made out of things which do not appear."* Even though faith means to believe without seeing, it doesn't mean that Christians must be clueless about the origins of their faith. On the contrary, Christians must learn about the Church's tradition, that is, two thousand years of interpreting the teachings of Christ within the Apostolic Succession and under the guidance of the Holy Spirit, Whom Christ promised to His Apostles. *(Jn 14:25)"The Advocate, the Holy Spirit, whom the Father will send in my name, will teach you everything, and remind you of all that I have said to you."*

We who attend Mass care about our souls. Therefore, it is appreciated when the preacher shows that he is aware of **our spiritual quests** and trials, and uses the homily to address issues that we encounter during our spiritual journey; for example, the need for self-denial and for fighting against the evil one. Homilies inspired by the life of saints such as Saint Padre Pio, or by writings of mystics such as Saint Teresa of Avila, or those of Pope John Paul II, are truly enlightening. Homelies inspired by the life and spirituality of saints can especially fill our souls with hope, joy, and faith, thus renewing our motivation to believe in God's Word and to live in accordance with the Gospel.

Since the homily comments on the Word of God, it should be **exhorting, but also uplifting**. *(Mt 11:30)"For my yoke is easy, and my burden light."* [NAB] The secular world is already giving us plenty of bad news. We need to hear the Good News. We come to Mass to hear that Jesus Christ is alive among us, that God loves us, that He always grants His children's prayers, and uses them to do good deeds in this world. We need to hear about the magnificent and eternal reward that awaits those who take care of their souls and strive to do the Father's will. *(1Pt 1:3-5)"Blessed be the God... who in his great mercy gave us a new birth to a living hope through the resurrection of Jesus Christ from the dead, to an inheritance that is imperishable, undefiled, and unfading, kept in heaven for you, who by the power of God are safeguarded through faith, to a salvation that is ready to be revealed in the final time."* [NAB]

We need to be reminded that the Holy Mass is the memorial of the sacrifice of Jesus Christ, and that Christ is truly present, Body and Blood, Soul and Divinity, in the Eucharist that we receive. We need to be regularly invited to attend Mass during the week. We also need to be regularly invited to go to confession. We need to be reminded that the sacrament of penance reconciles us with God for our failures to love, that the absolution we receive removes our guilt and heals our souls from the marks of sin; and that absolution brings us to a state of grace, which is required to receive the Eucharist.[29] *(1Co 11:27-30)"Therefore whoever eats the bread or drinks the cup of the Lord unworthily will*

---

29. State of grace: see Sacrament of Penance, CCC 1415.

have to answer for the body and blood of the Lord. A person should examine himself, and so eat the bread and drink the cup. For anyone who eats and drinks without discerning the body, eats and drinks judgment on himself. That is why many among you are ill and infirm, and a considerable number are dying." NAB

We need to be reminded that in the sacrament of confession it is Christ Himself in the person of His priest, Who gives absolution to the penitent. (Mk 2:10)"That you may know that the Son of man has authority on earth to forgive sins." (Jn 20:23)"If you forgive the sins of any, they are forgiven; if you retain the sins of any, they are retained." We need to be reminded that receiving absolution in the sacrament of reconciliation allows us to make peace with God, removes our guilt, and brings healing to our soul.

There are many basic elements of our faith that we need to be frequently reminded of because we humans tend to easily forget what God has given us, that is, salvation through His Son, His Word made flesh Who died for us. We need to be reminded often of the essence of Christ's teaching: (Lk 6:27-31.37-38)"Love your enemies, do good to those who hate you, bless those who curse you, pray for those who abuse you. To him who strikes you on the cheek, offer the other also; and from him who takes away your coat do not withhold even your shirt. Give to every one who begs from you; and of him who takes away your goods do not ask them again. And as you wish that men would do to you, do so to them. Judge not, and you will not be judged; condemn not, and you will not be condemned; forgive, and you will be forgiven; give, and it will be given to you; good measure, pressed down, shaken together, running over, will be put into your lap. For the measure you give will be the measure you get back."

We need to be exhorted to grow beyond the fact that living by the Gospel and following Jesus is demanding, and to reach the point of understanding that following Christ brings us freedom, all needed graces, peace, and the power to fight the evil one. We need to understand that the most important thing for our soul, and for the coming of God's kingdom, is for us to show compassion to others 'each time' that we become aware and have an opportunity to do so. It could be a smile, it could be a prayer, or it could be a material good. Isn't that the spirit of Christ's teaching? "O Jesus, my love, my vocation, at last I have found it. My vocation is LOVE!" 30

As a priest that I know often says: 'We Christians should keep in mind that our life is sometimes the only Gospel that will be read by some people.'

---

30. Saint Thérèse of the Child Jesus, Story of a Soul.

After the homily, the priest pauses for a moment so that, with the assistance of the Holy Spirit, what we just heard may take root in our souls. ✛ *"Any sort of haste that hinders recollection must clearly be avoided. During the Liturgy of the Word, it is also appropriate to include brief periods of silence in which, at the prompting of the Holy Spirit, the word of God may be grasped by the heart and a response through prayer may be prepared. It may be appropriate to observe such periods of silence, for example, before the Liturgy of the Word itself begins, after the first and second reading, and lastly at the conclusion of the homily."*[31]

PROFESSION OF FAITH: (Creed)

✛ *"The purpose of the* Symbolum *or Profession of Faith, or Creed, is that the whole gathered people may respond to the word of God proclaimed in the readings taken from Sacred Scripture and explained in the homily and that they may also call to mind and confess the great mysteries of the faith by reciting the rule of faith in a formula approved for liturgical use, before these mysteries are celebrated in the Eucharist."*[32] Usually, we recite the 'Nicene Creed', but the priest may also chose the 'Apostles' Creed', the "faithful summary of the apostles' faith" (CCC 194). Either way **let us stand** to respond to the Word of God by **proclaiming our faith** in these sacred mysteries.

THE APOSTLES' CREED

✛OM *"I believe in God, the Father almighty,*
Creator of heaven and earth.
I believe in Jesus Christ, his only Son, our Lord.
He was conceived by the power of the Holy Spirit
and born of the Virgin Mary.
He suffered under Pontius Pilate,
was crucified, died, and was buried.
He descended to the dead.
On the third day he rose again.
He ascended into heaven,
and is seated at the right hand of the Father.
He will come again to judge the living and the dead.

I believe in the Holy Spirit,
the holy catholic Church,
the communion of saints,
the forgiveness of sins,
the resurrection of the body,
and the life everlasting. Amen."

---

31. GIRM [33] 56, cf. *The Roman Missal, Lectionary for Mass, editio typica altera*, 1981, Introduction, no. 28.
32. GIRM [43] 67.

The Apostles' creed, which states the essential beliefs of the catholic faith, offers a lot on which to meditate. Let us take, for example, the passage that speaks of how, after being buried, Jesus descended to the dead. The version of the Apostles' Creed found in the *Catechism* (CCC) actually uses the words "He descended to hell."[33] Since Jesus never committed any sin, and that satan, who reigns in hell, is the enemy of Jesus, have you ever wondered why Jesus descended to hell? *"[Jesus] descended there as Savior, proclaiming the Good News to the spirits imprisoned there."*[34] *"Jesus did not descend into hell to deliver the damned, nor to destroy the hell of damnation, but to free the just who had gone before him."*[34a] *"He opened heaven's gates for the just who had gone before him."*[34b]

When Jesus Christ descended to hell, He made it obvious to satan and his allies that His mission was victorious; that He, the Christ, had just taken away satan's power over death; thus that He, the Christ, was The King of all and that all shall bow to Him. *(Heb 2:14.15) "Since, therefore, the children share flesh and blood, [Christ] himself likewise shared the same things, so that through death he might* **destroy the one who has the power of death***, that is, the devil, and free those who all their lives were held in slavery by the fear of death."* [bfa] *"Henceforth the risen Christ holds 'the keys of Death and Hades,' so that '***at the name of Jesus every knee should bow***, in heaven and on earth and under the earth, [***and every tongue confess that Jesus Christ is Lord***, to the glory of God the Father.]'"* [35]

33. CCC 633:"Scripture calls the abode of the dead, to which the dead Christ went down, 'hell' - *Sheol* in Hebrew or *Hades* in Greek - because those who are there are deprived of the vision of God (cf. *Phil* 2:10; *Acts* 2:24; *Rev* 1:18; *Eph* 4:9; *Pss* 6:6; 88:11-13). Such is the case for all dead, whether evil or righteous, while they await the redeemer: which does not mean that their lot is identical."
34. CCC 632, cf. 1 *Pet* 3:18-19.
34a. CCC 633, cf. Council of Rome (745): DS 587; Benedict XII, *Cum dudum* (1341): DS 1011;' Clement VI, *Super quibusdam* (1351): DS 1077; Council of Toledo IV (625): DS 485; *Mt* 27:52-53.
34b. CCC 637.
35. CCC 635, quoting *Rev* 1:18; *Phil* 2:10 [; *Phil* 2:11] (bold face added).

By His death, Jesus Christ abolished death. He brought freedom and eternal life to the souls of the just of all times, to those who have been, who are, and who will be faithful to God during their lives. Before Christ's victory, the souls of the faithful departed were held captive in Hades, the abode of the dead. But on the day that Jesus Christ died, many holy souls were awakened, and on the day of His resurrection these saints were able to embrace their freedom. *(Mt 27:52-53)"Tombs were opened, and the bodies of many saints who had fallen asleep were raised. And coming forth from their tombs after his resurrection, they entered the holy city and appeared to many."* NAB

When the glory of Christ shined in Hades that day, the souls that had been faithful to God were immediately released into Heaven, and a 'new rule' was established. That is, from that day, until the end of times, at the hour of death all souls who chose to follow Christ's way during their lives on earth would be free and able to go home to Heaven.

Christ said to Saint Peter that He would use him to build His Church, and that His Church was immortal. *(Mt 16:18)"You are Peter, and on this rock I will build my church, and the **powers of death shall not prevail against it**."* bfa Christ gave to His Vicar Peter the power to enforce this 'new rule' that gives souls access to Heaven. He gave him **the keys to our freedom**, that is, the sacraments and the teaching authority. *(Mt 16:19) "I will give you the keys of the kingdom of heaven, and **whatever you bind on earth** shall be bound in heaven, **and whatever you loose** on earth shall be loosed in heaven."* bfa And through Apostolic Succession, the Church still holds these keys and this power today.

THE NICENE CREED

✠OM *"We believe in one God,*
the Father, the Almighty,
maker of heaven and earth,
of all that is seen and unseen.

We believe in one Lord, Jesus Christ,
the only Son of God,
eternally begotten of the Father,
God from God, Light from Light,
true God from true God,
begotten, not made, one in Being with the Father.
Through him all things were made. [cf. Jn 1:2-4]
For us men and for our salvation
he came down from heaven:
by the power of the Holy Spirit
he was born of the Virgin Mary, and became man.

For our sake he was crucified under Pontius Pilate:
he suffered, died, and was buried.
On the third day he rose again
in fulfillment of the Scriptures:
he ascended into heaven
and is seated at the right hand of the Father.
He will come again in glory to judge the living and the dead,
and his kingdom will have no end.

We believe in the Holy Spirit, the Lord, the giver of life,
who proceeds from the Father and the Son.
With the Father and the Son he is worshipped and glorified.
He has spoken through the Prophets.
We believe in one holy catholic and apostolic Church.
We acknowledge one baptism for the forgiveness of sins.
We look for the resurrection of the dead,
and the life of the world to come. Amen."

The creed contains the essential beliefs of the Catholic faith. When we recite the creed we give assent to essential dogmas of faith such as: the miraculous conception of Jesus; the Virginity of Mary, Mother of God; man's salvation through Christ's death and resurrection; Christ's ascension into heaven; Christ's return; the apostolic succession of the Church... But do we know, understand, and believe what we are saying when saying the creed, or are we just reciting it mechanically? We should take time once in a while to reflect on the creed's content, because for one thing, one must believe what the Church teaches in order to be in full communion with the Church, which is a requirement before one can receive holy communion.

The **Nicene creed** was named after the Ecumenical Council that took place during the year 325 in Nicene, Asia Minor; this council defined the creed. The following excerpt from the New Testament is obviously one of the scriptural sources that the Church used to present the origins of Christ as defined in the Nicene Creed. *(Col 1:15-20)"He is the image of the invisible God, / the firstborn of all creation. / For in him were created all things in heaven and on earth, / the visible and the invisible, / whether thrones or dominions or principalities or powers; / all things were created through him and for him. / He is before all things, / and in him all things hold together. / He is the head of the body, the church. / He is the beginning, the firstborn from the dead, / that in all things he himself might be preeminent. / For in him all the fullness was pleased to dwell, / and through him to reconcile all things for him, / making peace by the blood of his cross / [through him], whether those on earth or those in heaven."* NAB

When we study the Nicene Creed,which has an interesting cosmic dimension, we find that it first defines the three persons of God the Trinity; God the Father, the maker of all things; Christ the only Son of God, the manifestation of God the Father; and the Holy Spirit, the giver of life. As we continue, we find that half of the creed talks about the Son, our Lord Jesus Christ. It presents Christ's divine origins and His role in the creation by saying that His Father, the maker of 'all seen and unseen,' made everything through Him, His Son the Christ. The creed then recapitulates Christ's successful mission of mercy. We are reminded that God was made flesh and lived among us as Jesus; and that after He suffered and died to free humanity - which He needed to do only once and for all... *(Rom 6:10)"The death he died, he died to sin, once for all;"* - then, Christ victoriously resurrected taking away satan's power over death. The creed then reminds us that Christ gloriously ascended into the heavens... *(Mk 16:19)"[Jesus] was taken up into heaven and sat down at the right hand of God."* ...and there, prepared a place for each and every soul who would follow His Way. *(Jn 14:3)"I go and prepare a place for you, I will come again and will take you to myself, so that where I am, there you may be also."* This is our hope and faith.

(Jn 12:32)"And I, when I am lifted up from the earth, will draw all people to myself." Since His ascension, Jesus has been faithfully, lovingly, and patiently offering to walk 'the way' back home to heaven with us. Heaven is our home, our place of origin, and our destiny. We are only pilgrims on earth. *(Heb 11:13)"They confessed that they were strangers and foreigners on the earth."* The creed reminds us that Jesus brings a great hope to those who choose to follow Him by promising them the priceless inheritance of resurrection and eternal life in heaven. This is the promise of Christ, in Whom we put our faith.

As the creed continues it talks about the divinity of the Holy Spirit and His continuous intervention in the life of God's people while speaking through His prophets. The Holy Spirit is the One who has been enlightening the minds of God's people. He is the giver of life to whom we owe our faith and our spiritual life. The creed then states that the Church is called to holiness through its apostolic mission to guide souls on Christ's path, starting with baptism and the forgiveness of sins. The Church is also called to spread the hope in the life hereafter by spreading the Good News that Christ has opened the gates of heaven and that we are now free to go home.

How wonderful is this faith that allows us to believe in extraordinary events such as: the beginning of time; the creation of heaven and earth; the incarnation of God in Jesus Christ two thousands years ago; and the return of Christ and how He will then reign over all the earth.

The creed concludes by reminding us of the starting and ending points of a redeemed life: the baptism in Christ that washes away our sins and leads us to resurrection in Christ to live with Him eternally. *"The Creed is like a conclusion of the sacred teaching which had been given to us in the Gospel."* [36]

GENERAL INTERCESSIONS: (Prayer of the Faithful)
✠ *"In the Prayer of the Faithful, the people respond in a certain way to the word of God which they have welcomed in faith and,* **exercising the office of their baptismal priesthood,** *offer prayers to God for the salvation of all... As a rule, the series of intentions is to be*
   a. *For the needs of the* **Church***;*
   b. *For* **public authorities** *and the* **salvation of the whole world***;*
   c. *For* **those burdened** *by any kind of difficulty;*
   d. *For the* **local community***.*

... **The people... stand** *and give expression to their prayer either by an invocation said together after each intention or by praying in silence."* [37]

These instructions from the *Roman Missal* were probably inspired by the following text of Saint Paul. *(1Tim 2:1-2)"First of all, then, I ask that supplications, prayers, petitions, and thanksgivings be offered for everyone, for kings and for all in authority, that we may lead a quiet and tranquil life in all devotion and dignity."* NAB

---

36. Translated from *'Nouveau Missel Quotidien'* (New Daily Missal), p. 365.
37. GIRM [45] 69, cf. SVEC, *Sacrosanctum Concilium,* Constitution on the Sacred Liturgy, no. 53.; GIRM [46] 70, [47] 71 (bold face added).

The General Intercessions, Prayer of the Faithful, are usually presented in the order described above - for the Church, the civil authorities, the salvation of all souls, those oppressed by various needs, and for the local community - , however, the content changes at every Mass.

Standing at his chair, the celebrating priest makes a brief introduction to invite the faithful to pray. Then, from the ambo, a member of the congregation, or the deacon, announces the prayer intentions. These are usually sober, succinct, and of communal character. After each intention, the congregation usually responds in unity with an invocation such as: 'Lord hear our prayer'. After the last intention the priest concludes with a prayer.[38]

Here is a representative example of the format of the *General Intercessions* (Prayer of the Faithful) said at Mass:

> For the needs of the **Church** and its leaders at all levels as they respond each day to the challenges of their ministry, we pray to the Lord:
> R. Lord, hear our prayer.
>
> For the **world leaders**, that they may seek the welfare of their people and to live in harmony with other nations, we pray to the Lord:
> R. Lord, hear our prayer.
>
> For all of **humanity**, that she may welcome her **Salvation in Jesus Christ** our Lord, we pray to the Lord:
> R. Lord, hear our prayer.
>
> For peace and healing among **people and nations,** especially where violence and **suffering** have prevailed for so long, we pray to the Lord:
> R. Lord, hear our prayer.
>
> For God's blessing on the activities of our **parish community** and for the various needs of all who serve in Jesus' name, we pray to the Lord:
> R. Lord, hear our prayer.

"...[On] weekdays, at Mass in the morning, the intercessions of morning prayer may replace the daily form of the general intercessions at Mass." [38a]

---

38. Cf. GIRM [47] 71.
38a. *General Instruction of the Liturgy of the Hours*, Congregation for Divine Worship, Feb. 2, 1971, Chapter II, no.94.

If the Mass is offered for the intention of someone who is still alive, the priest may mention the **intention of the Mass** at the end of the prayer of the faithful. Since most of the Masses are offered for the repose of a departed soul, the priest usually mentions the intention of the Mass at the time of the prayer of 'intercession for the dead' during the great Eucharistic prayer.

Since Jesus taught us that ... *(Mt 18:19)"If two of you agree on earth about anything for which they are to pray, it shall be granted to them by my heavenly Father,"*[NAB] ...you can imagine how powerful the united prayers of a whole congregation are. Now imagine all those catholic congregations in all the different dioceses and countries around the world united in prayer during the Sunday Masses. And now imagine all those Christian assemblies in the world praying together for peace and the coming of Christ's Kingdom. Imagine the power we have. Even though we may not understand or realize the power that the Father has given us through prayer, our loving and almighty heavenly Father still hears our prayers and grants them.

The conclusion of the 'General Intercessions' marks the end of the liturgy of the Word. At this time, **the congregation sits** and recollects in preparation for the liturgy of the Eucharist.

ECCE AGNUS DEI
THIS IS THE LAMB OF GOD

"The Mass is at the same time, and inseparably, the sacrificial memorial in which the sacrifice of the cross is perpetuated and the sacred banquet of communion with the Lord's body and blood. But the celebration of the Eucharistic sacrifice is wholly directed toward the intimate union of the faithful with Christ through communion. To receive communion is to receive Christ himself who has offered himself for us." (CCC 1382)

"*The altar,* around which the Church is gathered in the celebration of the Eucharist, represents the two aspects of the same mystery: the altar of the sacrifice and the table of the Lord." (CCC 1383)

AΩ Introduction to the Liturgy of the Eucharist

Through the liturgy of the Word, we had a dialogue with God. God spoke to us by means of the scripture readings and we responded with acclamations, praises and prayers. *(Heb 10:16)"I will put my laws on their hearts, and write them on their minds."* Since these words we exchanged with God have entered our consciousness and our hearts, we are now better prepared to celebrate the sacrifice of the altar, and partake in the Eucharistic meal. Receiving communion allows us to experience the presence of Christ in the intimacy of our soul, and to be transformed by Him.

With the liturgy of the Eucharist, our dialogue with God becomes an exchange of offerings. We offer ourselves and our gifts to the Father, and the Father gives us His Son in the Eucharist. On the altar of our inner temple we shall offer to God: our weaknesses and strengths; our joys and sorrows; our loved ones and those that we don't love enough; the fruits of our work; our health; our faith, doubts, and fears. And as the priest offers the sacrifice of the altar in our name, the Blood of Christ purifies all of our offerings. *(1Jn 1:7)"The blood of his Son Jesus cleanses us from all sin."* NAB We call upon the Holy Spirit to make our offerings acceptable to God for consecration. We pray for the mystical body of Christ: the living Church, the souls of our deceased loved ones, and all the souls in purgatory. We pray to be brought in communion with the heavenly body of Christ: Mother Mary, the angels, and the saints, whom we shall invite to join our celebration.

Celebrating the Eucharist is more than remembering what happened two thousand years ago. Each time we celebrate the Eucharist, we ask the Father to give us the life of His Son Jesus. And each time we ask, Christ gives us His life, redeeming and purifying us in His Blood. However, Christ doesn't have to die anymore to give us His life. He did that once and for all two thousand years ago. *(Rom 6:9.10)"We know that Christ, raised from the dead, dies no more; death no longer has power over him. As to his death, he died to sin once and for all."* NAB During the sacrifice of the Mass, out of pure love for us, Christ makes His sacrifice present, and allows the Eucharistic species to become His Body and Blood, Soul and Divinity, so that we may substantially receive His life; so that we, the members of His body, may be sanctified.

On the night His passion began, Christ instituted the Eucharist as a means to perpetuate His sacrifice of the cross, which was about to take place, so that the Blood that He was about to shed to wash away our sins would be continuously made present as a means of continuous salvation. Knowing human nature, Christ knew that our weaknesses would cause us to fall again into sin. *(Heb 4:15)"We do not have a high priest who is unable to sympathize with our weaknesses, but one who has similarly been tested in every way, yet without sin."* NAB

When Jesus Christ instituted the Eucharist at the Last Supper, He put an end to an old tradition that consisted in offering animals in sacrifice to God in order to be purified from sin. However, the only sacrifice that could ever take away sins is the sacrifice of Jesus Christ. *(Heb 9:13-14)"For if the blood of goats and bulls and the sprinkling of a heifer's ashes can sanctify those who are defiled so that their flesh is cleansed, how much more will the blood of Christ, who through the eternal spirit offered himself unblemished to God, cleanse our consciences from dead works to worship the living God."*NAB For Jesus is the Lamb of God. *(Jn 1:29)"Behold, the Lamb of God, who takes away the sin of the world!"* One can only imagine in a very limited way how precious the life and the Blood of the Son of God are.

Jesus came to save those sinners with repentant hearts. *(Mt 9:13)"I did not come to call the righteous but sinners [to repentance]."* NAB But Jesus can only save the life of those who want to be saved. What do we need to be saved from? We need to be saved from eternal death which is caused by sin, and which we are the slaves of as one who is the slave of an addiction. *(Rom 6:23)"For the wages of sin is death, but the free gift of God is eternal life in Christ Jesus our Lord."* It is by the grace of God alone that we may be saved from eternal death.

The liturgy of the Eucharist takes us back to the Last Supper, which is much more than a memorable meal. When Christ instituted the Eucharist the night before His death, the Last Supper was immortalized in time as it became one with the Sacrifice of the Cross. This Holy meal never ended, and it will continue until Christ comes again. Since the institution of the Eucharist, the people of God, whom are called by God, have continuously gathered to celebrate the memorial of Christ's sacrifice and to receive the divine food that sanctifies them and gives them life, that sanctifies and gives life to the Church.

During Mass, the mystery of the Sacrifice of the Cross is made present when the priest repeats the actions and words of Christ at the Last Supper. ✢*"For Christ took the bread and the chalice and gave thanks; he broke the bread and gave it to his disciples, saying, "Take, eat, and drink: this is my Body; this is the cup of my Blood. Do this in memory of me." Accordingly, the Church has arranged the entire celebration of the Liturgy of the Eucharist in parts corresponding to precisely these words and actions of Christ. / 1. At the Preparation of the Gifts, the bread and the wine with water are brought to the altar... / 2. In the Eucharistic Prayer, thanks is given to God... / 3. Through the fraction and through Communion, the faithful... receive... the Lord's Body and... Blood in the same way the Apostles received them from Christ's own hands."*[1]

---

1. GIRM [48] 72; cf. *Lk* 22:19-20, *Mt* 26:26-28, *Mk* 14:22-24.

Believing in the mystery of the Eucharist is not an easy thing to do. However, Christ is the One Who tells us that He is really present in the Eucharist. *(Mk 14:22.24)"This is my body, / this is my blood"*.

Mass is not a matter of symbolism, but a matter of faith that one just has to believe. *"We have been instructed in these matters and filled with an unshakable faith that that which seems to be bread, is not bread, though it tastes like it, but the Body of Christ, and that which seems to be wine, is not wine, though it too tastes as such, but the Blood of Christ."* [2]

St. Thomas Aquinas speaks of God's wisdom in giving us Jesus' Body and Blood in the form of bread and wine. *"It is evident to the senses that all the [aspects] of bread and wine remain after consecration. Such is the reasonable course of Divine providence, for it is abominable to eat human flesh and drink human blood. That is why Christ's Body and Blood are offered to us under the species of what we are accustomed to take, namely, bread and wine."* [3] Each time we eat the Body and Blood of Jesus Christ, we are truly transformed. *"We eat Jesus alive and glorious, and our eating neither divides nor harms him. Rather, He transforms us by, as if it were, inverse digestion."* [4]

At times God may bless us with spiritual experiences so that we can actually feel His presence in the Eucharist. Such experiences mainly happen to those with the heart and faith of a child. *(Mt 18:3)"Unless you turn and become like children, you will not enter the kingdom of heaven."* [NAB] *(Lk 17:21)"For behold, the kingdom of God is among you."* [NAB] In any case we may rightfully expect to experience in our life the fruits of receiving the Eucharist, such fruits as inner peace. The Eucharist is also known to lessen the hold that sin has on us.

Words chosen for the Liturgy of the Eucharist are holy, wise, and powerful. And when we take the time to read them, it helps us to put aside our doubtful adult reasoning that keeps us away from heavenly realities. If you invest yourself in the words and rituals that constitute the liturgy of the Eucharist, chances are that by the time you get to communion, your soul's vibrations are going to be quite high, and you will feel closer to God. So even if time is running and the homily might have been a little long, let us not hurry through the most important part of the Mass, that is, the liturgy of the Eucharist during which Christ truly becomes present on the altar.

---

2. Paul VI, *Mysterium Fidei*, quoting St-Cyril of Alexandria, *Catecheses*, 22, 9, *Myst.* 4: PG, 33, 1103.
3. *The Book of Catholic Quotations*, p. 311, quoting St.Thomas of Aquinas, *Summa Theologica*, 3, 75, 5. St. Thomas of Aquinas (1225-1274): doctor of the Church.
4. Germain Grisez, *The Way of the Lord Jesus*, Vol 1., *Christian Moral Principles*, Chap.33, Appendix: The bodily presence of Jesus in the Eucharist.

ΑΩ Liturgy of the Eucharist

(Jn 6:35)"I am the bread of life."
(Jn 6:53-55)"Unless you eat the flesh of the Son of Man and drink his
blood, you have no life in you. Those who eat my flesh and drink my
blood have eternal life, and I will raise them up on the last day.
For my flesh is food indeed, and my blood is drink indeed."
(Lk 22:19)"This is my Body, which will be given for you;
do this in memory of me." NAB

While the object of the liturgy of the Word is the teaching of the Word of God, a function that the priest partially shares with lay readers, the object of the liturgy of the Eucharist is to **make present the sacrifice of the cross**, a function reserved to the ordained priest. During the liturgy of the Eucharist, the most sacred aspect of the priestly ministry occurs. Indeed, as the liturgy prepares the faithful for the most sacred part of the Mass, the **consecration**, the priest becomes Christ's instrument to offer our gifts to the Father so that they may become the Body and Blood, Soul and Divinity of Christ.

The Eucharistic prayers are the means by which Christ, in the person of the priest, offers the sacrifice of the Mass to the Father. Thus, except for acclamations and responses that the congregation is expected to give, the **sacred words** of the Eucharistic prayers are **reserved to the priest** alone. However, since our baptism made us members of the royal priesthood of Christ - although nonordained members - we may and must join the priest spiritually in offering silently the sacrifice of the Mass, which makes present the sacrifice of the cross on the altar.

We will now take a closer look into what the Eucharist is. I do not pretend to explain here the mystery and miracle of the sacrament of the altar. Who could pretend to grasp the fullness of such a great mystery? But rather, I will present and explain the motions surrounding the liturgy of the Eucharist, and the ways in which the faithful are expected to participate. I hope that it will help you to better understand what happens during the sacrifice of the Mass, so that you may more fully benefit from this great gift from God.

Said simply, the main steps of the liturgy of the Eucharist happen as follows:[5] the altar is prepared; the priest receives our gifts of bread and wine, and presents them to the Father; the priest then offers the sacrifice of the Mass, during which the bread and wine become the Body and Blood of Christ; thereafter, the priest breaks one of the consecrated Hosts, the large Host, takes his communion, and then gives the other consecrated Hosts in communion to the faithful.

---

5. See Part Five, Appendix 'H', The Liturgy of the Mass Step by Step.

OFFERTORY RITES
PREPARATION OF THE GIFTS

The offertory rites, which are called the 'preparation of the gifts,' are the actions preparatory to the sacrifice of the Mass. The beginning of the offertory rites marks the beginning of the liturgy of the Eucharist, and is usually accompanied by an **offertory hymn**. The offertory rites start with the 'preparation of the altar', followed by the 'procession of the gifts', and the 'offertory', and concludes with the 'prayer over the gifts.' The people remain **sitting** until the 'prayer over the gifts'.

PREPARATION OF THE ALTAR:

At this point of the Mass, the altar is as it was set before the Mass started:[6] the altar is covered with a pure white cloth on which is set only a crucifix and two lighted candles. To prepare the altar for the sacrifice of the Mass, in one motion the servers bring the following from the credence table to the altar: the **chalice** with the **purificator**, the **paten** with the **large host**, the **corporal** with the **pall**, and any extra ciboria of bread that will not be carried in the procession of the gifts. A chalice veil and a burse of the liturgical color of the day may also be used: the burse, used to contain the corporal, sits on top of the paten and host, with the veil covering the burse and the chalice.

The priest, or server, unfolds the corporal at the center of the altar on the 'altar stone', [6a] places the chalice and purificator at the right side of the altar (the priest's right hand), and places the paten with the large host on the corporal. The extra ciboria of bread are placed on the outline of the corporal. The **Missal** is placed on its stand on the altar, on the left of the corporal, opened to the appropriate page. The servers bring the chalice veil and burse back to the credence.

PROCESSION OF THE GIFTS:

Once the altar is prepared, the offerings of bread and wine are presented to the priest, either by the servers or by members of the congregation. ✢*"It is praiseworthy for the bread and wine to be presented by the faithful. Even though the faithful no longer bring from their own possessions the bread and wine intended for the liturgy as in the past, nevertheless the rite of carrying up the offerings still retains its force and its spiritual significance."* [7]

When the gifts are to be presented to the priest by members of the congregation, before Mass, the offerings are set on the **'table of the gifts'**, which is usually placed in the nave near the front pews, or

---

6. See Part Two, Preparing Ourselves and the Temple, e) Preparing the Sanctuary.
6a. Since the corporal may have been used in a prior Mass and may contain particles of Host, never flick it open or shake it open in midair. How to unfold the corporal: see Part Five, Questions & Answers, Question 69. The Altar Stone: see Part Five, Church Norms, Arrangement and Furnishing of Churches, The Altar Stone.
7. GIRM [49] 73 (bold face added).

somewhere in the center aisle.[8] The offerings of bread and wine presented by members of the congregation consist of a **ciborium** of unconsecrated hosts and a **cruet**, or a decanter, **of wine**. The cruet of water is brought to the altar by a server at the time of the 'offertory', and the other needed vessels and linens are brought at a later time during the celebration.

The procession of the gifts begins when the celebrating priest leaves the altar with the servers and walks to the front of the sanctuary to receive the offerings. At this point, predetermined members of the congregation, usually two of them, reverently come out of their pew and take the gifts in procession from the 'table of the gifts' to the front of the sanctuary where they present the gifts to the celebrating priest. The servers assist the priest in bringing the gifts to the altar. Meanwhile, members of the congregation collect our money offerings for the needs of the Church, and especially the poor, and place them at a suitable place away from the altar.[9]

If a deacon is present, he is usually the one who prepares the altar, receives the gifts from the faithful, and prepares the gifts for the offertory. However, since **only an ordained priest** can celebrate the sacrament of the Eucharist, the priest, and not the deacon, is the one who offers the gifts and the sacrifice of the Mass to God.

At the time of the 'procession of the gifts,' if the **offerings** of bread and wine are **presented by the servers**, they first bring the ciborium *(ciboria)* containing the hosts to be consecrated for the communion of the faithful from the credence table to the altar. As the priest proceeds with the 'offertory',[10] the servers then bring him the offering of **wine** and the water contained in the cruets.

Let us take a closer look at the sacred vessels and linens.[11] The **pall** is a stiff square piece of cardboard or acrylic, covered with linen, used to cover the chalice during Mass. It is used to prevent dust or flying insects from falling into the wine of the Eucharist. The **corporal** is a small white linen, well pressed and folded, that the priest reverently unfolds on the altar and uses to prepare and to offer the sacrifice of the Mass. When brought to the altar, the corporal covers the **large host** contained in a small plate called the **paten**. The paten is used to consecrate the large host, and the **ciborium** is used to consecrate the small hosts. A larger paten may be used to contain both the large and

---

8. See Part Two, Preparing Ourselves and the Temple, e) Preparing the Sanctuary.
9. Money offerings away from the altar: cf. GIRM [49] 73. The collection of money offerings is to be interrupted during the consecration.
10. Offertory: see page 91.
11. Sacred vessels & linens: see picture on the next page; also see Part Three, After the Mass, the Sacristy and the Purification of the Sacred Linens.

the small hosts. At the time of the consecration the hosts become the Body of Christ. The **chalice** is used to contain and consecrate the wine mixed with water, which, at the time of the consecration, becomes the Blood of Christ. The **purificator** is another small white linen, which is used by the priest to wipe the chalice during the sacrifice, during communion, and after communion, in order to collect any remnants of the Blood of Christ. Since all of these sacred vessels and linens come in direct contact with the Body and Blood of Christ, they need to be handled with great reverence.

At the time of communion, ciboria of consecrated Hosts that are **reserved in the tabernacle**[12] may be brought to the altar for communion of the faithful. *"...[T]hey also participate in the same sacrifice to whom a priest distributes the Blessed Sacrament that has been reserved; however, the Church has not... ever forbidden, ... a celebrant to satisfy the piety and just request of those who, when present at Mass, want to become partakers of the same sacrifice, because **they likewise offer it** after their own manner... ."*[13] *"[It is a] more perfect form of participation in the Mass whereby the faithful, after the priest's communion, **receive** the Lord's Body **from the same sacrifice**... ."*[13a]

In many churches, the tabernacle is located outside of the sanctuary on a secondary altar.[14] The **sanctuary lamp**, located near the tabernacle, is kept lit as an indication to all of the real presence of God

12. See Part Three, Liturgy of the Eucharist, Communion Rite, The Eucharistic Reserve. Ciboria, Tabernacle, and Sanctuary Lamp: see Part Five, Catholic Glossary.
13. *Mediator Dei*, no. 118 (bold face added).
13a. CCC 1388, quoting *SC* 55 (bold face added).
14. See Part Five, Floor Plan of a Church in the Shape of a Latin Cross.

in the consecrated Hosts that are kept in the tabernacle. Since ciboria, Hosts, the tabernacle, and all the objects used to celebrate the Eucharist come in contact with or have become the Body and Blood of Christ, they are considered sacred and are to always be treated with the greatest respect, care, and reverence.

Sacred Silence

Once the gifts have been placed on the altar, the **offertory hymn** comes to an end. A sacred silence then takes place in the church as the priest recites the formulas of the offertory: *"Blessed are you, Lord, God of all creation... ."* Although he may say it silently, it is good for all to hear these sacred words. Indeed, since we, the faithful, are called to exercise our **priesthood of the laity** during the Mass, we need to be very attentive to all the sacred words said by the priest during the offertory, the sacrifice, the consecration, and during all of the other Eucharistic prayers. ✝*"In the celebration of Mass the faithful form a holy people, a people whom God has made his own, a royal priesthood, so that they may give thanks to God and **offer** the spotless Victim not only through the hands of the priest but also **together with him**, and so that they may learn to offer themselves."* [15]

Before going any further with the liturgy of the Eucharist, let us recall the kind of offerings that are pleasing to God, starting with a teaching from the Old Testament: *(Ps 51:17)"The sacrifice acceptable to God is a broken spirit; / a broken and contrite heart, O God, you will not despise."* In the Gospel, Jesus takes this teaching a step further when He tells us that showing love not only to God but also to our neighbor is an offering and a sacrifice that really pleases God. *(Mk 12:33)"To love [the Lord] with all your heart, with all your understanding, with all your strength, and to love your neighbor as yourself' is worth more than all burnt offerings and sacrifices."* [NAB]

While the priest presents our offerings of bread and wine to the Lord, we spiritually join him in offering the sacrifice of the Mass. We put on our inner altar, all that we have, material and spiritual, and everyone and everything that we carry in our hearts, and offer it all to God. We offer in a special way the people and the areas of our lives that need to be purified, healed, and saved. *(Mt 9:13)"I desire mercy, not sacrifice."* Once we have gathered our offerings on the altar of our souls, we spiritually put them on the paten and in the chalice on the altar, so that they may be offered to the Father within the sacrifice of the Mass. *(Sir 35:5)"The just man's offering enriches the altar / and rises as a sweet odor before the Most High."* [NAB] As we present our spiritual offerings we expose our heart to God and allow Him to touch

---

15. GIRM [62] 95, cf. SVEC, Constitution on the Sacred Liturgy, *Sacrosanctum Concilium*, no. 48; Sacred Congregation of Rites, Instruction *Eucharisticum mysterium*, On the worship of the Eucharist, 25 May 1967, no. 12: AAS 59 (1967), pp. 548-549 (bfa).

and heal us along with the people and the areas of our lives that we present to Him. Based on Jesus' teaching we believe that once the priest has offered the bread and wine to the Father for consecration, they become the Body and the Blood of Jesus Christ. We believe that the precious Blood of Jesus, which is the single most precious thing in the universe, purifies our spiritual offerings and makes them part of the mystical Body of Christ. It is a divine pattern. Everything we offer to God comes back to us consecrated and purified. How can it be otherwise?

"Let the souls of Christians be like altars on each one of which a different phase of the sacrifice, offered by the High Priest, comes to life again, as it were: pains and tears which wipe away and expiate sin; supplication to God which pierces heaven; dedication and even immolation of oneself made promptly, generously and earnestly; and, finally, that intimate union by which we commit ourselves and all we have to God, in whom we find our rest." [16]

OFFERTORY:

Let us continue with the celebration of the Mass. All is silent in the church. The paten containing the large host is sitting on the corporal and the priest is about to offer the gifts to the Father.

Offering of the Bread

With both hands the priest holds the paten, containing **the large host**, slighty raised above the altar and says quietly; [17]

✠[OM] *"Blessed are you, Lord, God of all creation.*
    Through your goodness we have this bread to offer,
    which earth has given and human hands have made.
    It will become for us the bread of life.
[We all answer quietly;] **Blessed be God for ever**.*"* [18] [bfa]
The priest then places the paten and host on the corporal.

Preparing of the Wine Oblation

The servers come to the right side of the altar, one with the wine cruet, and the other with the water cruet, and they assist the priest in preparing the wine oblation (offering). ✠*"After this, as the [server] presents the cruets, the priest stands at the side of the altar and **pours wine and a little water into the chalice**, saying quietly:*
    "By the mystery of this water and wine may we come
    to share in the divinity of Christ, who humbled himself
    to share in our humanity."" [19]

---

16. *Mediator Dei,* no. 152.
17. Cf. GIRM [102] 141.
18. All the Offertory and Eucharistic prayers are also found in the faithful's missal.
19. GIRM [102] 141, [103] 142, quoting *The order of Mass*, (bold face added).

When communion under both species is offered to all, the quantity of wine required is greater than usual. Thus, the wine offering might be presented in a **decanter** rather than in a cruet. If so, the priest might add the water to the wine offering directly into the decanter, before pouring the wine into the chalices for the consecration.

Since the sacrifice of the Mass is at the center of the liturgical celebration, the altar of the sacrifice is purposely positioned at the center of the sanctuary, so that **all may see the priest's actions at the altar**. Thus, as we, the faithful, see the priest adding water to the wine in the chalice, we spiritually add our humanity to the holy sacrifice, and ask the Father to sanctify us and our offerings in the Blood of Christ.

This is an exquisite opportunity to open up to the Father, to show Him our faith and hope in Him, and to be blessed by Him. As we put our humanity on the altar with the bread and wine, silently recalling some of **Jesus' promises** to those who follow His way may help in strengthening our faith and our hope. *(Mt 11:28)"Come to me, all you that are weary and are carrying heavy burdens, and I will give you rest." (Jn 14:13)"Whatever you ask in my name, I will do it."*

Jesus said in more than one way that **He came for the sick**, for what was broken. *(Lk 19:10)"For the Son of Man came to seek out and to save the lost."* But Jesus needs for us to offer Him our brokenness so that He may heal us, so that He may perfect our life as the Father intended our life to be. God created us free, and He never forces Himself on us. Thus, if we want God in our life, we need to invite Him.

At times, our love for God might make it difficult for us to offer Him **our brokenness** because we think in accordance with the world. Indeed, the world teaches us that when you love someone you usually do not offer him something that is broken, but rather, you offer him something nice, you want to give him the 'perfect' gift. Well, what makes sense to God usually does not make sense to the world. *(1Co 1:20)"Has not God made foolish the wisdom of the world?"* Our loving and almighty Father wants us to offer Him all that is broken and imperfect in our lives so that He may bless us with healing and purification, and give us perfect gifts. *(Jas 1:17)"Every generous act of giving, with every perfect gift, is from above, coming down from the Father of lights, with whom there is no variation or shadow due to change."*

While we meditate on what we need to offer to the Father, the priest continues with the **offertory** of the gifts.

OFFERING OF THE WINE OBLATION

✥*"[The priest] returns to the middle of the altar, takes the chalice with both hands, raises it a little, and says quietly;"* [20]

✥OM *"Blessed are you, Lord, God of all creation.*
Through your goodness we have this wine to offer,
fruit of the vine and work of human hands.
It will become our spiritual drink.
[We all answer:]   **Blessed be God for ever.**"

✥*"Then [the priest] places the chalice on the corporal and may cover it with a pall as appropriate. ...The priest bows profoundly and says quietly;"* [21]

✥OM *"Lord God, we ask you to receive us and be pleased with the sacrifice we offer you with humble and contrite hearts."*

INCENSING:

While incensing during Mass was somewhat put aside for the past decades, it is gratifying to now see more and more that the ritual of incensing is being reintroduced into the liturgy of the Mass. The use of incense has been part of the Catholic liturgical tradition for centuries. It is a sensible sign of our offerings and prayers rising up to God; a sign of prayer, sacrifice, and reverence for the people and the sacred objects being incensed. Incensation is one of the richest liturgical signs.

✥ "Incense may be used if desired in any form of Mass:
  a. *During the Entrance procession;*
  b. *At the beginning of Mass, to incense the cross and the altar;*
  c. *At the Gospel procession and the proclamation of the Gospel;*
  d. *After the bread and the chalice have been placed upon the altar, to incense the offerings, the cross, and the altar, as well as the priest and the people;*
  e. *At the showing of the host and the chalice after the consecration."*[22]

When incense is to be used during the Mass, the thurible is prepared ahead of time in the sacristy, and it is either carried in the entrance procession or brought into the sanctuary when needed. When it is time for incensing, assisted by the thurifer and a server, or a deacon, the priest puts incense into the thurible: *"The **thurifer** opens the **thurible** [censor] and holds it at a convenient level, ensuring that none of the chains impedes access to the bowl. The deacon [or server] presents the open **boat** [which contains the incense] and **spoon** at the level of the hands of the celebrant so that he may easily place **incense on the charcoal**."*[23]

---

20. GIRM [103] 142.
21. GIRM [103] 142; [104] 143.
22. GIRM [235] 276. Incensing: see also *Ps* 140 (141):2; *Rev* 8:3-4.
23. CMRR, chap. 6, 385. The thurible is prepared and placed at hand before Mass (bfa).

✠"*The priest, having put incense into the thurible, blesses it with the sign of the Cross, without saying anything. Before and after an incensation, a profound bow is made to the person or object that is incensed, except for the incensation of the altar and the offerings for the Sacrifice of the Mass.*"[24]

INCENSING THE OFFERINGS, THE ALTAR, AND THE PEOPLE
✠ "*...The priest may incense the **gifts** placed upon the altar and then incense the **cross** and the **altar** itself, so as to signify the Church's **offering and prayer rising like incense** in the sight of God. Next, **the priest**, because of his sacred ministry, **and the people**, by reason of their baptismal dignity, **may be incensed** by the deacon or another minister.*"[25] bfa

The Church's tradition of incensing, and even the manner of burning the incense, was adopted from Judaism. *(Lev 16:12.13)"He shall take a censer full of coals of fire... and two handfuls of crushed sweet incense, and he shall... put the incense on the fire before the LORD, that the cloud of the incense may cover the mercy seat that is upon the covenant."*

WASHING OF THE HANDS
After presenting the gifts of wine for the Offertory, the servers place the wine and water cruets back on the credence table, and then return to their places. Then, both servers go to the credence table and gather the vessels and linen needed for the ritual of the washing of the hands. One of the servers puts the **manuterge** (hand towel) on his left forearm and takes the **water cruet** with his right hand. The other server takes the **wash plate**. Together they walk to the side of the altar, at the right hand of the priest.

✠"*The priest then washes his hands at the side of the altar, a rite that is an expression of his desire for interior purification.*"[26] The priest then turns towards the servers and holds his hands over the wash plate. One of the servers pours a little bit of water on the priest's fingers, who then wipes his hands with the manuterge.

While washing his hands, the priest quietly says the following prayer:
✠OM "*Lord wash away my iniquity; cleanse me from my sins.*"

This ritual of 'the washing of the hands' enhances the importance of being pure before confecting, touching, or receiving the Eucharist. Since it is in our name that the priest offers the sacrifice of the Mass,

---

24. GIRM [236] 277.
25. GIRM [51] 75.
26. GIRM [52] 76.

it is also in our name that he washes his hands and prays for purification. So let us join the priest spiritually in this ritual and pray silently for our own purification.

As mentioned earlier, the Holy Mass is a sanctification process that starts with the 'penitential rite'. Saying silently this prayer with the priest during the rite of the 'washing of the hands' is among the many opportunities offered to us during the Mass to open our hearts to a deeper purification. We should seek and desire, that when the time comes to receive the Lord at communion, nothing stands between us and Him, that our inner temples are worthy to host Him. Seeking purification is seeking holiness. We should seek to be made holy enough to receive Him Who is holy.

Let us not hurry at this point of the Mass. Too often, the rhythm of the Mass accelerates after the liturgy of the Word. It is as though the most important part of the Mass was over, and we just hurry to communion. But in reality, the most important and **sacred part of the Mass is yet to come**, that is, the sacrifice of the Mass, the consecration.

Through the Catholic Church, the Holy Spirit has done magnificent work developing and organizing the liturgy of the Mass. **Let us not underestimate the spiritual effects** that each of the Eucharistic prayers and actions have on us, the faithful. For instance, let us think for a moment of how holy is the act of the priest elevating the Body and then the Blood of Christ for **adoration** by the faithful. We cannot humanly fully grasp the effect that adoration has on the soul, but we can experience some of the blessed effects that this act of worship has on us. As we kneel and bow even for a moment before the Eucharist, it brings our mind and soul to acknowledge and deepen the mystery and miracle of the real presence of God in the Body and Blood, Soul and Divinity of Christ in the Eucharist. When we adore, we come to realize that the power of God dwells much above our human perceptions and limits. We may also come to realize that it is only by humbling ourselves on our knees in front of God that we may have access to His dwelling. When we bow to adore God, we are affected beyond our understanding. Adoration enhances our expectations towards God, and there can't be any mistake in expecting the most from God and from His presence in the Eucharist.

Even though the Mass is rich in **symbolism**, do not give into the lie that the holy Mass is only symbolism. The sacrifice of the Mass truly makes present the sacrifice of the Cross. The Body and Blood, the Soul and Divinity of our Lord Jesus Christ truly become present on the altar at the time of the consecration. Therefore, let us not fall into the trap of letting Mass become a routine, but rather, let us take the time to celebrate the sacrifice of the altar with due reverence and faith.

PRAYER OVER THE GIFTS:

⊕"*Once the offerings have been placed on the altar and the accompanying rites completed, the invitation to pray with the priest and the prayer over the offerings conclude the preparation of the gifts and prepare for the Eucharistic Prayer. Upon returning to the middle of the altar, the priest, facing the people and extending and then joining his hands, invites the people to pray.*"[27] The **people stand**[28] as the priest says:

⊕OM "*Pray, brethren, that our sacrifice*
    may be acceptable to God, the almighty Father.

[The people respond:]
    May the Lord accept the sacrifice at your hands
    for the praise and glory of his name,
    for our good, and the good of all his Church."

⊕OM "[*With hands extended, the priest sings or says*
    the **prayer over the gifts**,...]
"*Almighty God,*
the saving work of Christ
made our peace with you.
May our offering today
renew that peace within us
and give you perfect praise.
We ask this in the name of Jesus the Lord."[29]

[...at the end of which the people respond:] **Amen!** "

This little word 'Amen' has much more power than we might realize. When we say 'Amen', we say 'Yes, I agree, let it be so'. This little word 'Amen' is a prayer in itself. Whether we realize it or not, our words and thoughts are the expression of our hearts, thus, they are our prayers, which are heard by God. *(Mt 15:18)*"*What comes out of the mouth proceeds from the heart.*" Fortunately for us, the Father only grants the prayers that meet His plan. *(Jer 29:11)*"*I know the plans I have for you, says the LORD, plans for your welfare and not for harm, to give you a future with hope.*" We invite into our lives what we think about and believe in. The more our thoughts and words are directed at knowing God, the more chance God has of revealing Himself to us. Let us give the Father a chance to give us the gifts He has intended for us to help us grow. Let us pay attention to the kind of thoughts that we nurture. *(Col 3:2)*"*Set your minds on things that are above, not on things that are on earth.*" Let us pray with confidence in God's love for us, let us say our 'Amen' as our 'Yes' to God, and let us watch God revealing Himself to us and improving our lives.

---

27. GIRM [53] 77, [107] 146.
28. Cf. GIRM [21] 43.
29. *The Order of Mass*, Christmas — Mass during the day, Prayer Over the Gifts.

THE EUCHARISTIC PRAYER:

✝*"Now the center and summit of the entire celebration begins: namely, the Eucharistic Prayer, that is, the prayer of thanksgiving and sanctification... The meaning of the Prayer is that the entire congregation of the faithful should join itself with Christ in confessing the great deeds of God and in the offering of Sacrifice."* [30]

✝*"...The Eucharistic Prayer demands, by its very nature, that **only the priest say it** in virtue of his ordination. The people... should associate themselves with the priest in faith and in silence, as well as through their parts... namely, the responses in the Preface dialogue, the* Sanctus, *the acclamation after the consecration, [and] the acclamatory* Amen *after the final doxology... ."* [31] [bfa] Although the Eucharistic prayers are reserved to the priest, you will notice that he uses the word 'we' when reciting these prayers. He, the ordained priest in Christ's royal priesthood, speaks in our name, 'we', the baptized members of Christ's royal priesthood, yet nonordained. Thus, we shall assume our priesthood by joining spiritually with the priest in his prayers and actions as he offers the sacrifice of the Mass to God the Father. ✝*"The nature of the "presidential" texts demands that they be spoken in a loud and clear voice and that everyone listen with attention. Thus, while the priest is speaking these texts, there should be **no other prayers or singing**, and the **organ or** other **musical instruments** should be silent."* [32] [bfa]

INTRODUCTORY DIALOGUE:

The introductory dialogue introduces the Eucharistic Prayer. From the offertory through communion, the priest stands at the middle of the altar facing the assembly while reciting the Eucharistic prayers. The priest extends his arms, and we join him in the following dialogue:

[The priest:]   ✝[OM] *"The Lord be with you.*
[The people answer:] **And also with you.**

[The priest:]   *Lift up your hearts.*
[The people:]   **We lift them up to the Lord.**

[The priest:]   *Let us give thanks to the Lord our God.*
[The people:]   **It is right to give him thanks and praise.**"

---

30. GIRM [54] 78.
31. GIRM [108] 147; cf. *Redemptionis Sacramentum* no. 52.
32. GIRM [12] 32. "It is a reminder of **wrong practices** that has greatly impeded and diminished the people's participation in this central part of the Mass. It is obvious that the... so-called **background music** often puts into the background what should be foremost and dominant. A "background" accompaniment of the priest's homily would be out of the question: but in the eucharistic prayer the word of the presider..., reaches the peak of its meaning." *Notitiae,* Sacred Congregation for Divine Worship, Notices on the GIRM, no.12, (1969-1981), *Not* 13 (1977) 94-95, no.2.

THE EIGHT CHIEF ELEMENTS [33]

There are **four Eucharistic Prayers** the priest may choose from, according to the circumstances. Each one of the Eucharistic Prayers includes the same **eight chief elements**, yet their forms and their sequences vary slightly from one Eucharistic Prayer to the other. To illustrate the eight chief elements, I have chosen to present here the **Eucharistic Prayer II**, which chief elements follow the sequence given in the GIRM, as listed bellow:

1- **Preface** - praise to the Father : *Thanksgiving*;
2- **Sanctus** - Holy Holy : *Acclamation*;
3- **Invocation of the Holy Spirit** : *Epiclesis*;
4- **The Lord's Supper** : *Institution Narrative and Consecration*;
5- **Memorial Acclamation** : *Anamnesis*;
6- **Memorial Prayer** : *Offering [of the Victim of the sacrifice]*;
7- *Intercessions* : **For the Church,**
                    : **For the dead,**
                    : **In communion with the saints**; and
8- **In praise of God** : *Doxology*.

"No person... may add, remove or change anything in the Liturgy... "[33a] especially the words of the chief elements of the Eucharistic Prayer.

1- PREFACE: (*Thanksgiving*)

According to the liturgical calendar, the celebrating priest chooses a Eucharistic preface that is suited for the mass of the day. There are **eighty-four** prefaces published in the *Roman Missal*. They all contain powerful words inspired from the Holy Scriptures, and each preface is as beautiful as the next. The prefaces have a three-part structure: the first part addresses **thanksgiving and praises** to God the Father; the second part relates the **work of salvation** by Jesus Christ; and the third part closes the thanksgiving prayer by declaring **our unity with the heavenly beings** and proclaiming **Gods' glory**. On a feast day, a distinct Eucharistic preface is read, which portrays the participation of either Mother Mary, a saint, or angels in the plan of salvation. The texts of the Eucharistic prefaces are true spiritual treasures. Read and meditate upon them at home when you have a chance; you will find them spiritually beneficial.

The following Eucharistic preface - Sundays in Ordinary Time I - is a good example of how the prefaces recall the work of salvation. Here, we are reminded that Christ brought us salvation through His passion, death, and resurrection; and that the Father's plan of salvation for us comes through our baptism in Jesus Christ, which makes us members of His royal and heavenly family.

---

33. Cf. GIRM [55] 79, [322] 365. Also see Part Five, Appendix 'H', Structure of the Eucharistic Prayers.
33a. *Inaestimabile Donum,* Foreword, cf. Second Vatican Council, Constitution on the Sacred Liturgy, *Sacrosanctum concilum,* nos. 22, 3.

As the celebrant stands at the middle of the altar with extended arm, a reverential silence flows through the **congregation standing** in the church. The celebrant then prays aloud to the Father in the name of all who are gathered in the church.[34]

PREFACE OF SUNDAYS IN ORDINARY TIME I [35]

✢OM *"Father, all-powerful and ever-living God,*
we do well always and everywhere to give you thanks
through Jesus Christ our Lord.
Through his cross and resurrection
he freed us from sin and death
and called us to the glory that has made us
a chosen race, a royal priesthood,
a holy nation, a people set apart.
Everywhere we proclaim your mighty works,
for you have called us out of darkness
into your own wonderful light. [cf. 1Pt 2:9]
And so, with all the choirs of angels in heaven
we proclaim your glory
and join in their unending hymn of praise:"

2- SANCTUS: (*Acclamation*: Holy, Holy)

✢*"...The whole congregation, joining with the heavenly powers, [the angels and the saints] sings the* Sanctus.*"*[35a] Let us sing! ♪

✢OM *"Holy, holy, holy Lord, God of power and might,*
heaven and earth are full of your glory. [cf. Rev 4:8]
Hosanna in the highest.
Blessed is he who comes in the name of the Lord.
Hosanna in the highest." [cf. Mt 21:9]

As far as I am concerned, the *Sanctus* is not meant to be said but to be sung. For one thing, the congregation has been quiet and mainly listening for a while, and singing allows the faithful to take a more active part in the liturgy. Then, we should sing the *Sanctus* because not only is singing praying twice,[36] but also, within the conclusion of the Eucharistic preface, we have just invited our allies, the angels, to sing this love song to God with us - a love song that praises God for his might, his holiness, and for the glory of His Son, Jesus Christ. We

---

34. Before reciting the Preface, the priest may mention which Eucharistic Prayer and Preface he has chosen in order to allow the faithful to follow in their missal.
35. Although the 'Eucharistic Prayer II' - which is here used to present the entire Eucharistic Prayer - has its own Preface, the 'Preface of Ordinary Time I' was chosen for illustrative purposes. Eucharistic Prayer II: see GIRM [322] 365b.
35a. GIRM [55b] 79b.
36. Singing is praying twice: cf. GIRM [19] 39.

should sing the *Sanctus* because at this point of the Mass, it is our last chance to raise our voices and souls' vibrations to better prepare our hearts before the priest starts the holy ritual of consecration.

The following biblical excerpts have surely inspired the Sanctus:
(Isa 6:2-3)"Seraphs were in attendance above him; each had six wings; And one called to another and said: / "Holy, holy, holy is the LORD of hosts; the whole earth is full of his glory."
(Rev 4:8)"Day and night they never cease to sing, / "Holy, holy, holy, is the Lord God Almighty, / who was and is and is to come!"
(Mk 11:9.10)"Those preceding [Jesus] as well as those following kept crying out: / "Hosanna! [37] */ Blessed is he who comes in the name of the Lord!... / Hosanna in the highest!""* NAB

Here are a few reminders for **choir directors** to improve participation of the faithful in singing the *Sanctus*.
- Try not to change the *Sanctus* hymn too often, participation of the faithful will be better if they already know the song;
- Try to choose a *Sanctus* hymn that is in an easy key for all to sing, and that you have noticed before seems to entice people to sing; [38] and
- Choose a *Sanctus* that uses the words of the *Sanctus* as found in the *Roman Missal*, not one that changes them.

I rejoice in the fact that the **angels** are mentioned in the liturgy of the Mass. Many of us have learned as a child that everyone has a guardian angel assigned to them for life, to look after us. But as we grow towards adulthood, it becomes unacceptable to either talk to or about this invisible heavenly friend of ours. Is believing in angels only part of a child's faith? When we look into the bible there are hundreds of references to the angels, whom act as God's messengers, as well as references to archangels, seraphim, and cherubim.

Most of us have heard about choirs of angels and have seen them depicted in masters' paintings, which were probably inspired by biblical texts. Even though heavenly beings are invisible to humans, angels and saints as well as the Mother of God are always present during the holy Mass, as they are always present to serve and worship the Lamb of God, wherever He is. Through the 'Eucharistic Prayer' we invite these heavenly hosts to join our celebration and to intercede for us. Just try to picture the angels standing near the altar and singing the *Sanctus* in harmony with us, and then, prostrating themselves before the Eucharist from the time of consecration until communion.

---

37. Hosanna: Hebrew for "save us now". It was the acclamation of the crowd when Jesus victoriously entered Jerusalem (Palm Sunday). It is a shout of joy and triumph.
38. Singing: see Part Two, Preparing Ourselves and the Temple, h) Choir director.

*(Ps 95:6)"O come, let us worship and bow down,
let us kneel before the LORD, our Maker!"
(1Jn 2:2)"He is the atoning sacrifice for our sins."*

🔔 CONSECRATION ✝

✝ *"...[The faithful]* **should kneel** *beginning after the singing or recitation of the* **Sanctus** *until after the* **Amen** *of the Eucharistic Prayer, except when prevented on occasion by reasons of health, lack of space, the large number of people present, or some other good reason. Those who do not kneel ought to make a profound bow when the priest genuflects after the consecration."* [39] bfa

It is with warmth in our hearts and veneration in our souls that we now go down on our knees as the priest prepares to say the words of consecration. At this time, everyone is being called upon to make a special leap of faith, to believe that by the power of the Holy Spirit, God the Father is going to alter the nature of the bread and wine offerings, and that they will become the Body and Blood of His Son, Jesus Christ. This great mystery and miracle is repeated each time the Holy Mass is celebrated.

Since the priest is instrumental to the consecration, sometimes I think that it must be somewhat more difficult for the priest than for us to make this leap of faith. But fortunately, Christ's presence in the Eucharist is independent of our level of faith. Christ, Who is One with God the Father and the Holy Spirit, is always truly and wholly present in the sacrament of the altar, despite the limits of our faith.

---

39. GIRM [21] 43, cf. SVEC, Constitution on the Sacred Liturgy, *Sacrosanctum Concilium*, no.40; Congregation for Divine Worship & the Discipline of the Sacraments, Instruction *Varietates legitimae*, 25 January 1994, no. 41: AAS 87 (1995), p. 304.

*"Christ having once died in a bloody manner cannot do so again. The Mass is therefore the unbloody renewal of the sacrifice of the Calvary. Christ does not die again in the Mass, but **his death is symbolized by the separate consecration of the bread and the wine** which is a figure of the separation of his Blood from his Body... the sacrifice of the Calvary is daily continued in the Mass. There, Christ renews innumerable times the offering of himself for the glory of God."* [40]

🔔 **PLEASE, RING THE LITTLE BELL!** 🔔

✝ *"A little before the consecration, when appropriate, a server rings a bell as a signal to the faithful. According to local custom, the server also rings the bell as the priest shows [elevates] the host and then the chalice."* [41] In some places it is still customary to also ring the big church bells at the time of the consecration to indicate to all that Jesus is being made present on the altar. A praiseworthy custom!

Unfortunately, it is not a standard practice to ring the bell during the Mass anymore as it was prior to the Second Council Vatican.[41a] Although it seems to be an insignificant element of the liturgy of the Mass, ringing the bell makes a difference in our worship. Omitting to ring the bell at the consecration and at each elevation takes away a sensible sign and certain sense of sacredness from the Mass. It takes away a certain spiritual impact from the communicants. When the bell rings, it seizes us in a way that makes us more aware of the moment and of God's presence in the Eucharist; and it calls upon us to submit to the Lord, and to render to Him immediate reverence and homage. So please, ring that little bell again! 🔔 If someone has gotten rid of it... buy a new one and offer it as a gift to the parish!

3- INVOCATION OF THE HOLY SPIRIT: *(Epiclesis)* [42]

Now, let us get back to the third chief element of the Eucharistic prayer, the *Epiclesis* or *Invocation of the Holy Spirit*. ✝ *"...The Church implores the power of the Holy Spirit that the gifts offered by human hands be consecrated, that is, become Christ's Body and Blood, and that the spotless Victim to be received in Communion be for the salvation of those who will partake of it."* [43]

---

40. Louis Trauffer, O.S.B. and Virgil Michel, O.S.B., *Orate Frates* 1 #3, 1927, Liturgical Press, 79.
41. GIRM [109] 150.
41a. Many signs and rituals that were removed from our churches and our liturgy after the Council were not mandated. Other changes: see Part Five, Church Norms, I-Arrangement and Furnishing of Churches, Changes in Arrangement and Furnishing.
42. The word 'Epiclesis' means 'invocation', here the priest invokes the Holy Spirit.
43. GIRM [55c] 79c.

This is the high point of the Mass, a very holy and powerful moment. Christ, represented by the priest, is about to offer Himself in sacrifice to the Father so that we may receive His life at communion. Therefore, throughout the Eucharistic prayer, which ends with the Doxology, it is on our knees that we will participate and honor His holy sacrifice. *(Rom 14:11)"Every knee shall bow to me." (Jas 4:10)"Humble yourselves before the Lord and he will exalt you."* ^{NAB}

While the **congregation is kneeling**, the priest stands in the center of the altar, and with arms extended, in the manner of Jesus on the Cross, begins to say the 'Invocation of the Holy Spirit':

✤^{OM} *"Lord, you are holy indeed,*
  the fountain of all holiness.

[The priest then joins his hands before laying them over the bread and the chalice.]
  Let your Spirit come upon these gifts to make them holy,
  so that they may become for us
  the Body ✠ ⁴⁴ *and Blood of our Lord Jesus Christ."*

As the priest blesses the offerings, the server rings the bell, thus making the faithful aware that this is the most important part of the Mass. The action of the priest 'laying on of his hands' over the offerings while saying these holy words of invocation, asking the Holy Spirit to make Christ present in the Eucharistic species, truly enhances the sense of power and holiness of the Eucharistic Prayer. Then, a brief moment of silence follows to allow us to meditate on the miracle of the Eucharistic consecration.

---

44. ✠ This sign marks the moment when the priest blesses the offerings by making the sign of the cross over them.

In the practice of his ministry, the priest uses the **'laying on of hands'** at different occasions, mainly when invoking the action of the Holy Spirit during the administration of a sacrament and the consecration or blessing of people or objects. The 'laying on of hands' is a tradition that the Church has inherited from the Apostles, who used it chiefly in the administration of the sacraments of Baptism, Confirmation, and Holy Orders. They considered the 'laying on of hands' as an unmistakable symbol of the outpouring of graces and gifts of the Holy Spirit. *(Acts 8:18)"The Spirit was given through the laying on of the apostles' hands."* It is in the name of Jesus and after His example that the Apostles practiced the 'laying on of hands' on those in need of physical and spiritual healing. *(Mk 8:25)"Jesus laid his hands on his eyes again; and he looked intently and his sight was restored, and he saw everything clearly."*

Just as the Apostles chiefly practiced the 'laying on of hands', the priest, who represents Christ, lays his hands over our offerings, and asks the Lord for our purification through the consecration of the sacrifice, whose Victim is Jesus. Then, as everything was created by the Words spoken by God, and as the Word was made flesh, the Eucharist is confected[44a] by the Word of Christ, which repeated by His minister, the priest, changes the bread and wine into the Body and Blood of Christ. *"We must therefore consider the Eucharist as:... the presence of Christ by the power of his word and of his* Spirit." [45]

> *"By the consecration the **transubstantiation** of the bread and wine into the Body and Blood of Christ is brought about. Under the consecrated species of bread and wine Christ himself, living and glorious, is present in a true, real, and substantial manner: his Body and his Blood, with his soul and his divinity."* [46]

Before returning to the liturgy of the Eucharist itself, I want to share with you an amazing and true story that happened in Lanciano, Italy, at the beginning of the 7th century. While celebrating Mass, the priest started doubting that Christ was really and substantially present under the eucharistic species on the altar. At this very moment, and in the presence of many witnesses the Host became a living piece of flesh of myocardium (heart), and in the chalice the consecrated wine became real blood which then coagulated into five clots of uneven size. These events are known as the **Eucharistic Miracle of Lanciano**. It is still possible to venerate these relics at Saint-Francis church, Lanciano, Italy. [47]

44a. To confect the Eucharist: uniting the matter with the form of the ritual, the priest morally and physically puts together the different materials for the Holy Sacrifice.
45. CCC 1358.
46. CCC 1413, cf. Council of Trent: DS 1640; 1651.
47. For more on the Miracle of Lanciano: see Part Five, Appendix 'B', Eucharistic Miracles.

4- THE LORD'S SUPPER: *(Institution Narrative and Consecration)*
The Last Supper is probably one of the best-known events of Jesus' life on earth, next to his birth and crucifixion. This is mainly due to the Church's tradition of celebrating the Mass, enhanced by the celebrations of Holy Week. Through the centuries, artists have also greatly participated in making these key events of our salvation well known, since a large number of them have depicted Jesus' birth, His Last Supper, and His Crucifixion. On the night of the Last Supper, although Jesus Christ knew that his holy passion was about to start, He chose that night to institute the Eucharist while sharing the traditional paschal feast with his Apostles. That night that was filled with the holiness and the peace of God, then became filled with the hatred and the violence of the world that led to Jesus' crucifixion. By the institution of the Eucharist at the Last Supper, Jesus taught His Apostles how, after His resurrection, they were to keep alive His victory of life over death until He returns. *(1Co 11:26)"For as often as you eat this bread and drink the cup, you proclaim the Lord's death until he comes."*

There were other instances before the Last Supper when Jesus talked about the Eucharist. For example, one day when Jesus was at Capernaum, as people were asking: *(Jn 6:30-33)'"What sign can you do, that we may see and believe in you?... Our ancestors ate manna in the desert, as it is written: / "He gave them bread from heaven to eat." / So Jesus said to them, 'Amen, amen, I say to you, it was not Moses who gave the bread from heaven; my Father gives you the true bread from heaven. For the bread of God is that which comes down from heaven and gives life to the world."'* [NAB] Then Jesus explained that He was the bread from heaven: *(Jn 6:49-51) "Your ancestors ate the manna in the desert, but they died; this is the bread that comes down from heaven so that one may eat it and not die. I am the living bread that came down from heaven; whoever eats this bread will live forever; and the bread that I will give is my flesh for the life of the world."* [NAB] Jesus goes further and reveals the precious life giving qualities of receiving communion. *(Jn 6:53.54.56)"Unless you eat the flesh of the Son of Man and drink his blood, you do not have life within you. Whoever eats my flesh and drinks my blood has eternal life, and I will raise him on the last day. ... Whoever eats my flesh and drinks my blood remains in me and I in him."''* [NAB] Blessed are you who believe and act upon these words of Christ. He remains in you forever.

Now that the Gospel has reminded us of the heart of the teachings of Jesus in regards to the Eucharist, let us keep His words in mind as we go to the *Sacramentary,* the *Roman Missal,* and see how the Catholic Church has carried out Jesus' instructions.

INSTITUTION NARRATIVE AND CONSECRATION

✛ *"...By means of words and actions of Christ, the Sacrifice is carried out which Christ himself instituted at the Last Supper, when **he offered** his Body and Blood under the species of bread and wine, **gave** them to his Apostles to eat and drink, and left them the **command** to perpetuate this same mystery."* [48]

CONSECRATION OF THE BREAD

Christ, the Word made flesh by whom all was created, makes Himself present in the Eucharist at the time of the consecration by the power of the Holy Spirit. *"The priest, in the role of Christ, pronounces these words, but their power and grace are God's. This is my body, he says. This word transforms the things offered."* [49] By repeating His own words through His minister, Christ changes the bread into His Flesh and the wine into His Blood at each and every Mass. The words of consecration were first pronounced by Jesus Christ at the Last Supper, then perpetuated by the Apostles when they celebrated Christ's memorial after His ascension, and later were recorded in the Gospel.[50]

At this point of the Mass, the atmosphere in the church is very holy. The congregation is on their knees and the priest stands at the center of the altar. He is carefully holding the Host with the fingertips of both of his hands slightly raised above the altar, when he says aloud to the Father while looking at the Host:

✛OM *"Before he was given up to death,*
a death He freely accepted,
He took bread and gave You thanks.
He broke the bread,
gave it to his disciples, and said:
[The priest bows slightly to say the words of consecration:]
Take this, all of you, and eat it:
This is my Body which will be given up for you.*"* [50]

🔔 ELEVATION OF THE HOST ✞

After the priest has finished saying the words of consecration, the server rings the little bell while the priest elevates the Host high above the altar, holding it still, showing it for everyone to see and to adore. The faithful then bow their heads and adore God, truly present in the Holy Host, by saying silently words of adoration such as: *(Jn 20:28)"My Lord and my God."* A sacred silence then takes place in the Church. The elevation recalls Christ, the divine Victim, elevated on the Cross, hanging between heaven and earth.

---

48. GIRM [55d] 79d.
49. CCC 1375, quoting St. John Chrysostom, *prod. Jud.* 1:6: PG 49, 380.
50. Consecration of the Eucharist: cf. Mt 26:26-28; Mk 14:22-24; Lk 22:19-20.

PIE · PELLICANE — JESU · DOMINE

With great reverence the priest silently places the Host back on the paten on the altar, bows and genuflects for a moment to adore God, and then rises again.

> (Ps 95:6)"O come, let us worship and bow down,
> let us kneel before the LORD, our Maker!"

The words of adoration that we say at elevation "My Lord and my God," were taken from the Gospel. They are the words of Saint Thomas to Jesus at the time of His second apparition to the Apostles after His resurrection. Thomas, who was absent the first time Jesus appeared to the apostles had declared: *(Jn 20:25)"Unless I see the mark of the nails in his hands and put my finger into the nailmarks and put my hand into his side, I will not believe."* [NAB] So the second time Jesus appeared to them, Thomas was present and Jesus said to him; *(Jn 20:27-28) "Put your finger here and see my hands. Reach out your hand and put it in my side. Do not doubt but believe. Thomas answered him, "My Lord and my God!"* Jesus then said: *(Jn 20:29)"Blessed are those who have not seen and have believed."* [NAB] How wonderful is the faith that allows us to believe that Jesus is truly present in the Eucharist.

How holy and inspiring it is to watch the celebrating priest offering the holy sacrifice of the Mass. This is especially true when the priest makes a point of keeping his eyes fixed on the Host and on the chalice while reciting the words of consecration: *"Take, eat; this is my body... this is my blood... ."* How holy it is to watch the priest keep his eyes fixed on the Eucharist during the elevation of the Body and of the Blood of Christ. It is as though his staring at and addressing the Host and then the cup of the Precious Blood, enhances the reality of God's presence in the Eucharist. At Masses when the priest looks at the faithful and addresses them instead of looking at the Eucharist while reciting the words of the consecration, it seems to bring our focus on the priest and away from the Eucharist.

CONSECRATION OF THE WINE

The priest now holds the chalice in the same manner and with the same reverence he used to hold the Host. All are still intensely staring at the altar. Looking at the cup the priest addresses the Father with the words that consecrate the wine into the Precious Blood of Christ.

✠OM *"When supper was ended, he took the cup.*
Again He gave You thanks and praise,
gave the cup to his disciples, and said:
[The priest bows slightly to say the words of consecration:]
Take this, all of you, and drink from it:
this is the cup of my Blood,
the Blood of the new and everlasting covenant.
It will be shed for you and for all men
so that sins may be forgiven.
Do this in memory of me." [51]

🔔 ELEVATION OF THE BLOOD ✠

As the priest elevates the chalice in the same manner that he did the Host, the server rings the bell again. On its knees, the congregation stares at the chalice while the priest shows the cup of the Precious Blood of Christ our Redeemer for everyone to see. Once more, the faithful then bow their heads and silently adore God:*(Jn 20:28)*"My Lord and my God." A sacred silence reigns in the Church. With great reverence the priest silently places the chalice back on the corporal on the altar, bows and genuflects for a moment to adore God, and then rises again. Oh what a holy moment this is!

(Ps 95:6) "O come, let us worship and bow down,
let us kneel before the LORD, our Maker!"

---

51. Words of Consecration: cf. Mt 26:26-28, Mk 14:22-24, Lk 22:19-20.

From this moment on, one can usually notice a greater reverence among the faithful, which is an indication of a greater influence of the Holy Spirit in those present. During the elevation, as we adore God in the intimacy of our souls, we add our own prayers and praises to Him. I love telling Him: *"My Lord and my God."* These are intimate words of love that can only be said to the divine being. As an intense sentiment of 'being here and now' often settles in at this point, I thank God for the grace of being able to attend Mass. I thank Christ for nourishing me with His life each time I receive the Eucharist; His precious life which He gave for us so that we can eventually go home. I praise and bless His Precious Blood, knowing well that there is nothing more precious and powerful in the whole universe; its value suffices to buy the lives of all human souls back from the evil one, and the power of its purity suffices to wash away all of our sins. *(Col 1:20)"Through him God was pleased to reconcile to himself all things, whether on earth or in heaven, by making peace through the blood of his cross."* During this holy moment, I often think about the mystery by which Christ is wholly and truly present in the smallest particle of the Eucharist in both species of the bread and wine. I then also often think about eucharistic miracles.

Although the priest has elevated only one Host and one chalice, all of the bread and wine offerings brought to the altar, for which the priest intended consecration, have now been changed into the Body and the Blood of Jesus Christ; all of our spiritual offerings have been received at the Father's altar in heaven, and purified by the Blood of the Lamb.

The God given psychology inherent in the liturgy of the Holy Mass is impressive in its ability to raise our consciousness, making us more sensitive to the miraculous presence of Jesus Christ in the Eucharist. Indeed, the liturgy aims to keep on raising our souls' vibrations towards a deeper state of grace so that by the grace of God we are as prepared as we can be to receive holy communion, and that we are as open and desirous as we can be to receive and to honor God in the Eucharist.

To continue our preparation, the liturgy brings us next to recall **Christ's** glorious victory of life over death; **a victory He obtained** through His **passion, death, and resurrection**, and that was glorified by His ascension into heaven where He reigns forever as the King of kings, head of the Body of Christ. Thereafter, the **intercessions** bring us to pray for all the members of the Church. *(Rom 12:5)"We who are many, are one body in Christ, and individually we are members one of another."* We intercede for the souls of our beloved departed ones, the souls in purgatory, and all of the members of the Church on earth; and we ask to be brought in eternal communion with the Church in heaven: Mother Mary, the saints, and the angels.

5- MEMORIAL ACCLAMATION *(Anamnesis)* [52]

✠ *"...The Church, fulfilling the command that she received from Christ the Lord through the Apostles, keeps the memorial of Christ, recalling especially his blessed Passion, glorious Resurrection, and Ascension into heaven."* [53]

At this point, all usually **keep on kneeling**, but in some dioceses it may be customary to stand to respond *[R.]* to the acclamation sung ♪ by the priest *[P]*. There are **four** acclamations the priest may choose from to acclaim Christ resurrected, alive, and awaited:

✠OM " *[P:] Let us proclaim the mystery of faith:*
A. *[R.]* **Christ has died,**
  Christ is risen,
  Christ will come again.
                    OR:
B. *[R.]* **Dying you destroyed our death,**
  rising you restored our life.
  Lord Jesus, come in glory.
                    OR:
C. *[R.]* **When we eat this bread and drink this cup,**
  we proclaim your death, Lord Jesus,
  until you come in glory.
                    OR:
D. *[R.]* **Lord, by your cross and resurrection**
  you have set us free.
  You are the Savior of the world." [bfa]

---

52. Anamnesis: Greek word for remembrance, memorial and proclamation. See CCC 1363-1364; cf. *Ex* 13:3; *Heb* 7:25-27; *LG 3*; *1Cor* 5:7.
53. GIRM [55e] 79e.

What a glorious moment this is! *(2Tim 1:10)"Our Savior Christ Jesus, ... abolished death and brought life and immortality to light through the gospel."* After recalling Christ's holy sacrifice, we now rejoice about the glorious success of His mission, His victory over death, and we declare our awaiting His return. We also rejoice because Christ just made Himself present on the altar.

(Jn 17:1-2)"Father, the hour has come. Give glory to your son, so that your son may glorify you, just as you gave him authority over all people, so that he may give eternal life to all you gave him." NAB

Reciting the 'Memorial Acclamation' produces a great sentiment of pride and hope towards Christ our Lord, and His victory. The Father truly gave Him all powers to succeed in His mission, but it is divine love that sustained Him until the end. And, filled with hope and faith in Christ's own promise, we await His return. *(Jn 14:3)"When I go and prepare a place for you, I will come back again and will take you to myself, that where I am you may be also."*

(Mt 24:23-24.26-27)"If anyone says to you then, 'Look, here is the Messiah!' or, 'There he is!' do not believe it. False messiahs and false prophets will arise, and they will perform signs and wonders so great as to deceive, if that were possible, even the elect. ... So if they say to you, 'He is in the desert' do not go out there; if they say, 'He is in the inner rooms' do not believe it. For just as lightning comes from the east and is seen as far as the west, so will the coming of the Son of Man be." NAB

6- MEMORIAL PRAYER: *(Offering of the Victim of the sacrifice)*
    ✢ *"...In this very memorial, the Church—and in particular the Church here and now gathered—***offers** *in the Holy Spirit **the spotless Victim to the Father**. The Church's intention... is that the faithful not only offer this spotless Victim but also learn to offer themselves... ."* [54] bfa

During the 'consecration', Christ, the Lamb of God, was made present on the altar. Now, as the priest extends his arms and says the 'memorial prayer', he intercedes for us in offering to the Father the Lamb of God, the Victim of the sacrifice of the Mass. At the same time, we offer ourselves to the Father, at each and every Mass, so that without holding back we come to say: *(Lk 22:42) "...[Father,] not my will but yours be done."*

---

54. GIRM [55f] 79f, cf. SVEC, Constitution on the Sacred Liturgy, *Sacrosanctum Concilium*, no. 48; Sacred Congregation of Rites, Instruction *Eucharisticum mysterium*, On the worship of the Eucharist, 25 May 1967, no. 12: AAS 59 (1967), pp. 548-549.

The 'Memorial Prayer' is powerful because by this prayer Christ continues to offer Himself to the Father for our salvation. Christ acts here as **Priest and Victim**. Through His Priest, Christ offers Himself to the Father as the only acceptable offering for man's redemption. As Victim, Christ says to God: **Look Father, it is I, Your Son**. For the sake of the Blood of My sacrifice, have mercy on your children.

Memorial Prayer

✢OM *"Father, calling to mind the death your Son endured for*
our salvation,
his glorious resurrection and ascension into heaven,
and ready to greet him when he comes again,
we offer you in thanksgiving this holy and living sacrifice.
Look with favor on your Church's offering,
and see the Victim whose death has reconciled us to yourself.
Grant that we, who are nourished by his body and blood,
may be filled with his Holy Spirit,
and become one body, one spirit in Christ." [54a]

Now that the sacrifice has become a life-giving banquet, we pray that our partaking of the Body and Blood of Christ fulfills God's will to make us one, one Body with one Head, the Christ. *(1Co 10:17.12:12) "Because there is one bread, we who are many are one body. For just as the body is one and has many members, and all the members of the body, though many, are one body, so it is with Christ."* We pray that unity comes among all members of the Body of Christ as we share the same life, the same spirit, the same faith, the same Father. *(Ep 4:4-6)"There is one body and one Spirit,...one hope..., one Lord, one faith, one baptism, one God and Father of all."* This unity cannot be achieved through human works, but only through the grace of God, by His giving us the Holy Spirit and the Life that we receive from the Eucharist. For as we eat Christ we gradually become more like Him. Our differences are lessened, the wounds of our sins are healed, and we are made whole and holy in Christ our Lord.

The reason that at every Mass we repeat the prayers that together form the great Eucharistic Prayer is not because God needs to be reminded of the mysteries of our salvation, but rather because we do. And if throughout the Mass the liturgy emphasizes the miracle of salvation that is present in the Eucharist, it is because these great spiritual realities do not naturally make sense to the human mind. We need to be told over and over again about these facts of our redemption in order to raise our faith and our spiritual convictions above human reasoning, and to increase our hope of one day entering the heavens, the spiritual realms in which God dwells.

54a. This 'Memorial Prayer' is taken from the Eucharistic Prayer III.

We need to be told over and over again that Christ gave His life to reconcile us with God, and that His sacrifice is continuously being made present on the altar through the sacrament of the Eucharist.

7- INTERCESSIONS:

Three intercessory prayers are said aloud by the priest alone: 'For the Church', 'For the dead' and 'In Communion with the Saints.' ✠*"...[These intercessions express] the fact that the Eucharist is celebrated in communion with the entire Church, of heaven as well as of earth, and that the offering is made for her and for all her members, living and dead, who have been called to participate in the redemption and the salvation purchased by Christ's Body and Blood."* [55]

For the Church

✠OM *"Lord, may this sacrifice,*
which has made our peace with you,
advance the peace and salvation of all the world.
Strengthen in faith and love your pilgrim Church on earth;
your servant, Pope Benedict XVI, our bishop, N.,
and all the bishops,
with the clergy and the entire people your Son has gained for you.
Father, hear the prayers of the family you have gathered
*   here before you.*
In mercy and love unite all your children wherever
*   they may be."* [55a]

The prayer of 'intercession for the Church' gives us an opportunity to pray for Our Pope and for all the clergy. I especially like the way this prayer talks about us, the Church, as being **pilgrims on earth**. I find it comforting that the liturgy reminds us of the fact that our life on earth is only a pilgrimage, and that this world is not our home. *(Heb 11:13)"...confessing that they are pilgrims and strangers on the earth."* [DR] It gives me spiritual and moral comfort for times when I can't make sense of this world. It refreshes my mind with the fact that our real home is in a much higher sphere of reality with God. There are many instances when the bible states that this world is not our home. Here is one example from the Gospel: *(Jn 15:19)"If you had been of the world, the world would love its own: but because you are not of the world, but I have chosen you out of the world, therefore, the world hateth you."* [DR]

---

55. GIRM [55g] 79g.
55a. While most of the other chief elements of this presentation were taken from Eucharistic Prayer II, this intercessory prayer for the Chuch is taken from Eucharistic Prayer III.

I like the way this prayer includes all of us by saying: *"Your children wherever they may be."* Is it presumptuous to claim these words as if they were for us, as if we were God's children, His chosen ones? I don't think so. There are many instances in the Gospel when Jesus calls His followers His own; for example: *(Jn 10:14)"I am the good shepherd, and I know mine and mine know me."* [NAB] According to the Gospel, whoever has a loving relationship with Jesus may claim to be known of Him, especially if this relationship brings him to live according to Christ's teaching. *(Jn 15:10)"If you keep my commandments, you will abide in my love."* We are the people that Jesus gained for the Father. *(Jn 17:24)"Father, I desire that those whom you have given me, may be with me where I am, to see my glory."* By our baptism our soul was cleansed from sin and received an **indelible mark**,[56] the seal of Christ. At our baptism, we were adopted by God as His children. Thus 'wherever we might be' we are part of the mystical Body of Christ, which has Jesus at its head. And Jesus, the Good Shepherd, looks after His sheep 'wherever they may be'.

FOR THE DEAD

As the priest continues, we now pray for departed souls, and we recall our faith in life after death and our hope for resurrection:

✚OM *"Remember our brothers and sisters*
who have gone to their rest
in the hope of rising again;
bring them and all the departed
into the light of your presence. ..."

It is usually at this point of the Mass, during the prayer of 'intercession for the dead', that the priest says aloud the **Mass' intention**. In other words, the priest mentions the name of the person for whom this sacrifice of the Mass is being offered, praying for this soul to rest in peace in heaven with God. Most Masses are offered for the soul of **beloved departed** ones. However, when the Mass is being offered for someone who is still alive, the priest may then mention the Mass' intention at the end of the 'General Intercessions', praying for this person to find God's peace in his life. Our faith and tradition teach us that souls in **purgatory**, as well as souls that are still on earth, greatly benefit from Masses said for them and for their intentions. *"As sacrifice, the Eucharist is also offered in reparation for the sins of the living and the dead and to obtain spiritual or temporal benefits from God."* [57] If we offer a Mass for a soul who happens to be already in heaven, my understanding is that the benefit is not lost, but rather, the Mass is used for another soul who needs it.

---

56. The indelible spiritual mark of Baptism, see CCC 1272.
57. CCC 1414. Arranging for Masses to be offered: see Part Three, Liturgy of the Eucharist, After the Mass, Conclusion of the Liturgy of the Mass.

Since this prayer of intercession for the dead says: *"remember our brothers and sisters who have gone to their rest...,"* this is a good time to remember those that we know and love that have passed to the other side. At this time of the Mass, I like to silently name in my heart, one after the other, all those that I know that have left this world, and as I name them, at times, the light that surrounds them allows me to see their faces. I can feel how happy they are that I remember them, and also how they are waiting for us to call upon them for help in our daily lives. I consider them to be my personal allies in heaven, next to the saints and the angels. *"Put this body anywhere! Don't trouble yourselves about it! I simply ask you to remember me at the Lord's altar wherever you are."* [57a] Praying for our departed loved ones and calling upon their help in our daily lives is a precious tradition. Not only are these souls able to help us, but their help brings them merit for their eternal lives. The holy souls in purgatory greatly appreciate our prayers, because it shortens their time of purification, and they pray for us in return. Pray for them, then pay attention to the blessings that come your way. Furthermore, praying for the souls of our departed ones keeps us aware of the reality that the soul lives on after leaving this world.

IN COMMUNION WITH THE SAINTS

✠OM *"...Have mercy on us all;*
make us worthy to share eternal life
with Mary, the virgin Mother of God,
with the apostles, and with the saints
who have done your will throughout the ages.
May we praise you in union with them,
and give you glory
through your Son, Jesus Christ."

I like this prayer because it sets for us the highest goal, sanctity. Such a goal could be looked at as being either incredibly ambitious, or a great **retirement plan**. Since we obviously are going to retire from this world sooner or later, we might as well plan for the future. The type of earthly retirement we can plan for is usually directly related to how much money we have put aside. Well, it is much the same way with eternal life, except for a couple of things. Eternal retirement lasts longer than earthly retirement; the two only available destinations are heaven or hell; and the only thing you can put aside in order to retire in heaven is the love you have shown for God and for your neighbors. *(Mt 7:21)"Not everyone who says to me, 'Lord, Lord,' will enter the kingdom of heaven, but only the one who does the will of my Father in heaven."* [NAB]

57a. CCC 1371, quoting St. Monica, before her death, to her sons, St. Augustine and his brother; *Conf.* 9, 11, 27: PL 32, 775.

(Mk 12:28.30.31)"Which commandment is the first of all? "You shall love the Lord your God with all your heart, and with all your soul, and with all your mind, and with all your strength. ...You shall love your neighbor as yourself. There is no other commandment greater than these.'"

No one could ever do enough good deeds to buy his way into heaven. If it was not for God's mercy, no one could ever enter heaven. But since our savior Jesus Christ came and died on the cross, it is now possible to plan on spending eternity in heaven in the company of the Father, Jesus Christ, Mother Mary, and all the other heavenly beings.

Being in communion of prayers with Mother Mary and the saints brings me peace and strength, and makes me feel loved. As I recall that we are truly part of Christ's family, and that heaven is our real home, the presence of the Holy Spirit then becomes more tangible. While in communion of prayer with the saints, I silently invite them to join us for the Eucharist. I picture saints and angels filling the sanctuary, kneeling or floating near the altar, surrounded by 'Christic' light and carried by angelic songs; and they join us in praising God and glorifying Christ for his victory of life over death.

8- IN PRAISE OF GOD: *(Doxology)* [58]
After the intercessory prayers, while the faithful are still kneeling, with one hand the priest takes the chalice containing the Precious Blood of Christ, and with the other hand he holds the large Host, the Body of Christ, slightly above the chalice. Then, he elevates the Host and the chalice together for everyone to see, and he either **says or sings alone** this praise to the Father:

DOXOLOGY ♪
✝OM *"Through him,*
with him,
in him,
in the unity of the Holy Spirit,
all glory and honor is yours,
almighty Father,
for ever and ever."

[All respond in singing in a common voice:] ♪ ***Amen!***

✝"[In the doxology,] the **glorification of God** is expressed and... is **confirmed** and concluded by the people's acclamation, **Amen.**" [59]

---

58. Doxology: from the Greek, *doxa* (glory) and *logos* (word), a formula of praise.
59. GIRM [55h] 79h (bold face added).

*"The proclamation of the Eucharistic Prayer, which... is the climax of the whole celebration, is proper to the Priest by virtue of his Ordination. ...Therefore [no] parts of the Eucharistic Prayer are [to be] recited by a Deacon, a lay minister ..., or by all members of the faithful together. The Eucharistic Prayer... is to be **recited by the Priest alone** in full."* [60]

After the 'Doxology', which **concludes** the great Eucharistic Prayer, the faithful stand for the 'Lord's Prayer.'

COMMUNION RITE

Next, the Lord's Prayer introduces the Communion Rite. The **posture** of the faithful during the Our Father varies according to the local custom. In some parishes family members, couples, and friends, hold each others hands; in other parishes the whole congregation holds hands; and in other parishes, each one recollects with joined hands, or uplifted hands, to pray to the Father. Since the Our Father is a prayer of adoration directed to the Father, the faithful have no obligation to hold hands.

Personally, I find that praying with uplifted hands helps me in directing my prayer to the Father and in making me more present to Him. *(1Tim 2:8)"I desire, then, that in every place the men should pray, lifting up holy hands."* So, let us remember that God is truly Our Father and pray to Him with **trust and confidence**!

---

60. *Redemptionis Sacramentum*, no. 52; cf. Pope John Paul II, Encyclical Letter, *Ecclesia de Eucharistia*, n. 28: AAS 95 (2003) p. 452; Missale Romanum, Institutio Generalis, n. 147; S. Congregation for Divine Worship, Instruction, *Liturgicae instaurationes*, n. 4: AAS 62 (1970) p. 698; S. Congregation for the Sacraments and Divine Worship, Instruction, *Inaestimabile donum,* n. 4: AAS 72 (1980) p. 334 (bold face added).

THE LORD'S PRAYER:
Standing at the altar, the priest joins his hands and says or sings one of the four introductions to the Lords' prayer;

✠^{OM} A)"*Let us pray with confidence to the Father*
        in the words our Savior gave us:

[Then the priest extends his hands to say, or sing, the Lord's Prayer with the people. Let us sing the Lord's Prayer! ♪]

        Our Father, who art in heaven,
        hallowed be thy name;
        thy kingdom come;
        thy will be done on earth as it is in heaven.
        Give us this day our daily bread;
        and forgive us our trespasses
        as we forgive those who trespass against us;
        and lead us not into temptation,
        but deliver us from evil. [61]

With hands [still] extended, the priest continues alone:
        Deliver us, Lord, from every evil,
        and grant us peace in our day.
        In your mercy keep us free from sin
        and protect us from all anxiety
        as we wait in joyful hope
        for the coming of our Savior, Jesus Christ.

The people end the prayer with the acclamation:
        For the kingdom, the power and the glory are yours,
        now and forever." [62]

---

61. The Lord's Prayer: cf. Mt 6:9-13; Lk 11:2-4.
62. Acclamation: cf. 1Ch 29:11; Dan 2:37; Jude 1:25; Rev 1:6.

(Lk 11:1)"[Jesus] was praying in a certain place, and when he had finished, one of his disciples said to him, "Lord, teach us to pray [63] *just as John taught his disciples."* [NAB] Thus, it was at the request of one of His disciples that **Jesus taught us how to pray** by giving us the 'Lord's Prayer'.

Have you noticed how the first half of the Lord's Prayer is dedicated to praising the Father - *hallowed be Thy name -,* and praying for His reign to come - *Thy will be done*? It is only in the second half of the Lord's Prayer that we present our petitions. More specifically, we make four requests to the Father.

In our first petition, we ask the Father to give us the necessary physical and spiritual food - *Give us our daily bread.* Indeed, we are not only asking for the bread that feeds our body, but also for the precious bread that comes down from Heaven to feed our soul. Yes, Jesus taught us to ask for **daily Eucharist**. ✣*"In the Lord's Prayer a petition is made for daily food, which for Christians means preeminently the **Eucharistic** bread, and also for **purification** from sin, so that what is holy may, in fact, be given to those who are holy".* [64] Thus, in the second, third, and forth petitions, we pray to the Father for **purification** as we ask Him for forgiveness of our sin, and protection and deliverance from evil.

Let us take a closer look. In our second petition, we pray to make our peace with God, as we ask the Father to **forgive** our sins. However, we ask Him to limit His mercy to the proportion of our own willingness to give mercy - *Forgive us as we forgive.* In our third petition we petition to be **protected** against our weaknesses and the limits of our own will, which cause us to sin - *Lead us not into temptation*; and in our forth and last petition, but not the least, we acknowledge our bondage to sin, and express our desire to be **made free** from the source of it - *Deliver us from evil.* Amen.

The 'Our Father', or 'Lord's Prayer', reminds me of the 'Maslow hierarchy of needs', [65] that places human needs in the sequence in which they have to be fulfilled in order for a person to reach happiness and self-realization. Maslow places physical needs - such as food, clothes, and dwelling - at the bottom of his 'hierarchy of needs'. Thus demonstrating that physical needs first have to be fulfilled before needs of an emotional, intellectual, and spiritual nature can be addressed; which we gradually encounter, and in that order, as we progress towards higher levels of 'Maslow's hierarchy of needs'.

63. For more of Jesus' teaching about prayer, see (Mt 6:1-8).
64. GIRM [56i] 81 (bfa).
65. Abraham H. Maslow, one of the founders of humanistic psychology in the 1960s.

Likewise, the Lord's Prayer contains a 'hierarchy of petitions'.[66] However, before we start presenting our petitions, the Lord's Prayer establishes first the greatness of the One to Whom we are praying to, God Our Father; thus raising our level of trust and faith that our prayer will be answered. Isn't that great psychology? The 'hierarchy of petitions' brings us to ask first for nourishment for our body and soul - *Give us our daily bread* -; before we go up one step and make petitions for our emotional needs, such as the peace and love that we seek from the Father's forgiveness - *Forgive us our trespasses*. We then move to a third level of the 'hierarchy of petitions', where we present the Father with an intellectual need, asking for His protection when our free will is challenged - *Lead us not into temptation.* How easily we are tempted and seduced away from God, and how often we choose to follow our plans, to do our will, rather than the Father's will.

As we progress in the 'hierachy of petitions', asking the Father to fulfill our needs for *daily bread*; for His love and His peace, which He grants us through His *forgiveness*; and for His protection against *temptation*; we are then strengthened in our faith and better prepared to go up to the last step, and acknowledge our bondage. We then ask the Father to *deliver us from evil.* With the 'Our Father', besides teaching us how to pray, Jesus also teaches us that we need to be made strong by the Father's love in order to persevere on our journey home to heaven.

At the end of the Lord's Prayer, the priest enhances the most precious petitions by basically asking the Father to grant us **inner peace**. A soul who has **faith** and inner peace is a free soul, one who has great potential to be happy. Without faith and inner peace, no matter who we are and what we possess, we are very limited. Let us consider, for example, a man who is healthy, skilled, and financially well off, and that also has a loving spouse and children. If this man does not have inner peace, nor faith in God, if he is tormented and anxious with no God to turn to with his torments, how can he enjoy any of what he has? Yet one can be sick, unskilled, broke, and without family, but if he has God's treasures of faith and inner peace, he may feel as though he is on the top of the world, and be **truly happy**. Of course, most people would rather be rich, healthy, and at peace, rather than broke, sick, and tormented. However, the point here is to realize that faith and inner peace allow one to live free and to grow, while torments and anxiety hold one captive.

As the priest concludes his petition to the Father, his prayer of awaiting with joyful hope the return of our Big brother, Jesus Christ, comes as a true exhortation to be steadfast in our journey of faith.

---

66. The Lord's Prayer: "This prayer not only teaches us to ask for things, but also in what order we should desire [and ask for] them." CCC 2763, cf. St. Thomas Aquinas, *STh* II-II, 83, 9.

The 'Our Father' is then concluded by this acclamation of the people: *For the kingdom, the power and the glory are yours, now and forever.* This acclamation is surely inspired by the following excerpt taken from the book of Revelation. Here, Saint John relates one of his amazing visions, during which the assembly of all beings ever created are glorifying as one voice the Lamb of God. *(Rev 5:13)"Then I heard every creature in heaven and on earth and under the earth and in the sea, everything in the universe, cry out: / 'To the one who sits on the throne and to the Lamb / be blessing and honor, glory and might, / forever and ever.'"* NAB

In the Gospel according to Saint Matthew, following the Lord's Prayer (cf. Mt 6:9-13), we find Christ insisting on the importance to forgive others. *(Mt 6:14-15)"For if you forgive others their trespasses, your heavenly Father will also forgive you; but if you do not forgive others, neither will your Father forgive your trespasses."* Jesus is teaching us a divine law: we can only receive what we are willing to give.

In the next chapter of the Gospel according to Saint Matthew, Christ continues His teaching about this divine law, the golden rule,[67] also known as **'the law of return'**. *(Mt 7:2)"For as you judge, so will you be judged, and the measure with which you measure will be measured out to you."* NAB *(Mt 7:12)"In everything do to others as you would have them do to you; for this is the law and the prophets."* In other words, we eventually harvest what we have sown. This law applies to forgiveness, love, compassion, joy... as well as to negative attributes such as indifference, meanness, rancor, hate... Thus, we should give what we want to receive. If you want to be loved and respected by others, you know what you need to do. However, Christ warns us to use discernment: *(Mt 7:6)"Do not throw your pearls before swine, or they will trample them under foot and turn and maul you."*

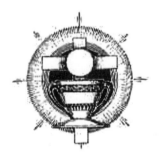

---

67. Other significant golden rules of life may be found in the Old Testament in books of wisdom such as *Proverbs*, *Ecclesiastes*, *Song of Songs,* and *Sirach* (*Ecclesiasticus*).

SIGN OF PEACE:

✝"*The Rite of Peace follows, by which the Church asks for peace and unity for herself and for the whole human family, and the faithful express to each other their ecclesial communion and mutual charity before communicating in the Sacrament.*" [68]

While **all are standing**, with arm extended standing in the center of the altar, the priest says the following prayer:

✝OM "*Lord Jesus Christ, you said to your apostles:*
I leave you peace, my peace I give you.
Look not on our sins, but on the faith of your Church,
and grant us the peace and unity of your kingdom
where you live forever and ever."

The people respond as one voice: **Amen**!

From the beginning of the Mass until now, all the prayers of the Mass were addressed to God the **Father.** But now that Jesus Christ is present on the altar under the Holy Species, starting with the above prayer for peace and until the Body and Blood of Christ are consumed at communion, the prayers of the Mass are addressed to Jesus Christ, the **Son** of God, the Lamb of God.

The priest continues by giving the greeting of peace to all:

✝OM "*The peace of the Lord be with you always.*
[The people respond:] **And also with you.**"

The priest, or deacon, then invites the congregation to exchange the Peace of Christ by saying:

✝OM "*Let us offer each other a sign of peace.*" [68a]

✝"*The priest may give the sign of peace to the ministers but always remains within the sanctuary, so as* **not to disturb the celebration**." [69] Likewise, without leaving their pews, the faithful turn to those near by and offer a sign of peace while saying: Peace be with you! ✝"*It is, however, appropriate that each person* **offer the sign of peace** *only to those who are* **nearest** *and in a* **sober** *manner.*" [69a] The rite of peace is not intended as an opportunity to socialize nor to demonstrate our affection to one another, but rather, it is a fraternal prayer. As we offer the 'sign of peace,' to those near by, we are telling them that we pray that peace, communion, and charity be in their hearts and ours before receiving Holy Communion.

---

68. GIRM [56b] 82.
68a. When a deacon is present, he is the one to invite us to share the sign of peace.
69. GIRM [112] 154 (bold face added).
69a. GIRM [56b] 82 (bold face added).

The word **peace** is encountered many times in the Old and New Testament. 'Peace be with you', **Shalom,** is a greeting that we, Christians, inherited from Judaism through Jesus Christ, the Prince of Peace. Jesus used this greeting, for example, the night after His resurrection: *(Jn 20:19)"...Jesus came and stood in their midst and said to them, 'Peace be with you.'"* NAB Then at another time, Jesus speaks of the kind of peace He gives us: *(Jn 14:27)"Peace I leave with you; my peace I give to you. Not as the world gives do I give it to you. Do not let your hearts be troubled or afraid."* NAB When we say: 'could I have some peace,' we usually mean: 'leave me alone.' But when Christ says: 'I give you my peace,' He means: 'do not worry, you are not alone, I am with you.' And if we believe in Him, we receive His peace. Just as life and faith, peace is a gift from God, a grace that keeps us untroubled at times of spiritual and temporal trials. Peace is a fruit of the Holy Spirit: *(Gal 5:22.23) "...the fruit of the Spirit is love, joy, peace, patience, kindness, generosity, faithfulness, gentleness, and self-control."* Peace is synonymous with serenity, calm and harmony. We should seek to be at peace with ourselves, with God, and with our neighbor.

THE BREAKING OF THE BREAD: (The Fraction)
Although during the consecration, the priest says: "He took bread... broke the bread...," it is only at this time of the Mass that the priest actually breaks the Host. Thus, holding the Host over the paten, which is sitting on the corporal on the altar, the priest reverently breaks the Host in two halves, taking all precautions that not one particle is lost. At this action, we the faithful, recall that Jesus **Christ was** physically and spiritually **broken for us** during His passion and sacrifice.

✢*"The priest breaks the Eucharistic Bread, assisted, if the case calls for it, by the deacon or a concelebrant.* **Christ's gesture of breaking bread** *at the Last Supper, which* **gave** *the entire Eucharistic Action* **its name in apostolic times**, *signifies that the many faithful are made one body. (1Co 10:17) ["Because there is one bread, we who are many are one body, for we all partake of the one bread."]"* [70]

✢*"Whenever a* **fragment of the host adheres** *to his fingers, especially after the fraction or the Communion of the faithful, the priest is to wipe [cleanse]* [71] *his fingers over the paten or, if necessary, wash them. Likewise, he should also gather any fragments that may have fallen outside the paten."* [72]

---

70. GIRM [56c] 83 (bold face added).
71. The priest gently rubs his forefingers and thumbs together over the paten.
72. GIRM [237] 278 (bold face added).

*"The **Eucharistic presence** of Christ begins at the moment of the consecration and endures as long as the Eucharistic species subsist.[73] Christ is present whole and entire in each of the species and whole and entire in each of their parts, in such a way that **the breaking** of the bread **does not divide Christ.**"* [74]

Breaking bread with friends is a wonderful and universal custom. And the fact that our Lord chose this **simple and well-known custom** to establish the ritual by which He would free us from sin and feed us with divine life reveals a lot about the **nature of God's love** for us. The Father makes it very simple for us, His children, to have access to Him and to His graces. All He asks of us is trust, faithfulness, and love; what could be more simple? However, our complicated reasoning often keeps us away from the Lord. We need to understand that God loves us as a father loves his children, yet, in a much more perfect way. *(Lk 11:13)"If you then, who are evil, know how to give good gifts to your children, how much more will the heavenly Father give the Holy Spirit to those who ask him!"* The Father can and will provide everything we need for our earthly life as well as for our eternal life, if we let Him.

THE EUCHARISTIC RESERVE

After the 'Fraction', the priest, or the deacon, might go to the eucharistic reserve - the tabernacle - to get a ciborium of Hosts that were consecrated during a prior Mass, so that these Hosts may be consumed by the faithful during the Communion. The priest opens the door of the tabernacle, and then genuflects before the Blessed Sacrament as a sign of adoration.[75] All are then reminded that Jesus is really present in the tabernacle, which is why we should **always genuflect to the tabernacle** whenever entering or leaving a pew in a church, and each time when passing in front of the Blessed Sacrament. Once the tabernacle is open, the priest moves aside the veil inside of the tabernacle, reaches in and brings out the ciborium.[75a] The priest closes the door of the tabernacle and brings the ciborium of Hosts to the altar, where he removes the ciborium's lid and the veil, if one is used.

Since the acolyte and the extraordinary ministers of Holy Communion are to receive the ciborium from the priest, they may not go to the tabernacle and bring the ciborium of Hosts to the altar (cf. GIRM 162). ✝*"In the first place, **it is the office of the priest... to minister holy communion...** ."* [76] Moreover, it generates **more reverence towards**

---

73. "As long as the Eucharistic species subsist" means; as long as the species exist.
74. CCC 1377, cf. Council of Trent: DS 1641 (bold face added).
75. Cf. GIRM [233] 274.
75a. If there are many ciboria to be taken out of the reserve, other ministers may assist the priest, who then reverently hands them the ciboria containing the Blessed Sacrament.
76. Sacramentary, second edition, Ministers of Communion, Foreword p.16 (bfa).

the Eucharist in the hearts of the faithful when a priest or a deacon handles the Eucharist, rather than a nonordained person. This is true for the handling of ciboria at the tabernacle, as well as for the distribution of Holy Communion. We must beware not to diminish the role of the priest by letting the nonordained fulfill these priestly functions during the Mass, except when it is truly needed.

The tabernacle is used to reserve the Eucharist for the sick who can't come to Mass, for Eucharistic adoration outside of Mass, and to insure that there is enough Hosts for the communion of all during the Mass. In the first place: ✢*"It is most desirable that the faithful, just as the priest himself is bound to do, receive the Lord's Body from hosts* **consecrated at the same Mass.**"[77] *"...[The] Church has not... ever forbidden... a celebrant to satisfy the piety and just request of those who, when present at Mass, want to become partakers of the same sacrifice, because they likewise offer it after their own manner... ."*[78]

AGNUS DEI: (LAMB OF GOD)

✢*"The supplication* Agnus Dei, *is, as a rule, sung by the choir or cantor with the congregation responding; or it is, at least, recited aloud. This invocation accompanies the fraction, [the breaking of the bread, and the commingling]."*[79] Let us pray to the One who gave His life to buy our freedom, and ask Him to have mercy on our poor souls, who do not know how to appreciate the true value of the sacrifice He made for us.

AGNUS DEI ♪

✢[OM] *"Lamb of God, you take away the sins of the world:*
    have mercy on us.
Lamb of God, you take away the sins of the world:
    have mercy on us.
Lamb of God, you take away the sins of the world:
    grant us peace."

(Jn 1:29)"Behold, the Lamb of God,
who takes away the sin of the world."

---

77. GIRM [56h] 85, cf. Sacred Congregation of Rites, Instruction *Eucharisticum mysterium*, On the worship of the Eucharist, 25 May 1967, nos. 31, 32; Sacred Congregation for the Discipline of the Sacraments, Instruction *Immensae caritatis*, 29 January 1973, no. 2: AAS 65 (1973), pp. 267-268, (bold face added).
78. *Mediator Dei*, 118.
79. GIRM [56c] 83. 'Agnus Dei' is Latin for 'Lamb of God'.

THE COMMINGLING:

The commingling is the action of mingling the Body and Blood of Christ. *"When the fraction is completed, the [priest] breaks off a small fragment of the Host with his right hand and reverently places it in the chalice [which contains the Blood of Christ]..., while his left hand rests on the corporal. This fragment is taken from the lower part of the left portion of a conventional Host."*[79a]

✤*"The priest breaks the Bread and puts a piece of the host into the chalice **to signify the unity of the Body and Blood** of the Lord in the work of salvation... ."*[80] This is a solemn yet joyful moment of the Mass. While the 'Breaking of the Bread' completes the unbloody representation of the Paschal sacrifice, the 'Commingling' completes the preparation of the Paschal banquet, of which we are about to partake.

The priest says inaudibly:
✤OM *"May this mingling of the Body and Blood of our Lord Jesus Christ bring eternal life to us who receive it."*

When communion under both species is distributed to all, it often requires the use of more than one sacred vessel to contain the Blood of Christ. Thus, at the time of the 'Preparation of the Gifts', the wine and water offering is poured into the sacred vessels for the consecration. Transferring the Blood of Christ from one vessel into other vessels at any time after the consecration is forbidden and may be considered a **sacrilege**. Of this, the Holy See reminds us in a recent document: *"The **pouring of the Blood of Christ** after the consecration from one vessel to another **is completely to be avoided**, lest anything should happen that would be to the detriment of so great a mystery."*[80a]

PRIVATE PREPARATION OF THE PRIEST:

After the *Agnus Dei,* the faithful usually **kneel**,[80b] those in the nave and those in the sanctuary, for the priest is about to elevate the Body and Blood of Christ. Yet, depending on local custom, in some parishes the faithful might keep standing. Personally, I can't keep from going down on my knees when the Blessed Sacrament is elevated before me. Kneeling at this time of the Mass helps us to recollect as the final preparation before receiving communion.

79a. CMRR, Chapter 5, no. 326; cf. GIRM [113] 155.
80. GIRM [56c] 83 (bold face added).
80a. *Redemptionis Sacramentum* no. 106 (bold face added).
80b. Cf. GIRM [21] 43.

Before his own communion, ✢*"The priest prepares himself by a prayer, said quietly, that he may fruitfully receive Christ's Body and Blood. The faithful do the same, praying silently."* [81] There are two prayers in the missal for the priest to choose from:

1-✢OM *"Lord Jesus Christ, Son of the living God, by the will of the Father and the work of the Holy Spirit your death brought life to the world. By your holy body and blood free me from all my sins, and from every evil. Keep me faithful to your teaching, and never let me be parted from you."*

OR

2- ✢OM *"Lord Jesus Christ, with faith in your love and mercy I eat your body and drink your blood. Let it not bring me condemnation, but health in mind and body."*

What beautiful prayers! In the first prayer, I especially like that we ask to be kept united to Christ forever. Then, the second prayer bears a great teaching: 'Let it not bring me condemnation, but health...', *(1Co 11:27-29)"Whoever, therefore, eats the bread or drinks the cup of the Lord in an unworthy manner will be guilty of profaning the body and blood of the Lord. Let a man examine himself, and so eat of the bread and drink of the cup. For any one who eats and drinks without discerning the body eats and drinks judgment upon himself."*

COMMUNION:

✢*"When the prayer is concluded, the priest genuflects, takes the [large] Host consecrated in the same Mass, and, holding it slightly raised above the paten or above the chalice, while facing the people, says,* **Ecce Agnus Dei** (This is the Lamb of God):*"* [82]

✢OM *"This is the Lamb of God
who takes away the sins of the world.
Happy are those who are called to his supper."* [83]

When the priest says, 'This is the Lamb of God,' it isn't a figure of speech. The priest is really holding and showing the Body and Blood of Christ for all to see, inviting all, who are properly disposed, to participate in the paschal meal. Then, using words from the Gospel, the priest together with the faithful humbly say:

✢OM **"Lord, I am not worthy to receive you,
but only say the word and I shall be healed***."*

---

81. GIRM [56f] 84.
82. GIRM [115] 157 (bold face added).
83. Cf. *Jn* 1:29 ; *Lk* 14:15.

This response we give at every Mass was probably inspired by the following words of the centurion. *(Lk 7:6.7)"..."Lord, do not trouble yourself, for I am not worthy to have you come under my roof; therefore I did not presume to come to you. But only speak the word, and let my servant be healed.""* Who can ever claim to be worthy of hosting God? *(Ps 103:21)"Bless the LORD, all his hosts, his ministers that do his will."* When we acknowledge that we are not worthy to receive Him, we humble ourselves, which helps to make room to let God into our heart and soul.

When at this time we say: *'Lord, I am not worthy... but only say the word and I shall be healed,'* I usually add in silence: Lord, please say a word to me now because today again I need to be healed. Then, I try to make myself most available to Him so that I may hear His word to me. And each time I ask Him, He blesses me with beautiful and intimate words of love, joy, hope, or faith. Often, the Lord's words to me are: 'I love you.' At other times He gives me words of guidance for a matter at hand that is important to me. Whatever His words are, they are simple and always either uplifting, edifying, or exhorting. At times, I carry and treasure His words in my heart for days afterwards. In all cases, Christ's words are enlightening and make me long even more to receive Him in the Eucharist. I carry His words in my heart as I walk towards the sanctuary to receive holy communion, where Christ feeds me with His life.

HOLY REMINDERS

At this moment, before the communion, the priest might remind the faithful that Christ is really wholly and truly present in the Eucharist: *"'That in this sacrament are the true Body of Christ and his true Blood is something that "cannot be apprehended by the senses," says St. Thomas, "but only by faith, which relies on divine authority." For this reason, in a commentary on Luke 22:19; ('This is my body which is given for you.'), St.Cyril says: "Do not doubt whether this is true, but rather receive the **words of the Savior** in faith, for since he is the truth, **he cannot lie.**""*[84] *"What seems to be bread is not bread, though it tastes like it, but the Body of Christ, and that what seems to be wine is not wine, though it tastes like it, but the Blood of Christ."*[85]

It is a favorable time for the priest to remind the faithful that Christ is wholly present even in the smallest part of the Eucharist: ✦ ***"Christ,***

---

84. CCC 1381, quoting St.Thomas Aquinas, *STh* III, 75, 1; cf. Paul VI, *MF* 18; St. Cyril of Alexandria, *In Luc.* 22, 19: PG 72, 912; cf. Paul VI, *MF* 18, (bold face added).
85. NCUBK no. 13, quoting St-Cyril of Jerusalem, cf.Paul VI, *Mysterium Fidei: On the Doctrine and Worship of the Eucharist* (September 3, 1965), no. 48 (in International Committee on English in the Liturgy, *Documents on the Liturgy, 1963-1979: Conciliar, Papal, and Curial Texts* (DOL 176, no. 1193).

***whole and entire**, and the true Sacrament, is received **even under only one species** [as much as under both species], and consequently that as far as the effects are concerned, those who receive under only one species are not deprived of any of the grace that is necessary for salvation.* "[86 bfa]

We need to be reminded about some of the blessings and graces that we receive through the reception of the Eucharist; graces such as the weakening of the hold that sin has over us, and the gradual **sanctification** of our souls. From time to time the faithful need to be reminded how to receive communion. The celebrating priest may simply remind the faithful why they should respond **'Amen'** when, at communion, the minister says: 'the Body of Christ', while presenting them with the Host. *"The act of Communion, therefore, is also an act of faith. For when the minister says, "The Body of Christ" or "The Blood of Christ," the communicant's "Amen" is a profession in the presence of the saving Christ, body and blood, soul and divinity, who now gives life to the believer."* [87] Thus, our 'Amen' means **I believe** that this Host is the Body and Blood, Soul and Divinity of Christ.

When communion is given under both species, it is important that the priest, from time to time, remind the faithful **how to receive the Blood** of Christ, in order to assure proper reverence, and especially so that **not one drop** of the Precious Blood is dripped on the floor.

COMMUNION OF THE CELEBRATING PRIEST

✠OM *"Facing the altar, the priest says quietly:*
'May the body of Christ bring me to everlasting life.'
He reverently consumes the body of Christ. Then he takes the chalice and says quietly:
'May the blood of Christ bring me to everlasting life.'
He reverently drinks the blood of Christ."

The priest usually consumes the large Host entirely. However, when the Host is very large or when concelebrating priests are present, he then shares the Host. As the priest consumes the Blood of Christ, he may save some for the purification[88] of the chalice. However, when a deacon or concelebrating priests are present, or when communion is distributed under both species to all, the priest shares the Blood, which is then entirely consumed during the communion.

86. GIRM [241] 282, cf. Council of Trent, session 21, *Doctrina de communione sub utraque specie et parvulorum*, 16 July 1562, chap.1-3: Denz-Schön, 1725-1729.
87. NCUBK no. 14.
88. The purification of the empty sacred vessels that were used during Mass is part of the post communion ritual. This ritual is discussed further on in this Part Three.

As the 'Communion Antiphon' begins, the extraordinary ministers of Holy Communion reverently approach the sanctuary. *"During the Communion of the celebrant, not earlier, **extraordinary ministers** come to the sanctuary. They first **genuflect** to the Eucharist on the altar. They may go to a credence table to cleanse their hands. They **stand at the side**(s) of the altar not around it, because they are not concelebrants, deacons or instituted acolytes. After "This is the Lamb of God...", the **celebrant** or deacon **gives them Communion** before the servers. They receive in both kinds, if the faithful receive in both kinds at that Mass. They do not give themselves Communion by taking the Eucharist from the altar. **The celebrant hands them the eucharistic vessel,** but they do not take it directly from the altar. These revised ceremonial signs truthfully define their ministry as "extraordinary" and hence dependent on the celebrant of the Eucharistic Sacrifice."* [89]

COMMUNION ANTIPHON: ♪

✣*"While the priest is receiving the Sacrament, the Communion chant is begun*. Its purpose is to express the communicants' union in spirit by means of the unity of their voices, to show joy of heart, and to highlight more clearly the "**communitarian**" nature of the procession to receive communion. The singing is continued for as long as the Sacrament is being administered to the faithful."* [90] Care should be taken to bring communion to the singers and musicians.

✣*"If there is no singing*, the Communion antiphon found in the Missal may be recited either by the faithful, or by some of them, or by a lector. Otherwise the priest himself says it after he has received Communion and before he distributes Communion to the faithful."* [90a]

The 'Communion Antiphon' is taken from the holy scriptures and is often an exhortation that is directly related to the readings of the day. Recitation of this antiphon brings forth, in our minds, a summary of the message carried in the 'liturgy of the Word' of the day. Here are some inspiring examples: *(Ps 42:1)"As a deer longs for flowing streams, / so my soul longs for you, O God." (Jn 6:27)"Do not work for food that perishes but for the food that endures for eternal life, which the Son of Man will give you."*[NAB] *(1Pt 1:18-19)"You know that you were ransomed from the futile ways inherited from your ancestors, not with perishable things like silver or gold, but with the precious blood of Christ, like that of a lamb without defect or blemish."*

---

89. CMRR, Revised Edition, 2005, Appendix 1, no. 781 (bfa) cf. GIRM [240-252] 162.
90. GIRM [56i] 86, cf. Sacred Congregation for the Sacraments and Divine Worship, Instruction *Inaestimabile donum*, 3 April 1980, no. 17: AAS 72 (1980), p. 338 (bfa).
90a. GIRM [56i] 87.

COMMUNION OF THE MINISTERS

After taking his own communion, the celebrating priest takes the ciborium to the communicants, starting with those present in the sanctuary, and in the following order: extraordinary ministers of Holy Communion, servers, and then readers. Since the Communion hymn is to be song until all have received, Communion may be brought to the cantor/ choir and musicians while the congregation receives, or they may come to the front of the church at the end to receive Communion.

Extraordinary ministers do not stand at or around the altar as do the priest(s), deacon, and acolyte. They wait for the priest to bring them the Eucharist. As mentioned earlier, if extraordinary ministers are to take part in the distribution of Communion, they would have entered the sanctuary at the time of the priest's Communion, and they would have purified their hands before taking up their position at the side of the sanctuary.

✟ *"The priest may be assisted in the distribution of Communion by other priests who happen to be present. If such priests are not present and there is **a very large number** of communicants, the priest may call upon extraordinary ministers to assist him, i.e., duly instituted acolytes or even other faithful who have been deputed for this purpose. [Extraordinary] ministers **should not approach** the altar before the priest has received Communion, and they are **always to receive from the hands of the priest** celebrant the vessel containing either species of the Most Holy Eucharist for distribution to the faithful."* [91]

*"The **acolyte** gives Holy Communion by virtue of his **institution**, thus taking **precedence** over other laity and religious authorized to distribute the Eucharist. **Extraordinary ministers** assist **only when** they are **needed** in addition to ordained ministers. Therefore clergy are not to remain seated at a celebration while acolytes or extraordinary ministers distribute Communion."* [92] *"This useful auxiliary ministry should not be trivialized by being required even at Masses where there are not great numbers of communicants... The **unnecessary multiplication** of extraordinary ministers may be motivated by a sincere desire "to involve the laity". But it may reflect a **confused theology** of laity and ministry, even the **false notion** that it is the "right" of the laity to give the Eucharist to others."* [93]

---

91. GIRM [118] 162, cf. Sacred Congregation for the Sacraments and Divine Worship, Instruction *Inaestimabile donum*, 3 April 1980, no. 10: AAS 72 (1980), p. 336; Interdicasterial Instruction on certain questions regarding the collaboration of the non-ordained faithful in the sacred ministry of priests, *Ecclesiae de mysterio*, 15 August 1997, art. 8: AAS 89 (1997), p. 871 (bold face added).
92. CMRR, Chap.10, no. 603, cf. Commission for the Authentic Interpretation of the Code of Canon Law, Appendix 1, par. 784 (bold face added).
93. CMRR, Appendix 1, no.787 (bold face added).

COMMUNION OF CONCELEBRANTS

In a concelebrated Mass, the concelebrating priests stand at the altar, together with the celebrating priest, throughout the Eucharistic Prayer; they share the celebrant's function by reading some of the prayers. Then after the communion of the celebrating priest, the concelebrants receive communion at the altar. ✢*"After the principal celebrant's Communion, the chalice is placed on another corporal at the side of the altar. The concelebrants approach the middle of the altar one after another, genuflect, and receive the Body of the Lord; then they go to the side of the altar and consume the Blood of the Lord."* [94]

The deacon - if one is present - receives communion under both species from the celebrating priest. Thereafter, the concelebrating priests usually share the large Host, the Body of Christ, and drink of the same cup of the Blood of Christ. With the preoccupation in mind that not one drop of the Blood of Christ may be dripped or spilled, and by respect for one another, the priests and deacon use the purificator to wipe the rim of the chalice after drinking from the cup.

COMMUNICANTS
Disposed to Receive

✢*"Since the Eucharistic Celebration is the Paschal Banquet, it is desirable that in keeping with the Lord's command, his Body and Blood should be received as spiritual food by the faithful who are **properly disposed**. This is the sense of the fraction and the other preparatory rites by which the faithful are led directly to Communion."*[94a]

We the faithful continue to prepare ourselves to receive communion by praying in silence. However, it is the gift of faith that allows us to believe in the real presence of Jesus Christ in the Eucharist, a belief that is enhanced by our being in a **state of grace**.

*"The celebration of the Eucharistic sacrifice is wholly directed toward the **intimate union** of the faithful with Christ through communion. To receive communion is to receive Christ himself who has offered himself for us."* [95]

*"The Church warmly recommends that the faithful receive Holy Communion each time they participate in the celebration of the Eucharist; she obliges them to do so **at least once a year** [during the Easter season]."* [96]

---

94. GIRM [205] 248.
94a. GIRM [56] 80 (bold face added).
95. CCC 1382 (bold face added).
96. CCC 1417; cf. CCC 2042, cf. CIC, can. 920; CCEO, cann. 708; 881 § 3 (bfa).

*"Anyone who desires to receive Christ in Eucharistic communion must be in the **state of grace**. Anyone aware of having sinned mortally must not receive communion without having received absolution in the sacrament of penance."* [97]

In reverence for the real presence of Christ in the Eucharist, for His Body and Blood, Soul and Divinity, and enlightened by the directives of the Church, who has been entrusted by Christ with the celebration of the memorial of His sacrifice, all should meet the following **conditions before receiving holy communion**:

- having received baptism;
- having received first communion and the appropriate catechesis;
- professing the creed of the Church and believing in the real presence of Jesus Christ in the Eucharist;
- being in a state of grace - free of mortal sin; and [98]
- having respected the one-hour Eucharistic fast. [99]
- Catholics who have been away from the Church for a while need to go to confession before receiving communion again.

For times when we forget the origins and the meaning of the Eucharist, or the necessity to be in a state of grace before receiving communion, here is an excerpt from the first letter to the Corinthians. Saint Paul here recalls the institution of the Eucharist, and explains some of the effects and consequences of receiving the Body and Blood of Christ, as well as the importance of being in a state of grace before we receive Jesus in holy communion:

*(1Co 11:23-31)"The Lord Jesus on the night when he was betrayed took a loaf of bread, and when he had given thanks, he broke it and said, "This is my body that is for you. Do this in remembrance of me." In the same way he took the cup also, after supper, saying, "This cup is the new covenant in my blood. Do this, as often as you drink it, in remembrance of me."For as often as you eat this bread and drink the cup, you proclaim the Lord's death until he comes. **Whoever, therefore, eats the bread or drinks the cup of the Lord in an unworthy manner will be answerable for the body and blood of the Lord**. Examine*

---

97. CCC 1415 (bold face added). Mortal sin (deadly sin): see Part Three, Liturgy of the Word, Penitential Rite, pp. 56-57, footnotes 16, 17, 18.
98. If one has doubts about being in the state of grace, he should consult a priest in the sacrament of confession before receiving communion.
99. Eucharistic fast consists in abstaining for at least one hour before communion from all food and drink, with the exception of water and medicine (cf. CCC 1387, cf. CIC, can. 919).

yourselves, and only then eat of the bread and drink of the cup. For all who eat and drink without discerning the body, eat and drink judgment against themselves. For this reason many of you are weak and ill, and some have died. But if we judged ourselves, we would not be judged." [bfa]

Since **it is not mandatory to receive communion** during the Mass, those who cannot receive, for one reason or another, may partake in the communion by **making a spiritual communion**[100] through which one receives spiritual blessings from the Lord. If you desire to receive the Eucharist, but a personal life situation prevents you from receiving, then be assured that the Church can help you to regulate your situation, what ever it is, so that you may become able to receive the Life that Christ wants to give you.

For those who are disposed to receive communion, here is a quote from the Catechism, which states some of the **spiritual fruits** that you receive when receiving communion. *"Communion with the Body and Blood of Christ **increases** the communicant's **union** with the Lord, **forgives** his **venial sins**, and **preserves** him **from grave sins**. Since receiving this sacrament **strengthens the bonds of charity** between the communicant and Christ, it also reinforces the unity of the Church as the Mystical Body of Christ."* [101]

---

100. See Part Five, Appendix 'F', Essential Catholic Prayers, Prayers for Communion and Private Eucharistic Adoration, Spiritual Communion.
101. CCC 1416 (bold face added).

COMMUNION PROCESSION

♪ At this time, the communion song has usually been playing since the priest's communion, and will continue playing throughout the communion of the faithful. The choir director has chosen a song that allows all to sing and inspires them to rejoice in receiving the Bread of life. Here is an excerpt taken from the Sacramentary regarding the communion song: ✦*"[The purpose of the communion chant] is to express the communicants'* **union in spirit** *by means of the* **unity of their voices***, to show* **joy of heart***, and to highlight more clearly the* **"communitarian" nature** *of the procession to receive Communion."* [102]

As Saint Don Bosco (1815-1888) strongly and clearly stated, it is most **imperative that the faithful are not directed to communion** by letting people out of their pews row by row. Such a practice may wrongly encourage those who are not in a state of grace to receive communion. Thus the communion procession should be done freely, even though if somewhat disorderly. In any case, we should not worry about what others may think if we do not go to communion, but rather what God will think if we receive Him improperly disposed.

Once the priest(s), the deacon, and the ministers have received their own communion, then the **faithful** reverently come out of their pews to **form procession lines in the different aisles** of the church. With a recollected attitude, they walk toward the front of the sanctuary where they receive the Eucharist. While walking in procession to communion, one should be longing to receive Christ, and pray to be totally absorbed by Him when receiving the Eucharist.

The priest(s) and other ministers assisting in the distribution of holy Communion reverently come out of the sanctuary, each carrying a ciborium of Hosts. It is appropriate for the celebrating priest to be the first one to come out of the sanctuary, followed by the other priest(s), the deacon, and last, the extraordinary ministers. They each then take their position at the head of an aisle to distribute communion to the faithful.

In order to insure that holy Communion is distributed in an orderly and reverent manner, and by reverence for the Blessed Sacrament, it is desirable that the positions assumed by each of the ministers be agreed on before the Mass starts. Usually, the celebrating priest stands at the head of the main aisle, while the other priest(s), the deacon, and the extraordinary ministers position themselves at the head of secondary aisles. Those who remain in the sanctuary kneel and contemplate the miracle of the divine life that they have just received.

---

102. GIRM [56i] 86 (bold face added).

As I walk towards the sanctuary, as a final preparation, I often ask Mother Mary to come and make sure that my soul is nice and clean to receive Her Jesus. And each time I ask, I can feel Her putting her Motherly touch on my soul. I also pray to the Holy Spirit: 'Lord I believe in the real presence, but increase my faith.' The Holy Spirit comes to my aid by reminding me of some of Christ's living words such as: *(Jn 6:51)"I am the living bread that came down from heaven. Whoever eats of this bread will live forever; and the bread that I will give for the life of the world is my flesh."*

At times, I ask Christ to allow me to feel His presence in the Eucharist, knowing well that no matter what I may or may not feel, He is there truly and wholly present. Whenever Christ blesses me with feeling His presence in the Eucharist, it raises my consciousness of Him to the point of becoming blissfully overwhelmed. When that happens, I usually can't help shedding tears of joy, as if overflowing from a too full heart. While self-consciousness may tend to hold my tears back, Christ's presence and love makes all resistance melt away. Oh! How I cherish this intimate union! *(Ps 27:4)"One thing I ask of the LORD; / this I seek: / To dwell in the LORD's house / all the days of my life, / To gaze on the LORD's beauty, / to visit his temple."* NAB

COMMUNION OF THE FAITHFUL

Standing in line, the communicants approach one by one, and receive communion in the following manner:

✛ OM *"[the priest takes a host, raises the host slightly and shows it to each, saying:]* The Body of Christ. *[each communicant replies:]* **Amen**.*"*

✛ *"... [T]he communicant **bows** his or her head before the Sacrament as a gesture of reverence and receives the Body of the Lord from the minister. The consecrated host may be received either on the tongue or in the hand, at the discretion of each communicant."* [103] *"The act of Communion... is also an act of faith. For when the minister says, "The Body of Christ" or "The Blood of Christ," the communicant's **"Amen"** is a profession in the presence of the saving Christ, body and blood, soul and divinity, who now gives life to the believer."* [104]

In the past decades, the faithful have been encouraged to receive communion in the hands rather than on the tongue. However, as mentioned in the above and following excerpts from the Sacramentary, it is at the discretion of the communicant to receive communion either on the tongue or in the hands, where it is permitted.

---

103. GIRM [117] 160 (bold face added).
104. NCUBK, Part I, no. 14 (bold face added).

✢ *"In the distribution of* **communion** *the custom of placing the consecrated bread* **on the tongue** *of the communicants* **should be maintained***, since it is based on a traditional practice of several centuries. Nevertheless episcopal conferences may decree, with confirmation of the decisions by the Apostolic See, that* **communion may** *also* **be given** *in their territory by placing the consecrated bread* **in the hands** *of the faithful,* **provided that** *precautions are taken against danger of insufficient reverence or false doctrines about the Eucharist arising in the minds of the faithful."* [105] bfa

COMMUNICANTS
Manner to receive the Host

Those who choose to receive communion in the hands should do so with great reverence. The manner in which communicants should receive the Body of Christ in the hand is as follows: if the communicant is right handed, he places his left hand slightly in front of his heart with the palm open and upwards, and he puts his right hand underneath, in a manner so that both palms are facing upwards and **forming a safe receptacle** for the Host. Then standing in front of the minister, he slightly raises his hands to receive the holy Host in the palm of his left hand. Upon receiving the Host, and while still standing in front of the minister, without haste the communicant carefully takes the Host with the fingers of his right hand and puts the Host on his tongue. Out of reverence for the Eucharist and as a rule to prevent any possibilities of dropping the Host, one may **never walk away** from the minister **before consuming the Host.**

✢ *"As soon as the communicant receives the host, he or she consumes it entirely."* [106] If a communicant should witness that a Host or a particle of a Host has fallen on the ground, he should make sure that it is picked up, by informing one ministering the Eucharist. *"If a **Host** falls to the ground, **the minister, not the communicant,** must retrieve it at once."* [107]

"...[W]hen receiving [communion] in the hand, the communicant should be guided by the words of St. Cyril of Jerusalem: 'When you approach, take care not to do so with your hand stretched out and your fingers open or apart, but rather place your left hand as a throne... as befits one who is about to receive the King. Then receive Him, taking care that nothing is lost.'" [108]

---

105. Sacramentary, Second Edition, Forward, p.16, Manner of Ministering Communion.
106. GIRM. [117] 161. Also see Part Three, Communion Rite, Profanation of the Blessed Sacrament.
107. CMRR, Chapter 10, no. 611 (bold face added).
108. NCUBK, no. 41, quoting St. Cyril of Jerusalem.

In some parishes, when communion is received on the tongue a server stands near the priest with a **Communion-plate**, which he places under the chins of the faithful as the priest gives them communion, thus securing the Host in case it may be dropped. *"The Communion-plate for the Communion of the faithful should be retained, so as to avoid the danger of the sacred host or some fragment of it falling."* [108a]

The **manner** for communicants **to receive the Body of Christ on the tongue** is as follows: after saying 'Amen', the communicant opens his mouth slightly and advances his tongue slightly on the lower lip, without putting it out, so that it is easier for the priest or minister to place the Host on his tongue. Whether the communicants receive communion in the hand or on the tongue, out of reverence for the Eucharist, they should **let the Host melt** on their tongue rather than chew it like ordinary food; which may cause particles of the Host to stick to the teeth instead of being ingested right away. After receiving communion, since the Lord is now substantially present in the faithful, they return to their pews walking in a recollected manner, looking down to prevent distraction.

When standing to receive communion[109] the communicant should make a **sign of reverence** before he receives, by bowing his head or making a deep bow towards the ciborium or chalice that contains the Body and Blood of Christ. At times, we see people who right after receiving communion walk away from the priest or minister who gave them the Eucharist, to go and make the sign of the cross while looking at the crucifix in the sanctuary. Unfortunately, this practice, which tends to disrupt the procession, indicates a confusion. If the idea is to make a sign of reverence to the Lord, then why not make this sign to Christ who is present in the ciborium held by the priest? When the faithful are **allowed to kneel** to receive communion, there is no need to make any other sign of reverence.

After consuming the Host, communicants who receive the Eucharist in the hand should make sure that **no particles of the Host are left** on their hands. If such is the case, one should consume these particles. Unfortunately, very few communicants know to look for particles of the Host on their hands. Mother Teresa of Calcutta has said: *"The thing that makes me saddest is watching people receive communion in the hand."* What a stunning statement coming from this Blessed who has seen so much suffering.

108a. *Redemptionis Sacramentum* no. 93 (bold face added).

109. In most parishes the communicants stand to receive communion, but there are shrines and parishes were people can kneel at the communion rail to receive communion. Both manners are approved by the Church (cf. *Redemptionis Sacramentum*, 90).

A person may not receive the **Eucharist more than once on the same day**, except in the circumstances specified in liturgical norms, which are as follows: the faithful may receive communion a second time on the same day only when attending a Mass for **special occasions** such as a marriage, funeral, baptism, confirmation... or a catholic congress, special meeting or sacred pilgrimage, and only if attending the whole Mass.[110]

EXTRAORDINARY MINISTERS OF HOLY COMMUNION

"... [T]he **ordinary** *minister of Holy Communion is the Bishop, the Priest and the Deacon.* **Extraordinary** *ministers of Holy Communion are those instituted as acolytes and the faithful so deputed... ."* [111] Therefore, it is ordinarily the office of the priest to distribute communion, and it is extraordinary to depute a lay minister to give Holy Communion.

"This **function is to be understood strictly** *according to the name by which it is known, that is to say, that of extraordinary minister of Holy Communion, and not "special minister of Holy Communion" nor "extraordinary minister of the Eucharist" nor "special minister of the Eucharist", by which names the meaning of this function is unnecessarily and improperly broadened."* [111a]

Many bishops in the United States encourage that communion under both species be given at all Masses in their dioceses, and they entrust extraordinary ministers, at communion during the Mass, to assist in ministering ciboria of Hosts as well as chalices of the Blood of Christ. However, it is required that: *"**Extraordinary ministers** of Holy Communion should **receive sufficient** spiritual, theological, and practical **preparation** to fulfill their role with knowledge and reverence."* [112] This requirement applies to all extraordinary ministers of Holy Communion, whether they give communion under both species or under the species of bread alone.

It is necessary for extraordinary ministers to be in a **state of grace**, not only to receive communion, but also, to distribute communion. Extraordinary ministers must have a most **reverent and sacred attitude** towards the Eucharist, whether they are distributing holy communion during the Mass, or bringing communion to the sick. They are to set a proper example for the congregation. They must also

---

110. Cf. *The Sacramentary*, Second Edition, Foreword, p.15, Communion More than Once a Day.
111. *The Collaboration of the Non-Ordained Faithful in the Sacred Ministry of Priest*, Congregation For The Clergy, Practical Provisions, Article 8, § 1, The Extraordinary minister Of The Holy Communion (bold face added), cf. *CIC*, can. 910 § 2.
111a. *Redemptionis Sacramentum,* no. 156 (bold face added).
112. NCUBK, Part II, No. 28 (bold face added).

handle with great reverence the sacred **vessels** and the sacred **linens**, before, during, and after the Mass. Unfortunately, some liturgical lay ministers show a lack of reverence towards the Eucharist. This statement is motivated by disconcerting attitudes and comments that I have witnessed; for example, some lay ministers seem to be unable to refer to the Blessed Sacrament as the Body and the Blood of Christ, and only refer to the Blessed Sacrament as the **bread and wine**, and this without even qualifying the species as being 'holy' or 'consecrated'. I have heard lay ministers referring to the purification and/or the washing of the sacred vessels as **doing the dishes**. In some cases, lay ministers have been directed to rinse the sacred vessels **without** these being first **purified**. Then, there is that **false concept** among some lay ministers that they have a right given by God to minister Holy Communion. It makes you wonder what kind of training some of them might have received, if any training at all.

Extraordinary ministers
Manner to give the Host
Here are some practical recommendations concerning the distribution of the Body of Christ that extraordinary ministers should know:

*"Those who minister the Eucharist should **never be hasty**, because this leads to accidents and implies both a lack of reverence for the Eucharist and of respect for those who receive the Lord. The minister **should say "The Body of Christ"** clearly so that the communicant hears the words and can respond, but **it is not necessary** for others in the church to hear these words; **nor** is it **desirable that several voices be heard** saying "The Body of Christ" when ministers are distributing Holy Communion at the same time. If the **number of Hosts will not suffice** for all the communicants, the minister [113] should **go to the altar** or another place and discreetly break the particles so that all who approach the altar may communicate. But it is **neither becoming** nor convenient to attempt **to break** them **while distributing** Holy Communion. As already noted, at the fraction of the Mass, during the Agnus Dei, **only a priest may assist** the celebrant in breaking Hosts."* [113a]

*"It seems preferable to keep the thumb on the upper part of the Host and the forefinger beneath it, so as to **maintain control**."* [113b] Handling the Host in this manner gives better control to set the Host on the tongue or in the palm of the communicant. No one should distribute Holy Communion without proper practical and spiritual **training**, and official approval from the local Bishop or the Pastor.

---

113. The breaking of Hosts is reserved to the ordinary (ordained) ministers.
113a. CMRR, Chapter 10, 610 (bold face added).
113b. CMRR, Chapter 10, 605.

COMMUNION OF THE FAITHFUL UNDER BOTH SPECIES [114]

✦ *"Holy Communion has a fuller form as a sign when it is distributed under both kinds. For in this form the sign of the Eucharistic banquet is more clearly evident and clear expression is given to the divine will by which the new and eternal Covenant is ratified in the Blood of the Lord, as also the relationship between the Eucharistic banquet and the eschatological banquet in the Father's Kingdom."* [115]

However, by respect for the Precious Blood of Christ, communion under both holy species during the Mass is to be practiced with great reverence and may be **reserved for special communicants and occasions** as follows:

- Adults at the Mass which follows their **baptism or confirmation**;
- Baptized persons **being received into the Church**;
- Bride and Bridegroom at their **wedding** Mass;
- Ordained at their **ordination** Mass;
- Lay missionaries when publicly **receiving their mission**;
- Sick person and all present when **viaticum** is administrated;
- Godparents, parents, wife or husband, and lay catechists of a newly baptized adult at the **Mass of initiation**.[115a]

✦ *"In addition to those cases given in the ritual books [same cases as the ones given in the above list], Communion under both kinds is permitted for:*
*a) **Priests** who are **not able to celebrate** or concelebrate Mass;*
*b) The deacon and others **who perform some duty at the Mass**;*
*c) **Members of communities** at the **conventual Mass** or "community" Mass, along with **seminarians**, and **all** who are engaged in a **retreat** or are taking part in a spiritual or **pastoral gathering**."* [116]

As you can see, the Holy See permits communion under both species only on special occasions in the life of members of the Church, thus emphasizing the fact that these events are special. However, the Bishop may, under certain conditions, allow communion under both holy species in his diocese on occasions other than those mentioned above.

114. For a history of communion under both species: see Part Five, Appendix 'C', Origin of Communion Under Both Species.
115. GIRM [240] 281, cf. Sacred Congregation of Rites, Instruction *Eucharisticum mysterium*, On the worship of the Eucharist, 25 May 1967, no. 32: AAS 59 (1967), p. 558.
115a. Cf. *The Roman Missal,* second edition, GIRM [242].
116. GIRM [242] 283 (bold face added).

✢ *"The Diocesan Bishop may establish norms for Communion under both kinds for his own diocese... The Diocesan Bishop is also given the faculty to permit Communion under both kinds whenever it may seem appropriate to the priest to whom, as its own shepherd, a community has been entrusted, provided that the* **faithful have been well instructed** *and there is* **no danger of profanation** *of the Sacrament or of the rite's becoming difficult because of the large number of participants or some other reason."* [117]

General Norms for Communion Under Both Kinds
✢ *"When* **Communion** *is distributed* **under both kinds**,
  a. *The chalice is usually administered by a* **deacon** *or, when no deacon is present, by a priest, or even by a duly instituted acolyte or another extraordinary minister of Holy Communion, or by a member of the faithful who, in* **case of necessity**, *has been entrusted with this duty for a single occasion;*

  b. *Whatever may remain of the* **Blood of Christ** *is* **consumed at the altar** *by the priest or the deacon or the duly instituted acolyte* **who ministered the chalice**. *The same then purifies, wipes, and arranges the sacred vessels in the usual way.*

Any of the faithful who wish to receive Holy Communion under the species of bread alone should be granted their wish." [117a]
"Christ, whole and entire, and the true Sacrament, is received even under only one species... ." [118]

Variations in the Procedure
At Masses where communion is given **under both species** rather than under the form of **bread alone**, variations in the procedure are encountered before, during, and after the Mass. Here are **some guidelines** addressing these variations:
  - **A quantity of wine** that will suffice for the number of communicants expected needs to be prepared before the Mass.

  - **Additional vessels** and **purificators** needed to minister the Blood are to be set on the credence table before the Mass. *"Sacred vessels for containing the Body and Blood of the Lord must be made in strict conformity with the norms of tradition and of the liturgical books.* **Reprobated**, *therefore, is any practice of using vessels made from* **glass, earthenware**, *clay, or other materials that break easily."* [118a]

---

117. GIRM [242] 283 (bold face added).
117a. GIRM [-] 284 (bold face added).
118. GIRM [241] 282, cf. Council of Trent, session 21, *Doctrina de communione sub utraque specie et parvulorum*, 16 July 1562, chap.1-3: Denz-Schön, 1725-1729.
118a. *Redemptionis Sacramentum*, no. 117 (bold face added).

- At the procession of the gifts, a **decanter** containing the **wine** to be used for all the communicants is brought to the altar, as well as the **additional chalices**.

- At the time of the **offertory**, the priest pours the wine into the chalices, and **consecrates the wine** directly **in the chalices** that will be used for the communion. *"Never to be used **for** containing the Blood of the Lord are flagons, bowls, or other vessels that are not fully in accord with the established norms."* [118b] *"The **pouring of the Blood** of Christ after the consecration from one vessel to another is completely to be avoided, lest anything should happen that would be to the detriment of so great a mystery."* [119]

- At the *Agnus Dei* (Lamb of God) the servers bring to the altar the **additional purificators**.

- After the priest's communion, the **extraordinary ministers** approach the altar to receive from the priest communion under both species; after their communion, the extraordinary **ministers receive from the hand of the priest** a **ciborium** of Hosts, **or a chalice** of the Precious Blood with a purificator. [119a]

- After the communion of the faithful, the ministers who ministered a chalice are expected to **consume** what happens to remain of **the Blood of Christ** in their chalice at the altar, and, in some cases, to purify the chalices at the credence, and to wipe them dry and arrange them properly on the credence table.

- After the Mass, since all of the **sacred vessels and linens** used for the Eucharist have come in contact with the Body and Blood of Christ, they should be **handled with great reverence**, and they should all be **purified** before they are washed, and put away.

118b. *Redemptionis Sacramentum*, no. 106 (bold face added).
119. *Redemptionis Sacramentum*, no. 106 (bold face added).
119a. Cf. GIRM [240-252] 162.

COMMUNION OF THE BLOOD OF CHRIST

✢"If Communion of the Blood of Christ is carried out by communicants' drinking from the chalice, each communicant, **after receiving the Body** of Christ, moves and stands facing the minister of the chalice. The minister says, ...(The Blood of Christ), the communicant responds, Amen, and the minister hands over the chalice, which the communicant raises to his or her mouth. Each communicant drinks a little from the chalice, hands it back to the minister, and then withdraws; the minister wipes the rim of the chalice with the purificator." [120] The minister of the chalice is first a deacon, a priest other than the celebrating priest, an instituted acolyte, and last an extraordinary minister of Holy Communion.

Following are instructions regarding the proper manner to distribute communion of the Blood of Christ to the faithful when **drinking from the chalice**.
- "The chalice may **never** be left on the altar or another place to be picked up by the communicant for **self-communication** (except in the case of concelebrating bishops or priests), nor may the chalice be passed from one communicant to another. There shall always be a minister of the chalice.
- After each communicant has received the Blood of Christ, the minister carefully **wipes both sides** of the rim of the chalice with a purificator. This action is a matter of both reverence and hygiene. For the same reason, the minister **turns the chalice** slightly after each communicant has received the Precious Blood." [121]
- "When giving the Blood of the Lord to **elderly** people or **children**, it seems better to **keep hold** of the chalice and to guide it carefully to the lips." [122]

COMMUNION OF THE BLOOD BY INTINCTION

The manner for the faithful to communicate under both kinds by intinction of the Host is described in the Sacramentary as follows: ✢"If Communion from the chalice is carried out by intinction, each communicant, holding a **communion-plate under the chin**, approaches the priest who holds a [ciborium of Hosts], a minister standing at his side and holding the chalice. **The priest takes a host, dips** it partly **into the chalice** and, showing it, says,... (The Body and Blood of Christ). The communicant responds, Amen, receives the Sacrament **in the mouth** from the priest, and then withdraws." [123]

---

120. GIRM [244-245] 286 (bold face added).
121. NCUBK, Part II, nos. 44, 45 (bold face added).
122. CMRR, Chapter 10, 606 (bold face added).
123. GIRM [246-247] 287 (bold face added).

*"The **communion plate is required** when the Eucharist is ministered by intinction, lest drops of the Precious Blood fall. It is still used in some churches whenever Communion is distributed."* [124]

In some dioceses, communion under both species by intinction of the Host is practiced as follows: after receiving the Host in the hand, the communicant walks to the minister of the chalice who then presents him the chalice with the words, 'the Blood of Christ.' After saying 'Amen,' the communicant 'dips' his Host in the Blood of Christ contained in the chalice which is held by the minister, and then consumes the holy species. However, the **Holy See** has **forbidden** this practice. *"The communicant **must not be permitted to intinct the host himself** in the chalice, nor to receive the intincted host in the hand."* [124a]

Allow me to relate a personal experience over which I became heart broken due to the lack of reverence and of consciousness that I witnessed during a Easter Mass while serving as an extraordinary minister of Holy Communion. In a parish where communion is usually distributed under the species of bread alone, with the intention of enhancing the celebration of the Easter Mass, the pastor invited the faithful to receive communion under both species. First, the pastor 'forgot' to prepare the faithful spiritually by informing them on how to receive the Body and Blood of Christ - there given by intinction; then, he 'forgot' to give communion to the extraordinary ministers and to hand them the sacred vessels containing the Eucharist. Therefore, the extraordinary ministers were left to pick up the sacred vessels from the altar, since the priest had already gone to distribute communion. Then, as the unprepared communicants came to receive communion, some of them after 'dipping' their Host in the Blood were rushing off while 'dripping' the Blood of Christ on the floor. I was shocked. Seeing this, as I presented the other communicants with the cup saying, 'The Blood of Christ,' I would quickly add, 'take your time please.' Once communion was over, I went back to my place with a saddened heart, and found myself praying to God in the words of Jesus; *(Lk 23:34) "Father, forgive them; for they do not know what they are doing."*

I am sure that many priests, or religious and lay people acting as extraordinary ministers, also at times witness a lack of consciousness and reverence towards the Blessed Sacrament, and therefore can understand how I felt. Please, **let us not be silent** in the face of those who demean the most precious gift from God, the Eucharist, **which is more precious than life itself**.

---

124. CMRR, Chapter 2, 114, cf. GIRM [80c] 118, [246b, 247b] 287; *CB*, no. 125 (bfa).
124a. *Redemptionis Sacramentum*, no. 104 (bold face added).

Let us voice lovingly this urgent need for an increase of reverence towards the Eucharist, towards each drop of Christ's Blood and each little particle of His Body. ✢ *"If a **host** or any particle **should fall**, it is to be picked up reverently. If any of the **Precious Blood is spilled**, the area where the spill occurred should be washed with water, and this water should then be poured into the sacrarium in the sacristy."*[125]

Either we believe that the Eucharist is Jesus Christ's Body and Blood, and that Christ is really present in the Eucharist, **or we do not**. And if we do not believe in His presence in the Eucharist, then we might be better not to receive the Eucharist. Our heavenly Father does not require that we understand how Jesus makes Himself present in the Eucharist for us to receive Him. But the Father does require that we believe that Jesus is present as Jesus, Himself, said that He is: (Mk 14:22.24)*"This is my body... . This is my blood."* [NAB] Let us keep in mind that if we drip or spill the Blood of Christ on the floor and neglect to attend to it, or even later walk on it, we are profaning the Precious Blood, **a sacrilege**. It is also a sacrilege when consecrated Hosts or particles of Hosts are ignored and left behind unconsumed, or even end up on the floor, including the particles that are left in the palm of the hand after communion.

PROFANATION OF THE BLESSED SACRAMENT

Profanation means a blasphemous act, an act of irreverence towards God or something sacred. A sacrilege is a conscious or unconscious act of violation of a sacred thing, especially in regards to the mishandling or mistreating of the Blessed Sacrament, which is a mortal sin. Some acts of profanation are committed out of negligence or **ignorance**, but others are committed **consciously**, thus making them graver sacrileges. It is most tragic that Jesus' vulnerability in the Eucharist is abused by some who throw out particles of Hosts and remains of the Blood, or worse, by some who commit despicable sacrilegious acts. It is specifically to prevent the profanation of the Body and Blood of Christ that the Church has defined norms regarding the manner to minister and to receive Holy Communion: *"If a person takes the Host but does not eat it, the **minister must retrieve it**, if necessary calling on the assistance of others to avoid profanation."* [126] *"[When communion is given in the hand], special care should be taken to ensure that the **host is consumed** by the communicant **in the presence of the minister**, so that no one goes away carrying the Eucharistic species in his hand. If there is a risk of profanation, then Holy Communion should not be given in the hand to the faithful."* [126a]

---

125. GIRM [239] 280 (bold face added). Sacrarium: See Part Five, Catholic Glossary and Part Three, Sacristy, Purification of the Sacred Linens.
126. CMRR Chapter 10, 611 (bold face added).
126a. *Redemptionis Sacramentum*, no. 92, Congregation for Divine Worship and the Discipline of the Sacraments, Dubium: *Notitiae* 35 (1999) pp. 160-161.

The practice of giving Communion of the Precious Blood to all usually means a multiplication of purificators that come in contact with the Blood of Christ; and these are not always attended to as they should be after the Mass. Thus, it **opens the door to profanation**. Communion under both species presents more risks of profanation than communion under the form of bread alone. If we do not have all the resources to practice communion under both species with all due reverence, then a good way to **prevent profanation** of the Eucharist is to have communion under the form of bread alone. Moreover, a good way to make sure that all Hosts and particles of Hosts are being consumed is to have communion on the tongue. God comes first.

HOLY REMINDERS

From time to time, people need to be reminded how to proceed at the time of communion. In some cases, people need to be reminded on **how to join the communion procession** to the sanctuary and which aisle to use to go back to their pews, so that communion takes place in an orderly manner, thus allowing for reverence and recollection. This is especially true for Masses during conventions, at places of retreats, and at shrines where pilgrims are only passing through. Yet, it might also be needed in some parishes. Once in a while, the priest should remind the faithful of the **importance of saying 'Amen'**, when receiving the Eucharist. Whether communion is given under both species or under the form of bread alone, pastors should remind the faithful, once in a while, to **consume the Host right away,** and that no one should go away carrying the Eucharistic species in his hand. We need to be reminded that the **state of grace** is required to receive communion. And we especially need to be reminded regularly that **Christ is truly and really present in the Eucharist**, even in the smallest particle, and that this is why we must receive the Holy Host and the Precious Blood with the greatest of **reverence**.

When serving as an extraordinary minister during Mass, there were times when I was stunned by the attitude of communicants. Some seemed distracted, and quite a few did not respond 'Amen' when addressed with the words 'the Body of Christ', as they were presented with the holy Host. We need to be reminded that by our 'Amen' we acknowledge and confess our faith in Christ's real presence in the Eucharist. *(1Co 10:16)"The cup of blessing that we bless, is it not a sharing in the blood of Christ? The bread that we break, is it not a sharing in the body of Christ?"* As a communicant, I sometimes wonder about those who distribute communion in haste or in a casual manner. We need to make sure that all ministers and communicants understand that communion is a holy and sacred moment and take the time to give and receive the Eucharist in a reverent manner.

AFTER COMMUNION:

After receiving the Eucharist, the communicants go back to their pews and kneel.[127] ✢*"When the distribution of Communion is finished, as circumstances suggest, the priest and faithful spend some time praying privately. If desired, a psalm or other canticle of praise or a hymn may also be sung by the entire congregation."*[128] ♫ This time of silent prayer after communion is reserved to give praise and thanksgiving to the Father Who has made it possible for us to again receive the Life of His Son, Jesus, by the means of the Eucharist. It is a time to contemplate on Jesus Christ Who has made Himself really present in the Eucharist, and Who is now really present within us, with His Soul and His Divinity. This is a blessed opportunity for a moment of intimacy with Christ, and for experiencing His magnificent gifts of peace and joy while listening for His voice in our hearts. Since the beginning of the Mass, the liturgy has prepared us for this moment. **This is the time to** ignore all that surrounds us and **be with God**.

Once everyone has received the Eucharist, the priest(s) and the ministers go back into the sanctuary. **All ciboria and chalices** must be brought **back to the altar** after communion. None of the remaining consecrated Hosts may be transferred from one ciborium to another except by the priest, or deacon, and only at the altar and over the corporal.

CLEANSING OF THE HANDS

As the priest purifies his fingers after distributing Communion Hosts, extraordinary ministers who distributed Hosts must also purify their fingers after the Communion. Before returning their ciboria, *"If fragments of the Host adhere to the fingers after distributing Communion, [the extraordinary] minister gently rubs the thumb and forefinger together so as to cleanse them over the... ciborium."*[129] Then, while the priest gathers the remaining Hosts and consumes the remaining Blood, the extraordinary ministers go to the credence and 'rinse' their fingers. *"[After the **extraordinary ministers** of the Holy Communion have distributed] the Eucharist according to local practice, then they give the vessel to the celebrant, deacon or acolyte, or place it on the altar. Each genuflects and goes to the credence table to cleanse his fingers before returning to [their] places among the assembly. They do not purify the sacred vessels."*[130]

---

127. After communion, people may either kneel, sit or stand. It is a matter of option, not of obligation. Those who have already received Communion do not have to remain standing until everyone has received. The GIRM does not say that people must stand until all have received, nor does it say that an individual priest or bishop can demand this. Cf. *Adoremus Bulletin*, Vol. IX, no.1: March 2003, Adoremus.org.

128. GIRM [56j] 88.

129. CMRR, Chap. 5, no. 343, cf. GIRM [237] 278.

130. CMRR, Appendix 1, no. 782 (bold face added) cf. GIRM [238] 279.

When I served as an extraordinary minister, while it was customary to wash our hands in the wash plate at the credence table before distributing Communion, no one ever indicated that we should 'cleanse' our fingers after distributing communion Hosts. I thought that a better practice would be for extraordinary ministers to 'rinse' their fingers in the wash plate, and to drain this water into the sacrarium after the Mass. Then, while working on this book I found that this is the recommended practice. The purpose for extraordinary ministers to 'cleanse' their fingers after they have distributed communion Hosts is to make sure that any particles of the Host that may remain on their fingers find their way into the sacrarium. Thus, it is a matter of reverence and of preventing profanation of the Blessed Sacrament.

PURIFICATION OF THE SACRED VESSELS:
The priest may purify the sacred vessels at the altar or at the credence table, but always over a corporal. *"Moreover... a duly instituted acolyte [may carry] the sacred vessels to the credence table and there purifies, wipes and arranges them..."*[131] The purpose of this ritual is to make sure that not one particle of Host, no matter how little, nor one drop of the Precious Blood, no matter how small, are left behind as if they were ordinary bread crumbs and wine residues.

Immediately after returning to the altar, the priest or minister entirely **consumes** what might remain of the **Blood** of Christ. When communion is distributed under both species, *"...extraordinary ministers of Holy Communion ... may consume what remains of the Precious Blood from their chalice of distribution... ."*[131a] After he has **gathered** the remaining consecrated **Hosts** in a ciborium, the priest puts the ciborium **in the tabernacle**, closes and locks the door of the tabernacle for safe keeping, and then genuflects. Thus, protecting the Hosts against danger of profanation. The Blood may never be reserved, and is always to be entirely consumed right after the communion.[132] The pastor, deacon or sacristan has the custody of the key of the tabernacle, which is kept in a safe place.[132a]

The priest then proceeds to the purification of the sacred vessels. **First**, the priest **wipes his fingers** over the paten. ✟*"Whenever a fragment of the host adheres to his fingers, especially after the fraction or the Communion of the faithful, the priest is to wipe his fingers over the paten or, if necessary, wash them. Likewise, he should also gather any fragments that may have fallen outside the paten."*[133]

---

131. *Redemptionis Sacramentum*, no. 119 (bold face added).
131a. NCUBK, no. 52. Also cf. GIRM [244] 284.
132. Cf. *Redemptionis Sacramentum*, 107; GIRM [120] 163, [242] 284, [238] 279.
132a. Cf. CMRR, Chapter 1, no. 73, cf. CIC, Canon 938 §3.
133. GIRM [237] 278.

Second, with the purificator wrapped around his fingers, the priest purifies the **paten** and empty **ciboria** by gently brushing into his chalice - which contains remnants of the Blood of Christ - the remaining fragments of Hosts from the paten and empty ciboria that were used to consecrate and to distribute the Eucharist.

✢"...*Then, standing at the altar or at the credence table, he purifies the paten or ciborium over the chalice, then purifies the chalice, saying quietly...*" [134]
  ✢OM "*Lord, may I receive these gifts in purity of heart.*
    May they bring me healing and strength, now and for ever."

Third, the next step is the purification of the **chalice(s)**, that is to 'rinse' the chalice to collect Host and Blood residues. ✢"*The sacred vessels are purified by the priest, the deacon, or an instituted acolyte after Communion or after Mass, insofar as possible at the credence table. The purification of the chalice is done with water alone or with wine and water, which is then drunk by whoever does the purification.*" [134a] At the purification of the chalice, the priest cleanses (purifies) his consecrated fingers, that he used to touch the Eucharistic bread. "*While a server **pours** a reasonable amount of **water** into the chalice or ciborium, the celebrant may place his **fingers over the vessel** so that fragments adhering to his fingers are washed into the cup. He may remove his fingers as a signal for the server to stop pouring. He dries his fingers [with the purificator] and if necessary **revolves** the vessel to ensure that fragments are detached from the inner surface of the cup. (If necessary he uses his fingers to dislodge fragments adhering to the vessel.) He then **drinks** the ablution.*" [135] Then, the priest completes the purification of his chalice by **wiping it dry** with the purificator.

In the same manner, the priest, deacon, or acolyte purifies each of the other chalices that were used to minister the Blood of Christ. He pours water into the sacred vessel, revolves the water to collect the residues of the Blood, and drinks the ablution. The vessels are then wiped dry, and placed on the credence covered with a purificator.

Once the purification is completed, the celebrating priest folds the purificator, and places it over the chalice with the paten on top. Then, he carefully folds the corporal on the altar, collecting in its center any Eucharistic particles or remnants. The corporal is the sacred linen used for the Body of Christ. As the body of Jesus Christ was placed on the shroud, so the Eucharist is always placed on a corporal. And as

---

134. GIRM [120] 163.
134a. GIRM [238] 279 (bold face added).
135. CMRR, Chapter 5, no. 346 (bold face added).

the Body of Christ was wrapped in the shroud after His death, small particles of Hosts are collected and wrapped in the corporal after the Mass. Thus, the corporal must never be shaken.

Next, the priest sets the folded corporal on the top of the purified sacred vessels, and, if the purification is done at the altar, the priest places the sacred vessels on the side of the altar to his right. The **servers** then **remove the vessels** and take them to the credence table.[136] Therefore, after the purification of the sacred vessels, only the altar cloth and the candles, and sometimes a crucifix, are left on the altar. The altar is now as it was before the sacrifice of the Mass was offered. The celebrant goes to his seat for a time of silent thanksgiving to God.

In answer to a request from the U.S. Conference of Catholic Bishops, the Sacred Congregation for Divine Worship and the Discipline of the Sacraments issued a decree by which "*... for grave pastoral reasons, the faculty may be given by the diocesan Bishop to the priest celebrant to use the assistance... of extraordinary ministers in the [purification] of sacred vessels after the distribution of Communion... in the celebration of Mass. This faculty is conceded for a period of three years [from March 22, 2002] as a dispensation from the norm of the* Institutio Generalis, editio typica tertia *of the Roman Missal.*" [137]

DEFERRING THE PURIFICATION

When communion to the faithful is given under both kinds, the number of sacred vessels to be purified can be significant. Thus, purification might be deferred until after the Mass. For the benefit of those assisting the priest in his liturgical work, here are some practical norms regarding deferring the purification. ✞*"It is also permitted, especially if there are several vessels to be purified, to leave them suitably covered on a corporal, either at the altar or at the credence table, and to purify them **immediately** after Mass following the dismissal of the people."* [138] When the purifications are deferred until after Mass, "*...the celebrant (deacon, acolyte) returns immediately after Mass to carry out the purifications, assisted by servers. This practice seems preferable only if there are many vessels to purify. However, it presents some problems, for example, the celebrant or other minister may forget to cleanse the vessels after Mass or servers may take them to the sacristy before they have been purified. The **purifications should not be carried out in the sacristy**.*" [138a]

---

136. After Mass, the sacred vessels will be washed in the sacristy, and the sacred linens will there be purified. See Part Three, The Sacristy.

137. NCUBK, Decree, March 22, 2002 (Prot. 1382/01/L), (bold face added).

138. GIRM [120] 163 (bfa). See also, Part Three, Liturgy of the Eucharist, Sacristy.

138a. CMRR, Chapter 5, no. 349 (bold face added).

If the purification is deferred until after the Mass, the chalices must first be purified in the sanctuary; rinsing them with water, consuming the ablution, and wiping them dry. Then only, may the chalices be brought back into the sacristy to be rinsed at the sacrarium. *"The reverence due to the **Precious Blood** of the Lord demands that it be fully consumed after Communion is completed and **never be poured** into the ground or the sacrarium."* [139] It is a **sacrilege** to throw the remains of the Blood of Christ or even residues from the purification of the chalice into the sacrarium. *"...'one who throws away the consecrated species or takes them away or keeps them for a sacrilegious purpose, incurs... **excommunication**... .' Anyone... [who] for example [casts] the sacred species into the sacrarium or in an unworthy place or on the ground, incurs the penalties laid down... ."* [139a]

PRAYER AFTER COMMUNION:

After a silent time of thanksgiving, the priest rises, opens his arms inviting the **congregation to stand** together. ✣*"Then, standing at the chair or at the altar and facing the people the priest, with hands joined says,* Oremus (Let us pray*); then, with hands extended, he recites the prayer after Communion."* [140]

✣*"To bring to completion the prayer of the People of God, and also to conclude the entire Communion Rite, the priest says [or sings] the Prayer after Communion, in which he prays for the fruits of the mystery just celebrated. ... The people make the prayer their own by the acclamation,* **Amen**.*"* [141]

The prayer after communion is usually brief, but filled with exhortation and expectations towards the living gift we have just received.

✣OM *"Lord,*
   you give us Christ, the King of all creation,
   as food for everlasting life.
   Help us to live by his gospel
   and bring us to the joy of his kingdom,
   where he lives and reigns for ever and ever." [141a]

All together we consent to this prayer by responding *"**Amen**!"*

---

139. NCUBK, PART II, 55, Purification of Sacred Vessels (bold face added).
139a. *Redemptionis Sacramentum*, no. 107 (bfa), cf. *CIC*, can. 1367; Pontifical Council for the Interpretation of Legislative Texts, Response to dubium, 3 July 1999: AAS 91 (1999) p. 918.
140. GIRM [122] 165.
141. GIRM [56k] 89 (bold face added).
141a. The *Roman Missal*, the Order of Mass, Solemnity of Christ the King, Prayer after Communion.

CONCLUDING RITE

✢ *"The concluding rites consist of*
  *a. Brief **announcements**, if they are necessary;*

  *b. The priest's **greeting and blessing**, which on certain days and occasions is enriched and expressed in the prayer over the People or another more solemn formula;*

  *c. The **dismissal of the people** by the deacon or the priest, so that each may go out to do good works, praising and blessing God;*

  *d. The **kissing of the altar** by the priest and the deacon, followed by a profound bow to the altar by the priest, the deacon, and the other ministers."* [142]

At this time, the pastor or the deacon stands at the ambo and makes brief announcements of community interest. These may concern the Mass schedule, parish finances, nomination of a deacon, recruiting of volunteers... anything that concerns the life of the parish or of the Church. These announcements may also be made by a layperson representing a parochial committee or organization such as a member of the parish council, or a member of a parochial charitable organization. *"If instruction or testimony [are given] by a layperson in a Church concerning the Christian life, it is preferable that this be done outside Mass. Nevertheless, for serious reasons it is permissible that [these] be given after the Priest has proclaimed the Prayer after Communion."* [142a] Announcements are a good opportunity to invite parishioners to volunteer to take part in the actions of the Body of Christ in their own parish. *(Jas 2:26)"For just as the body without the spirit is dead, so faith without works is also dead."*

The announcements may include an invitation to come to socialize in the community hall after Mass while sharing coffee and doughnuts, which usually draws a good crowd. It is a great opportunity to get to know each other better, and also for people to learn more about the parochial activities and how they can get involved. Furthermore, inviting people to the community hall to socialize reinforces the fact that the church is not the place for socializing. Thus, it is a good time to remind people to leave the church silently out of respect for God who is present in the tabernacle, and for those who wish to stay for a while after the Mass to enjoy a quiet moment of prayer with God. After all, a church is the house of God, which is first a house of prayer. *(Jn 2:17)"Zeal for thy house will consume me."*

---

142. GIRM [57] 90 (bold face added).
142a. *Redemptionis Sacramentum*, no. 74.

GREETING AND BLESSING:

The verb 'to bless' means to call upon Heaven's protection unto people, and the word 'blessing' is defined as the invocation of God's favor. So let us receive this blessing with the attitude of one who is ready to receive Heaven's protection and God's favor.

Standing at his chair facing the congregation, the priest extends his hands to greet the people and to give them God's blessing.

⳨ᴼᴹ *"The Lord be with you.*
[The people answer:]
And also with you.
[The priest joins his hands and then places his left hand upon his breast, raises his right hand and blesses the people:]
May almighty God bless you,
[the priest then makes the sign of the cross over the people - who silently listen as the priest alone says:]
the Father, and the Son, ✠ *and the Holy Spirit.'*
[The people answer:] **Amen.**"

On certain feast days, solemnities, and special occasions - such as baptisms, marriages, or funerals - the priest usually recites a solemn blessing or a prayer over the people taken from the *Roman Missal*.[143] The priest, or the deacon if one is present, first says:

⳨ᴼᴹ *"Bow your heads and pray for God's blessing."*

Then the priest extends his hands and prays over the people using one of the twenty solemn blessings found in the Sacramentary as the occasion directs. All these blessings are composed in a four-part formula, and after each part the people answer, Amen. Here is an example:

⳨ᴼᴹ *"Through the resurrection of his Son*
God has redeemed you and made you his children.
May he bless you with joy. **R. Amen.**

The Redeemer has given you lasting freedom.
May you inherit his everlasting life. **R. Amen.**

By faith you rose with him in baptism.
May your lives be holy,
so that you will be united with him for ever. **R. Amen.**

May almighty God bless you,
the Father, and the Son,✠ *and the Holy Spirit.* **R. Amen.**"[144]

---

143. Cf. GIRM [124] 167. *The Roman Missal* offers the priest a choice of twenty solemn blessings and twenty-six prayers over the people.
144. *The Roman Missal*, Solemn Blessing no. 7, Easter Season.

DISMISSAL: (A, B, or C)

Immediately after the blessing, with hands joined, the deacon, or in his absence the priest himself, signifies the end of the Mass by dismissing the people using one of the following three forms:

✙ᴼᴹ "A. *Go in the peace of Christ.* [or]

   B. *The Mass is ended, go in peace.* [or]

   C. *Go in peace to love and serve the Lord.*

[And in unison the congregation answers:] ***Thanks be to God*****!***"

The word 'Mass' comes from the Latin word '*missa*' which means 'dismissal'. And the meaning of the words used for the dismissal are taken from the Latin '***Ite, Missa est***', 'Go, you have been sent'. Where are we being sent? We are being sent to proclaim Jesus by our actions and words.

The concluding response given by the faithful, 'Thanks be to God', in Latin '*Deo Gratias*', summarizes the nature of the Eucharistic celebration. Mass is a prayer of **Thanksgiving** to the Father. We thank Him for saving our lives by giving us the life of His Son Jesus Christ, a gift that God renews at every Mass through the Eucharist. We give thanks to God for the Mass, the priest, and the Eucharist.

♪ As the **recessional hymn** starts, the priest is standing behind the altar. ✙*"Then, as a rule, the priest **venerates the altar** with a kiss and, after making a profound bow with the lay ministers, departs with them."* [145] After venerating the altar, the priest walks to the front of the altar, turns his back to the standing congregation, and together with the ministers bows to the altar. Then, while the priest, deacon, and lay ministers leave the sanctuary in a procession, it is expected and appropriate that the **faithful let the procession pass** before leaving their pews. Besides, why hurry away when the choir director is concluding Mass with a joyful hymn that exhorts us to rejoice in being sent out to share our faith in Christ. ♪ Let us start sharing our joy by singing together the recessional hymn, and ringing the church bells for the whole parish to hear! ♪ 🔔

---

145. GIRM [125] 169 (bold face added).

LEAVING THE CHURCH

Just as the priest gives reverence to the altar before leaving the sanctuary, the faithful give reverence to Jesus present in the tabernacle by genuflecting when leaving their pews. Most of the time, the celebrating priest goes to position himself at the back of the church - or outside depending on the weather - to greet his parishioners personally. It is a good opportunity to introduce yourself to your pastor if you have not yet done so. Also, since your pastor usually invests a fair amount of time preparing his homily, he will surely appreciate your telling him that you enjoyed his homily. Let us tell our pastors that we appreciate their devotion towards our congregation. Pastors need and appreciate the support of the faithful.

At the end of the Mass, we give thanks to the Lord for the life, the joy, and the peace that we just received, and we leave the church carrying these precious treasures in our hearts and souls. If we are attentive, we will notice that people's eyes shine as they walk out of the church. It is the reflection of their souls refreshed by the divine graces that God gave them during the Mass, and especially by the life they received in the Eucharist. *(Jn 6:53)"...Unless you eat the flesh of the Son of Man and drink his blood, you have no life in you."* Whether we perceive it or not, Mass increases the level of sanctity of souls, including ours.

Let us try to keep a loving spirit as we go back home and into the world. The world surely needs it! Let us start by holding the church door open for one another, and being especially nice to each other, and thoughtful of others while driving home from church.

It is **precious** to be able at times to stay in church after the Mass, or to visit the Blessed Sacrament between Masses, to have a quiet time alone with the Lord when most people have left and the **church is completely silent**. Unfortunately, because of the lack of respect towards the house of God encountered in our society, some parishes can not leave the doors of their church unlocked between Masses. Thus the faithful who wish to stay with God after the Mass are often allowed only a few minutes before the sacristan locks the doors. Some parishes have solved this problem by allowing parishioners to let themselves out using an emergency door, a door that looks itself as it closes. Praise be to God!

AFTER THE MASS

THE SACRISTY: [146]

While everyone is leaving the church, the sacristan starts assuming his functions again. He puts out the candles[146a] at the altar and brings back to the sacristy the objects used during the Mass; he picks up from the credence table the sacred vessels and linens, the cruets, the wash plate(s), and the little bell. He also brings back to the sacristy the Mass books and the thurible. Although the sacristan's work consists of various responsibilities, at this time let us focus on the care he gives to sacred vessels and sacred linens right after the Mass.

If the extraordinary ministers purified their fingers in the **wash plate** after communion, then this **water** now contains remnants of Hosts and shall be poured into the sacrarium, along with the water left in the **cruet**, if the priest has blessed it. The **sacrarium** is a basin with a **drain** that goes **directly to the earth**, and the reason why these are installed in every sacristy is to make sure that none of the holy remnants from the Eucharist, nor the holy water, end up in a regular sink, which drains into the sewage. ✦*"The practice is to be kept of building a sacrarium in the sacristy, into which is poured the water from the purification of sacred vessels and linens."* [147]

What the sacristan needs to do now in the sacristy is to **'wash'** the sacred vessels and to **'purify'** the sacred linens. Since the **sacred vessels** were already 'purified' at the altar, or at the credence table (first step), the sacristan may now rinse them with regular water (second step) and, out of reverence for the residues of the Blessed Sacrament, **pours** this **rinse water** into the **sacrarium**. If needed, the sacristan may now 'wash' the sacred vessels with soap and water (third step) and dry them with a regular cloth before putting them back in their secure places in the sacristy.

If you recall, after communion the priest proceeded to the 'purification' of the sacred vessels: he used a sacred linen called the **purificator** to wipe into the chalice remnant particles of Hosts from the paten and ciborium. Then, after pouring some water from the cruet [148] into the chalice and on his fingers, the priest wiped his fingers with the **purificator** and drank the ablution. Finally, the priest wiped the chalice dry with the **purificator**. Thus, the purificator used by the priest now contains **remnants of the Body and the Blood of Christ**, and **all the purificators** used to give communion of the Blood to the faithful

---

146. See Part Five, Church Norms, III- Norms for the Sacristy.
146a. Use a snuffer to put out the candles; it is more dignified and prevents wax drips.
147. GIRM [-] 334, cf. GIRM [239] 280.
148. Usually the water and wine in the cruet are blessed at the altar before being used for the Holy Sacrifice. Thus, they became sacramentals and should be treated as such.

also now contain remnants of the Blood of Christ. Thus, these **purificators** now need to be 'purified' before they are 'washed.' Special attention must also be given to the **corporal**, a small sacred linen placed on the altar on which sit the Eucharistic species during the liturgy of the Eucharist. Its purpose is to collect particles of Host that might fall during the 'Fraction' or when transferring Hosts and drops of Blood that might drip during the priest's Communion or at the 'Purification'. Unless there are Blood stains on it, the corporal does not need to be 'purified' and 'washed' after every Mass; but it should always be **handled with great reverence**, and since it may contain particles of Host, it may **never be shaken.**

The **corporal** and the **purificators** used during Mass should always be **handled with great reverence**, they should not be **left sitting** for days in a hamper bag in the sacristy before they are attended to, **nor** should they be **washed** in the washing machine or by hand in a regular sink - both of which drain into the sewage - **until** they have been '**purified**.'

PURIFICATION OF THE SACRED LINENS
To proceed with the purification of the sacred linens in the sacristy:
- first **soak** the linens in cold water for one hour or overnight;
- then **pour this water** into the sacrarium;
- **rinse** the linens **and pour** the rinse water into the sacrarium;
- then **hang** the linens **to dry**.

By pouring this water into the sacrarium, we return to earth any remnants from the Eucharistic meal, and by hanging the linens to dry we allow the Eucharistic residual in this water to evaporate in the air. After they have been 'purified', the sacred linens may be '**washed**' with soap and water, and **dried**, and properly **ironed** and **folded** [148a] before they are put back in their proper place in the sacristy.

Since it is not easy to remove **lipstick** marks from purificators, women should be considerate in this matter when they intend to drink from the chalice. A stain removing agent or a little chlorine may be used during the 'wash' to eliminate persistent stains. Out of reverence for these sacred linens try using milder detergent or pure soap.

The **manuterge** (hand towel) used by the priest to wipe his fingers before the consecration does not usually contain remnants of the Body and Blood of Christ. Thus, it does not need to be 'purified' before it is 'washed'. The same applies to the **pall,** which is used to

---

148a. Folding and ironing the sacred linens: see Part Five, Questions and Answers, B) For Those attending to Sacred Vessels and Linens, Question 69.

cover the chalice after the consecration of the Blood. Since the pall usually does not come directly in contact with the Body or Blood of Christ, it may be put back in its place in the sacristy after the Mass.

*"Let Pastors take care that the **linens for the sacred table**, especially those which will receive the sacred species, are always kept clean and that they are **washed in the traditional way**. It is praiseworthy for this to be done by pouring the water from the first washing, done by hand, into the church's sacrarium or into the ground in a suitable place. After this a second washing can be done in the usual way."* [148b]

Following are other practical directives concerning the care of sacred linens: *"If the Precious **Blood has spilled** on the **altar cloth**, the appropriate part of the cloth should be **soaked** in water and the cloth **hung out to dry**. Later the whole cloth will be washed. The surface of the altar is treated as above with a damp towel, which is soaked and later washed. The **water** in which these cloths or towels have been soaked is **poured** into the **sacrarium**, or down the drain of the [holy water] font, or into the garden.*

*The respectful care of altar linen should be maintained in all churches. Before they are washed, **corporals and purifiers** should always be rinsed first and the water should be disposed of as described above, in the sacrarium. Then they are washed. For obvious practical reasons, purifiers should never be made of a nonabsorbent synthetic fabric. Unlike the corporal, they should not be starched."* [149]

In Quebec, I know of the **Sisters of Saint Joan of Arc** whose vocation includes the care of church linens. In many dioceses of the United States, I know that members of the **Altar Society** volunteer to take care of the sacred linens at home. For those who do not have a sacrarium in the sacristy of their church, or attend to **care of the linens at home**, you should either **water your plants** with the rinse water used to soak and rinse the sacred linens, or **pour it** directly **on the earth** in an appropriate area outside of your house, but never pour it down the regular sink which drains into the sewage.

While doing research for this book, I have come to realize that the purpose and the manner used to purify the sacred linens are **widely misunderstood** among the sacristans and lay ministers whom attend to the care of the sacred linens. Many seem to think that taking care of the sacred linens means to get them as clean and white as possible, well folded and ironed. Many seem unaware of the purpose for the purification of the sacred linens, which is to make sure that **no**

148b. *Redemptionis Sacramentum*, no. 120 (bold face added).
149. CMRR, Appendix 6, nos. 854-855 (bold face added).

remnants of the Body and Blood of Christ are profaned by being mistreated or left behind either on the altar, or in the sacred vessels and linens.

Some even told me that these remnants are too insignificant for God to be there present!? It is as though, because Mass is over, some people think that God's presence in the eucharistic species suddenly vanishes from these sacred linens and vessels. When I discussed this matter with some of the people involved, I was told that one should not go off the deep end about these linens. Please! We **venerate relics** because they have **touched the body of saints.** How much more reverence should we show for the **sacred linens** that **touch the Body and Blood of Christ**, Mass after Mass? The sacred linens are like little shrouds of Christ.

But it seems that all to often, after the Mass, the sacred linens are put into a **laundry bag** in the sacristy closet **where they end up sitting for weeks at a time**. When I realized this, I thought no wonder some people do not believe in the real presence of Christ in the Eucharist any more. How logical is it to go through all the reverences of consecration, communion and purification, if we are to throw the sacred linens into a laundry bag after the Mass, and let them sit there for days before throwing them in the washing machine like ordinary laundry? If we cannot purify the sacred linens with the reverence they deserve, then we might as well use paper towels for corporals and purificators and burn them reverently right after the Mass. But since the use of paper towels is not appropriate, and even forbidden, then the rites of purification of the sacred linens must be performed in a timely and proper fashion.

If the number of people available to purify and wash the sacred linens is limited, then we might consider limiting the number of purificators, by limiting the number of Masses at which communion is given under both species to the faithful, which multiplies the purificators and the risk of profanation of the Body and Blood of Christ.

CONCLUSION OF THE LITURGY OF THE MASS

With this book, I do not presume to say everything there is to say about the Holy Mass and the sacrifice of Jesus Christ. But I do hope that it brings a better appreciation of the Mass, of its liturgy, and its rituals, that it increases our reverence for the Blessed Sacrament and our desire to worship God. No one could ever say everything that there is to be said about the Mass and the mystery of the Eucharist. However, Mass after Mass, the rich tradition of the Church and the Holy Spirit reveal to us more about the mystery of Christ's Holy Sacrifice.

Great blessings are granted to us when we invest ourselves in the celebration of the Mass. The Mass then becomes a more sacred and alive experience, which allows us to better understand that receiving Jesus in the Eucharist sanctifies our soul, and that, receiving Him daily sanctifies us a little more every day. The liturgy of the Mass is so rich and the Word of God is so alive, that at each Mass, one can discover something new about God and the mystery of the Eucharist by which Christ gives us His Body and His Blood. *(Jn 15:5)"I am the vine, you are the branches. Those who abide in me and I in them bear much fruit, because apart from me you can do nothing."*

Let us give thanks to the priests who consecrate their lives to celebrate the Eucharist for us. Because of them we are allowed to commune with the Body and the Blood of Christ; without them, there is no Eucharist. What a precious gift they are! Let us not take them for granted.

The word Eucharist means Thanksgiving, and Mass is a prayer of Thanksgiving. But also, it is *"a dogma of the Catholic Faith that the Mass... is a true sacrifice and a representation in an unbloody manner of the sacrifice of Christ."* [150] *"As sacrifice, the Eucharist is also offered in reparation for the sins of the living and the dead and to obtain spiritual or temporal benefits from God."* [151]

Our soul is the most precious thing we have. Our bodies are mortal and whatever we have on this earth is temporary. Yet, our soul is immortal; it is the only thing that we will have for eternity. Thus, we should focus on giving our soul the best care possible, and receive the sacraments often, especially Confession and the Eucharist. We can make arrangements for having Masses offered for our soul while we are alive and for after we die; we can also have Masses offered for the souls of beloved ones, departed or alive. Nothing is as powerful as the Precious Blood of Christ, which can deliver souls on earth from the worst situations as well as It can deliver souls from purgatory.[152]

---

150. CE, Sacrifice of the Mass.
151. CCC 1414.
152. Purgatory: see Part Five, Catholic Glossary.

To offer a Mass for someone, you need to contact or visit a parish rectory, or a religious community of priests. There, they have a book in which each Mass is scheduled with the name of a specific person for whom the Mass will be offered. The usual offering (stipend) for a Mass that is 'read' is about ten to fifteen dollars, and for a Mass that is 'sung' is about fifteen to twenty dollars. You may schedule a Mass where you will be present so that you may join in the prayer. Let us make it clear that we do not 'buy' a Mass, but rather we make a money offering to the priest as a compensation for his earthly needs.

When I talk to people about offering a Mass, many say, "I offer my Mass for my beloved ones from my seat. What difference does it make that the priest reads their names from the Mass register?" Well, it is not the same thing. Of course, God hears the prayer of our heart, but when the priest offers the Mass for the intention of a specific soul, then the intercession is done through the power of the sacrament of Holy Orders. Thus, when the priest presents the offering at the altar it is as though Christ Himself is offering the Mass for that intention. Think of how during the Mass God changes the bread and wine offered by the priest into the Body and Blood of Christ. Well, God also receives in a more special manner the intention of the Mass for a specific soul when presented to Him by the priest.

The '**Gregorian Mass**' is a powerful form of Mass offering. It is a series of thirty Masses offered on thirty consecutive days for the intention of a specific soul. The usual offering for a Gregorian Mass is about one hundred and seventy-five dollars. However, most parishes are not able to provide this series of Masses, because of the limited number of priests and of daily Masses. Thus, to arrange for a Gregorian Mass, you should contact or go to the house of a religious community of priests, especially missionary priests. The Gregorian Mass is believed to be very effective in shortening the time needed in purgatory for the reparation of sins of departed souls so that they may reach heaven as soon as possible and rest in peace in the Lord.

We can make arrangements for a Gregorian Mass to be offered for our soul right after we pass away. In their wills and trusts, many provide for Masses to be offered for themselves and others after they pass away. Sometimes provisions are made for Masses to be said over an extended period of years. You may have Masses said, single Masses or Gregorian Masses, for anyone you wish, a Catholic or a non-Catholic. Since everyone has a soul, all can benefit from having a Mass offered for them. It is the most precious gift we can give.

As we approach the house of the Lord to attend Mass, let us remember that we are a chosen race, a royal priesthood, who have been invited to gather at the table of the Lord, the King of Kings, where the finest of food is served to us. Indeed, the Lord feeds us with His Word, His love, and His Body and Blood. Christ instituted the Eucharist *"in order to perpetuate the sacrifice of the Cross throughout the centuries until He should come again, and so to entrust to His beloved spouse, the Church, a memorial of His death and resurrection: a sacrament of love, a sign of unity, a bond of charity, a paschal banquet in which the Christ is eaten, the mind is filled with grace, and a pledge of future glory is given to us."* [152a]

Since we, the Church, are the bride of Christ, then as a bride who is filled with love and expectation towards her bridegroom makes herself as beautiful as possible before meeting him at the altar, let us make ourselves as beautiful as we can, body and soul, to meet Christ, our bridegroom at the altar. Let us not only dress our body with our Sunday clothes, but also, let us make sure that our soul is spotless and ready to receive our Lord. Then, as the bride who gives herself to her bridegroom without holding back, let us give ourselves to Christ during the celebration of His Holy Sacrifice, and also during our day-to-day life. Let us have confidence in our Lord that He takes us for better and for worst. Let us marry our soul to His so that we may be transformed to become more and more holy, that we may become more like Christ.

As we approach the house and the table of our Lord, let us always remember that Christ gave His life for us. Let us also remember that the reason why Christ made this priceless and holy Sacrifice was to free us from the bondage of satan, and to make it possible for us to go home to the Father in heaven. *(1Pt 1:18-19)"...you were ransomed from the futile ways inherited from your ancestors, not with perishable things like silver or gold, but with the precious blood of Christ, like that of a lamb without defect or blemish."*

152a. *SC* 47, cf. St. Augustine, *Tractatus in Ioannem*, VI, n. 13; quoting *Roman Breviary*, feast of Corpus Christi, Second Vespers, antiphon to the Magnificat.

"THE INFINITE VALUE OF THE HOLY MASS

The Holy Mass is the highest form of worship. It is the sacrifice of Calvary renewed. One Mass gives God more praise and thanksgiving, makes more atonement for sin, and pleads more eloquently than does the combined and eternal worship of all the souls in heaven, on earth and in Purgatory. In the Holy Mass, it is Jesus Christ, God, as well as Man, who is our Intercessor, our Priest, and our Victim. Being God - as well as Man - His prayers, merits, and His offerings are infinite in value.

WHY SHOULD WE HEAR HOLY MASS?

The Mass is the best means we have:

1- To render God the highest form of worship.
2- To thank Him for all His blessings.
3- To make reparation for all our sins.
4- To obtain all the blessings we desire.
5- To release souls from Purgatory and to shorten our own time there.
6- To preserve us from all dangers to soul and body.
7- To be consoled at the hour of death, for at that moment their memory will be our greatest consolation.
8- To intercede for us at the Judgment Seat of God.
9- To bring down God's blessings; therefore, try to assist at Mass every day, or as often as possible, and twice on Sundays.
10-To better understand the sublimity of the Passion of Christ, and, therefore to increase our love for Him.

OFFERING TO THE ETERNAL FATHER

Eternal Father, we offer Thee the Blood, the passion, and death of Jesus Christ, the sorrows of Mary most holy, and of Saint Joseph, in satisfaction for our sins, in aid of the holy souls of Purgatory, for the needs of holy Mother Church, and for the conversion of sinners."

Nihil Obstat, Rev. Robert M. Kelly, S.J., Censor Deputatus
Imprimatur George Cardinal Mundelein

EUCHARISTIC ADORATION

Since Jesus is truly and really present in the Holy Eucharist, the Church encourages us to come to the church, outside of the Mass, to visit with the Lord. We may come individually to spend some quiet time before the tabernacle to worship Him, and we may gather for adoration before the Blessed Sacrament exposed in the monstrance on the altar. *"'The worship of the Eucharist outside the Sacrifice of the Mass is a tribute of inestimable value in the life of the Church.' ...The faithful 'should not omit making visits during the day to the Most Holy Sacrament [in the tabernacle or exposed], as a proof of gratitude, a pledge of love, and a debt of the adoration due to Christ the Lord who is present in it.'..."* [153]

On the first Friday of every month, public eucharistic adoration is held in many parishes, sanctuaries and chapels. Religious communities, who have frequent periods of exposition of the Blessed Sacrament, often welcome those who wish to join them for adoration. Some religious communities are dedicated to perpetual adoration, thus they have permanent exposition of the Blessed Sacrament, with attendance day and night. Oh, how precious and holy is the time that we spend with Jesus Christ, the Lamb of God, present in the Blessed Sacrament!

"Exposition of the Most Holy Eucharist must always be carried out in accordance with the prescriptions of the liturgical books. ... [,and]... the Most Holy Sacrament, when exposed, must **never be left unattended** *even for the briefest space of time... ."* [153a bfa] The three main parts of Eucharistic adoration are: **Exposition with Adoration, Benediction, and Reposition.** Exposition should always include readings of the Word of God, songs, prayers and silent periods for adoration. The ordinary minister of the exposition is a bishop, priest, or deacon. An acolyte or a special minister, who has a devotion to Eucharistic adoration, may be appointed to expose and repose the Blessed Sacrament, but they may not give Benediction.[153b]

---

153. *Redemptionis Sacramentum*, nos. 134, 135, quoting *Ecclesia de Eucharistia, n. 25: AAS 95 (2003) pp. 449-450; Mysterium fidei: AAS 57 (1965) p.771.*
153a. *Redemptionis Sacramentum*, 137, 138, cf. *RR, Holy Communion and Worship of the Eucharist Outside Mass, 82-100; Missale Romanum, GIRM 317; CIC, can. 941 § 2.*
153b. Cf. *Eucharistiae Sacramentum*, nos. 82-100; *Inaestimabile Donum*, nos. 20-27; Canon 941 §2; CIC, Canon 943.

Whenever the Blessed Sacrament is exposed, the following principles should also be observed:

a) **Silence** is always maintained except for singing and responding to prayers that are part of the ceremony;

b) One should **never sit or stand with his back turned** to the exposed Blessed Sacrament, and;

c) The **genuflection** is made whenever passing in front of the monstrance, or on entering and leaving the church.[154]

Let us look at the Eucharistic devotion known as the 'Holy Hour', a ceremony inspired by Christ's words: *(Mt 26:40)"So you could not keep watch with me for one hour?"*[NAB], during which the Blessed Sacrament is exposed for adoration for a period of one hour. The faithful gather a few minutes before the appointed time for the Holy Hour. An altar server or an acolyte prepares the sanctuary. He places a **corporal** on the altar, lights four to six **candles** near the altar, and brings the **thurible** into the sanctuary ready to be used. Then, as the ceremony begins, all stand as the priest, or deacon, wearing a **cope** over his alb and stole, walks into the sanctuary holding the **monstrance**.

The priest places the monstrance on the corporal at the center of the altar, goes to the tabernacle, opens it, and genuflects.[155] All then kneel while singing a eucharistic hymn such as *'O Saving Victim'*.[156] The priest takes out the pix, which contains the large consecrated Host kept in a lunette.[156a] He reverently brings the pix to the altar, places it on the corporal, opens the little glass window at the center of the monstrance, and **exposes the Blessed Sacrament** by placing therein the Host contained in the lunette. Then, he reverently and precisely places the monstrance at the center of the corporal, as on a throne, facing the people. He genuflects, and goes to kneel before the Blessed Sacrament in front of the altar.

Once the Blessed Sacrament is in **Exposition**, it is **time for Adoration**. Assisted by the thurifer, the priest incenses the Blessed Sacrament while all bow and silently adore **the Lord present** in the Host. During exposition, the faithful participate in prayers and songs. The 'Divine Praises'[156] are often recited. They also listen to scripture readings and a homily that directs their attention to the worship of Christ the Lord. Eucharistic adoration always includes generous periods of **silent prayer**. If 'Vespers' are celebrated during the 'Holy Hour', its texts and hymns are then incorporated.[157]

---

154. Cf. CMRR, chapter 11, no. 683.

155. If the tabernacle is at a distance from the altar, the priest wears the humeral veil to carry the Host to the altar. Humeral Veil: Part Five, Church Norms, Sacred Vestments.

156. See footnote 156 on next page.

156a. Lunette and Pix: see Part Five, Catholic Glossary.

157. Cf. *Eucharistiae Sacramentum,* nos. 95,96. Vespers: see Part Five, Catholic Glossary, Liturgy of the Hours.

Towards the end of exposition, the priest **incenses the Blessed Sacrament** for a second time while all kneel and sing a hymn, usually *'Tantum Ergo'*. If 'Vespers' are celebrated during the 'Holy Hour', a song of the Magnificat such as *'Mary's Song,'* [156] is then also sung. After the incensing, the celebrant rises and sings or says the following:

Priest: *You have given them bread from heaven.*

   All: *Containing in itself all delight.*

Priest: *Let us pray,...*

Priest: *Lord Jesus Christ / you gave us the Eucharist*
     as the memorial of your suffering and death.
     May our worship of this sacrament of your body and blood
     help us to experience the salvation you won for us
     and the peace of the kingdom
     where you live with the Father and the Holy Spirit,
     one God, for ever and ever.

   All: *Amen.*

The priest may then sing or say alone another Eucharistic prayer.

Then the time comes for **Benediction**. After the prayers, the priest puts on the **humeral veil**, goes to the altar, genuflects before the Blessed Sacrament, enfolds his hands in the veil, and picks up the monstrance with both hands. Without a word, the priest elevates the Blessed Sacrament while facing the faithful, thus inviting them to a deeper adoration. He slowly makes the sign of the cross several times over the people with the monstrance. This action, known as 'Eucharistic Blessing' or 'Benediction of the Blessed Sacrament', concludes the time of adoration.[158] After the blessing, the priest places the monstrance back on the altar, genuflects, removes the Host from the monstrance, and places the Host in the pix.[158a] He reverently walks to the tabernacle, places the Blessed Sacrament therein, and genuflects before closing and locking the door. During this action, known as **Reposition**, the eucharistic hymn *'Holy God'* [156] is usually sung.

The Blessed Sacrament may also be exposed for only a **'brief period'**, for example after the Mass, in a ceremony known as '**Eucharistic Benediction**'. This ceremony, which only lasts about twenty minutes, includes the Exposition with Adoration, Benediction, and Reposition of the Blessed Sacrament. The incensing is done in the same manner as during the 'Holy Hour', and the hymns and prayers used, and their sequence, are the same as those of the 'Holy Hour.' However, the readings are omitted and the periods of silence are shorter.

---

156. 'O Saving Victim', 'Tantum Ergo', 'Mary's Song', 'Divine Praises', 'Holy God': see Part Five, Appendix 'F', Essential Catholic Prayers, Hymns and Prayer for Holy Hour.
158. Just as liturgical ceremonies are concluded by a blessing, Eucharistic Adoration is concluded with the Eucharistic Blessing. Thus, it is the last action before Reposition, cf. *Eucharistiae Sacramentum,* nos. 99, 100.
158a. The priest may also leave the pix at the tabernacle and carry the Host in the lunette in his hands wrapped in the humeral veil, holding the Host close to his heart.

Periodically, monthly or yearly, the Blessed Sacrament may be exposed for '**lengthy periods of adoration**', which traditionally was for forty-hours in memory of the hours between the death and the resurrection of Christ our Lord. Today's lengthy periods of adoration are usually of twenty-four hours, and the faithful must be scheduled to be **present at all times.** There must **always** be someone present, at every moment, while the Blessed Sacrament is exposed. The faithful usually sign up for a whole hour or two at a time. *(Mt 26:40)"So you could not keep watch with me for one hour?"* NAB Unless vocal prayers or hymns are directed by a minister, sacred silence is observed by all who visit the Blessed Sacrament during 'lengthy periods of adoration.'

Eucharistic procession is another form of Eucharistic adoration. It takes place after a Mass or after a 'lengthy period of adoration.' Adoration begins once the Host is exposed in the monstrance, and continues as the priest solemnly carries the monstrance outside of the church and through the streets of the parish, accompanied by the faithful singing hymns of adoration; thus, the faithful give public witness of their faith and devotion towards the Blessed Sacrament, and the world is exposed to the Eucharist. At the end of the procession, the benediction takes place outside of the church, for example, on the front steps. The procession must be well planned so that proper reverence is given to the Blessed Sacrament at all times.

When we expose ourselves to the Blessed Sacrament, Christ's divinity and love shines upon us, filling us with His peace, and healing us. Jesus desires and awaits our coming and spending time with Him. A friend of mine, Sylvie, once had an inspiring vision during Eucharistic adoration. She saw Jesus behind the monstrance with His divine heart located right on the Host. The Host is the divine heart of Jesus.

"The Church and the world have a great need for Eucharistic worship. Jesus awaits us in this sacrament of love. Let us not refuse the time to go to meet him in adoration, in contemplation full of faith, and open to making amends for the serious offenses and crimes of the world. Let our adoration never cease." Pope John Paul II.

"With a delicate and jealous attention the Church has regulated Eucharistic worship to its minutest details. She does not rely on anyone to take in hand the matter of honoring her divine Bridegroom; for everything is important, significant, and divine when there is a question of the Real Presence of Jesus Christ." St. Peter Julian Eymard.

NOTES: Prayers for private adoration: Part Five, Appendix 'F', Essential Catholic Prayers, Prayers for Communion and Private Eucharistic Adoration.
The Catholic faith in regards to the Eucharist: see *CCC*, The Sacrament of the Eucharist, nos. 1322-1419. *"The Catechism is an authentic and sure guide to the Catholic faith for Christians today and for generations to come."* Pope John Paul II.

Part Four

A Tribute

to the

Holy Mass

✠ OM *"When we eat this Bread and drink this Cup*
We Proclaim your Death Lord Jesus
Until You Come in Glory."

*In loving memory of Rev. Father Felix Migliazzo (1921- ordained 1949- 2005),
here celebrating Easter Mass 2004 at Ave Maria Chapel in Monterey, California,
assisted by his faithful altar servers Philippe (left) and Chino (right) Abatol.*

A Tribute to the Holy Mass

The Holy Mass is the celebration of nothing less than the most important event ever to take place on the face of the earth, Christ's passion, death, and resurrection. The Holy Mass makes present the sacrifice of the cross. Through His passion, Christ took our sins upon Himself; through His death, He destroyed our sins and our eternal death sentence; and through His resurrection, Christ gave us access to eternal life. In the same manner, during the sacrifice of the Mass, Christ takes upon Himself the sins that we offer Him; and, once the Holy Spirit changes the bread and wine into the Body and Blood of Christ, Christ, through His priest, offers Himself as victim to the Father so that our sins may be washed away anew in His Blood. Then, as we receive the Eucharist, Christ gives us life anew.

There is nothing more precious than the Blood of the Lamb of God, which bought freedom and eternal life for all souls. However, freedom and life cannot be forced on any one, not even by God. Indeed, since God gave us free will, He will not take it away from us. As for all heavenly blessings, God needs our consent to give us eternal life. When Jesus taught us how to pray the 'Our Father', He taught us how to give our will and consent to God; and when He instituted the Eucharist at the Last Supper, Jesus taught us how to receive His life.

The Holy Mass is the celebration of Christ's victory over death. By His Precious Blood, Christ took away from satan the power he had over us fallen souls. By His death, Christ destroyed death forever, and by His resurrection and ascension, He opened the 'gates of heaven' for us, and gave us access to the 'bridged way' that leads home to heaven where we will live for eternity. Only then will our salvation be complete.

Although we have been saved by Christ, because of our fallen nature staying on 'the path' that leads home to heaven is not easy. Our Father and creator knew that we would need constant reminders and continuous access to Him. Thus, God provided us with the Holy Spirit and the Holy Scriptures. *(Jn 14:26)"...[The] Holy Spirit, whom the Father will send in my name, will teach you everything, and remind you of all that I have said to you."* God has also installed reminders within our souls. *(Heb 10:16)"I will put my laws in their hearts, and I will write them on their minds."* The Father gave us prayer as a continuous means of communication with Him, and the sacraments as a continuous means of distribution of His graces. But the most precious gift of all is the sacrament of the Eucharist through which we can continuously receive His divine life. *(Jn 6:53)"Unless you eat the flesh of the Son of Man and drink His blood, you have no life in you."* Each time we receive communion, God builds up our inner temple and nourishes with divine life the Christ child dwelling within us. *(1Co 3:16)"Do you not know that you are God's temple and that God's Spirit dwells in you?"*

The liturgy of the Mass teaches us how to relate to God; how to enter into His court; how to speak to Him; and what gifts to offer Him. The liturgy of the Word teaches us Who God is and what He expects of us. The liturgy of the Eucharist teaches us the spirit of thanksgiving, which we should adopt not only during the Mass, but also in our daily lives. The liturgy teaches us to give thanks to the Lord for everything that we are and have. By changing the simple food of bread and wine into the Body and Blood of Christ, God teaches us that His ways are simple and awesome. He uses simple things to show us His mighty power.

The liturgy teaches us about God's love for us. As the Mass begins, we are invited to turn away from our sins and to turn repentantly to God for forgiveness. There we find God the Father faithfully and lovingly awaiting us with open arms and heart, as did the father of the prodigal son. Freed from our sins, we may then enter into God's grace, and truly be fed and sanctified by His Word and His Eucharist. When we spend time with God by attending Mass and receiving Him in communion regularly, even daily, we gradually begin to think like Him, while our love for Him increases constantly. Seeing this, God showers us with His love through His blessings and graces. Although **spiritually** present in His gathered people and in the proclamation of His Word, God has chosen the Eucharist to make Himself **substantially** present to us.

Prior to the Mass, some priests make themselves available to hear confessions to allow penitents to attain a 'state of grace', which is required for receiving Holy Communion. The one who, with a contrite heart, seeks God's forgiveness and reconciliation in the sacrament of confession will receive from God absolution for his sins. In the sacrament of reconciliation, it is Christ who speaks through the priest. It is He Who absolves the penitent with the words: I absolve you from your sins, in the name of the Father, and of the Son, and of the Holy Spirit. Go in peace. How comforting these words are to the soul! *(Jn 8:11)"Go, and do not sin again."* God's forgiveness is always given to the contrite heart. *(Ps 130:3-4)"If you, LORD, mark our sins, / Lord, who can stand? / But with you is forgiveness / and so you are revered."* [NAB] *(Ps 103:12.13) "As far as the east is from the west, / so far have our sins been removed from us. / As a father has compassion on his children, / so the LORD has compassion on the faithful."* [NAB]

Absolution of grave sins can only be sought in the sacrament of penance. But, if there is nothing heavy on your heart, and you are at peace with your Creator, then the 'penitential rite' will help you adopt the attitude of humility that is essential in order to attain a 'state of grace'. To be brought closer to God during the Mass, we first need to humble ourselves so that we may look up to God as a child does to his father. Then, we shall seek to realize how merciful, perfect, almighty and trustworthy the Father is and abandon ourselves into His love. To truly commune with God, we must acknowledge that we need Him, and that we are lost without Him. *(1Co 4:7)"What do you have that you did not receive?"*

The liturgy is designed to bring us to a 'state of grace' right from the beginning of the Mass. Then, as the liturgy develops, it takes us into a process that allows us to work on opening our heart, so that we may become more and more receptive to the spiritual gifts that God is offering us during the Mass. Through hymns, prayers and acclamations, the liturgy strives to bring the congregation together as one body, which, in fact, is what we are. We are the members of the Body of Christ, Christ's living Church. *(Ep 5:23)"Christ is the head of the church, the body of which he is the Savior." (Rom 12:5)"We, who are many, are one body in Christ, and individually we are members one of another." (1Co 10:17)"We who are many are one body, for we all partake of the one bread."* And when we are gathered as a Church, Christ is among us. *(Mt 18:20)"For where two or three are gathered in my name, I am there among them."*

The liturgy then develops into a dialogue between God and us. By the means of the scripture readings, God reminds us that He is almighty and that He loves us. As we answer Him with the psalm and the acclamations, we nurture our hope and our faith in His love for us. With the words of wisdom and love contained in the Holy Scriptures, God teaches us the golden rules to be kept safe from the traps of this world, and those to be kept in His grace and to receive His innumerable blessings. *(Jn 14:21)"They who have my commandments and keep them are those who love me; and those who love me will be loved by my Father, and I will love them and reveal myself to them."*

We cannot receive love or any other spiritual gifts if our heart is closed, no more than we can receive a material gift if our hands are closed. The door of our heart opens from the inside. *(Rev 3:20)"Listen! I am standing at the door, knocking; if you hear my voice and open the door, I will come in to you and eat with you, and you with me."* All of the prayers, scripture readings, homily, singing and offering rituals, all of these have an effect on opening our hearts and purifying our souls. They make us more available to receive God's love and blessings, which He offers us more especially by the means of the Eucharist.

Mass after Mass, we present our offerings to the Father, which the Father accepts because it is Jesus who presents our offerings to Him. Mass after Mass, by the power of the Holy Spirit, our offerings of bread and wine are changed into the Body and Blood of Jesus Christ, and our spiritual offerings are sanctified at the Father's altar. And Mass after Mass, as we receive Him in the Eucharist, God keeps on nourishing and sanctifying our souls with the Body and Blood of Christ.

What should we offer to God? Well, as it is written the offering that is pleasing to God is a loving and contrite heart. *(Mt 12:7)"I desire mercy, not sacrifice."* [NAB] Since the Precious Blood of Christ purifies everything that it touches, during the Holy Sacrifice of the Mass we should offer to God all that is wrong within us and in our lives. *(Mk 2:17)"Those who are well do not need a physician, but the sick do. I did not come to call the righteous but sinners."* [NAB] Since all pain is rooted in sin, we should especially offer to God our pains and weaknesses, and all the people we know who are suffering, and all those who are making others suffer. We should offer to God all the sinful situations of this world such as abortion and all other forms of evil. When we are in a state of grace, our prayers and spiritual sacrifices are especially efficient in uprooting sin and evil, and in obtaining graces.

Through our baptism, God makes us members of Christ's royal priesthood, thus, giving us the power that allows us and exhorts us to offer spiritual sacrifices that are acceptable to God; sacrifices of prayer and intercession, and the offering of our daily joys and crosses. However, since the Holy Mass is the most perfect prayer and sacrifice there is, our spiritual sacrifices are most efficient when offered in union with the Holy Mass. Only a pure soul can enter heaven, and to satisfy the need of atonement for our sins, no sacrifice sanctifies the soul and pleases God like the sacrifice of the Mass. Our spiritual sacrifices are magnified by the sacrifice of Jesus Christ, which the ordained priest offers to the Father in our name. ✝[OM] *"...Look with favor on your Church's offering / and see the Victim whose death has reconciled us to yourself. /... Lord, may this sacrifice, / which has made our peace with you, / advance the peace and salvation of all the world."*[1] Our baptism allows us and exhorts us to pray not only for our conversion and purification, but also for those of all souls, wherever they may be, on earth or in purgatory.

The sacrifice of the Mass cleanses us anew from sin. *(Heb 9:14)"The blood of Christ, who through the eternal spirit offered himself unblemished to God, cleanse our consciences from dead works to worship the living God."* [NAB] Cleansed from sin, we are then able to receive the life and the peace of Christ. We become free to do the will of the living God, to worship Him and to praise Him, and to thank Him for His love and for all the blessings that He bestows on us in our daily lives.

God uses His servants, the priests, to give us access to the greatest sacrament of all, the Eucharist. The degree of holiness of this sacrifice does not depend on the state of grace, the faith, nor the holiness of the priest and of the assembly of the faithful. Fortunately for us, when God manifests Himself He is always Whole and Perfect. However, our ability to commune with God does depend on our degree of holiness,

---

1. ✝ *The Order of Mass*, Eucharistic Prayer III, excerpt from the Memorial Prayer.

on our degree of purity. Unless we are in a state of grace, we are not in a state to receive God in the Eucharist.

Just before the communion, the priest elevates the Body and Blood of Christ and says: ✝"*This is the Lamb of God / who takes away the sins of the world... .* [And we answer:] *Lord, I am not worthy to receive you, / but only say the word and I shall be healed.*" [2] Our answer is one of a cleansed soul who, in all humility, acknowledges the weakness of its human nature. It is more likely that our human nature will cause us to fall and sin again, and that we will then need to be cleansed all over again by the Precious Blood of the holy sacrifice of Jesus. Each time that we receive this divine cleansing, the Father takes us deeper into the consciousness of the mystery of our redemption brought to us by His Son Jesus Christ.

Through the sacrament of Holy Orders, the Father uses His priests as instruments to give graces to His people by the means of the sacraments. [3] The sacraments that consecrate the important stages of our Christian lives are usually celebrated during the liturgy of the Mass. It is often during a Mass that, soon after our birth, we initially receive Christ's life in the sacrament of Baptism. Later in life, often when we are of grammar school age, we are initiated into the sacrament of Confession, where we seek and receive God's forgiveness for our sins; initiated into this sacrament we then prepare for the day when, during a Holy Mass, we will receive our first Holy Communion. As we become adolescents and chose to officially confirm our faith in Christ, it is usually during a solemn Mass celebrated by the Bishop that we receive the sacrament of Confirmation, which consists in seeking and receiving a special outpouring of the Holy Spirit.

Later on during our adult life, it is again in the midst of the liturgy of the Mass that we celebrate the sacrament of Marriage, during which a couple seeks and receives God's blessing for their union. For those who are called to a religious vocation, it is during a celebration of the Holy Mass that they are received into the sacrament of Holy Orders or consecrate themselves to a Religious life. For those who receive the sacraments of Baptism and Confirmation during adulthood, it is again during the liturgy of the Mass that these significant events in their lives are usually celebrated. When illness strikes, the sacrament of Anointing of the Sick, which may be celebrated during a Mass, is there to bring graces such as peace and strength, and at times even physical or spiritual healing. Then, at the end of our earthly life, the funeral Mass helps our soul to peacefully depart this world and reach heaven to be with God; for those who are there gathered, it also nourishes their hope and faith towards the resurrection and the life everlasting.

---

2. ✝ *The Order of Mass*, excerpt from the Communion Rite; cf. Jn 1:29; Lk 7:6-7.
3. The 7 sacraments: see CCC 1210-1666; Part Five, Questions & Answers, Question 32.

As for the Holy Scriptures, the liturgy of the Mass reflects a great understanding of the human mind, revealing that their author is God and Creator. The Creator knows that we need to subject our minds to His in order to become present to Him and to receive His grace. The way in which the liturgy of the Mass gradually prepares us to receive Holy Communion reveals that the Creator knows how to subject our minds. Right from the beginning of the Mass, the 'Introductory Rites' tend to create a unity among the faithful by having us stand, pray, and sing together as One; thus taking the focus away from our differences, and bringing us to identify ourselves as members of the Body of Christ. Next, the 'Penitential Rite' allows us to reconcile with God, to get closer to Him, and to open our hearts to Him; thus making us more receptive to what the Lord wants to tell us during the 'Liturgy of the Word.' Then, with its hymns, prayers, and rites the 'Liturgy of the Eucharist' aims to raise our consciousness of Christ's redemptive sacrifice, so that by the time we receive 'Communion' we are fervently receptive to the Presence of Christ in the Eucharist; thus, we may have great expectations towards Christ, and open widely the door of our hearts to welcome Him. And when Christ knows that He is welcome, He always has a way to surpass our expectations.

When we bestow the liturgy of the Mass with the value that it has, and really invest ourselves in the Mass, it raises our potential to reach a state of soul that allows us to experience God's presence, to personally encounter Him. God is always present to us, but we are not always present and receptive to Him. We may encounter God at any time during the Mass. It might be while listening to His Word during the scripture readings, or while singing praises to Him, but it is especially at the time of communion that God may allow us to encounter Him as we receive Him in the Eucharist.

The liturgy of the Mass works to transform the soul, and the outcome tends to be directly related to our participation. During the Mass, we are called to let go of our reasoning, to trust God, and entrust to Him the control of all the events in our lives.

Having a perpetual missal or a subscription to a monthly missal, such as the 'Living with Christ' or the 'Magnificat', [4] allows families, couples, and individuals to study and discuss the scripture readings that are read during the Mass. It gives us the opportunity to become more familiar with the beautiful and powerful texts of the prayers of the Mass, especially those of the liturgy of the Eucharist, that we would

---

4. Subscription to a monthly missal: see the last page of this book. One may also purchase from a Catholic bookstore a perpetual Weekly Missal and/or Sunday Missal that includes all the Masses of the Roman Catholic calendar with all the prayers and scripture readings as described in: Part Five, Church Norms, Requisites for celebrating the Mass, Cycles for Holy Scripture Readings.

not otherwise meditate on or read. As a matter of fact, even though we repeat some of these texts at every Mass, there is never enough time during the celebration to appreciate their content. Having a missal at home allows us to read and reflect on the scripture readings of the daily Mass. This is a good way to fulfill, in a few minutes, our soul's daily need for the Word of God and for praising Him, especially, if we have not had the chance to attend Mass.

The liturgy of the Mass is a religious practice that we have inherited from the early Church. After enduring the changes that this world has experienced throughout the centuries, the celebration of the Holy Mass is still at the center of the faith and of the religious practice of the Church of the twenty-first century. Thus, one may rightfully conclude that not only was the liturgy of the Mass constituted on solid basis, but that its authors were truly inspired by the Holy Spirit. Indeed, the liturgy of the Mass is solidly based on the Holy Scriptures, on the Institution of the Eucharist by Jesus Christ, and on His Sacrifice of the Cross. The Holy Mass makes present the Sacrifice of the Cross. Since the mysteries of the Eucharist and of the Sacrifice of the Cross are rooted in eternity, the Holy Mass does not need to fear the passage of time. According to Saint Paul, the Holy Sacrifice of the Mass will be celebrated until Christ comes again; *(1Co 11:26)"For as often as you eat this bread and drink the cup, you proclaim the Lord's death until he comes."* Saint Paul is only repeating here what Jesus Christ promised; *(Jn 14:3)"And when I go and prepare a place for you, I will come again and will take you to myself, that where I am you may be also."*

These days many people in our society look at the Holy Mass as a vestige from the past for which the participants are nostalgic for an old tradition. Unfortunately, this kind of thinking has influenced some of the people of Christ, and they have started to look at the Mass in a more secular way. Some secular people consider that we who attend Mass suffer from a lack of evolution. Others think that Mass is merely symbolism and that there is no reality to it. If only they understood about the life and the blessings that are freely being given by God through His Word and His Eucharist, they would all fight to get a front row seat at Mass to hear Christ's teaching, and they would want to be the first in line to receive His Body and Blood. *(Jn 4:10)"If you knew the gift of God."*

Today's children mainly depend on their parents and/or grandparents to learn about the Holy Mass and its rituals. Learning about the liturgy of the Mass can be a wonderful family experience from which everyone can benefit. Taking the time to study the liturgy of the Mass is in itself a tribute to the Holy Mass. When I was a child, once we were back home from church, my father used to ask us kids: 'Tell me one thing that you remember about Mass today.' Since I knew that my father was going to ask us about the Mass, and since I enjoyed these Sunday conversations, it was a great incentive for me to pay better attention to what occurred during the Mass. Furthermore, I loved the kind of attention that I would get from my parents for coming out with good answers. If you are not a kid anymore, become childlike again. *(Mt 18:3)"Unless you change and become like children, you will never enter the kingdom of heaven."* Each Mass is a unique experience that deserves to be shared, even if briefly, and having someone to share the experience with after the Mass is such a great blessing.

"The liturgy: the prayers, the readings, the ceremonies, the rites that form the liturgy, was born from the effort brought forth by the Church to offer a public cult to the Father by Jesus Christ, and that would be worthy of Him while sanctifying the souls. ... Sanctifying men: such is the second role of the liturgy. The grace giving sacraments, the sacramentals, the various prayers, and thanksgiving ceremonies, ... create, repair, and expand the supernatural being in us which is submitted to Christ. This new man is called a Christian. ...The liturgy educates men. It takes the soul of the Christian, kneads his intellect and his heart. By its colors, readings, and songs, the liturgy forms within the Christian complex sentiments, which, in the soul of the baptized, shall bring the soul of Jesus to bloom." [5]

---

5. Text translated and taken from the *Nouveau Missel Quotidien,* La liturgie, pp. 46-47 (see Part Five, Bibliography).

Part Five

Elements for Catechesis
on the
Holy Mass

Let Us Test Our Knowledge

ECCE · PANIS · ANGELORUM

IHS

AQUILA - PASCHA - JUDA

*(Heb 9:1-7)"**Even the first covenant had regulations for worship and** an earthly **sanctuary**. For a tent was constructed, the first one, in which were the lampstand, the table, and the bread of the Presence; this is called the Holy Place. Behind **the second** curtain was a tent called the **Holy of Holies**. In it stood the golden altar of incense and the ark of the covenant overlaid on all sides with gold, in which there were a golden urn holding the manna, and Aaron's rod that budded, and the tablets of the covenant; above it were the cherubim of glory overshadowing the mercy seat. ... preparations having been made, the priests go continually into the first tent to carry out their ritual duties; but **only the high priest goes into the second,** and he but once a year, and not without taking the blood that he offers for himself and for the sins committed unintentionally by the people."* bfa

The Judaic norms for the sanctuary - the tabernacle (the ark), altar, incense, sanctuary lamp, sacred vessels, liturgical vestments and colors; for the priests - ordination, conduct, and sanctity; for the sacrifices - offerings, showbreads, rituals, and sacrifice intentions; and for the liturgical traditions - worship, days of penance, and feast days - were given by God to Moses on Mount Sinai and are found in the Bible in the books of *Exodus* (chapters 25 to 40) and throughout the book of *Leviticus*.

CHURCH NORMS

To insure that the Holy Mass is celebrated in an environment worthy of its sacredness and in accordance with its institution, the Church has established norms regarding the following: the construction and arrangement of churches and their sanctuaries; furnishings and images and objects of veneration; the sacristy and the place for the reservation of the Blessed Sacrament; the place for the clergy, the faithful, and the choir and musical instruments; the sacred vessels and vestments; and the matter used for the sacraments.

The Gospel relates how Jesus Christ gave directions to the Apostles when the time came to chose a place where He would institute the Eucharist. *(Lk 22:12)"He will show you a large room upstairs, already furnished. Make preparations for us there."* Thus—✞*"The Church has always regarded this command as applying also to herself when she gives directions about the preparation of people's hearts and minds and of the places, rites, and texts for the celebration of the Most Holy Eucharist."* [1] For example, the Church has established that the Eucharist is to be celebrated in a church, and if there is no church available, the chosen place should be suitable for the sacredness of the Mass and the participation of the faithful.[2]

ARRANGEMENT AND FURNISHING OF CHURCHES

Church norms for the arrangement and the furnishing of churches require that churches be adorned with noble materials that promote the dignity of these sacred buildings, and with signs of heavenly realities that foster the instruction of the faithful and promote worship. Churches are usually blessed and dedicated to, and named after, God the Trinity, our Lord Jesus Christ, Mother Mary, archangels, or patron saints;[2a] for example: the church of Christ the King or of Our Lady of Grace.

PLAN & ARCHITECTURE

✞*"For the proper construction, restoration, and remodeling of sacred buildings... consult the diocesan commission on the sacred Liturgy and sacred Art."*[3] Most of the older Catholic churches were built in a classic architectural style with the floor plan in the shape of the Christian cross. Often, the sanctuary is located in the head of the cross, facing east, and the main entrance is located at the foot of the cross, facing west. In the arms of the cross, the transept, there are usually secondary (minor) altars placed against the walls.[4]

---

1. GIRM [I] 1.
2. Cf. GIRM [253] 288.
2a. Cf. GIRM [255] 290, [279] 292.
3. GIRM [256] 291, cf. SVEC, Constitution on the Sacred Liturgy, *Sacrosanctum Concilium*, no.126; Sacred Congregation of Rites, Instruction *Inter Oecumenici*, On the orderly carrying out of the Constitution on the Sacred Liturgy, 26 September 1964, no.91: AAS 56 (1964), p.898.
4. See 'Floor Plan of a Church' on page 183.

The sanctuary represents the head of Christ, the transept His arms, and the nave His Body. Traditionally, the structure of the churches in the shape of a Christian cross consisted of a fairly high lengthwise central nave, which reminds us of an upside down ship. A center aisle and side aisles separate the pews that cover most of the floor of the nave. Together, the center aisle and the open space in front of the pews, in the transept, form the shape of the cross on the floor of the church.[4a] In some churches, galleries are built over the side aisles to offer more seating for the faithful. These side galleries are usually connected to the organ and choir loft, which is usually located at the center rear of the church above the main entrance. The location of the organ loft allows the sound of the organ and the voices of the choir to carry naturally and evenly throughout the church.

One of the architectural highlights of churches are their bell towers that stretch up high above the roof with their crosses on top pointing towards the heavens. These bell towers, which in classical architecture often come in sets of two, shelter carillons whose sound varies depending on whether they are announcing a regular Mass, a funeral, a baptism, the Angelus, or a marriage. The most spectacular carillon sound is the one for Easter that joyfully announces the celebration of Christ's resurrection. Another architectural highlight of churches is undoubtedly their stained glass windows, whose beauty can really be appreciated only from the inside of the church, especially when rays of sunlight are plunging through them. Traditionally, they depict events of the lives of Jesus, Mary, and the saints.

CHANGES IN THE ARRANGEMENT AND FURNISHING OF CHURCHES

Following the Second Vatican Council, important changes were made in the liturgy of the Mass. Prior to the Second Council, the priest celebrated the Mass in Latin, facing an altar that was placed against the center wall of the sanctuary, and with his back to the faithful. Now, most priests celebrate the Mass in a popular language, at an altar placed in the middle of the sanctuary, and while facing the faithful. The manner of receiving communion has also changed. Prior to the Second Council, the faithful knelt at the communion-rail [5] and received communion on the tongue from the priest who stood in the sanctuary. Now, most of the time, the faithful stand and receive the Eucharist in the hand from the priest, or a minister, who stands out and in front of the sanctuary. Since the need for communion-rails seemed to have disappeared, these were removed from most churches.

4a. See 'Floor Plan of a Church' on page 183. The tradition of using the central aisle and transept to form the shape of a cross on the floor has been incorporated in the architecture of many modern churches.
5. Communion-rail: see 'Floor Plan of a Church' on page 183; Part Five, Catholic Glossary.

FLOOR PLAN OF A CHURCH IN THE SHAPE OF A LATIN CROSS

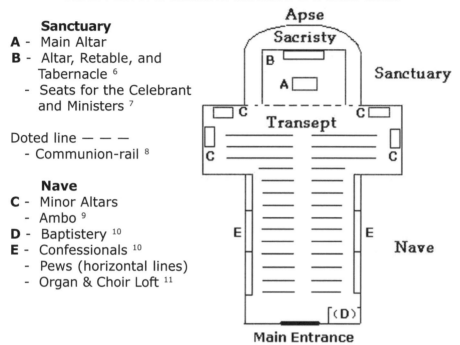

Sanctuary
A - Main Altar
B - Altar, Retable, and
 Tabernacle [6]
 - Seats for the Celebrant
 and Ministers [7]

Doted line — — —
 - Communion-rail [8]

Nave
C - Minor Altars
 - Ambo [9]
D - Baptistery [10]
E - Confessionals [10]
 - Pews (horizontal lines)
 - Organ & Choir Loft [11]

✠ *"The **sanctuary** is the place where the altar stands, where the word of God is proclaimed, and where the priest, the deacon, and the other ministers exercise their offices. It should suitably be marked off from the body of the church either by its being somewhat elevated or by a particular structure and ornamentation. It should, however, be large enough to allow the Eucharist to be celebrated properly and easily seen."* [12]

---

6. Altar, Retable, and Tabernacle as they were located in the churches prior to the Second Vatican Council: see picture on p. 186.
7. The location in the sanctuary for the seats of the celebrating priest & ministers varies with the church's architecture. The celebrant's chair ought to stand as a symbol of his function of presiding over the assembly and of directing prayer. "Any appearance of a throne is to be avoided." GIRM [271] 310, cf. Sacred Congregation of Rites, Instruction *Inter Oecumenici*, On the orderly carrying out of the Constitution on the Sacred Liturgy, 26 September 1964, no 92: AAS 56 (1964), p. 898.
8. Communion-rail: low railing installed at the front of the sanctuary for the communion of the faithful; also see Part Five, Catholic Glossary.
9. In the old churches, the ambo was mounted on a wall of the nave several feet above the floor, with a little roof overhead to help carry the priest's voice throughout the church. Today, in most churches, the ambo is located at floor level in the sanctuary.
10. Traditionally, the baptistery was located at the back of the church, and the confessionals on the sides of the nave. Now, their places vary with the church's design.
11. The organ & the choir often shared a loft located over the church's main entrance. Now, their location varies, but it may never be in the sanctuary. See Part Five, Quest.121
12. GIRM [258] 295, cf. Sacred Congregation of Rites, Instruction *Inter Oecumenici*, On the orderly carrying out of the Constitution on the Sacred Liturgy, 26 September 1964, no. 91: AAS 56 (1964), p. 898 (bold face added).

THE ALTAR

The following excerpts from the Roman Missal discuss the norms for the construction and the use of the altar, the table of the Lord. ✛*"The altar on which the Sacrifice of the Cross is made present under sacramental signs is also the table of the Lord to which the People of God is called together to participate in the Mass, as well as the center of the thanksgiving that is accomplished through the Eucharist. / The celebration of the Eucharist in a sacred place is to be carried out on an altar; but outside a sacred place, it may be carried out on a suitable table, always with the use of a cloth, a corporal, a cross, and candles. / An altar whether fixed or movable is dedicated according to the rite prescribed in the Roman Pontifical; but it is permissible for a movable altar simply to be blessed."* [13]

Since the center of the Mass is the Eucharistic Sacrifice, and the Eucharistic Sacrifice is offered on the altar, the altar, and not the celebrant's chair, should always be at the center of the liturgical celebration. The celebrant's chair should never be placed in front of the altar, nor should it be placed in a manner to become the center of the liturgical celebration to the detriment of the altar.

Here are some interesting **historical facts** concerning the altar:
- In the Bible, the Hebrew word for 'altar' comes from a word meaning 'to slaughter for sacrifice.'
- In the early Church, the Eucharist was celebrated on a table in homes. When churches were first built, altar tables were often made of wood and moved in by deacons for the liturgy and then moved out after the liturgy.
- The use of fixed altars diminished with the end of Temple Judaism and the decline of paganism. It then became possible for the early Church to use fixed stone altars without provoking controversy; their altars were usually marble and square in shape.
- The relics of the saints became associated with altars because the early Christians celebrated the Eucharist at the grave sites of the martyrs to honor them. *(Rev 6:9)"I saw under the altar the souls of those who had been slaughtered for the word of God and for the testimony they had given."* Later in the fourth century, churches and altars were built over martyrs tombs and out of this association came much later the tomb-shaped altar and the medieval practice of hollowing out a hole in the top of the altar for the placement of relics. During the papacy of Paul VI, relics were no longer required to be part of the altar, although it was still recommended that relics be enclosed in or under the altar. The new Code of Canon Law reiterates that the placing of relics in fixed altars is to be preserved (cf. CIC, can. 1237 § 2).

13. GIRM [259] 296, [260] 297, [265] 300.

- Since about the fifth century and until the time of the Second Vatican Council, in a church, the altar was built against the center wall of the sanctuary which often faced eastward. Above the altar was mounted a highly ornate retable[14] in which was incorporated the tabernacle for reservation of the Blessed Sacrament. Therefore, the priest celebrated Mass while facing the tabernacle.

THE ALTAR STONE

✠ *"In keeping with the Church's traditional practice and the altar's symbolism, the table of a fixed altar is to be of stone and indeed of natural stone. In the dioceses of the United States of America, however, wood which is worthy, solid, and well-crafted may be used, provided that the altar is structurally immobile. .../ The practice of placing relics of Saints, even those not Martyrs, under the altar to be dedicated is fittingly retained. Care should be taken, however, to ensure the authenticity of such relics."* [15] The altar stone is a symbol of Christ Who is the 'corner stone' and the 'rock' foundation of the Church of which we are the 'living stones'. It also recalls the stone altars used at the time of the Old Testament to offer sacrifices to God.

While doing research for this book, I was fascinated to find out that relics were incorporated in the mesa (top) of altars. With my pastor's permission I looked under the altar cloth to see the altar stone. There it was, a six-inch square altar stone with a little cross engraved at each corner and one in the center, inlaid in the top surface of the wooden altar. However, the relics inlaid in the altar stone were not visible. My pastor explained that during the Mass, at the time of the preparation of the gifts, the priest sets the corporal directly on the altar stone, and places the offerings of bread and wine on it. Therefore, **the sacrifice of the Mass is offered on the altar stone**. How holy!

The relics that are incorporated in altars are known as 'first class relics', which usually means that they are pieces of bones from the body of a saint or a martyr who gave his life for Christ. Relics are holy objects that radiate the holiness of the saints to whom these objects belong. Although they do not have the sanctifying power of the sacraments, as any other sacramentals, relics have the power to *"...prepare us to receive grace and dispose us to cooperate with it. ..."*[15a] The relics incorporated in altars radiate vibrations of saints and/or martyrs, whose holy vibrations participate in raising the level of holiness of the altar on which the sacrifice of the Mass is being offered. *(Mt 23:19)"For which is greater, the gift or the altar that makes the gift sacred?"*

---

14. Retable / reredos: see picture on next page and the 'Floor Plan of a Church' on page 183. See also Part Five, Catholic Glossary.
15. GIRM [263] 301, [266] 302.
15a. CCC 1670.

As illustrated on the 'Floor Plan of a Church' on page 183, the altar is located in the center of the sanctuary. In churches built prior to the Second Vatican Council, the retable is often fixed to the center wall of the sanctuary, reminding us of a time when the priest celebrated Mass with his back to the assembly while facing the Blessed Sacrament in the tabernacle. In some of these churches, the tabernacle is still located in the retable, but in many cases it has been relocated to a minor altar outside of the sanctuary, either in the transept, the nave, or in an adjoining chapel.

THE TABERNACLE
-The Eucharistic Reserve-

The tabernacle is the place in a church where Jesus Christ is substantially truly present.[16] The Church recommends that the Blessed Sacrament be kept in a tabernacle that is placed in a part of the church that is **beautifully** adorned, easily **visible** to the faithful, and appropriate for **silent prayer**[17] - such as in the retable of the sanctuary. The Blessed Sacrament is not to be kept on an altar on which Mass is celebrated. The tabernacle is to be made of inviolable material, solid

and none-transparent; and immovable and kept locked in order to protect the Blessed Sacrament from profanation as much as possible. A sanctuary lamp, fueled with oil or wax, is to be kept lit at all times near the tabernacle to indicate and honor the presence of Christ.[18] The purpose of the tabernacle is to reserve the Blessed Sacrament for Communion for the sick, and for Eucharistic worship outside of Mass.

On the left, a picture of the altar, retable and tabernacle of the San Carlos Borromeo Carmel Mission Basilica in Carmel, California. Blessed Junipero Serra (who is buried in the sanctuary) and his Franciscan friars built the original church in 1793.

16. At Fatima, the Angel of Portugal, appearing to the children, reminded to all that Jesus is truly present in all of the tabernacles of all the churches in the world.
17. Cf. GIRM [276] 314, [-] 315.
18. Cf. GIRM [277] 314, [-] 316.

Norms for 'The Place for the Reservation of the Most Holy Eucharist' are found in ✝Chapter V of the *General Instruction of the Roman Missal* titled 'The Arrangement and Furnishing of Churches for the Celebration of the Eucharist', [19] along with norms for the following:

The Altar and its Appointments;
The Ambo;
The Chair for the Priest Celebrant and Other Seats;
The Places for the Faithful;
The Place for the Choir and the Musical Instruments; and
Sacred Images.

Let us look at the norms for the Ambo and for the central element of decoration of the sanctuary, the Crucifix.

THE AMBO

As for other furnishings and sacred vessels, the ambo of a Church is usually blessed before its first use. ✝*"The dignity of the word of God requires that the church have a place that is suitable for the proclamation of the word and toward which the **attention** of the whole congregation of the faithful **naturally turns** during the Liturgy of the Word."* [19a] As for any assembly, a congregation of faithful is more receptive to a message when the speaker is visible and audible.

THE CRUCIFIX

The main decoration of the sanctuary of a Catholic church is a large crucifix placed high above for everyone to see, either mounted on the central wall of the sanctuary or hanging from the ceiling. The crucifix is placed in this manner so that it dominates the assembly. A crucifix may also be carried in the entrance procession and placed in its stand in the front of the sanctuary for all to see. A small crucifix is also placed on the altar for the priest to see while he offers the sacrifice of the Mass.

✝*"There is also to be a cross, with the figure of Christ crucified upon it, either on the altar or near it, where it is clearly visible to the assembled congregation. It is appropriate that such a cross, which calls to mind for the faithful the saving Passion of the Lord, remain near the altar even outside of liturgical celebrations."* [20] *"...In the context of the Roman liturgy, "cross" means a crucifix. A figure of the risen Christ behind an altar cannot be regarded as a substitute for the cross... The liturgical crucifix... is a sign in the midst of the eucharistic assembly proclaiming that the Mass is the same Sacrifice as Calvary."* [20a]

---

19. Cf. GIRM, Chapter Five, [253] 288 through [280] 318. Also see Part Two, e) Preparing the Sanctuary. Sanctuary: Part Five, Catholic Glossary.
19a. GIRM [272] 309, cf. Sacred Congregation of Rites, Instruction *Inter Oecumenici*, On the orderly carrying out of the Constitution on the Sacred Liturgy, 26 September 1964, no. 92: AAS 56 (1964), p. 899 (bold face added).
20. GIRM [270] 308.
20a. CMRR, Chapter 1, 64-65, see RR, *Book of Blessings, Blessing of a Cross*, no 1235.

REQUISITES FOR THE CELEBRATION OF THE MASS

The norms for 'The Requisites for the Celebration of Mass' found in ✦Chapter VI of the GIRM include the following: norms for 'SACRED VESSELS', norms for 'The Bread and Wine for Celebrating the Eucharist', here presented under THE MATTER OF THE SACRAMENTS (Eucharist and Sacred Oils); and norms for 'Sacred Vestments', here presented under SACRED VESTMENTS and LITURGICAL SEASONS AND RELATED COLORS.

SACRED VESSELS

✦"...the sacred vessels are held in special honor, especially the chalice and paten, in which the bread and wine are offered and consecrated, and from which they are consumed.

Sacred vessels are to be made from precious metal...

...sacred vessels may also be made from other solid materials that, according to the common estimation in each region, are precious, for example, ebony or other hard woods, provided that such materials are suited to sacred use and do not easily break or deteriorate... This applies to all vessels which hold the hosts...

As regards chalices and other vessels that are intended to serve as receptacles for the Blood of the Lord, they are to have bowls of nonabsorbent material. ..." [21]

From the 'Ceremonies of the Modern Roman Rite', here is a more detailed presentation of requirements for the sacred vessels that expresses both the practical and spiritual aspects of these requirements.

"91. **The chalice and paten** are blessed by a bishop or priest... (cf. CB, no. 986 and references). The chalice should be a truly beautiful vessel, a worthy offering of human art. In itself it is the most characteristic expression of the **majesty** of the Eucharistic Sacrifice. If possible, a church should possess various chalices for different occasions and a larger chalice for concelebrations.

92. The **traditional** form of **chalice** seems preferable; with a suitable **cup**, a convenient **node** and a very stable **base**. Not only is it always easier to use, but it is already a familiar eucharistic symbol in the minds of our people. Chalices which **resemble secular objects** may provoke a profane association of ideas. A chalice is a unique sacred cup reserved for the Eucharist.

---

21. GIRM [289] 327, [294] 328, [290-292] 329, [291] 330. Sacred Vessels: see also Part Three: Liturgy of the Eucharist, Offertory Rites, Procession of the Gifts; Communion Rite, After Communion, Purification of the Sacred Vessels; After the Mass, The Sacristy. See also Part Five, Catholic Glossary.

*93. A **glass or ceramic chalice** is easily **breakable** and is **thus excluded** as also are chalices with cups made of absorbent material or material which deteriorates easily [cf. GIRM [290, 291] 329]. Moreover, it may well be argued that a priest should never celebrate the Sacred Mysteries in vessels less worthy than those he would use at his own table. The contrived "poverty" of chalices made of wood or pottery seems to end up expressing only a **lack of esteem** for the Eucharist itself. ...But what has always distinguished the eucharistic vessels is that they are partly defined and identified as "sacred vessels" by being of significant material value. Secular vessels are never to be used for the Eucharist (Inaestimabile Donum, no. 16)." [22]*

THE MATTER OF THE SACRAMENTS

The Church has established norms concerning the choice and the preparation of the matter used for the Eucharist, as well as for the matter used for other sacraments. These norms were established for both spiritual and practical reasons. For example, since Jesus used unleavened bread and grape wine to institute the Sacrament of the Eucharist, thus, the Church has established that the bread used for the Eucharist should be unleavened and that the wine should be from grapes. Such norms reflect the Church's concern to be faithful to the actions of Christ, and also the concern to use only the best quality matter in rendering worship to God.

---

22. CMRR, Chapter 2, nos. 91, 92, 93 (bold face added).

A) THE MATTER OF THE EUCHARIST

"*144. **The bread** for the Eucharist in the Roman Rite is unleavened wheaten bread (CIC, Canons 924 §2, 926; G.I.R.M. [282] 320). It should be made from the **finest quality plain wheat flour mixed with pure water**. It should be carefully baked so as to be a palatable food that is neither too hard nor uncooked. [It must be recently baked, cf. G.I.R.M. [-] 320].*

*145. It is prudent always to use bread prepared professionally by those who observe Church law and custom rather than to allow others to bake bread according to "recipes"... [A]dding other kinds of flour, chemical colorings, oil, shortening, salt, sugar, honey, etc., renders the matter **invalid or at least doubtful**.*

*146.The traditional **round form** of the host is always required (cf. G.I.R.M. [283] 321 "forma tradita confectus"; Inaestimabile Donum, no.8), a simple evocative **symbol of unity and perfection**. The large bread may be of the traditional dimensions... (just over 7cm or 2-7/8 inches diameter in Rome). Such a host also fits the lunette of a monstrance. It customarily bears some sacred symbol [IHS] and is usually marked in such a way as to be divided at the fraction, with a section marked on the left side to form the particle to be placed in the chalice. ...*

147. [The large host may also] have a diameter of between 15 to 20 cm (about 6-8 in.)... It should not be of exaggerated proportions, which could cause ridicule and obvious inconvenience. ...

148. [The peoples' hosts] should be of substantial texture and of reasonable proportions (3.5 cm or 1-3/8 in diameter in Rome).

*149. The **bread** for the Eucharist should always be fresh. ...care should be taken to **renew** the particles [Hosts] in the tabernacle at least **every two weeks**, preferably more frequently. (A reasonable way of observing CIC, Canon 939.)...*

*150. The wine used for the Eucharistic Sacrifice must be **natural and pure grape wine** (cf. CIC, Canon 924§3; G.I.R.M. [284] 322). The color of the wine is a matter of personal choice. However red wine obviously seems to have a better sign value than white wine, favored in the Western Rites perhaps because of convenience in washing altar linen.*

151. Priests should use only wine authorized by the bishops in accord with the Church law and custom. ... The wine should be carefully stored in the sacristy in a secure and cool place. ...

B) The Matter of Sacred Oils

*153. The Sacred Oils are made of **pure olive oil** or another pure vegetable oil when this cannot be procured easily (cf. CIC, Canon 847§1... in an emergency, a priest may bless any vegetable oil, e.g., to anoint a dying person). In the making of Chrism, before or during the rite of consecration, some fragrant balsam or a fine perfume essence is added to the oil and carefully blended to produce a symbolic fragrance. The distinctive fragrance also helps to identify Chrism in the pastoral situation.*

*154. The priest in charge of the Oils should see that they are **renewed annually**, soon after the Chrism Mass.*[23] *The Oils from the previous year should be burned. Larger quantities may be consumed in one of the lamps. The validity of sacramental anointing is in no way affected if Oils from an earlier year are used, but this should only happen in case of necessity (cf. Canon 847§2). At the celebration of Christian Initiation at Easter, it is obviously of deeper significance to use the Chrism which has been recently consecrated by the bishop.*

*155. The principles of quality which apply to the matter of the sacraments should extend to the wax, incense, charcoal and any other material substances which are used in the celebration of the liturgy (...incense: CB. no.85 ... 'pure sweet scented incense...' ... 'frankincense' should be preferred... .). Only the **best fruits of creation** should be **set aside for God** in the worthy celebration of this sacrifice of praise and thanksgiving."* [24]

*"Since the Liturgy has great pastoral value, the liturgical books have provided for a certain degree of adaptation to the assembly and to individuals, with the possibility of openness to the traditions and culture of different peoples. The revision of the rites has sought a noble simplicity and signs that are easily understood, but the desired **simplicity must not degenerate into an impoverishment of the signs**. On the contrary, the signs, above all the sacramental signs, must be easily grasped but carry the greatest possible expressiveness. Bread and wine, water and oil; and also incense, ashes, fire and flowers, and indeed almost all the elements of creation have their place in the Liturgy as gifts to the Creator and as a contribution to the dignity and beauty of the celebration."* [24a]

---

23. Chrism Mass: see Part Five, Catholic Glossary, Chrism Mass.
24. CMRR, Chapter 2, Matter of the Sacraments, nos. 144-155 (bold face added). See also GIRM [281-286] 319-324; *Redemptionis Sacramentum* nn. 48-50.
24a. Pope John Paul II, *Vicesimus Quintus Annus,* Part III, no. 10, December 4, 1988, On the 25th Anniversary of the document on Liturgical Constitution, *Sacrosanctum Concilium*, December 4, 1963; cf. *Sacrosanctum Concilium,* nos. 34, 37-40.

SACRED VESTMENTS

The tradition of priests wearing sacred vestments to celebrate the Mass originates in the Judaic heritage. *(Lev 6:10)"The priest shall put on his linen garment." (Ex 39:41)"The finely worked vestments for ministering in the holy place, the sacred vestments for the priest Aaron."* The Mass brings us in contact with God, and liturgical vestments remind us that the Mass is not an ordinary action. ✝*"The vestment proper to the priest celebrant at Mass and other sacred actions directly connected with Mass is, unless otherwise indicated, the chasuble, worn over the alb and stole."*[25] The diversity of vestments allows us to recognize the function of each minister. For example, to be differentiated from the priest, the deacon wears his stole on the left shoulder, crossed and fastened at his right side.

Alb: Long white/cream pastoral robe, often made with a hood and worn with a *cincture*. The **priest** may wear the alb with only a stole to administrate certain sacraments, but to celebrate the Mass, the priest wears a chasuble on top of the alb and stole. *"The* alb *should be ample... Whether or not it is worn over a cassock [or habit], it should fall to the ankles and come to the wrists. A collar on the alb to replace the amice should conceal the everyday dress of the priest... ."* [26] The alb is also worn at Mass by **deacons, servers,** and **acolytes.**

Amice: Rectangular piece of white cloth worn around the neck, tucked into the collar and falling over the shoulders; worn by **celebrating priest** when the alb does not completely cover the ordinary clothing at the neck.

Cassock: A non-liturgical, full-length, close-fitting robe that used to be worn by all **diocesan** priests and seminarians as ordinary daily clothes, but worn today by only a few of them. Cassocks are black for priests and seminarians, purple for bishops and other prelates, red for cardinals, and white for the Pope.

Chasuble: Overall liturgical vestment worn by the **priest** to celebrate the Mass. This large mantle of traditional liturgical colors is often highly decorated with, for example, a full size cross on the back and on the front. Its color determines when it will be used according to the liturgical color of seasons and feasts. *"...the chasuble is seen to represent the* **charity** *of Christ which "covers all things" (cf. Col 3:14). In the context of celebrating the Eucharistic Sacrifice, this symbol of charity should surely take precedence over the symbol of authority."* [27]

---

25. GIRM [299] 337.
26. CMRR, Chapter 2, no. 122.
27. CMRR, Chapter 2, no. 126.

Cincture: A cord that serves as a belt for holding the alb and the priest's stole close to the body.

Cope: Mantle-like vestment open in front and fastened at the neck, worn over the alb and stole by the sacred minister for Eucharistic benediction and processions, and other ceremonies.

Dalmatic: Proper liturgical vestment for the **deacon** to wear at Mass in place of a chasuble. It is a loose tunic that reaches the ankles worn over all the other vestments; its sleeves are loose and its sides are open from the waist down. The dalmatic is also worn by the **bishop** when he is ordained and when he celebrates a solemn Mass.

Habit: Garb worn by members of religious orders as everyday wear.

Humeral Veil: Rectangular shawl worn over the cope by the sacred minister to cover his arms and his hands while holding and/ or carrying the Blessed Sacrament in the monstrance during a Eucharistic procession or Eucharistic Benediction.

Maniple: Handkerchief-like ornament that the celebrating priest used to wear on the forearm as a sign of being a servant of God.

Stole: Long scarf worn around the neck that hangs down in front to the knees, that the celebrating **priest** wears over the alb and under the chasuble. Usually, the stole and the chasuble are of a matching color chosen according to the liturgical season or feast. When the priest concelebrates Mass, or administers other sacraments, he wears a stole on top of the alb. **Deacons** wear the stole on the left shoulder and across to the right. *"...Because the stole is the symbol of the sacramental and teaching authority of those in Sacred Orders, it is worn only by bishops, priests and deacons... ."* [28]

The sacristan may lay out the liturgical vestments ahead of time on the vesting table in the sacristy so that it is easier for the priest to vest for the Mass. The vestments should be laid out in the reverse order to that followed by the priest in putting them on. Thus, the first vestment to be placed on the vesting table is the chasuble, the stole is laid on top of the chasuble, and the alb is laid on top of it all. The alb is the first vestment that the priest puts on. These three liturgical vestments worn by priests to celebrate the Mass are the minimum in required liturgical vestments. To celebrate the Mass, monks and friars wear these three liturgical vestments on top of their 'habit'.

---

28. CMRR, Chapter 2, no. 124.

Traditionally, the priest would follow a ritual of prayers before and after celebrating the Holy Mass. This prayer ritual included a thirty-minute meditation before the Mass and recitation of the 'vesting prayer' as he dressed with the liturgical vestments. In the 'vesting prayer,' the priest asks the Lord for the grace to be made worthy to celebrate the memorial of the sacrifice of Jesus Christ. Then, after the Mass, the priest would make a ten-minute thanksgiving. Today, this ritual for priests is usually limited to a brief recollection before Mass and a brief thanksgiving after the Mass. However, as they vest for Mass, some priests still say the traditional 'vesting prayer', which is posted in many sacristies.[29]

VESTING PRAYER

"While he **washes his hands**, let him say:
Give strength to my hands, Lord, to wipe away all stain, so that I may be able to serve you in purity of mind and body.

As he places the **amice** over his head, let him say:
Lord, set the helmet of salvation on my head to fend off all the assaults of the devil.

As he puts on the **alb:**
Purify me, Lord, and cleanse my heart so that, washed in the Blood of the Lamb, I may enjoy eternal bliss.

As he ties the **cincture**:
Lord, gird me about with the cincture of purity and extinguish my fleshly desires, that the virtue of continence and chastity may abide within me.

As he places the **maniple** over his left arm: *Lord, may I worthily bear the maniple of tears and sorrow so as to receive the reward of my labor with rejoicing.*

As he puts the **stole** around his neck:
Lord, restore the stole of immortality, which I lost through the collusion of our first parents, and, unworthy as I am to approach your sacred mysteries, may I yet gain eternal joy.

As he assumes the **chasuble:**
Lord, you said, "my yoke is easy and my burden is light". Grant that I may be able to wear this vestment so as to obtain your grace. Amen." [30]

(Lev 16:32)"The priest who is anointed and consecrated as priest... shall make atonement, wearing the linen vestments, the holy vestments."

---

29. Also see Part Two, Preparing Ourselves and the Temple, g) Vesting for the Mass.
30. CMRR, Appendix 10, no. 892 (bold face added). The maniple is not worn anymore.

LITURGICAL SEASONS AND FEASTS *

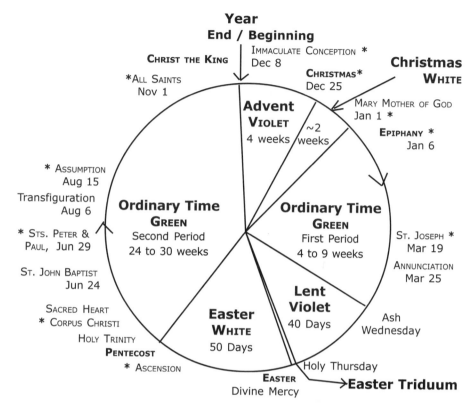

THE LITURGICAL YEAR begins on the first Sunday of Advent (closest Sunday to Nov. 30) and ends with the week following the Feast of Christ the King. The year is divided into five **SEASONS** plus the Triduum: Advent, Christmas, Ordinary Time (2 periods), Lent, Easter Triduum, and Easter. Each season has its own color for liturgical vestments.

EASTER is celebrated on the 1st Sunday after the 1st full moon following the spring equinox.[30a] The date for Easter determines most of the dates for the liturgical seasons and for many feasts.

The dates for the celebration of the following **SOLEMNITIES** change yearly: Easter, Ascension, Pentecost, Holy Trinity, Corpus Christi, Sacred Heart, and Christ the King. Solemnities are first in order of importance, followed by Feasts, and Memorials: obligatory and optional.

The asterisks * mark Holy Days of Obligation (def. Part Five, Catholic Glossary; cf. CCC 2177). Some of these feasts can be moved to a Sunday or abolished by a conference of bishops. Calendar for Solemnities, Feasts and Memorials: see the *Roman Missal*, a perpetual missalet, or *The Ordo* (liturgical calendar) published for your diocese.
30a. The spring equinox occurs between March 22 and April 25. Equinox: see Part Five, Catholic Glossary; Appendix 'A', Comparative Calendar of Catholic and Judaic Feasts.

Color: *symbol*	LITURGICAL SEASONS & RELATED COLORS
Green: *Hope & Vitality*	**Ordinary Time:** (33-34 weeks over two periods) - the 1st period starts on the Monday following the Sunday after *Epiphany*, and lasts until the Tuesday before *Ash Wednesday* (1st day of Lent). - the 2nd period starts Monday after *Pentecost* (end of Easter season) and ends with the week that follows the feast of *Christ the King* (last Sunday of liturgical year). The beginning and closing dates of these two periods vary each year according to the date of Easter.
Violet/Purple: *Prayer & Penance*	**Advent:** (4 weeks) starts on the Sunday after *Christ the King* and lasts until *Christmas Eve*. **Lent:** (40 days before Easter - March/April) from *Ash Wednesday* to before the eve of *Holy Thursday;* violet on *Holy Saturday*. Violet, white or black may be used at funeral Masses and for Masses for the Dead.
White: *Purity and Integrity of Life & Faith*	**Christmas Season:** lasts from *Christmas Eve* until the Sunday after *Epiphany* (~2 weeks). **Easter Season:** (50 days) from *Easter* Sunday to the Saturday before *Pentecost*. White is also used on *Solemnities* (including the eve of *Holy Thursday,* excluding the Lord's Passion), feasts of the Blessed Virgin Mary, the Holy Angels, and the Saints (except feast of the Martyrs).
Red: *Blood of Christ & Martyrs, and Holy Spirit Fire*	**Palm Sunday, Good Friday, Pentecost,** celebrations of the **Lord's Passion**, and feasts of the Apostles, Evangelists and **Martyr Saints**.
Rose: *Joy of Anticipation*	***3rd Sunday of Advent* & *4th Sunday of Lent*.** During these periods of penance rose expresses the joy in waiting for Christmas and then Easter.

THE LITURGICAL SEASONS determine the colors used for the liturgical vestments worn by the priest to celebrate the Mass (chasuble and stole), as well as the color chosen for sanctuary adornments (ornament for the tabernacle, the ambo, the altar, the burse, and chalice veil). Throughout the seasons the color of the liturgical vestments changes for solemnities, feast days and special occasions (baptism, funerals...).
LITURGICAL COLORS: cf. GIRM [308] 346.

The norms for Holy Scripture readings to be read during the Mass are found at ✟ Chapter VII, of the third edition of the GIRM, titled *'The Choice of the Mass and Its Parts', nos.* 356-362.[31]

CYCLES FOR HOLY SCRIPTURE READINGS

At Mass, the Holy Scripture readings are read from a book called the Lectionary, which is composed of two volumes:
- **Volume One** contains the readings for **Sundays** and **solemn feasts**, which are arranged in a three-year cycle: **Years A, B & C.**
- **Volume Two** contains the readings for weekdays, the feasts of the saints, and various occasions (no cycle). The **weekday** readings are arranged in a two-year cycle: **Years I & II**; the readings for the **feasts of the saints** and for the weekdays of Advent, Christmas, Lent, and Easter are arranged in a **one-year cycle**.

The first edition of the Lectionary was published in 1969 and the second edition in 1981. Since 2002, Volume Two is available in a three volume format: Year I, Year II, & Ritual Masses for Various Needs and Votive Masses. The selections of Holy Scripture readings contained in the volumes of the Lectionary include the first reading, the second reading - whenever there are two readings -, the responsorial psalm, the Gospel acclamation versicle, and the Gospel reading.

The cycles for Holy Scripture readings are structured according to the liturgical year calendar, as described in the two prior pages. These cycles of readings and their selection of readings are observed by the whole Catholic Church. This means that on any given day, millions of Catholics in countries around the world are being united through hearing and meditating upon the same teachings and words of God.

The following calendar may be useful to lay ministers assisting in the liturgy as well as to the faithful who have a perpetual missal.[31a]

Calendar of Cycles for Holy Scripture Readings

Sundays and Solemn Feasts Year			Weekdays Year	
A	**B**	**C**	**I**	**II**
2002	2003	2001	*odd*	*even*
2005	2006	2004	2005	2004
2008	2009	2007	2007	2006
2011	2012	2010	2009	2008
2014	2015...	2013	2011...	2010

31. In the 2nd edition of the GIRM, the norms for Holy Scripture readings are found in Chapter VII titled *'Choice of Mass Texts,'* [318-320].
31a. Perpetual missal: see the last page of this book.

NORMS FOR THE SACRISTY

*"79. While not strictly part of the liturgical setting, the sacristy plays an **important role in the preparations for worship** and in its worthy accomplishment. According to European tradition, the major sacristy is a **kind of chapel** and may even include a fixed altar. It should be spacious and conveniently located near the sanctuary or the entrance to the church. A distinct vesting room near the door to the church is desirable (see CB. no. 53).*

*80. **A crucifix** or some other sacred image should be the central focus of the major sacristy, as this is customarily venerated by clergy and servers before and after liturgical celebrations. A card should be displayed bearing the **names** of the **Pope** and the diocesan **bishop** and the **title of the church**, for the information of visiting celebrants. **Holy water** should be available in a stoup at the door into the church. A **bell** may be hung on the wall near this door to alert the people when a procession is about to enter the church.*

*81. ...a **spacious table** or bench for setting out vestments, ample **cupboards** and **drawers**, a **secure safe** for sacred vessels and the tabernacle key, a **sink** with hot and cold water and towels, a second small sink leading directly into the earth (**sacrarium**), a place for storing bread and wine, a **bookcase** for the liturgical books, safer custody for sacramental registers, a fixed place for the current "**Ordo**" or calendar, a **clock**, a bracket for the **processional cross**, a place for **reserving the Eucharist** during the Easter ceremonies, and a repository [ambry]... for the **Holy Oils**, if they are not kept in the baptistery.*

*83. ...**Silence** before (during) and after a liturgical celebration should be required of all who assist in the sacristy (cf. CB. nos. 37, 38)."*

*162. [The **sacristan**]... is responsible for the sacristies, the care of precious objects and cleanliness and order within the church. ... (cf. CB. nos. 38"* [32]

32. CMRR, Chapter 1, nos. 79, 80, 81, 83, 162 (bold face added). See also Part Three, Liturgy of the Eucharist, the Sacristy.

Appendixes

Abbreviations for
The Books of the Bible

Old Testament

Pentateuch

Gen	Genesis
Ex	Exodus
Lev	Leviticus
Num	Numbers
Deut	Deuteronomy

Historical Books

Josh	Joshua
Judg	Judges
Ru	Ruth
1 Sam	1 Samuel
2 Sam	2 Samuel
1 Kg	1 Kings
2 Kg	2 Kings
1 Ch	1 Chronicles
2 Ch	2 Chronicles
Ezra	Ezra
Neh	Nehemiah
Tob	Tobit
Jdt	Judith
Esth	Esther
1 Macc	1 Maccabees
2 Macc	2 Maccabees

Wisdom Books

Job	Job
Ps	Psalms
Prov	Proverbs
Eccl	Ecclesiastes
Sg	Song of Songs
Wis	Wisdom
Sir	Sirach

Prophetic Books

Isa	Isaiah
Jer	Jeremiah
Lam	Lamentations
Bar	Baruch
Ezek	Ezekiel
Dan	Daniel
Hos	Hosea
Joel	Joel
Am	Amos
Ob	Obadiah
Jon	Jonah
Mic	Micah
Na	Nahum
Hb	Habakkuk
Zeph	Zephaniah
Hg	Haggai
Zech	Zechariah
Mal	Malachi

New Testament

Gospels

Mt	Matthew
Mk	Mark
Lk	Luke
Jn	John

Acts

Acts	Acts of the Apostles

Pauline Letters

Rom	Romans
1 Co	1 Corinthians
2 Co	2 Corinthians
Ga	Galatians
Ep	Ephesians
Ph	Philippians
Col	Colossians
1 Th	1 Thessalonians
2 Th	2 Thessalonians
1 Tim	1 Timothy
2 Tim	2 Timothy
Ti	Titus
Philem	Philemon
Heb	Hebrews

Apostolic Letters

Jas	James
1 Pt	1 Peter
2 Pt	2 Peter
1 Jn	1 John
2 Jn	2 John
3 Jn	3 John
Jude	Jude
Rev	Revelation

Appendix 'A'
COMPARATIVE CALENDAR OF CATHOLIC AND JUDAIC FEASTS [33]

CATHOLIC	DATES	JUDAIC	JEWISH MONTHS
ADVENT * Preparation period for Christmas, begins 4 weeks before Christmas Eve	November	....	Heshvan
CHRISTMAS Celebrates the birth of our Lord Jesus Christ. *"I am the light of the world."* Octave / 8 days of Christmas	December 25 January	**FEAST OF LIGHTS** ***HANUKKAH*** Dedication of the temple Joyful 8 days feast	Kislev Tebeth
PRESENTATION 40 days after Jesus' birth Judaic tradition	February 2 March 14-15	**FEAST OF PURIM** Celebrates God's victory over the Haman's plot to destroy the Jews	Shebat Adar
LENT * Period of atonement, begins 40 days before Easter, ends on Holy Thursday [33a]	April 14 15 21	**PASSOVER** Unleavened Bread Closing Passover	Nisan
EASTER * Celebrates the Resurrection of our Lord Jesus Christ	May		Iyyar
PENTECOST * Celebrates the sending of the Holy Spirit and the foundation of the Church (50 days after Easter)	June 6 July August September October 1-2	**Feast of Pentecost** Celebrates Moses receiving the Law on Mount Sinai (50 days after Passover) **Feast of Trumpets** Begins the civil year	Sivan Tammuz Ab Elul Tishri
	10	**Day of Atonement** ***YOM KIPPUR***	
NOTE: *variable feast dates	15-21	**Feast of Tabernacles** Memorial for Israelites wandering in the desert[34]	
The Day of the Lord	Sunday	**Sabbath**	Saturday

33. The origins of these Judaic feasts are found in *Leviticus* 23, except for the feasts of Purim (*Esther* 9) and Hanukkah (*1Macc* 4).
33a. The Holy Week: *Holy Thursday eve*, celebration of the Institution of the Eucharist and Holy Orders. *Good Friday*, celebration of the Passion and Death of our Lord. *Holy Saturday* (day), Mass is not celebrated, communion is distributed from the reserve. The Church awaits Her Lord in front of opened and empty tabernacles. *Holy Saturday* (night) Easter Vigil; liturgy of the light, and Baptism of new members of the Church.
34. Tabernacles: syn. Booths or Tents. The forefathers lived in tents while in the desert.

Appendix 'B'
EUCHARISTIC MIRACLES

The Eucharist is a Mystery and a Miracle. For times when we may doubt that the Eucharist is truly the Body and Blood of Christ, the Lamb of God, here are the true stories of some Eucharistic miracles.

The Eucharistic Miracle of Lanciano

Italy has been blessed many times with extraordinary spiritual events as well as with great saints such as Saint Francis and Saint Clare of Assisi, Saint Catherine of Sienna, Saint Don Bosco, Saint Gemma Galgani, Saint Padre Pio and many others. Here is the story of an especially blessed and extraordinary event that took place in Lanciano, Italy, at the beginning of the 8th century. This amazing and true story can not leave anyone indifferent, especially those of us who receive the Body and Blood of Jesus Christ in communion.

While celebrating Mass, the priest was doubting that the Body and Blood of Christ was really present and substantial in the host and chalice.

At this very moment, and in the presence of many witnesses, the host became a living piece of flesh, and in the chalice, the consecrated wine became real blood that coagulated into five clots of uneven size. This event is known as the **Eucharistic Miracle of Lanciano.**

Both the miraculous Flesh and the Blood were saved and underwent several analyses throughout the centuries. In February of 1574, the five clots - still intact after more than eight hundred years - were weighed. Although each of the clots are of different sizes, each clot then had a weight that equaled the total weight of the five clots together.

The 1713 monstrance in which are enshrined the holy relics of the Eucharistic Miracle of Lanciano.

This supernatural phenomenon was interpreted as a sign that Christ wanted to confirm the Church's teaching; that not only is Christ really and wholly present in the Eucharist, but that He is so even in the smallest particles of the consecrated bread and wine.

Strict scientific tests done during 1970 and 1971 revealed the following; the tests confirmed that the miraculous Flesh and Blood clots were really human flesh and blood, and that both were of the same AB blood type. The Flesh comes from the myocardium (heart) and, as for the Blood, it is still as fresh as if taken as a sample that same day. No traces of preservative were found and the state in which the piece of Flesh was found presupposes that only a practitioner of exceptional abilities could have performed this dissection. Finally, despite the fact that these relics have been exposed for centuries to atmospheric and biologic elements, no trace of decomposition was found. It is still possible to venerate these relics today at Saint-Francis church, in Lanciano, Italy.

The extensive study of the Shroud of Turin done in 1978 by 44 scientists revealed among other things that marks of fresh bleeding wounds on the cloth from the unwashed body are of the AB blood type, the same blood type discovered in the relics of the Lanciano Eucharistic miracle.

MIRACULOUS RECEPTION OF HOLY COMMUNION

In October of 1917 in **Fatima, Portugal,** before the children received the apparitions of the Blessed Mother, the Angel of Portugal appeared to them as the *Angel of Peace*. In his third and final appearance, the

Angel brought with him a chalice and suspended above it, a Host. Before offering the Host to Lucia, the only one who had received First Communion, he prostrated himself on the ground and said a prayer.[35]

The *Angel of Peace*, repeated this prayer three times and then rising up, lifted the Host before his eyes and said: "Take and drink the Body and the Blood of Jesus Christ, horribly insulted by ungrateful men. Make reparation for their crimes and console your God." With this, he gave the Host to Lucia and let the other children drink from the Chalice.

---

35. See Part Five, Appendix 'F', Essential Catholic Prayers, Prayers for Communion and Private Eucharistic Adoration, Eucharistic Prayers from Fatima, 1) Angel's prayer.

In **Garabandal, Spain**, some fifty years after the apparitions of Fatima, another child visionary of Marian apparitions received communion in a miraculous way. It was midnight on July 18, 1962, when Conchita, one of the four young girl visionaries from Garabandal, entered into ecstasy. She went out into the street at a short distance from her house, then she fell down on her knees in the midst of a crowd of locals and visitors. Bright lights were focused on her. She put out her tongue, upon which there was nothing as everyone could see. Then, suddenly, a Host appeared on her tongue and remained there for a few minutes. Don Alejandro Damians, then standing about three feet from Conchita, filmed amazing pictures of the miracle, including clear pictures of the Host on Conchita's tongue.

Throughout the history of the Church, there are many occurrences of the miraculous reception of holy Communion, and often, angels were the ones ministering the Eucharist. Such is the case, for example, for Saint Clement (4th c.) while in jail; Saint Pascal Baylon (d. 1592) while working in the field; Saint Bonaventure (d. 1274) while keeping away from Communion out of humility; Catherine of Jesus (d. 1594) while longing for the Eucharist; and Saint Catherine of Sienna (d. 1380) who experienced several miraculous receptions of the Eucharist.

MIRACULOUS EUCHARISTIC BLOOD STAINS

Eucharistic miracles are of different types of phenomena. Here is a case where spots of the Precious Blood appeared on a corporal. This series of events is known as the Eucharistic miracle of **Stich, Germany.** On the evening of June 9, 1970, a visiting priest who was celebrating Mass noticed a small red spot on the corporal at the place where the chalice containing the precious Blood had been resting. The priest touched the base of the chalice, but found it absolutely dry. During this time the small spot was expanding and was now the size of a dime. When Mass was over, the priest inspected everything on the altar and found that everything was normal. He could not find even a remote cause for this red stain. He took the stained corporal and locked it in a safe place.

Two days later, after the priest discussed the matter with the pastor and examined the corporal, the cloth was photographed and sent to the University of Zurich for chemical analysis. The conclusion of four different analyses revealed that the stain was human blood which contained the biochemical markers of a man in agony. About a month later, on July 14th, the phenomenon repeated itself at the same chapel in Stich. Four red spots appeared on the corporal after the Consecration. Several days later, the pastor sent the stained corporal for analysis to the District Hospital at Cercee. Once more, the test revealed that the stains were human blood.

Bleeding Hosts

Here is the story of a bleeding Host that took place in the village of **Santarem, Portugal**, some 35 miles south of Fatima. In the early 13th century, a woman had stolen a Host to give to a sorcerer in payment for putting a curse on her unfaithful husband. While she was still in the church, the Host she had hidden in her veil began to bleed. She hurried home and hid it in a chest. During the night the Host began to emit such a brilliant beam of light that the woman had to reveal everything to her husband. The Host was brought back to the church, and news of this miracle quickly spread throughout the country and beyond its borders. One can still venerate today in Santarem the bleeding Host of this Eucharistic miracle.

Here is another story of a bleeding Host. In 1263, Father Peter of Prague, a German priest stopped in **Bolsena, Italy**, on a pilgrimage to Rome. Although he was a pious priest, he had difficulty believing in the real presence of Christ in the Eucharist. He was celebrating Mass at the church of Saint Christina when, as he completed the words of consecration, blood started to seep from the consecrated Host. The blood ran down over his hands, onto the altar and the corporal. In a state of confusion, Father Peter first attempted to hide the blood, but then he interrupted the Mass, and went to Orvieto, where Pope Urban IV was then residing. After hearing Father Peter's story, the Pope absolved him for having doubts and sent representatives to Bolsena to investigate. The investigation confirmed all that the priest had related. The Host and the corporal bearing the blood stains were brought to the Pope, and in a solemn procession the relics were brought into the cathedral. One year later, in August 1264, Pope Urban IV **instituted the feast of Corpus Christi**, Body of Christ. The corporal bearing the spots of blood is still exhibited in the Cathedral of Orvieto.

Eucharistic Miracles in the 1990s

Eucharistic miracles do not only belong to the medieval history of the Church. On the contrary, throughout the 1990s the number of reported Eucharistic miracles is greater than ever before witnessed in the whole history of the Church in such a short period of time. These reports, which come from all over the world, surely deserve our attention. Here are the stories of some of these fairly well known Eucharistic miracles.

In **Betania, Venezuela**, a Eucharistic miracle took place on December 8, 1991, while Father Otty was celebrating the midnight Holy Mass in honor of the Feast of the Immaculate Conception. After he had finished the Consecration and broken the large Host into four pieces, he took one piece of the Host for his communion. As he placed the remaining portions of the Host on the paten on the altar, to his amazement he saw what seemed to be blood coming out from the Host. He later described it as if the blood was spurting from a wound. Father Otty placed the bleeding Host in a chalice, which he locked in the tabernacle for the night. When he looked at it again at 6 am the next morning, he found the Host still bleeding. He then placed the bleeding Host in the monstrance and brought the Host into the church to show the people who had gathered for Mass.

People saw the Host bleeding and blood accumulating at the bottom of the Monstrance. Among those present, a man who had a camcorder, filmed this miraculous event. After Bishop Ricardo of Los Teques was informed, he had the Host tested in Caracas. The analyses revealed that the red substance was, in fact, human blood. The Miraculous Host was taken to the convent of the Augustinian Nuns in Los Teques for safekeeping, adoration, and visitation by pilgrims. On November 13, 1998, a visiting pilgrim recorded the bleeding Host on video. What he saw and recorded is even a greater miracle. The bleeding Host of Los Teques appeared to be a burning, bleeding, and beating heart; and it is all on videotape!

THE EUCHARIST AS ONLY FOOD

In **Worcester, Massachusetts (U.S.A.),** a series of miraculous events surround a young girl who was brain-damaged in a swimming pool accident when she was 3 years old. The girl, Audrey Santo, is confined to her bed, unable to walk or talk. As of 2002, the only solid food she has been able to eat for the past **nine years** is the Holy Communion, which she receives daily. Some years ago, the local Bishop permitted the Blessed Sacrament to be reserved in a tabernacle kept in Audrey's room. On several occasions the two gold angels engraved on the tabernacle door have wept fragrant oil. The testing of the oil by different chemical laboratories has revealed that the makeup and origin of the oil are unknown. Religious statues and pictures in Audrey's room have wept oil and sometimes blood. On three occasions, consecrated Hosts taken from the tabernacle in Audrey's room have seeped a red fluid. The fluid that has been examined by an independent laboratory was found to be human blood. On Good Friday 1996, the tabernacle in Audrey's room began bleeding. Audrey now bears the **stigmata** - the visible wounds of Jesus. Some, who have visited Audrey, have reported miraculous healings and conversions, among whom are three of Audrey's nurses. Through Audrey, God has given the world extraordinary signs letting us know that He, the Almighty, is really present in the Eucharist.

Another amazing eucharistic story involves the French mystic **Marthe Robin** from **Drome, France** (1902-1981). She was confined to bed in her twenties, crippled and gradually paralysed. Marthe spent **50 years** in bed in an increasingly painful and unchangeable position, without eating or drinking, without sleeping, blind, suffering from the pains of the **stigmata** and the physical attacks of the devil. Her only nourishment was the Holy Eucharist. She read hearts and suffered the agony of the Passion every Friday. She offered her sufferings for the sins of modern man, the good of mankind and the 'Foyers of Charity', which she founded with the help of Father Georges Finet.

MORE BLEEDING HOSTS

After Marlboro, New Jersey, U.S.A., had been the site of Marian apparitions for ten years, on the feast of Divine Mercy of April 10, 1994, a miraculous event occurred in a nearby town called **Yardville, N.J.** Father Robert Rooney was celebrating morning Mass at Saint Vincent de Paul Church. After saying the words of consecration, as he raised the Host for adoration, blood came out of the Host. The server and some of the parishioners saw this occur. Father Rooney was understandably shaken by the bleeding Host. After showing the Host to the parish priest, it was decided that the bleeding Host would be kept in the tabernacle while they waited for the instructions of the local Bishop. After a few days, Bishop Reiss decided not to investigate this phenomenon. Fr. Rooney then gave the Host to his spiritual director Father Valenta, who had the Host photographed and examined by two medical doctors using non-invasive microscopic analysis.[36] The doctors stated: "There is no scientific explanation, the red material came from within the Host and it has the microscopic characteristics of human blood; the Church must make the determination as to any miracle."

A few months later, on the feast of Corpus Christi, June 6, the Blessed Virgin appeared to Father Rooney and told him that her Son had sent him a gift - the bleeding Host - and that from now on his spiritual director would take care of everything. Father Rooney died six weeks later on July 16, 1994 - the feast of Our Lady of Mount Carmel. Father Valenta brought the bleeding Host to Bishop Reiss of the Diocese of Trenton where, as of 2002, the Host still resides.

In 1995, **Methuen, Massachusetts (U.S.A.)** was the site of another miraculous Eucharistic miracle. In preparing to distribute Communion, an extraordinary minister of Holy Communion at Our Lady of Mount Carmel Church discovered a bleeding consecrated Host inside the tabernacle. The bleeding Host was transferred to a sacred vessel and kept in the tabernacle until further examination. The bleeding Host was eventually sent to Dr. B. Lipinski, a biochemist, for non-invasive examination. He confirmed that the red substance was human blood. A small sample of the crusted blood was then sent to the California Laboratory of Forensic Sciences. After several preliminary tests confirmed the presence of blood, a crossover electrophoresis test conducted on the sample confirmed the substance to be human blood.

---

36. Non-invasive techniques were used since a bishop's approval is required for any invasive examination.

OTHER MIRACULOUS RECEPTIONS OF HOLY COMMUNION

Rome, Italy. Since 1971, Marisa Rossi, an Italian Marian visionary, has been receiving locutions and signs from Our Blessed Mother, presenting herself as the 'Mother of the Eucharist', and asking for humanity to change its ways and return to God and especially to the Eucharist. On September 14, 1995 on the feast of the Exaltation of the Cross, after praying in the chapel, Marisa, who is wheelchair-bound, stood and kissed the crucifix, which Don Claudio Gatti had removed from the altar in preparation for a procession. Marisa saw a Host emerge from the side of the corpus on the cross and fall into her hand. Many around her saw the Host. Then in April of 1996, Marisa was photographed as a Host suddenly appeared in her outstretched hands during an apparition of the Blessed Virgin.

Naju, Korea. While concelebrating the Holy Mass on September 22, 1995, Ukrainian Catholic Bishop Roman Danylak, of the Eparchy of Toronto, Canada; Rev. Father Aloysius Chang, parish priest of the Kwangju Archdiocese in Korea; and Rev. Father Peter Finn, retired priest of the Diocese of London, Canada witnessed, along with the eleven faithful present, the following event: during the holy Communion, the Host received by the Korean, **Julia Kim**, was miraculously changed into a round piece of living and bleeding flesh. All present had the opportunity to view and venerate silently the miraculous Host before Julia consumed it. This was not Julia's first experience of such a miracle.

Although the Catholic Church does not officially recognize most of these Eucharistic miracles, the least we can say is that these wonderful events produce a great enthusiasm around the world, especially among Catholics, increasing their faith and reverence for the Real Presence of Jesus Christ in the Eucharist. From October to November 2005, Rome hosted a public photographic exhibition of 80 of the most important Eucharistic miracles. The exhibition coincided with the closing of the 'Year of the Eucharist' and the Synod of Bishops on the Eucharist, held in Rome by Pope Benedict XVI.

For those who believe no explanation is necessary,
but for those who do not believe... no explanation is sufficient.

Appendix 'C'
ORIGIN OF COMMUNION UNDER BOTH SPECIES

"From the first days of the Church's celebration of the Eucharist, Holy Communion consisted of the reception of both species in fulfillment of the Lord's command to "take and eat... take and drink." The distribution of Holy Communion to the faithful under both kinds was thus the norm for more than a millennium of Catholic liturgical practice.

The practice of Holy Communion under both kinds at Mass continued until the late eleventh century, when the custom of distributing the Eucharist to the faithful under the form of bread alone began to grow. ...This practice spread until the Council of Constance in 1415 decreed that Holy Communion under the form of bread alone would be distributed to the faithful.

In 1963, the Fathers of the Second Vatican Council authorized the extension of the faculty for Holy Communion under both kinds in *Sacrosanctum Concilium*:

> The dogmatic principles which were laid down by the Council of Trent remaining intact, Communion under both kinds may be granted when the bishops think fit, not only to clerics and religious, but also to the laity, in cases to be determined by the Apostolic See (*SC*, no. 55).

The Council's decision to restore Holy Communion under both kinds at the bishop's discretion took expression in the first edition of the *Missale Romanum* and enjoys an even more generous application in the third typical edition of the *Missale Romanum*:

> "Holy Communion has a fuller form as a sign when it is distributed under both kinds. For in this form the sign of the Eucharistic banquet is more clearly evident and clear expression is given to the divine will by which the new and eternal Covenant is ratified in the Blood of the Lord, as also the relationship between the Eucharistic banquet and the eschatological banquet in the Father's Kingdom." [37]

The extension of the faculty for the distribution of Holy Communion under both kinds does not represent a change in the Church's immemorial beliefs concerning the Holy Eucharist. Rather, today the Church finds it salutary to restore a practice, when appropriate, that for various reasons was not opportune when the Council of Trent was convened in 1545 (GIRM [241] 282). ..." [37a]

---

37. GIRM [240] 281, cf. Sacred Congregation of Rites, Instruction *Eucharisticum mysterium*, On the worship of the Eucharist, 25 May 1967, no. 32: AAS 59 (1967), p. 558.
37a. NCUBK, Congregation for Divine Worship and the Discipline of the Sacraments, and USCCB, March 2002, Prot. 1383/01/ L., Part I, nos. 17-21.

Appendix 'D'
THE ROMAN CURIA

The Roman Curia serves the Pontiff in exercising his power in the Church. Its departments, in which the Cardinals serve, perform their duties in the name and authority of the Pope. The structure of the Roman Curia, according to the Vatican's website (09/2005), is as follows:

Secretariat of State: *provides the Pope with the closest assistance.*

Congregations: (9) exercise the Church's authority & competence.
- Catholic Education: *supervisory competence over institutions of Catholic education.*
- Causes of Saints: *handles matters for causes of beatification and canonization.*
- Evangelization of Peoples: *directs and coordinates world wide missionary works.*
- Oriental Churches: *has competence in matters of Eastern Catholic Churches.*
- Doctrine of the Faith: *has duty to safeguard the doctrine of the faith and morals.*
- Divine Worship and the Discipline of the Sacraments: *supervises all aspects related to the promotion and regulation of the liturgy, principally the sacraments.*
- Institutes of Consecrated Life & Societies of Apostolic Life: *has competence over institutes of Religious, secular institutes, societies of apostolic life & third (secular) orders.*
- Clergy: *has competence regarding the life, discipline, rights and duties of the clergy.*
- Bishops: *has functions relating to bishops and the jurisdictions in which they serve.*

Tribunals (3)

Pontifical Councils: (11)
- Laity: *supports the laity in their participation in the life and mission of the Church.*
- Promoting Christian Unity: *handles proper interpretation & execution of ecumenism.*
- Family: *urges Christian families to fulfill their educative & apostolic mission.*
- Justice and Peace: *promotes world justice and peace according to the Gospel.*
- 'Cor Unum': *informs and coordinates Human and Catholic development.*
- Pastoral Care of Migrants and Itinerant peoples: *also tourists and travelers.*
- Health & Pastoral Care: *promotes the work of intl. Catholic health organizations.*
- Legislative Texts: *interprets the universal laws of the Church.*
- Inter-religious dialogue: *between Christians and non-Christians.*
- Culture: *relations with unbelievers who are open to cooperation.*
- Social Communications: *usage of media to communicate the message of salvation.*

Synod of Bishops: assembly of Bishops that counsels the Pope.

Offices: (3)

Pontifical Commissions: (7)
- Cultural Heritage of the Church: *preserves the Church's patrimony of art & history.*
- 'Ecclesia Dei': *the return of full ecclesial communion of priests of Msgr. Lefebvre.*
- Sacred Archaeology.
- Pontifical Biblical Commission.
- International Theological Commission.
- Interdicasterial Commission for the Catechism of the Catholic Church.
- Pontifical Commission for Latin America.

Swiss Guard and **Labour Office of the Apostolic See.**

Institutions Connected with the Holy See: (8)
- Fabric of St. Peter: *administration and care of the basilica.*
- 'Latinitas' Foundation: *promotes and studies the Latin language.*
- Office of Papal charities.
- 'Peregrinatio ad Petri Sedem': *assistance to pilgrims coming to Rome.*
- Pontifical Institute of Sacred Music.
- Pontifical Musical Chorus of the Sistine Chapel.
- Vatican Press.
- Vatican Publishing House.

Pontifical Academies: (5) Life, Science & Social Sciences in light of Church's doctrine.
- 'Culturum Martyrum': *study of ancient and modern martyrs.*
- Ecclessiastical: *prepares priests to diplomatic services; Nuncios & Secretary of State.*
- Life: *study and inform on biomedical and law issues in relation with promoting life.*
- Science: *promotes progress of mathematic, physic, and natural science.*
- Social Sciences: *promotes progress of economic, sociology, law, and political sciences.*

Pontifical Committee for Eucharistic Congresses.

Appendix 'D'

CATHOLIC CLERGY HIERARCHY   AND   CORRESPONDING CHURCH

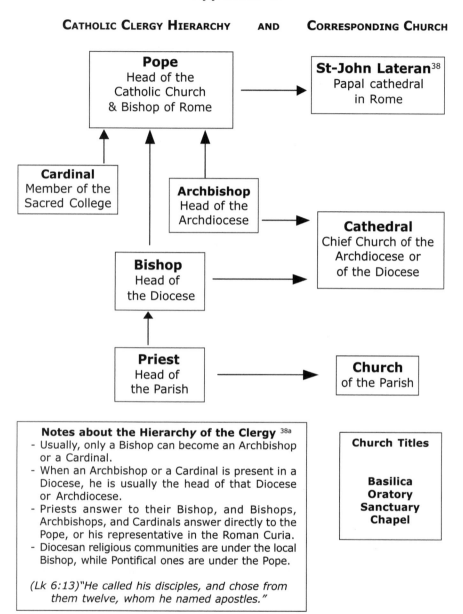

Pope
Head of the
Catholic Church
& Bishop of Rome

St-John Lateran[38]
Papal cathedral
in Rome

Cardinal
Member of the
Sacred College

Archbishop
Head of the
Archdiocese

Cathedral
Chief Church of the
Archdiocese or
of the Diocese

Bishop
Head of
the Diocese

Priest
Head of
the Parish

Church
of the Parish

Notes about the Hierarchy of the Clergy [38a]
- Usually, only a Bishop can become an Archbishop or a Cardinal.
- When an Archbishop or a Cardinal is present in a Diocese, he is usually the head of that Diocese or Archdiocese.
- Priests answer to their Bishop, and Bishops, Archbishops, and Cardinals answer directly to the Pope, or his representative in the Roman Curia.
- Diocesan religious communities are under the local Bishop, while Pontifical ones are under the Pope.

(Lk 6:13)"He called his disciples, and chose from them twelve, whom he named apostles."

Church Titles

**Basilica
Oratory
Sanctuary
Chapel**

---

38. The Basilica of Saint Peter of Rome, is the second chief church after Saint John Lateran, which is the papal cathedral.

38a. Documents from early Church Fathers such as St. Ignatius of Antioch (himself a Bishop martyred in 107) show that the Church already had an established clergy hierarchy as early as the 1st century.

NOTE: Chapel: building or part of a building used for divine worship; a portion of a church set aside for the celebration of Mass or some special devotion. Definitions for the above clergy and church titles: see Part Five, Catholic Glossary.

Appendix 'E'
THE COMMANDMENTS

God gave us His commandments so that we may have a good life and stay in His grace. The Ten Commandments, Jesus' commandments of love and life, and the precepts and teachings of the Church are all given to us by the Lord. As Catholics, we are required to examine our conscience, in the light of all of God's commandments, on a daily basis and more specially before approaching the sacrament of reconciliation.

THE TEN WORDS OF GOD
Decalogue (cf. Ex 20:2-17, Deut 5:6-21) [38b]

CCC 2067 "The Ten Commandments state what is required in the love of God and love of neighbor. The first three concern love of God, and the other seven love of neighbor."

Love of God
1. I am the Lord your God: you shall not have strange gods before me.
2. You shall not take the name of the Lord your God in vain.
3. Remember to keep holy the Lord's Day.

Love of neighbor
4. Honor your father and mother.
5. You shall not kill.
6. You shall not commit adultery.
7. You shall not steal.
8. You shall not bear false witness against your neighbor.
9. You shall not covet your neighbor's wife.
10. You shall not covet your neighbor's goods. [39]

CCC 2056 "... the word 'Decalogue' means literally 'ten words' " (cf. Ex 34:28; Deut 4:13; 10:4).
CCC 2057 "...the 'ten words' point out the conditions of a life freed from the slavery of sin. The Decalogue is a path of life."

THE SCHEMA: fundamental truth and duty of Judaism. [39a]
(Deut 6:4)"...the LORD is our God, the LORD alone." (Truth)
(Deut 6:5-9)"You shall love the LORD your God with all your heart, and with all your soul, and with all your might. Keep these words that I am commanding you today in your heart. Recite them to your children and talk about them when you are at home and when you are away, when you lie down and when you rise. Bind them as a sign on your hand, fix them as an emblem on your forehead, and write them on the doorposts of your house and on your gates." (Duty)

38b. Decalogue, related texts CCC 2083-2557.
39. The Ten Commandments, Traditional Catechetical Formula, CCC pp. 496, 497.
39a. Schema: also see Par Five, Catholic Glossary.

JESUS' COMMANDMENTS OF LOVE AND LIFE

Jesus says that He did not come to abolish the law or the prophets, but to fulfill it (cf. Mt 5:17). Jesus has elevated the law of the Old Testament to a higher commandment that teaches **charity, mercy, and life**.

(Mk 12:33)"'To love [the Lord your God] with all the heart, and with all the understanding, and with all the strength,' and 'to love one's neighbor as oneself,'--this is much more important than all whole burnt offerings and sacrifices."

(Mt 7:12)"Whatever you wish that men would do to you, do so to them; for this is the law and the prophets."

Jesus teaches that it is better to give life, rather than not to kill, to act out of love, rather than out of obligation. Some of Jesus' most significant teaching on the commandments of love and life are found in 'The Sermon on the Mount' (cf. Mt 5-7), which includes the eight 'Beatitudes' (cf. Mt 5:3-12). Here are some excerpts.

(Mt 5:11-12)"Blessed are you when people revile you and persecute you and utter all kinds of evil against you falsely on my account. Rejoice and be glad, for your reward is great in heaven. ..."

(Mt 5:39-42.44)"...Do not resist one who is evil. But if any one strikes you on the right cheek, turn to him the other [cheek] also; and if any one would sue you and take your coat, let him have your cloak as well; and if any one forces you to go one mile, go with him two miles. Give to him who begs from you, and do not refuse him who would borrow from you. ...Love your enemies and pray for those who persecute you."

(CCC 1966)"The New Law is the grace of the Holy Spirit given to the faithful through faith in Christ. It works through charity; it uses the Sermon on the Mount to teach us what must be done and makes use of the sacraments to give us the grace to do it:... ."

Jesus calls us to holiness!

(Mt 5:48)"Be perfect, therefore, as your heavenly Father is perfect."
(Lk 6:35.37-38)"Do good, and lend, expecting nothing in return.... "Do not judge, and you will not be judged; do not condemn, and you will not be condemned. Forgive, and you will be forgiven; give, and it will be given to you. A good measure, pressed down, shaken together ...for the measure you give will be the measure you get back.""

(Mt 25:34-36)"'Come, O blessed of my Father, inherit the kingdom prepared for you from the foundation of the world; for I was hungry and you gave me food, I was thirsty and you gave me drink, I was a stranger and you welcomed me, I was naked and you clothed me, I was sick and you visited me, I was in prison and you came to me.'"

(2 Pet 3:14)"Therefore, beloved, while you are waiting for these things, strive to be found by him at peace, without spot or blemish."

Other bible references for examination of conscience: Mt 5:21-22; 27-28; Mk 7:21-23; Lk 16:13; Rom 13:13-14; 1Cor 6:9-11; Ep 4:25-27; 5:3-5; 6:1-4; Col 3:12-14.

The [5] Precepts of the Church

"The precepts of the Church are set in the context of a moral life bound to and nourished by liturgical life. ... [These positive laws are] meant to guarantee to the faithful the very necessary minimum in the spirit of prayer and moral effort, in the growth in love of God and neighbor:

[1.]..."You shall attend Mass on Sundays and on holy days of obligation." [39b] ...

[2.] ... "You shall confess your sins at least once a year."...

[3.] ... "You shall humbly receive your Creator in Holy Communion at least during the Easter season."...

[4.] ... "You shall keep holy the holy days of obligation."...

[5.] ..."You shall observe the prescribed days of fasting and abstinence."...

The faithful also have the duty of providing for the material needs of the Church, each according to his abilities." [39c]

VIRTUES		VICES	
4 Cardinal	**3 Theological**	**7 Capital Sins**	
Prudence	Faith	Pride	Lust
Justice	Hope	Avarice	Gluttony
Fortitude	Charity	Envy	Sloth,
Temperance		Wrath	or Acedia
see CCC 1805-1809, 1812-1829.		*see CCC 1865-1869, 2534-2540.*	

"The human [cardinal] virtues are stable dispositions of the intellect and the will that govern our acts, order our passions, and guide our conduct in accordance with reason and faith. / The theological virtues dispose Christians to live in a relationship with the Holy Trinity. / The gifts of the Holy Spirit... complete and perfect the virtues of those who receive them. They make the faithful docile in readily obeying divine inspirations. / The fruits of the Spirit are perfections that the Holy Spirit forms in us as the first fruits of eternal glory." [39d]

7 Gifts of the Holy Spirit	**12 Fruits of the Spirit**	
Wisdom	Charity	Generosity
Understanding	Joy	Gentleness
Counsel	Peace	Faithfulness
Fortitude	Patience	Modesty
Knowledge	Kindness	Self-control
Piety	Goodness	Chastity
Fear of the Lord		
see CCC 1831, 1266, 1299;	*see CCC 1832, 736;*	
cf. Isa 11:1-2.	*cf. Gal 5:22-23.*	

39b. Holy days of Obligation: Sundays and other feasts as listed by the Church (cf. CCC 2177); see, Part Five, Church Norms, II, Liturgical Seasons & Feasts.
39c. CCC 2041-2043, cf. CIC, cann. 1246-1248; CCEO, can. 881§1, §2, §4.; CIC, can. 989; CCEO, can. 719.; CIC, can. 920; CCEO, cann. 708; 881§3; CIC, can. 1246; CCEO, cann. 881§1, §4; 880§3.; CIC, cann. 1249-1251; CCEO, can. 882.; CIC, can. 222.
39d. Excerpts taken from CCC 1834, 1840, 1831, 1832.

Appendix 'F'
ESSENTIAL CATHOLIC PRAYERS
(The prayers found in this Appendix are taken from
different prayer books and missals.)

THE SIGN OF THE CROSS: (sign yourself, then join your hands.)
In the name of the Father (on the forehead),
and of the Son (the chest),
and of the Holy (left shoulder) *Spirit* (right shoulder), *Amen.*

BLESSING BEFORE MEALS:
*Bless us, O Lord, and these thy gifts, which we are about to
receive from thy bounty, through Christ, our Lord, Amen!*

OUR FATHER: (The Lord's Prayer)   *(cf. Mt 6:9-13; Lk 11:2-4)*
*Our Father, who art in heaven, hallowed be thy name;
thy kingdom come; thy will be done on earth as it is in heaven.
Give us this day our daily bread; and forgive us our trespasses
as we forgive those who trespass against us; and lead us not
into temptation, but deliver us from evil. Amen.*

THE APOSTLE'S CREED:
*I believe in God, the Father almighty, creator of heaven and earth.
I believe in Jesus Christ, his only Son, our Lord. He was conceived
by the power of the Holy Spirit and born of the Virgin Mary. He
suffered under Pontius Pilate, was crucified, died, and was buried.
He descended into hell. On the third day he rose again. He
ascended into heaven and is seated at the right hand of the
Father. He will come again to judge the living and the dead.
I believe in the Holy Spirit, the holy catholic Church, the communion
of saints, the forgiveness of sins, the resurrection of the body,
and the life everlasting. Amen.*

HAIL MARY: (Ave Maria)
*Hail Mary, full of grace, the Lord is with thee; blessed are thou
among women, and blessed is the fruit of thy womb, Jesus.
Holy Mary, Mother of God, pray for us sinners, now and at the
hour of our death. Amen.*

*(Lk 1:26-28) "...the angel Gabriel was sent from God to a city
of Galilee named Nazareth, to a virgin betrothed to a man whose
name was Joseph, of the house of David; and the virgin's name
was Mary. And he came to her and said, "Hail, O favored one,
the Lord is with you!"*

(Lk 1:41-42)"*When Elizabeth heard Mary's greeting, the child leaped in her womb. And Elizabeth was filled with the Holy Spirit and exclaimed with a loud cry, "Blessed are you among women, and blessed is the fruit of your womb."*

The origins of the third part of the Hail Mary are as follows: the words '*Holy Mary, Mother of God*' come from the Council of Ephesus in 431 to explain the term 'Theotokos' (God bearer). Heretics of the time believed that Mary was the mother of Christ, but not of God. However, the people of Ephesus rioted, carrying torches into the streets and shouting, '*Holy Mary Mother of God, pray for us sinners*'. It is believed this part of the prayer came into common usage during the 16th century. Later, the prayer was completed with '*now and at the hour of our death.*' The official *Catechism of the Council of Trent* (1545-1563) states that the third part of the 'Hail Mary' has been framed by the Church.

THE ANGELUS:
V: The Angel of the Lord declared unto Mary:
R: *And she conceived by the Holy Spirit.* (cf. Lk 1:26-37)
    Pray one **Hail Mary,** full of Grace the Lord is with thee...
V: Behold, the handmaid of the Lord:
R: *Be it done unto me according to thy word.* (cf. Lk 1:38)
    Pray one **Hail Mary,** full of Grace the Lord is with thee...
V: And the Word was made flesh:
R: *And dwelt among us.* (cf. Jn 1:14)
    Pray one **Hail Mary,** full of Grace the Lord is with thee...
V: Pray for us, O holy Mother of God,
R: *That we may be made worthy of the promises of Christ.*
V: Let us pray.
All: *Pour forth, we beseech thee, O Lord, thy grace unto our hearts, that we, to whom the Incarnation of Christ, thy Son, was made known by the message of the Angel, may by His Passion and Cross be brought to the glory of His Resurrection, through the same Christ, our Lord. Amen.*   In conclusion pray one 'Glory Be'.

The Angelus commemorates the mystery of the Incarnation of Our Lord. Traditionally, the Angelus was celebrated three times a day: at 6 am, (dawn) as monastery bells rang for morning prayer; at 12 noon, as church bells rang to recall the crucifixion of Our Lord (especially on Fridays); and at 6 pm (dusk).[40]

GLORY BE:
Glory be to the Father, and to the Son, and to the Holy Spirit. As it was in the beginning, is now, and ever shall be, world without end. Amen. (cf. Rev 1:8)

---

40. Daily hours for prayer: see Liturgy of the Hours, Part Five, Catholic Glossary.

PRAYERS OF THE ROSARY

O MY JESUS: (Our Lady gave this prayer at Fatima and requested that we recite it after each decade of the Rosary.)
O my Jesus, forgive us our sins, save us from the fires of hell, and lead all souls to Heaven, especially those most in need of Your mercy.

PRAYER FOR A NEW PENTECOST:
(may be recited after each decade of the Rosary)
Come, Holy Spirit, come by means of the powerful intercession of the Immaculate Heart of Mary, your well-beloved Spouse.

O SACRAMENT, MOST HOLY:
(may be recited after each decade of the Rosary)
O Sacrament, Most Holy, O Sacrament Divine;
All praise and all thanksgiving, Be every moment thine.

PRAYER OF THE MIRACULOUS MEDAL: (prayer to conclude the rosary)
"O Mary conceived without sin,
Pray for us who have recourse to Thee."
(The Miraculous Medal with the above prayer was received in 1830 by St. Catherine Laboure, a Sister of Charity, during Marian apparitions on Rue du Bac, Paris.)

HAIL, HOLY QUEEN: *Salve Regina* (prayer to conclude the rosary)
Hail, Holy Queen, Mother of Mercy; our life, our sweetness, and our hope. To thee do we cry, poor banished children of Eve; to thee do we send up our sighs, mourning and weeping in this valley of tears. Turn, then, most gracious Advocate, thine eyes of mercy toward us; and after this, our exile, show unto us the blessed fruit of thy womb, Jesus; O clement, O loving, O sweet Virgin Mary.
V: Pray for us, O Holy Mother of God.
R: That we may be made worthy of the promises of Christ.
(Composed by 'Herman the Cripple')

O GOD, WHOSE ONLY BEGOTTEN SON: (recited to conclude the rosary. This prayer is the collect from the Mass of the Blessed Virgin of the Rosary, celebrated on October 7th..)
Let us pray - O God, whose only begotten Son, by His life, death and resurrection has purchased for us the rewards of eternal life, grant, we beseech Thee, that meditating upon these mysteries of the most Holy Rosary of the Blessed Virgin Mary, we may imitate what they contain, and obtain what they promise, through the same Christ our Lord. Amen.
V: May the divine assistance remain always with us.
R: And may the souls of the faithful departed, through the mercy of God, rest in peace. Amen.

PRAYER TO ST. MICHAEL THE ARCHANGEL:[40a] (recited to conclude the rosary)
Saint Michael, the Archangel, defend us in battle, be our safeguard against the wickedness and snares of the Devil. May God rebuke him, we humbly pray; and do thou, O Prince of the Heavenly Host, by the power of God, cast into hell satan and all the other evil spirits who prowl about the world seeking the ruin of souls. Amen.

PRAYER TO DEFEAT THE WORK OF SATAN: (prayer to conclude the rosary)
O Divine Eternal Father, in union with your Divine Son and the Holy Spirit, and through the Immaculate Heart of Mary, I beg You to destroy the power of your greatest enemy - the evil spirits. Cast them into the deepest recesses of hell and chain them there forever. Take possession of your Kingdom which You have created and which is rightfully yours. Heavenly Father, give us the reign of the Sacred Heart of Jesus and of the Immaculate Heart of Mary. I repeat this prayer out of pure love for You with every beat of my heart and with every breath I take. Amen.

THE MEMORARE: (recited to conclude the rosary or at any time)
Remember, O most gracious Virgin Mary, that never was it known that anyone who fled to your protection, implored your help, or sought your intercession was left unaided. Inspired by this confidence, I fly unto you, O virgin of virgins, My Mother! To you I come, before you I stand sinful and sorrowful. O Mother of the Word incarnate, despise not my petitions, but in your mercy hear and answer me. Amen.

AN ACT OF CONSECRATION TO THE IMMACULATE HEART: (said at any time)
O Mary, my Mother, your heart is a shrine of holiness.
I consecrate myself entirely to your Immaculate Heart. I reject satan and all of his works. I give you my very being and my whole life: all that I have, all that I love, and all that I am. Keep me and guard me as your property and possession. Amen.

PRAYER FOR THE SOULS OF PURGATORY:
V: Eternal rest give unto them, O Lord,
R: And let perpetual light shine upon them.
*   May they rest in peace. Amen.*

40a. The prayer to Saint Michael was composed by Pope Leo XIII in 1884 after he received a revelation informing him of Satan's plan to try to destroy the Church and bring all souls to their ruin. Pope Leo XIII then instructed all priests and faithful to say the Saint Michael's prayer after each Mass. The practice was abandoned in the 1960's.

AN ACT OF CONTRITION: (to be recited in sacramental confession)
O my God! I am heartily sorry for having offended You, and I detest all my sins, because I dread the loss of heaven and the pains of hell, but most of all because they offend You, my God, who art all-good and deserving of all my love. I firmly resolve with the help of Your grace, to confess my sins, to do penance, and to amend my life. Amen.

COME, HOLY SPIRIT: (to be recited before beginning intellectual work)
Come, Holy Spirit, fill the hearts of thy faithful and enkindle in them the fire of thy love. Send forth your Spirit and they shall be created; and you shall renew the face of the earth.
Let us pray: O God, who instructs the hearts of your faithful by the light of your Holy Spirit, grant us by the same Holy Spirit to be truly wise and ever to rejoice in his consolation. Through Christ our Lord. Amen

• •

DIVINE MERCY CHAPLET

This chaplet was given by Jesus to Saint Faustina (1905-1938) with the promise that special graces will be granted to those who recite this chaplet at the holy hour of 3 pm The devotion to the Divine Mercy also includes a novena said in preparation for the feast of Divine Mercy, celebrated the Sunday after Easter. Ask about it in your parish.

Introductory prayer:
O Blood and Water, which gushed forth from the Heart of Jesus as a fount of mercy for us. I trust in You!

The Chaplet: (to be prayed on the rosary beads) *Sign yourself; then recite one Our Father, one Hail Mary, and the Apostle's Creed.*

Before each of the five decades, on the large bead say:
V: Eternal Father, I offer You
the Body and Blood, Soul and Divinity
of Your dearly beloved Son, Our Lord Jesus Christ,
R: In atonement for our sins and those of the whole world.
On the small beads of each decade, say:
R: For the sake of His sorrowful Passion,
V: Have mercy on us and on the whole world.

Concluding Prayer, after the fifth decade repeat three times:
Holy God, Holy Mighty One, Holy Immortal One,
Have mercy on us and on the whole world.

In conclusion say three times: *Jesus! I trust in You!*

PRAYER OF THE LADY OF ALL NATIONS
Prayer for Peace given in Amsterdam by Our Lady,
Our Co-Redemptrix, Mediatrix and Advocate,
to Ida Peerdeman during Marian apparitions (1945-1959).

Lord Jesus Christ, Son of the Father,
send now your Spirit over the earth.
Let the Holy Spirit live in the hearts of all nations,
that they may be preserved against
degeneration, disaster and war.
May the Lady of All Nations, who once was Mary,
be our Advocate. Amen.

● ●

THE CALL TO PRAYER
"God calls man first. *Man may forget his Creator or hide far from his face; he may run after idols or accuse the deity of having abandoned him; yet the living and true God tirelessly calls each person to that mysterious encounter known as prayer. In prayer, the faithful God's initiative of love always comes first; our own first step is always a response. As God gradually reveals himself and reveals man to himself, prayer appears as a reciprocal call, a covenant drama. Through words and actions, this drama engages the heart. It unfolds throughout the whole history of salvation."* [41]

THE TRADITION OF PRAYER
"Prayer cannot be reduced to the spontaneous outpouring of interior impulse: in order to pray, one must have the will to pray. Nor is it enough to know what the Scriptures reveal about prayer: one must also learn how to pray. Through a living transmission (Sacred Tradition) within 'the believing and praying Church,' the Holy Spirit teaches the children of God how to pray." [42]

Prayer is an essential activity of our life of faith. It brings us into a relationship with God, nourishes our soul and brings us peace. Prayer is a dialogue. There is a time to speak to God, to present Him our petitions and thanksgivings, but there is also a time to listen to what God has to say to us. Pray at all times and for all things: to offer your day, to bless your food, to give thanks to God, to ask for help in your work, when you need to be comforted, when you need help to control yourself, before you go to sleep... Pray in all things and Praise Him.

The greatest of all prayers is the Holy Mass.

---

41. CCC 2567.
42. CCC 2650, cf. *DV* 8.

Prayers for Communion
and Private Eucharistic Adoration

An Act of Faith in the Real Presence
(may be recited before or after communion, or during adoration.)

Lord Jesus Christ, I believe you are as truly present in this holy sacrament, under the signs of bread and wine, as you were when dying upon a cross for the salvation of all mankind, or as you are now enthroned in glory in heaven at the right hand of the Father.

You said that you would give us yourself as the bread of life, which if we eat, we shall live forever. I believe this truth because you are truth itself. With confidence in your loving forgiveness therefore, I approach your altar, conscious that my unworthiness to receive you is outweighed by your desire to be united with my soul. You desire to nourish it on its earthly pilgrimage, until the day when I shall be with you in the eternal banquet, to feed on the unveiled beauty of your presence forever.

Act of Thanksgiving:
(may be recited after communion or during private adoration.)

From the depths of my heart I thank you, dear Lord, for your infinite kindness in coming to me. How good you are to me! With your most holy Mother and all the angels, I praise your mercy and generosity toward me, a poor sinner. I thank you for nourishing my soul with your Sacred Body and Precious Blood. I will try to show my gratitude to you in the Sacrament of your love, by obedience to your holy commandments; by fidelity to my duties, by kindness to my neighbor, and by an earnest endeavor to become more like you in my daily conduct.

Ecce Panis Angelorum (prayer)
Behold the bread of angels, is become the pilgrim's food.
Truly the bread of children must not be thrown to dogs.
You were foretold in ancient symbols; Isaac was to be sacrificed,
You were selected as the Paschal Lamb, Manna given to the Fathers.
O Good Shepherd you are truly bread,
Jesus have mercy on us. Feed us and guard us.
Enable us to see good things in the land of the living.
You know and are able to do all things;
Here you feed us, there we shall dine together as coheirs
and companions of the heavenly court. Amen.

Note: See Part Three, Liturgy of the Eucharist, After the Mass, Eucharistic Adoration.

Soul of Christ / Anima Christi   (prayer)

Soul of Christ, sanctify me. / Body of Christ, save me.
Blood of Christ, inebriate me. / Water from the side of Christ, wash me.
Passion of Christ, strengthen me. / O good Jesus, hear me.
Within thy wounds hide me.
Suffer me not to be separated from thee.
From the malicious enemy defend me.
In the hour of my death call me, / and bid me come to thee,
That with thy saints I may praise thee / for ever and ever. Amen!

Anima Christi, sanctifica me. / Corpus Christi, salva me.
Sanguis Christi, inebria me. / Aqua lateris Christi, lava me.
Passio Christi, conforta me. / O bone Iesu, exaudi me.
Intra tua vulnera absconde me.
Ne permittas me separari a te. / Ab hoste maligno defende me.
In hora mortis meae voca me, / et iube me venire ad te,
ut cum Sanctis tuis laudem te / in saecula saeculorum. Amen.

Spiritual Communion: *(prayer when unable to receive communion)*

Most loving Jesus, I adore You with a lively faith. You are present in this Sacrament by virtue of Your infinite power, wisdom, and goodness. Although conscious of my unworthiness, I place all my hope in You. I love You, O Lord, with all my heart and I desire to receive You now spiritually. Come therefore, O Lord, to me in spirit. Feed me, for I am hungry; strengthen me, for I am weak; enliven and sanctify me with Your sacred Body and Blood. Deliver me from all sin and make me always obedient to Your commands. Let me never be separated from You, my Savior, who with the Father and the Holy Spirit live and reign one God forever and ever. Amen.

Eucharistic Prayers from Fatima:

(may be said during silent time of private or public adoration)

1. Angel's prayer: (from the Angel of Portugal)
   O most Holy Trinity, Father, Son and Holy Spirit, I adore Thee profoundly. I offer Thee the most precious Body, Blood, Soul and Divinity of Jesus Christ, present in all the tabernacles of the world, in reparation for the outrages, sacrileges and indifference by which He is offended. By the infinite merits of the Sacred Heart of Jesus and the Immaculate Heart of Mary, I beg the conversion of poor sinners. Amen.

2. Pardon prayer: (from the Angel of Portugal)
   My God, I believe, I adore, I hope, and I love You. I beg pardon of You for those who do not believe, do not adore, do not hope, and do not love You. Amen.

3. The Eucharistic Prayer: (from Our Lady)
   Most Holy Trinity, I adore you! My God, my God, I love you in the Most Blessed Sacrament. Amen.

Hymns and Prayers for Holy Hour [42a]

O Saving Victim / O Salutaris (hymn)
*O Saving Victim, opening wide, the gate of heaven to us below!
Our foes press on from every side;
Your aid supply, your strength bestow.*
*O salutaris hostia, Quae caeli pandis ostium;
Bella premunt hostilia, Da robur fer auxilium.*

*To your great name be endless praise,
Immortal Godhead, One in Three;
O grant us endless length of days, when our true native land we see.*
*Uni trinoque Domino, Sit Sempiterna gloria;
Qui vitam sine termino, Nobis donet in patria.*

During silent adoration, one may choose to say the *Eucharistic Prayers from **Fatima*** that are found on page 222. The children received these prayers from Our Lady and from the Angel of Portugal, the Angel of Peace, during the apparitions of Fatima in 1917.

Come Adore / Tantum Ergo (hymn) [42b]
*Down in adoration falling,
Lo! The sacred host we hail;
Lo! O'er ancient forms departing,
Newer rites of grace prevail;
Faith for all defects supplying,
Where the feeble senses fail.*
*Tantum ergo Sacramentum, / Veneremur cernui
Et antiquum documentum, / Novo cedat ritui:
Praestet fides supplementum, / Sensuum defectui.*

*To the everlasting Father,
And the Son who reigns on high,
With the Holy Spirit proceeding,
Forth from Each eternally,
Be salvation, honor, blessing.
Might, and endless majesty. Amen.*
*Genitori Genitoque, / Laus et jubilatio,
Salus, honor, virtus quoque, / Sit et benedictio:
Procedenti ab utroque, / Compar sit laudatio. Amen.*

42a. Liturgy for Holy Hour: see Part Three, Liturgy of the Eucharist, After the Mass, Eucharistic Adoration.
42b. These are the two last verses of *Pange lingua,* with an English version.

Mary's Song (hymn)
Inspired by the Canticle of Mary, the *Magnificat* (cf. Lk 1:46-55)
Sometimes sung when Vespers are celebrated during 'Holy Hour'.

My soul doth glory in your love, O Lord. (bis)
For you gazed on your servant with compassion,
And you reached out and took me by the hand.
> *Great is our God and holy is his name.*
> *His mercy reaches to the end of time.*
> *Ah, the lowly he raises to the heavens,*
> *And the proudhearted have no part with him.*
>> *Ah, how he fills the hungry with his love.*
>> *With empty hands the rich are sent away.*
>> *He will always be mindful of his mercy,*
>> *As he promised our fathers long ago.*
My soul doth glory in your love, O Lord. (bis)
For you smiled on your servant with compassion,
And you reached out and took me by the hand.

Divine Praises (prayer)
Blessed be God.
Blessed be his Holy Name.
Blessed be Jesus Christ, true God and true Man.
Blessed be the Name of Jesus. Blessed be his most Sacred Heart.
Blessed be his most Precious Blood.
Blessed be Jesus in the most Holy sacrament of the Altar.
Blessed be the Holy spirit, the Paraclete.
Blessed be the great Mother of God, Mary most holy.
Blessed be her holy and Immaculate Conception.
Blessed be her glorious Assumption.
Blessed be the name of Mary, Virgin and Mother.
Blessed be Saint Joseph, her most chaste spouse.
Blessed be God in his angels and in his saints.

Holy God, We Praise Thy Name (hymn)
Holy God, we praise thy name! / Lord of all, we bow before thee;
All on earth thy scepter claim, / All in heaven above adore thee;
Infinite thy vast domain, / Everlasting is thy reign. (bis)
> *Hark! the loud celestial hymn, / Angel choirs above are raising;*
> *Cherubim and Seraphim, / in unceasing chorus praising,*
> *Fill the heavens with sweet accord; / Holy, holy, holy Lord! (bis)*
Holy Father, Holy son, / Holy Spirit, Three we name thee,
While in essence only One, / Undivided God we claim thee,
And adoring bend the knee, / While we own the mystery. (bis)

THE WAY OF THE CROSS

The 'Stations of the Cross' are part of the furnishings of churches and of most chapels. They are usually mounted on the walls, on both sides of the nave, presented in the form of paintings or low-reliefs. In some cases, they may also be found outdoors on the grounds of churches, sanctuaries or in cemeteries in the format of large sculptures or large low-reliefs. Typically, the 'Stations of the Cross' are placed several feet from each other in order that, while doing the devotion called the 'Way of the Cross', after pausing in front of each station to pray silently we walk a few steps to the next station, **as Our Lord walked His Way to the Cross**. There are **fourteen 'Stations of the Cross'** (sometimes fifteen), and they represent the **Passion and the Death** (and the Resurrection) of **Our Lord Jesus Christ**. The Stations are titled and numbered as follows:

1st Station: **Jesus is condemned to death.**

2nd Station: **Jesus takes his Cross.**

3rd Station: **Jesus falls for the first time.**

4th Station: **Jesus meets His Blessed Mother.**

5th Station: **Simon helps Jesus carry His Cross.**

6th Station: **Veronica wipes the face of Jesus.**

7th Station: **Jesus falls for the second time.**

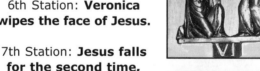

8th Station: **Jesus speaks to the women of Jerusalem.**

9th Station: **Jesus falls for the third time.**

10th Station: **Jesus is stripped of his garments.**

11th Station: **Jesus is nailed to the Cross.**

12th Station: **Jesus dies on the Cross.**

13th Station: **Jesus is taken down from the Cross.**

14th Station: **Jesus is placed in the tomb.**

Each station is engraved with its **own** roman **numeral** and usually adorned with a small **cross on top**. When pausing in front of each station, we recall its title, sign ourselves and/or genuflect, and **pray**: *"We adore You, O Christ, and we praise You. Because by Your holy cross, You have redeemed the world."* After the last station, we pray one 'Our Father', one 'Hail Mary', and one 'Glory Be.' The 'Way of the Cross' may be done before the Mass as a preparation for the celebration of the memorial of Our Lord's sacrifice. This spiritual work, which gives **plenary indulgences**, may be done at any time when visiting a church.

The vestiges of what seems to be the oldest 'Stations of the Cross' were found near 'Mary's house' near Ephesus, inspiring us to think that Mother Mary started this devotion. This house, where Mother Mary lived for the last nine years of her life, and these 'Stations of the Cross' were discovered through the writings of the visions received by the stigmatized mystic Sister Anne Catherine Emmerich (1774-1824).

Appendix 'G'
THE ROSARY

The Rosary is a summary of the Gospel that brings us to meditate on the story of our salvation. Indeed, as we recite the Rosary, we meditate on the joyous, luminous, sorrowful, and glorious mysteries of the life of Jesus and Mary, recalling how Jesus bought freedom and eternal life for all souls. Decade after decade we recall the birth, the life, the passion, and the death of Our Lord Jesus Christ, as well as how the Father glorified Him by His resurrection, His ascension into heaven, and the sending of His Spirit. The Rosary brings us to meditate on the purity, the obedience, and the faith of Mary, Virgin and Mother of God; as well as on the sorrows She suffered during the passion of Her son Jesus, and on Her glorious assumption into heaven and Her crowning as Queen of Heaven, Queen of all the angels and saints.

The Rosary is a simple prayer, humble like Mary, that all of us can say together with Her, Our Mother. As we pray the 'Hail Mary', we ask Her to 'Pray for us poor sinners', and since Our Lady always comes to the aid of Her children, we know that She joins Her prayer to ours. She makes our prayers most efficient because Jesus can never refuse anything His Mother asks of Him. During Her many apparitions, Our heavenly Mother has repeatedly asked us to pray the Rosary, and often repeated that it is a powerful weapon against evil. By praying the Rosary from the heart, we can drive away many dangers and many evils from ourselves, our home, our life, and our homeland. With our prayer made together with Mother Mary, we can obtain a change of hearts and conversion for ourselves and for many others. Praying the Rosary brings lasting peace.

THE HISTORY OF THE ROSARY

The prayers that compose the Rosary, and the mysteries under which they are gathered, have their origin in the Gospel. However, the origin of the devotion of praying the Rosary can be traced to the ninth century in Ireland when monks used to recite daily the 150 *Psalms of David,* a practice that the surrounding lay population wished to share. However, since many of them could not read, the monks suggested instead that they recite 150 *Our Fathers*. In order to keep count, people used pebbles and then strings on which they had made 150 knots, or 50 knots. The name given to this string of beads was the *Paternoster.*

In the mid-eleventh century in Italy, Saint Peter Damian spread the practice of reciting 150 *Angelic Psalters*,[43] thus, repeating 150 times: *(Lk 1:28)"Hail, full of grace, the Lord is with thee: blessed are thou among women"*. [DR]

---

43. *'Angelic'* because it is the salutation of the Archangel Gabriel to Mary: 'Hail, full of grace...', and *'Psalter'* because the complete rosary then had the same number of *Hail Marys* as there are psalms in the Book of the *Psalms of David*, that is 150.

In the early 13th century, Saint Dominic (1170-1221), who had sought Our Lady's help to fight the Albigensians' heresy in France, received apparitions of Our Lady near Toulouse. The Virgin Mary instructed him to preach the *Angelic Psalter* and how to preach it. She told him that the *Angelic Psalter* was the weapon to be used against heresy and sin. Inspired by the Holy Spirit, Saint Dominic preached the Rosary for the rest of his life. He founded the 'Order of Preachers' known as the 'Dominicans', whom have always been the foremost promoters of the Rosary. Saint Dominic also founded the 'Confraternity of the Holy Rosary', which retained its first fervor only for a century.

In 1261, Pope Urban VI added the salutation of Elizabeth to the Angelic Salutation: *(Lk 1:42)'Blessed are thou among women, and blessed is the fruit of thy womb',* to which he added the word 'Jesus'. Through the 1300s, many series of meditations were composed to accompany the *Angelic Psalter.* In the mid-fourteenth century, the 150 Salutations were grouped into decades preceded by the Our Father. Later (c. 1460-75), Our Lady chose the Dominican Bl. Alan de la Roche to revive the Confraternity of the Holy Rosary. He spread anew the devotion of the Rosary throughout Western Christendom, while promoting the 3 sets of mysteries grouped into 15 decades. It is at that time that the devotion was first referred to as the *Rosary,* which means *crown of roses*. Our Lady has revealed to some devotees that each time they say a Hail Mary they are giving Her a beautiful rose; each complete Rosary of fifteen (twenty[44]) decades makes Her a crown of roses, and each chaplet of five decades is a little wreath of flowers or a little crown of heavenly roses that we place on Jesus' head and on Hers.

In 1568, following the Council of Trent, the third part of the Hail Mary was added to the Angelic Salutation: *Holy Mary Mother of God...* (see p. 216). In 1569, Pope Pius V, himself a Dominican, established the 15 mystery Rosary as the official Church version. October 7th, the feast of 'Our Lady of the Rosary', commemorates the day in 1571 when - after Pope St. Pius V had asked the Christians to pray the Rosary for victory - Christian forces defeated the Turkish Moslems on the coast of Lepanto, Greece. In the 1700s, St. Louis-Marie Grignion de Montfort composed a set of rosary meditations, one for each of the mysteries, that to this day is still one of the most popular. Like many Pontiffs before him, (c. 1883) Pope Leo XIII declared Saint Dominic the institutor of the Rosary.

According to a popular belief, the daily recitation of the 15 decades of the Rosary honor in one year the number of wounds suffered by Our Lord during His Passion, 5,475 (365 X 15); one decade for each wound.

---

44. In his Apostolic letter of Oct.16th, 2002 *'Rosarium Virginis Mariae',* Pope John Paul II promotes anew the beauty and the power of the Rosary, and gives us a new series of mysteries, the five Mysteries of Light, bringing the rosary to a total of twenty decades.

PRAYING THE ROSARY AND THE CHAPLET

Traditionally, the recitation of the Rosary consists in praying 15 decades, and each decade is recited while honoring one of the 15 holy mysteries of the life of Our Lord and of Our Lady. Each mystery is meditated on, bead by bead, while saying one 'Our Father', ten 'Hail Marys', and one 'Glory be' during each decade. On October 16th 2002, Pope John Paul II added a new set of 5 mysteries to the Rosary, bringing to 20 the number of mysteries of the Holy Rosary. These new mysteries are known as the 'Luminous Mysteries' or the 'Mysteries of Light'.

The recitation of the chaplet tends to be more popular among devotees. This shorter form consists of the recitation of 5 decades while meditating on one set of 5 mysteries; either the joyful, the luminous, the sorrowful, or the glorious mysteries. The decades may be recited separately if the entire rosary, or chaplet, is completed on the same day.

When we say the Rosary, we pray to the Lord through the intercession of Our Lady, whom we should always invite to pray with us. We usually offer our recitation of the Rosary, or chaplet, for personal and specific petitions, and for Mother Mary's intentions such as peace, the conversion of sinners, and the return of Jesus Christ.

The Twenty Mysteries of the Holy Rosary [45]

THE JOYFUL MYSTERIES
(recited on Monday and Saturday)
1. The Annunciation, *(Lk 1:26-38).*
2. The Visitation, *(Lk 1:39-56).*
3. The Nativity of Our Lord, *(Mt 1:18-25; Lk 2:1-20).*
4. The Presentation of Our Lord, *(Lk 2:21-39).*
5. The Finding of the Child Jesus in the Temple, *(Lk 2:41-52).*

THE LUMINOUS MYSTERIES
(recited on Thursday)
1. Baptism of Jesus in the Jordan, *(Mt 3:17; Mk 1:9-11; Jn 1:29-36).*
2. Self-manifestation of Jesus at the wedding of Cana, *(Jn 2:1-12).*
3. Proclamation of the Kingdom of God and the Call to conversion, *(Mt 4:17; Mk 1:14-15; Lk 4:18-19.43; Jn 3:5).*
4. The Transfiguration of Our Lord, *(Mt 17:1-8; Mk 9:2-8; Lk 9:28-36).*
5. The Institution of the Eucharist at the Last Supper, *(Mt 26:26-30; Mk 14:22-26; Lk 22:14-20).*

---

45. In this presentation, the days recommended for the recitation of each set of mysteries are given according to the tradition of the Rosary, and according to Pope John Paul II's Apostolic letter *Rosarium Virginis Mariae.*

THE SORROWFUL MYSTERIES
(recited on Tuesday and Friday)
1. The Agony in the Garden,
   (Mt 26:38-46; Mk 14:32-41; Lk 22:40-46).
2. The Scourging at the Pillar,
   (Mt 26:67-68; Mk 14:65;Lk 22:63-65; Jn 19:1).
3. The Crowning with Thorns,
   (Mt 27:27-31; Mk 15:16-20; Jn 19:2-3).
4. The Carrying of the Cross,
   (Mt 27:31-32; Mk 15:20-22; Lk 23:26-31; Jn 19:16-17).
5. The Crucifixion and Death,
   (Mt 27:33-54; Mk 15:23-39; Lk 23:33-47; Jn 19:18-37).

THE GLORIOUS MYSTERIES
(recited on Wednesday and Sunday, except:
Sundays of Advent, the Joyful; Sundays of Lent, the Sorrowful)
1. The Resurrection of Our Lord,
   (Mt 28:1-10; Mk 16:1-11; Lk 24:1-12; Jn 20:1-18).
2. The Ascension of Our Lord,
   (Mk 16:19; Lk 24:50-51; Acts 1:9-11).
3. The Descent of the Holy Spirit,
   (Acts 2:1-4.41; Ps 104:30).
4. The Assumption of the Blessed Virgin Mary,
   (Rev 12:14; Jdt 13: 17-20; Ps 45:14-15).
5. The Coronation of Our Lady as Queen of Heaven,
   (Rev 12:1; Jdt 15:9-10; Sir 24:2-6).

Do you know about the Cenacles of the Marian Movement of Priests? The Cenacles are meetings whose purpose is to pray the Rosary while meditating on the mysteries, and also to read the messages that the Rev. Fr. Don Stefano Gobbi received from Our Lady between 1973 and 1997. Our Lady gave guidelines that favor peaceful and holy meetings, and that help deepen our understanding of the Gospel. The Cenacles are for everyone: priests, religious, laity, families, and children. For more information and documentation contact the Marian Movement of Priests, St. Francis, Maine, www.mmpusa.net, (207) 398-3375.

How to Pray the Rosary [46]

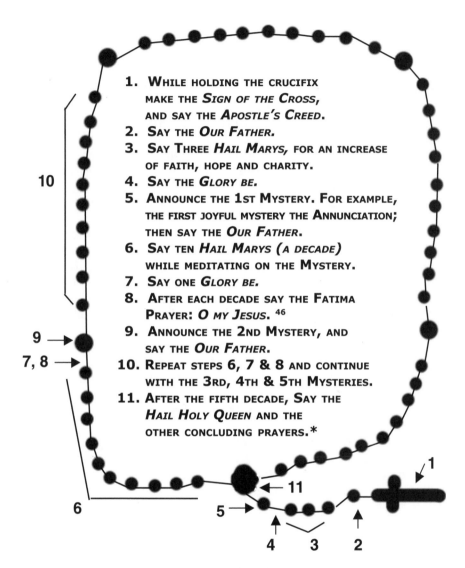

1. **While holding the crucifix make the *Sign of the Cross*, and say the *Apostle's Creed*.**
2. **Say the *Our Father*.**
3. **Say Three *Hail Marys*, for an increase of faith, hope and charity.**
4. **Say the *Glory be*.**
5. **Announce the 1st Mystery. For example, the first joyful mystery the *Annunciation*; then say the *Our Father*.**
6. **Say ten *Hail Marys* (a decade) while meditating on the *Mystery*.**
7. **Say one *Glory be*.**
8. **After each decade say the Fatima Prayer: *O my Jesus*. [46]**
9. **Announce the 2nd Mystery, and say the *Our Father*.**
10. **Repeat steps 6, 7 & 8 and continue with the 3rd, 4th & 5th Mysteries.**
11. **After the fifth decade, Say the *Hail Holy Queen* and the other concluding prayers.***

*Other concluding prayers:[46] 'O God, whose Only-begotten Son', and 'Prayer to Saint Michael.' Also pray: 'Sacred Heart of Jesus, have mercy on us'; 'Immaculate Heart of Mary, Pray for us'. Then, pray for the intentions of the Pope [47] saying: one *Our Father*, one *Hail Mary*, one *Glory be*. At the end make *The sign of the Cross*.

---

46. See Part Five, Appendix 'F', Essential Catholic Prayers, Prayers of the Rosary.
47. A plenary indulgence can be obtained under the usual conditions for praying for the intentions of the Pope, or for reciting the Rosary in a church or a chapel, or as a family or group. Plenary Indulgence and Conditions: see Part Five, Questions & Answers, Question 25; Catholic Glossary.

THE FIFTEEN PROMISES OF THE VIRGIN MARY
TO THOSE WHO RECITE THE ROSARY

1. Whoever shall faithfully serve me by the recitation of the Rosary shall receive signal graces.
2. I promise my special protection and the greatest graces to all those who shall recite the Rosary.
3. The Rosary shall be a powerful armor against hell, it will destroy vice, decrease sin, and defeat heresies.
4. It will cause virtue and good works to flourish; it will obtain for souls the abundant mercy of God; it will withdraw the hearts of people from the love of the world and its vanities, and will lift them to the desire of eternal things. Oh, that souls would sanctify themselves by this means.
5. The soul which recommends itself to me by the recitation of the Rosary, shall not perish.
6. Whoever shall recite the Rosary devoutly, applying themselves to the consideration of its Sacred Mysteries shall never be conquered by misfortune. God will not chastise them in His justice, they shall not perish by an unprovided death; if they be just, they shall remain in the grace of God, and become worthy of eternal life.
7. Whoever shall have a true devotion for the Rosary shall not die without the Sacraments of the Church.
8. Those who are faithful to recite the Rosary shall have during their life and at their death the light of God and the plenitude of His graces; at the moment of death they shall participate in the merits of the Saints in Paradise.
9. I shall deliver from purgatory those who have been devoted to the Rosary.
10. The faithful children of the Rosary shall merit a high degree of glory in Heaven.
11. You shall obtain all you ask of me by the recitation of the Rosary.
12. All those who propagate the Holy Rosary shall be aided by me in their necessities.
13. I have obtained from my Divine Son that all the advocates of the Rosary shall have for intercessors the entire celestial court during their life and at the hour of death.
14. All who recite the Rosary are my children, and brothers and sisters of my only Son, Jesus Christ.
15. Devotion of my Rosary is a great sign of predestination.

October 2002 to October 2003 was the Year of the Rosary
"Say the Rosary every day, to obtain peace for the world."
— *Our Lady of Fatima, 1917*—

Our Lady gave these promises to St. Dominic & Bl.Alan de la Roche. The Archbishop of New York (1919-1938) gave the Imprimatur for this English translation by P. J. Hayes.

THE TWELVE PROMISES OF JESUS CHRIST
TO THOSE DEVOTED TO HIS SACRED HEART

St. Margaret Mary Alacoque, herself consecrated to the Sacred Heart as a child, was given these promises while receiving visions of the Sacred Heart (1673-1675) at Paray-le-Monial, France. Her confessor, St. Claude de la Colombiere, helped promote the devotion and the promises.

1. *I will give them all the graces necessary in their state in life.*
2. *I will establish peace in their homes.*
3. *I will comfort them in all their afflictions.*
4. *I will be their secure refuge during life and, above all, in death.*
5. *I will bestow abundant blessings upon all their undertakings.*
6. *Sinners shall find in my Heart the source and the infinite ocean of mercy.*
7. *By devotion to my Heart tepid souls shall grow fervent.*
8. *Fervent souls shall quickly mount to high perfection.*
9. *I will bless every place where a picture of my Heart shall be set up and honored.*
10. *I will give to priests the gift of touching the most hardened hearts.*
11. *Those who promote this devotion shall have their names written in my Heart, never to be blotted out.*
12. *I will grant the grace of final penitence to those who communicate (receive Holy Communion) on the first Friday of nine consecutive months.*

The devotion to the Sacred Heart first consists in becoming aware of the love that our heavenly Father continuously pours out through the Sacred Heart of Jesus, pierced for us on the cross. As we become conscious of this infinite fount and ocean of mercy that is offered to us, then we seek to honor the Sacred Heart of Jesus. We may start by offering our own heart to Jesus and praying: 'Sacred Heart of Jesus, have mercy on us, I trust in You.' As we honor the Sacred Heart, our hearts open more deeply to receive God's love and to become more compassionate.

Besides placing and honoring a picture of the Sacred Heart (9), promoting the devotion (11), receiving communion on nine first Fridays (12), and meditating on the twelve promises, we may honor the Sacred Heart through devotions such as: the Prayer, the Litanies, and the Consecration to the Sacred Heart; the 'Efficacious Novena to the Sacred Heart of Jesus' (said daily by St. Pio); and the family enthronement to the Sacred Hearts of Jesus and Mary. Besides devoting the month of June to the Sacred Heart, the Church celebrates the solemnity of the 'Sacred Heart' on the third Friday following the feast of Pentecost, and the 'Divine Mercy Sunday' on the first Sunday after Easter.[47a]

47a. Feasts of the Sacred Heart, the Immaculate Heart, and Divine Mercy Sunday: see Part Five, Church Norms, II- Requisites for the celebration of the Mass, Liturgical Seasons & Feasts; and the 'Divine Mercy Chaplet' (received by St. Faustina, see p. 218).

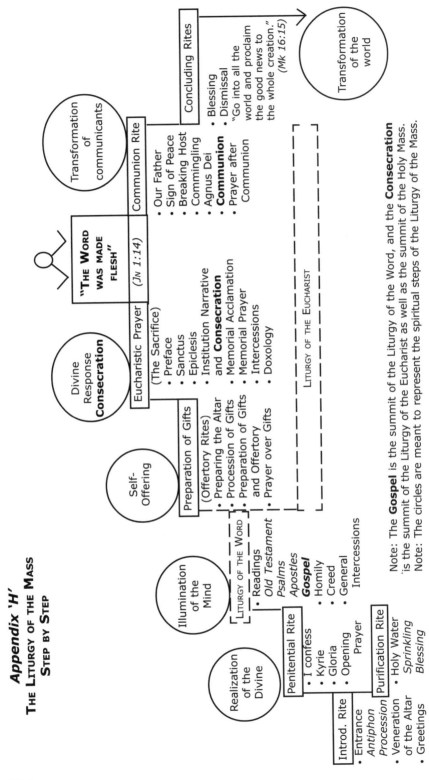

Appendix 'H'
THE LITURGY OF THE MASS
STEP BY STEP

LITURGY OF THE WORD

Realization of the Divine

Introd. Rite
- Entrance *Antiphon*
- *Procession*
- Veneration of the Altar
- Greetings

Penitential Rite
- I confess
- Kyrie
- Gloria
- Opening Prayer

Purification Rite
- Holy Water *Sprinkling Blessing*

Illumination of the Mind
- Readings *Old Testament Psalms Apostles* **Gospel**
- Homily
- Creed
- General Intercessions

LITURGY OF THE EUCHARIST

Self-Offering

Preparation of Gifts
(Offertory Rites)
- Preparing the Altar
- Procession of Gifts
- Preparation of Gifts and Offertory
- Prayer over Gifts

Divine Response **Consecration**

Eucharistic Prayer
(The Sacrifice)
- Preface
- Sanctus
- Epiclesis
- Institution Narrative and **Consecration**
- Memorial Acclamation
- Memorial Prayer
- Intercessions
- Doxology

"THE WORD WAS MADE FLESH" *(JN 1:14)*

Transformation of communicants

Communion Rite
- Our Father
- Sign of Peace
- Breaking Host
- Commingling
- Agnus Dei
- **Communion**
- Prayer after Communion

Concluding Rites
- Blessing
- Dismissal
"Go into all the world and proclaim the good news to the whole creation." *(MK 16:15)*

Transformation of the world

Note: The **Gospel** is the summit of the Liturgy of the Word, and the **Consecration** is the summit of the Liturgy of the Eucharist as well as the summit of the Holy Mass.
Note: The circles are meant to represent the spiritual steps of the Liturgy of the Mass.

234

Appendix 'H'
STRUCTURE OF THE EUCHARISTIC PRAYER
THE EIGHT CHIEF ELELMENTS

Chief Elements \ Eucharistic Prayer	I - Roman Canon	II	III	IV
May be used	Always, Feasts of Apostles & Saints therein mentioned; and Octave of Christmas & Easter.	Weekdays, Mass for the Dead, and special circumstances.	Sundays, Feast days, and Masses for the Dead.	Sundays in Ordinary Time, and Masses with no specific Preface.
1. Preface	None of its own - Any.	Its Own, or Any.	None of Its Own - Any.	Its Own - Unchangeable.
2. Sanctus	YES	YES	YES	YES
1. Praise to the Father	YES	NO	YES	YES
7. Intercession:	: for the Church : for the Living : for the Saints	NO	NO	NO
3. Invocation of the Holy Spirit	YES	YES	YES	YES
4. Institution Narrative and Consecration	YES	YES	YES	YES
5. Memorial Acclamation	YES	YES	YES	YES
6. Memorial Prayer	YES	YES	YES	YES
7. Intercession:	: for the Dead : for the Saints	: for the Church : for the Dead : for the Saints	: for the Saints : for the Church : for the Dead	: for the Church : for the Dead : for the Saints
8. Doxology	YES	YES	YES	YES

Note 1: The Eucharistic Prayer is also known as the *anaphora*, meaning 'repetition for effect'. These prayers are repeated at every Mass.
Note 2: The 8 chief elements of the Eucharistic Prayer: see GIRM [55] 79; Part Three, Liturgy of the Eucharist, the 8 chief elements.
Note 3: According to the occasion, the priest chooses one of the 4 Eucharistic Prayers, see GIRM [322] 365.
Note 4: According to the occasion, the priest chooses from among the 84 Prefaces found in the *Sacramentary, Roman Missal.*
Note 5: Eucharistic Prayer: also see *Redemptionis Sacramentum,* nos. 51, 54, 56.

235

Appendix 'I'
Redemptionis Sacramentum

INSTRUCTION: ON CERTAIN MATTERS TO BE OBSERVED OR TO BE AVOIDED REGARDING THE MOST HOLY EUCHARIST. CONGREGATION FOR DIVINE WORSHIP AND THE DISCIPLINE OF THE SACRAMENTS (03/ 25/ 2004).

- SOME HIGHLIGHTS-

Note: this text is not a strict quotation, but rather, excerpts taken from the Instruction *Redemptionis Sacramentum* (bfa).

[4] The liturgical reform inaugurated by the [Second] Council has greatly contributed to a more conscious, active and fruitful **participation** in the Holy Sacrifice of the Altar on the part of the faithful. [However] **abuses** against the nature of the Liturgy and the Sacraments, [and] the tradition and the authority of the Church [have developed]. [5] The liturgical words and rites, are a faithful expression, **matured over the centuries**, of the understanding of Christ, and they teach us to think as he himself does. [6] Abuses [which] contribute to the **obscuring** of the Catholic faith and doctrine concerning this wonderful sacrament, [7] are [often] rooted in a **false** understanding of **liberty**. [8] Yet the Eucharist is too great a gift to tolerate ambiguity or depreciation. [9] Abuses are often based on ignorance, [and] involve a rejection of those elements whose deeper meaning is not understood and whose **antiquity** is not recognized, [and of] practices received universally from apostolic and **unbroken tradition**.

[10] The Church herself has no power over those things which were **established by Christ** himself and which constitute an unchangeable part of the Liturgy. [11] The Mystery of the Eucharist is too great for anyone to permit himself to treat it according to his **own whim**. [12] The Catholic people have the right that the Sacrifice of the Holy Mass should be celebrated for them in an **integral manner**, according to the entire doctrine of the Church's Magisterium.

[27] As early as the year 1970, the Apostolic See announced the cessation of all **experimentation** as regards the celebration of Holy Mass and reiterated the same in 1988. [36] The Christian people, a chosen race, a **royal priesthood**, a holy people, a people God has made his own, manifests its coherent and **hierarchical** ordering. For the common priesthood of the faithful and the ministerial or hierarchical Priesthood, though they **differ in essence** and not only in degree, are ordered to one another, for **both partake**, each in its own way, of the one Priesthood of Christ. [37] All of Christ's faithful, **freed from their sins** and incorporated into the Church through Baptism may **offer themselves** as a living and holy sacrifice pleasing to God, by their works, giving witness to Christ.

[37] **Participation** of the lay faithful in the Eucharist cannot be equated with mere presence, and less a passive one, but is rather to be regarded as a **true exercise** of faith and of the baptismal dignity. [38] When stripped of its **sacrificial** meaning, [Mass] is understood as if a simple fraternal banquet. [39] For promoting an active **participation** [of the faithful] the Council fostered acclamations, responses, psalmody, antiphons, and canticles, actions or movements and gestures, and called for sacred silence. In the songs, the melodies, the choice of prayers and readings, the homily, the prayer of the faithful, the decoration of the Church building according to the **various seasons**, there is ample possibility for introducing a **certain variety** by which the riches of the liturgical tradition will also be more clearly evident.

[40] It does not follow that everyone must necessarily have something concrete to do beyond the actions and gestures, as if a specific liturgical ministry must **necessarily** be given to the individuals to be carried out by them. Catechetical instruction should strive to instill anew a **sense of deep wonder** before the greatness of the mystery of faith that is the Eucharist. The Church prostrates herself in **adoration** before the Lord who was crucified, suffered and died, was buried and arose, and perpetually exclaims to Him who is clothed in the fullness of his divine splendor: "My Lord and my God!"

[41] For promoting and nourishing [the proper] understanding of **liturgical participation,** the celebration of the Liturgy of the Hours, the use of the sacramentals and exercises of Christian **popular piety** are extremely helpful. [42] The Church has not come together by human volition; rather, she **has been called** together by God in the Holy Spirit, and she responds through faith.

[43] It is appropriate that a number of persons distribute among themselves and exercise various ministries or different parts of the same ministry. [44] The most important of these ministries are those of **acolyte and lector**, as well as the functions of **preparing the hosts, washing the liturgical linens**. All should do exclusively and fully that which pertains to them. [46] The lay faithful called to assist at liturgical celebrations should be **well instructed** and must be those whose **Christian life, morals and fidelity to the Church's Magisterium** recommend them. [47] It is laudable to maintain the custom by which **boys** or youths, customarily termed servers, provide **service of the altar** after the manner of acolytes, and receive catechesis regarding their function. A great number of [**vocations**] over the centuries have come from among boys such as these.

Appendix 'J'
SUNDAY CELEBRATIONS IN THE ABSENCE OF A PRIEST

When no priests are available to celebrate the **Sunday Mass**, the faithful may gather for a service that includes the Sunday readings and the distribution of communion provided that the gathering takes place in a church or a chapel, that it is conducted in accordance with the Church's norms, and that the authorization of the local Bishop has been given. Since celebrations in the absence of a priest do not include the Mass, the faithful should make every possible effort to attend the obligatory Sunday Mass at a nearby parish.

REDEMPTIONIS SACRAMENTUM, 164 -166, Congregation for Divine Worship and the Discipline of the Sacraments, March 25, 2004, excerpts.

*[164] Sunday celebrations [in absence of a priest], are **to be considered** altogether **extraordinary**. [165] It is necessary to avoid any sort of confusion between this type of gathering and the celebration of the Eucharist. The diocesan Bishops, therefore, should prudently discern whether Holy Communion ought to be distributed in these gatherings. [164] Deacons or lay members of Christ's faithful who are assigned a part in such celebrations by the diocesan Bishop should strive "to keep alive in the community a genuine '**hunger' for the Eucharist**, so that no opportunity for the celebration of Mass will ever be missed." [165] It will be preferable, moreover, when both a Priest and a Deacon are absent, that the **various parts be distributed among several faithful** rather than having a single lay member of the faithful direct the whole celebration alone. **Nor is it ever appropriate** to refer to any member of the lay faithful as "presiding" over the celebration. [166] The diocesan Bishop, must **not easily grant permission for such celebrations to be held on weekdays**, especially in places where it was possible or would be possible to have the celebration of Mass on the preceding or the following Sunday.* bfa

DIRECTORY FOR SUNDAY CELEBRATIONS IN THE ABSENCE OF A PRIEST, Chap. III: Order of Celebration, Congregation for Divine Worship and the Discipline of the Sacraments, June 2, 1988, International Commission on English in the Liturgy, excerpts.

*35. The order to be followed in a Sunday celebration that **does not include Mass** consists of two parts, the celebration of the word of God and the giving of holy communion. Nothing that is proper to Mass, and particularly the presentation of the gifts and the eucharistic prayer, is to be inserted into the celebration. 38. When a **deacon presides** at the celebration, he acts **in accord with his ministry** in regard to the greetings, the prayers, the gospel reading and homily, the giving of communion, and the dismissal and blessing. He wears the vestments* *proper to his ministry, that is, the alb with stole, and, as circumstances suggest, the dalmatic. He uses the presidential chair.*

*39. The **layperson is not to use words that are proper to a priest or deacon** and is to omit rites that are too readily associated with the Mass, for example, greetings - especially **"The Lord be with you"** - and dismissals. [The layperson does not kiss the altar.] 40. The lay leader wears vesture that is suitable for his or her function or the vesture prescribed by the bishop. He or she does not use the presidential chair, but another **chair prepared outside the sanctuary**. Since the altar is the table of sacrifice and of the paschal banquet, its only use in this celebration is for the rite of communion, when the consecrated bread is placed on it before communion is given.*

41. The following is an outline of the elements of the celebration.
> *a. **Introductory rites**. The purpose is to form the gathered faithful into a community and for them to dispose themselves for the celebration.*
> *b. **Liturgy of the word**. [In order that the participants may retain the word of God, there should be an explanation of the readings or a period of silence for reflection on what has been heard.]*
> *c. **Thanksgiving**. [The faithful praise the glory and mercy of God.]*
> *d. **Communion rites**. These are an expression and accomplishment of communion with Christ and with his members, especially with those who on this same day take part in the eucharistic sacrifice. [The faithful are to be frequently reminded that even when they receive communion outside Mass they are united to the eucharistic sacrifice.]*
> *e. **Concluding rites**. These point to the connection existing between the liturgy and the Christian life.* bfa

CEREMONIES OF THE MODERN ROMAN RITE, Chapter 10, A Sunday Celebration in the Absence of a Priest. (In the following quoted articles, the abbreviation DSCAP is used for: Directory for Sunday Celebrations in the Absence of a Priest, which is referred to on page 238 - bfa.)

*"653. If an **instituted acolyte** leads the service, he wears an alb. A **lay person** who leads this act of worship wears vesture which is suitable for his or her function or vesture prescribed by the bishop (cf. DSCAP, 40). Extraordinary ministers or licensed catechists may wear some **symbol** of their office, where this is customary. **Religious** wear their habit. All of these persons are described below as the "leader".*

*654. The celebration **builds on the rite for Holy Communion outside Mass**, and the same preparations are made. However, in the celebration of this rite, the following significant variations should be noted.*

*655.1. To symbolize the absence of an ordained minister,... in some places a **stole** is draped over the **empty chair** as a reminder.*

*656.2. During the rite, the leader "acts as **one among equals**" (cf. DSCAP, 39). He or she does not use priestly greetings, such as "The Lord be with you", and rites readily associated with the Mass are omitted, especially any kind of "Eucharistic Prayer" or similar prayer. Therefore, **a different form of greeting is used** at the beginning of the rite, and at the conclusion **a lay form** of the blessing is used as the leader makes the sign of the cross on himself.*

*657.3. The Liturgy of the Word [readings] is taken **from the Sunday Mass**. However, as **only a priest or deacon may preach**, it is desirable that the leader read a homily prepared by the pastor, but only according to the decision of the episcopal conference in such a matter (cf. DSCAP, 43). The **General Intercessions** are to follow an established series of intentions, not forgetting intentions proposed by the bishop and prayer for vocations to Holy Orders (cf. DSCAP, 44).*

*658.4. A **thanksgiving** is to be part of the celebration. **All stand and face the altar** for the thanksgiving, perhaps a **psalm**, a **hymn** such as the Gloria, a **canticle** such as the Magnificat, or a **litany**. But the thanksgiving is not to resemble or take the form of a Eucharistic Prayer or Preface taken from the Roman Missal. The corporate [communal] thanksgiving may be made either after the General Intercessions or after Communion **and/or** as an act of corporate **adoration before Communion** (cf. DSCAP, 45).*

*659.5. **Before the Lord's Prayer**, the leader brings the Eucharist from the place of reservation, **places the ciborium on the altar** and genuflects. The thanksgiving in the form of corporate eucharistic adoration may follow. This **time of adoration** includes a suitable hymn or psalm or a litany addressed to the Eucharistic Lord. The leader and the assembly kneel during the adoration (cf. DSCAP, 45.2). This act underlines the fact that **the Eucharist is already here**, already "given" by God through the hands of a priest. Therefore it seems to be an option which should be favored strongly at these celebrations. After adoration, all stand and the leader introduces the **Lord's Prayer**, which is sung or said by all. At a Sunday celebration when Holy Communion is not given, the Lord's Prayer is still to be part of the rite (cf. DSCAP, 48).*

*660.6. If possible, **bread consecrated on that same Sunday** should be used.(cf. DSCAP, 47). But this is usually not feasible in the situations where these celebrations are authorized. Nevertheless, where the Eucharist is reserved for these celebrations, every effort should be made to ensure that the consecrated Species is fresh [less than two weeks old].*

*661. The **texts of rites to be used** on these occasions are to be drawn up by the episcopal conference in collaboration with the Holy See. The diocesan **bishop will provide other directives** concerning the role of the lay person who leads this act of eucharistic worship."*

SUMMARY OF THE DIRECTORY FOR
SUNDAY CELEBRATIONS IN THE ABSENCE OF A PRIEST

(For these celebrations, the only time lay ministers may be in the sanctuary is for the readings of the Holy Scriptures and to place and remove the ciborium of Hosts from the altar. They are not to lead from the sanctuary nor stand at the altar.)

Introductory Rites:
    The Entrance Antiphon of that Sunday, and/or a Hymn;
    The Sign of the Cross;
    A Greeting - a lay greeting must be a different formula than the
        one from the Order of Mass: 'The grace of Our Lord...';
    The Penitential Rite is omitted.

Liturgy of the Word: readings found in the Lectionary for that Sunday.
    First Reading; Responsorial Psalm; and Second Reading;
    Gospel Acclamation;
    Gospel Reading - omit the greeting:'The Lord be with you...';
    Homily - if prepared by the pastor may be read by a layperson;
    Period of Silence;
    Recitation of the Creed;
    The Prayer of the Faithful - as established for that Sunday.

Thanksgiving (standing) - may be done before or after the communion;
    Suggestions: Psalm 100, 113, 118, 136, 147, or 150; a hymn -
    such as the Gloria; or a canticle - such as the Canticle of Mary.

Communion Rite: the Eucharistic Prayer is omitted.
    The Eucharist is placed on the altar - no layperson stands at the
        altar during the prayers; all kneel for a time of adoration, an
        adoration hymn is sung or the Divine Praises may be recited;
    The Lord's Prayer - intro: e.g. Let us pray the Our Father;
    The Sign of Peace - intro: e.g. Let us wish peace to one another;
    The Agnus Dei is followed by the 'Lord I am not worthy...' ;
    Communion Antiphon - the extraordinary minister takes his own
        communion at the altar, and after a moment comes to the faithful;
    Communion - a hymn may be sung during communion;
    Period of silence, then a psalm or song of praise may be sung.

Concluding Rite:
    Dismissal - only if a deacon is present;
    Blessing - a lay form of blessing: e.g., May the Good Lord bless us,
    (signing himself) The Father, The Son & the Holy Spirit, Amen.;
    Concluding Hymn - a hymn may be sung.

Catholic
Glossary

Ambo: lectern, pulpit, furnishing of the church's sanctuary, stand from which the holy scripture readings are read, the homily is preached, and the prayer of the faithful is offered.

Anointing: ancient custom by which is made sacred the person, place, or thing anointed, dedicating them to God; e.g., priests, kings, prophets, church... (cf. 1Sam 16:13, 2Co 1:21.22, 1Jn 2:20). Christ is the Anointed One, the Messiah. Anointing with oil is a sign of joy and honor, the oil representing the Holy Spirit. In the Church, the faithful are anointed with sacred oil during the sacraments of baptism, confirmation, holy orders and anointing of the sick. The ministry of anointing is reserved to the priest. Consecration of the anointing oils: see Chrism Mass.

Anointing of the sick and/or of the dying: *"The sacrament of Anointing of the Sick is given to those who are seriously ill [or dying] by anointing them on the forehead and hands with duly blessed oil."* [48] Also known as 'extreme unction', this sacrament is part of the 'Last Rites': the sacraments of *"Penance, the Anointing of the Sick and the Eucharist as viaticum constitute at the end of Christian life 'the sacraments that prepare for our heavenly homeland' or the sacraments that complete the earthly pilgrimage."* [48a]

Apostolic Succession: *"authoritative and unbroken transmission of the mission and powers conferred by Jesus Christ on St. Peter and the Apostles from them to the present pope and bishops."* [48b]

Archbishop: title given to a bishop in charge of an archdiocese.
Archdiocese: an ecclesiastical jurisdiction headed by an archbishop. An archdiocese is usually a metropolitan see, i.e., the principal diocese of a group of dioceses comprising an ecclesiastical province.

Baptistery: in a church, a chapel for the baptismal fonts, thus, a place for administering Baptism. Traditionally, baptisteries were adjacent or near the church's entrance, a position symbolizing the fact that through this sacrament, the faithful are received into the Church and incorporated in Christ. To emphasize the relationship of Baptism to the Eucharist, contemporary pastoral and liturgical practice favors placement of the baptistery near the sanctuary and altar, or the use of a portable baptismal font in the same location.

Basilica: church endowed by the pope with this special title, because of its antiquity, dignity, historical importance or significance as a center of worship. The presence of a yellow and red stripped umbrella indicates that the basilica bears privilege of giving indulgences.

48. CCC 1513, cf. CIC, can. 847 §1.
48a. CCC 1525. See also in this Glossary; Viaticum and Chrism Mass.
48b. *A Catholic Dictionary*, see Part Five, Bibliography.

Bishop: (Ordinary) priest who has received plenitude of sacerdoce (priesthood/holy orders) and who has authority and responsibility to ordain, confirm, and govern the diocese, giving it spiritual direction.

Blessed Sacrament: the Eucharist, consecrated bread and wine hosting the real presence of God; Body and Blood, Soul and Divinity. The Blessed Sacrament is consecrated and distributed during the Holy Mass. Hosts of the Blessed Sacrament are kept in the Eucharistic reserve, the tabernacle, to be brought to the sick who could not attend Mass. A large Host is kept in the tabernacle for worship and adoration.

Book of the Gospels: as for the Lectionary, the Book of the Gospels is the official compilation of Holy Scripture readings for the Mass, but specifically those chosen for the Gospel readings. The Book of Gospels is carried by the deacon, or a lay reader, in the entrance procession at the beginning of the Mass.

Bread of offering, bread of the Presence, (cf. Lev 24:5-9; 1Sam 21:4). Twelve cakes of unleavened bread, representing the twelve tribes of Israel dedicated to divine service, were placed on a table set before the Ark of the Covenant. On each Sabbath day, the priests would eat the bread of the Presence in the holy place, and replace it with fresh bread.

Cardinal: prelate of the Church who usually was first a bishop, and then became a member of the Sacred College, the College of Cardinals. Cardinals are appointed by the Pope to act as his counselors. Gathered in conclave, Cardinals elect the Pope.

Catechesis: the process of 'echoing' the Gospel, of introducing young people or adult converts to the main elements of the Christian faith. The Catechesis is based on scripture, tradition and liturgy, as well as on the teaching authority and life of the Church. Its purpose is to develop a living, explicit, and active faith through the liturgical and sacramental life of the Church.

Catechism: Book that contains explanations of dogmas and morals, that instructs on principles and mysteries of the Christian faith.

Catechumen: an unbaptized person who is undergoing catechesis in preparation for entrance into the Church through the sacrament of baptism. A Catechumen is one who studies the Catechism.

Cathedra: official chair/throne of the bishop found in the sanctuary of a Cathedral.
Cathedral: episcopal church of the diocese, proper to the bishop. When a Cardinal has office in a diocese, then he, who is first a bishop, is the head of that diocese, and his church is the local cathedral.

Catholic: The word Catholic, which means general or universal, first occurs in Christian use in letters of St-Ignatius of Antioch (d. 107) to the Smyrnaeans: *'Wheresoever the bishop shall appear, there let the people be, even as where Jesus is, there is the Catholic Church.'*

Catholicism: religion of Christians who acknowledge the Pope's authority concerning doctrines of faith and morals because he is the successor and spiritual heir of St. Peter, whom was appointed by Jesus Christ. The essentials of the Catholic faith are contained in the Creed.[49] Catholics believe that by the means of the sacraments, of which there are seven, God gives them graces of redemption that Christ obtained through His passion, death and resurrection. Catholics believe that in receiving the sacrament of the Eucharist, the greatest of the sacraments, they truly receive the Body and Blood, the Soul and Divinity of Jesus Christ.

Chalice: sacred vessel used by the priest during the Holy Mass to consecrate the wine into the Blood of Christ.

Chrism Mass: Mass that takes place at all cathedrals on Holy Thursday gathering around the bishop: priests, deacons, religious and lay ministers of the diocese, and during which the bishop consecrates the oils (olive/vegetable) for the whole diocese. They are: 1- the sacred chrism (oil mixed with balm), used for anointing at baptism, confirmation, ordination of priests and bishops, and dedication of churches and altars; 2- the oil for catechumens, used at baptism before the anointing with chrism, and poured with chrism into the baptismal water blessed in Easter Vigil ceremonies; and 3- the oil used for anointing the sick. The sacred chrism and oils are reserved in an **ambry** in all the parish churches. [49a]

Christians: those who have been baptized in the name of Jesus Christ: 'In the name of the Father, and the Son, and the Holy Spirit', and choose to live according to His Gospel. *(Acts 11:26)"It was in Antioch that the disciples were first called Christians."* [NAB]

Church: *"The word 'Church' means 'convocation'. It designates the assembly of those whom God's Word 'convokes', i.e., gathers together to form the People of God, and who themselves, nourished with the Body and Blood of Christ, become the Body of Christ."* [49ab]
Church: a place of Christian worship.

Ciboria: plural of ciborium. **Ciborium:** sacred vessel with a lid in the shape of a canopy used by the priest to consecrate Hosts and distribute them to the faithful at Communion. Consecrated Hosts are reserved in a ciborium in the tabernacle for worship outside of Mass and for the sick.

49. Creed (Nicene and Apostle's): Part Three, Liturgy of the Word, Profession of Faith.
49a. Cf. CCC 1183, 1241, 1289, 1294-1297, 1574.
49b. CCC 777.

Communion-plate: liturgical vessel in the shape of a small metal plate with a handle that the server places under the communicants' chin to secure the Host during communion. Its use is especially recommended for those receiving communion on the tongue.

Communion-rail: altar rail, found mainly in churches built prior to Vatican II. It is a low decorative railing installed across the front of the sanctuary that has two functions. First, it separates the sanctuary from the nave, as a reminder that the sanctuary is a place set apart for the Lord; it is the holy place where the sacrifice of the Mass takes place and where the Lord Himself dwells in the tabernacle. The sanctuary used to be reserved for the clergy and the servers. Secondly, the communion-rail is an extension of the main altar. As the faithful kneel side by side at the altar rail to receive Holy Communion, it is as though they receive from the altar of the sacrifice itself. Kneeling at the altar rail was the universal way to receive communion prior to the Second Vatican Council. This form of receiving communion has been maintained in some churches and shrines.

Confessional, Reconciliation room: the place designated for the celebration of the sacrament of Penance. The confessional appeared after the Council of Trent to give more secrecy and anonymity to the penitent. Confessionals are booth-like structures built along the walls of the nave for the purpose of hearing confessions. They have separate compartments for the priest and the penitent, and a window with grating or screen between them. Since Vatican II, confessionals have been replaced or supplemented by small reconciliation rooms arranged so that the priest and the penitent can sit and speak face to face.

Congregation for Divine Worship and the Discipline of the Sacraments: one of the nine congregations (governing agencies) of the Roman Curia that serve the Vatican and the local Churches with authority granted by the Pope. The role and authority of this congregation is to supervise everything pertaining to the promotion and regulation of the liturgy, primarily the sacraments.

Corporal: from the Latin *corpus,* body. The corporal is a small sacred linen, white, square, and with an embroidered cross, on which the priest prepares and offers the Sacrifice of the Mass. It is also used as a 'throne' for the monstrance during Exposition of the Blessed Sacrament.[49c]

Credence: table for the service at the altar on which are placed the vessels and the linens used during the Mass. The credence is located along the sanctuary wall to the left of the altar as seen from the nave.

49c. Corporal: see Part Three, Liturgy of the Eucharist: Offertory Rites, Preparation of the Altar and Procession of the Gifts; Communion Rite, Purification of the Sacred Vessels; and After the Mass, The Sacristy, and Eucharistic Adoration.

Crucifix: a cross bearing the figure of the body of Christ, representative of the Sacrifice of the Cross.

Doctrine, Catholic: body of revealed and defined truth/dogma regarding faith and morals that the Church teaches according to the authority She received from Christ through the Apostles.
Dogma, Catholic: fundamental element of truth revealed by God that one must believe in order to be saved.

Ecumenical Council: assembly of the college of bishops that must be held with and under the presidency of the pope, which has supreme authority over the Church in matters pertaining to faith, morals, worship and discipline. They gather to discuss and plan common action for doctrinal and pastoral good of the whole Church. The Council of Jerusalem (51) *(Acts 15)* was a preamble to the Church's Ecumenical Councils. Here are some of them: the first council was **Nicene I** (325), defined the Nicene Creed;[50] **Ephesus** (431), defined Mother Mary to be *Theotokos* - Mother of God, thus, condemning the Nestorian heresy; **Nicene II** (787), condemned Iconoclasm which considered the veneration of holy images idolatry; **Lateran IV** (1215), ordered annual reception of the sacraments of penance and of the Eucharist and defined the term 'transubstantiation'; **Trent** (1545-1563) reasserted traditional Catholic doctrine in reaction to the Protestant reformation, begins the counter reformation; **Vatican I** (1869-1870), defined the pope's infallibility; and **Vatican II** (1962-1965), - 21st and latest Council - sought to modernize its forms and institutions, produced 16 documents reflecting pastoral orientation towards renewal and reformation in the Church, emphasizing the full development of the Church - of all the faithful - and the fulfillment of its mission.

Epistle: from the Greek word for 'letter', the 21 Epistles are books of the New Testament that were written as letters to early Christian communities to exhort them and instruct them on doctrine and morals.

Eucharist: from the Greek *eucharistia*, meaning 'thanksgiving', the Eucharist is the **Blessed Sacrament**, the **sacrament of the Body and Blood of Jesus Christ**. During the liturgy of the Eucharist we give thanks to the Father for our salvation and give Him due worship. The Eucharist is confected during the Holy Mass when the offerings of bread and wine, presented by the priest, are transformed into the Body and Blood of Christ (see 'transubstantiation'). Christ is then made substantially present in the Eucharist and given in Holy Communion to the faithful. The sacraments of the Eucharist and of Holy Orders were instituted by Jesus Christ at the Last Supper to perpetuate His sacrifice until He comes again. The Eucharist is the food that keeps the Church alive.

---

50. Nicene Creed: see Part Three, Liturgy of the Word, Profession of Faith.

Evangeliary: in French *Evangile,* from the Greek *euaggelion: eu*=good, *aggelion*=announce or news. The Evangeliary is better known as the Book of the Gospels (see Glossary).

Equinox: days of the year when the hours of day light are equal to the hours of night. This happens twice a year, at spring and at fall. The date for Easter is set on the first Sunday following the first full moon after the spring equinox.[51] The dates for the beginning and end of the liturgical seasons and for many feasts are set in reference to the date of Easter.

Ex Cathedra: the pope is said to speak *Ex Cathedra* when, in virtue of his office as shepherd of the Church, he defines a doctrine of faith or morals. He is then infallible, as defined by the First Vatican Council.

Gospel: from the Anglo-Saxon term 'god-spell' meaning 'good news' or 'good tidings'. In Christian use, Gospel means the Good News of salvation proclaimed by Jesus Christ and handed on in written form by the Evangelists St. Matthew, St. Mark, St. Luke, and St. John. The Church teaches and proclaims the Gospel as the summit of divine revelation. (Also see Part Three, Liturgy of the Word, Gospel).

Gregory I, the Great, Saint: (540-604) Born in Rome, the 64th pope (590-604); we owe to him the compilation and arrangement of liturgical chant, which was named after him, *Gregorian chant.* It is a form and style of sacred chant and music that was a highly regarded standard of liturgical music for centuries. Pope Gregory 1st the Great introduced the custom of *Gregorian Mass*, that is a set of thirty Masses said for the soul of a deceased on thirty consecutive days, which are believed to help getting holy souls out of purgatory[51a] and into heaven.

Gregory XIII: (c. 1502-1585) born in Bologna, the 226th Pope (1572-1585). For a century, the Church had supervised the reform of the Julian calendar (from Julius Caesar), which by the 1500's was ten days out of step per year. Pope Gregory XIII insured the completion of the work and gave us our actual calendar, the Gregorian calendar, in 1582. It was quickly adopted in most European countries. The Gregorian calendar is considered accurate to within one day in 20,000 years.

Host: from the Latin *hostia*, victim. Communion bread that has been consecrated by the priest during the holy Sacrifice of the Mass.

Holy Days of Obligation: days of the year on which Catholics are bound to attend Mass. The days of obligation are: All Sundays, and the feasts of Christmas, Epiphany, Ascension, Body and Blood of Christ

---

51. References to Equinox: Part One, Judaic Heritage, p. 9, footnote 11; Part Five, Church Norms, Liturgical Seasons and Feasts, footnote 30a.
51a. See: Purgatory & Plenary Indulgences in this Glossary; Offering Mass on p. 162.

(Corpus Christi), Mary Mother of God, Immaculate Conception, Assumption, and the feast days of St. Joseph, the Apostles St. Peter and St. Paul, and the feast of All Saints.[52]

Holy Hour: Eucharistic devotion that consists in exposing the Blessed Sacrament for one hour to allow the faithful to adore the Lord and to meditate on the Eucharistic mystery, including the Passion of Our Lord.[52a]

Indulgence: see Plenary Indulgence.

IHS: in Greek, first three letters in the name of Jesus. This monogram is widely used in the Church to honor the name Jesus. IHS has also come to mean: Iesus Hominum Salvator, Jesus Savior of Humanity.

Jews: originally this word denoted one belonging to the tribe of Judah. Later it was applied to anyone of the Hebrew race who returned from the Babylonian captivity. Since most of the exiles came from Judah, and since they were the main historical representatives of ancient Israel, the term 'Jew' eventually came to include the entire Hebrew race. The spoken language of Judah is called 'Jewish'. In the Gospels, the word 'Jews' is the usual term for Israelites.

Judaism: religion of the Jewish people. Its teachings come from the Old Testament, especially the Ten Commandments, the Law of Moses, - *Exodus* 20 to *Deuteronomy* -, and the tradition of their elders. The principal elements of Judaism include circumcision, a strict monotheism, abhorrence of idolatry, and Sabbath-keeping. (Also see Pentateuch).

Lectern: see Ambo.
Lectionary: the Church official compilation of Holy Scripture readings for the Mass, including the Psalm Responsories and the Gospel Acclamation versicles. There are two volumes: Volume I contains readings for Sundays and Solemn feasts, and Volume II contains readings for Weekdays, for the feasts of Saints, and ritual Masses for various needs and votive Masses.[52b]

Liturgical Year: starts with the first Sunday of Advent and ends with the week following the feast of Christ the King. It comprises 5 liturgical seasons, [52c] whose periods are set in relation to Easter.

---

52. Holy Days of Obligation: see CCC 2177, 2192; Part Two, p.32; Part Five, Church Norms, Requisites for the Celebration of the Mass, Liturgical Seasons & Feasts.
52a. Holy Hour: Part Three, Liturgy of the Eucharist, After the Mass, Eucharistic Adoration.
52b. Lectionary: Part Five: Church Norms, Requisites for the Celebration of the Mass, Cycles for Holy Scripture Readings; Questions & Answers, Questions 53, 55, 91-100. NOTE: In the USA, VOLUME II of the Lectionary is also published in a 3 volume format: Liturgical Year I, Year II, and Ritual Masses for Various Needs and Votive Masses.
52c. See Part Five: Church Norms, Requisites for Celebrating the Mass, Liturgical Seasons & Feasts; Questions & Answers, Question 52; and Glossary, Equinox.

Liturgy: from the Greek 'leitourgia', service of worship; a rite or body of rites prescribed by the Church for public worship. The liturgical prayer is the prayer of the assembly joined together as God's people. The liturgy includes the celebration of the seven sacraments, especially the Eucharist. The three main purposes of the liturgy are as follows: to give glory and honor to God through prayer; to build up the faith of the people; and to teach and instruct the faithful in the meaning of Christ's word through the sacred mysteries.

Liturgy of the Hours (priorly Divine Office): public prayer of the Church for praising God and sanctifying the day that priests and professed religious have a sacred obligation to celebrate daily, and in which the laity are exhorted to participate. This liturgy may also be celebrated in private. The 'Liturgy of the Hours', as revised by Vatican II, is celebrated as follows: Morning Prayer (Lauds - at dawn); Office of Readings (at any time); Daytime Prayer (to be observed by contemplative communities: Terce -9 am, Sext -12 noon, and None -3 pm); Evening Prayer (Vespers - at dusk); and Night Prayer (Compline - before retiring). In a general form, the 'Liturgy of the Hours', which may be sung or said, comprises: antiphons, hymns, psalms, biblical readings (biblical and non-biblical readings for the Office of Readings), a canticle - of Zechariah *(Benedictus)* at Lauds, *Te Deum* with the Office of Readings, of Mary *(Magnificat)* at Vespers, and of Simeon *(Nunc Dimittis)* at night -, and prayers. The complete 'Liturgy of the Hours' can be found in the *Roman Breviary*, and also in the book titled *The Liturgy of the Hours*. The monthly missal for Mass *Magnificat* also provides the daily 'Liturgy of the Hours' for the Morning, Evening, and Night Prayer (see Bibliography).

Liturgy of the Mass, Roman rite: ceremony that comprises two main parts, the liturgy of the Word and the liturgy of the Eucharist. Its actual form was constituted according to the Vatican II document *Sacrosanctum Concilium, The Constitution of the Sacred Liturgy*, which promotes a liturgical renewal that brings forth the spirit of sacredness of the Mass, and a greater participation of the laity in the liturgy of the Mass.

Lunette: from the Latin *luna,* moon; a set of two discs of glass—each mounted on a hinged metal ring—used to contain the large Host that is exposed in the monstrance for adoration of the Blessed Sacrament. The Host contained in the lunette is reserved in a **pix** in the tabernacle.

Mass:*"The Mass is at the same time, and inseparably, the sacrificial memorial in which the sacrifice of the cross is perpetuated and the sacred banquet of communion with the Lord's body and blood. But the celebration of the Eucharistic sacrifice is wholly directed toward the intimate union of the faithful with Christ through communion. To receive communion is to receive Christ himself who has offered himself for us."* [53]

---

53. CCC 1382. Mass: see also 'Eucharist' and 'Sacrifice of the Mass' in this Glossary.

Missal: book of prayers used for the liturgy of the Mass. The priest's missal, the '*Roman Missal*', is also known as the '*Sacramentary*'.[53a] The missal used by the faithful, the missalet, contains the prayers and the holy scripture readings read and said during the Mass.

Monstrance: from the Latin '*monstrare*', to show; sacred vessel used for Exposition of the Blessed Sacrament, for Eucharistic Benediction, and for Eucharistic procession. "*The purpose of the monstrance, or ostensorium, is to prolong the sacred moment of "showing" [the Host] at the elevations, and so to present Our Lord to His People for adoration. The monstrance takes various forms, always with a convenient lunette or gilded clip to hold the sacred Host for exposition, and usually equipped with a glass door on a hinge. It should be a glorious throne for Our Lord, because the splendor of the vessel contrasts with the simplicity of the appearances of bread, through which He presents Himself to us for adoration. ... By custom, a light veil or white cover is provided for the monstrance when it is not in use.*" [54]

Novena: popular Catholic devotion that has been practiced since the seventeenth century. It derives from the **nine days** that Our Lady and the Apostles spent in prayer, between the Ascension of Our Lord and the feast of Pentecost, awaiting the coming of the Holy Spirit as promised by Jesus Christ (cf. Acts 1:5). A novena, private or public, is offered over nine consecutive days—or one day a week over nine weeks—and consists in presenting a particular petition to the Father, by the recitation of a prayer offered in the name of Our Lord Jesus, through the intercession of Our Lady, or a favorite saint. A novena may also consist in offering the Masses that we attend over nine consecutive days.

Oratory: from Latin '*ore*', prayer. An oratory is first a place of prayer.

Paten: sacred vessel in the shape of a small dish, and usually made of fine metal, that the priest uses to contain and consecrate the large Host during the Mass.

Pentateuch: from the Greek *penta*, five, the first five books of the Old Testament: Genesis, Exodus, Leviticus, Numbers and Deuteronomy. In Hebrew, *Torah,* the Law of God as revealed in the Mosaic Law; it includes the civil, moral and religious laws of the Israelites. The Pentateuch contains the history of the Israelites and their ancestors, of their faith in God's Revelation and His covenant with them, His chosen people. Since Jesus Christ established a New Covenant between man and God, the people of God, who were first exclusively the Israelites, now extends to and also includes Christians.

53a. Also see *Sacramentary* in this Glossary.
54. CMRR, Chapter 2, no. 99. Illustration of a monstrance and Eucharistic adoration: see Part Three, Liturgy of the Eucharist, After the Mass, Eucharistic Adoration.

Pius V: (1566-1572) Pope who enforced the many decrees issued from the Council of Trent concerning doctrinal matters opposed by the Protestant Reformers and organized the Counter-Reformation.

Pix: little case, made of fine metal, used by the priest to bring Holy Communion to the sick. A larger pix is used, in the tabernacle, to contain the *lunette* that holds the large Host that is reserved for exposition of the Blessed Sacrament.

Plenary Indulgence: remission before God of the entire temporal punishment - reparation time in purgatory - due for sins already pardoned. Sins that have been repented by the sinner and forgiven (pardoned) by the intercession of the Church in the sacrament of penance, still require reparation, which can be done while on earth through plenary indulgences. Such indulgences may be acquired by means of prescribed devotions done under the usual conditions.[54a]

Pope: Holy Father, Vicar of Christ, successor of Saint Peter, and bishop of Rome; the Pope is the elected chief of the Roman Catholic Church, the highest Catholic prelate. Since the Pope is chosen to guide the people of God on earth by the power of the Holy Spirit, all clergy and laity owe him obedience. The Magisterium (teaching authority) of the Church is personalized in the pope and his bishops, together and in unity with him (also see Apostolic Succession in Glossary).

Prelate: high-ranking member of the Church clergy; bishop, archbishop, cardinal, and the pope.
Priest: a man who was received into the sacrament of Holy Orders.

Protestant Reformation: religious movement instigated by Martin Luther in the 16th century that caused a schism in the Church bringing millions of Catholics in Europe to reject the Church's traditions, doctrines, and practices, and to refuse obedience to the Pope. Reformers promoted *Scriptura Sola,* Holy Scriptures alone, thus rejecting 1500 years of the Church's interpretation of the Holy Scriptures through the guidance of the Holy Spirit. The protestant reformation gave birth to Protestant Churches where everyone has their own interpretation of the scriptures; to this day they promote *Scriptura Sola* and reject the *Magisterium*.

Purgatory: according to the Catholic faith and tradition, it is the "final purification of the elect" (CCC 1031), who are then temporarily and partially alienated from God while their love is made perfect and they give satisfaction (reparation) for their sins.[55] This belief also holds that the prayers of the faithful on earth for holy souls who are in purgatory are efficacious in shortening these souls' time of final purification.

54a. Plenary Indulgence: also see Part Five, Questions & Answers, Questions 12, 25.
55. Reparation of sins: also see Plenary Indulgence in this Glossary.

Retable/reredos: vertical structure of highly decorated paneling, that - in churches built prior to the Council Vatican II - is mounted on the central wall of the sanctuary above the main altar. The main ornament of the retable is the tabernacle. Relics of saints and martyrs are usually incorporated in the retable.[55a]

Roman Rite: *"the manner of celebrating Mass, administration of the sacraments and sacramentals, recitation of the Divine Office and other ecclesiastical functions authorized for the Diocese of Rome and governed by the Roman Ritual. The Roman Rite is the dominant rite of Western Catholicism and the one most widely used throughout Christianity"* (*CE*).

Sacrament: sacred sign instituted by Christ to bring sanctifying graces to those receiving it. There are seven sacraments in the Church: *Baptism* and *Confirmation*, which may be received only once; *Reconciliation* and *Eucharist*, which may and should be renewed regularly; *Matrimony*, may be received more than once if a spouse dies or if the marriage is declared null by the Church; *Holy Orders*, may be received only once; and *Anointing of the Sick*, given to those seriously sick and the dying.

Sacramentals: "*...sacred signs instituted by the Church. They prepare men to receive the fruit of the sacraments and sanctify different circumstances of life. Among the sacramentals, blessings occupy an important place...* ."[55b] Sacramentals are any object, prayer or action that can put us in touch with God's grace in Christ. Like sacraments, sacramentals make available to us the stream of divine grace, which flows from the Paschal mystery of the passion, death and resurrection of Christ. An object becomes a sacramental when a priest blesses it by an intercessory prayer. A sacramental may also be the simple gestures and prayers of the Church imploring God's blessing on person or things. Here are some examples of sacramentals: the priest making the sign of the cross on our brow, signing ourselves, holy water, scapulars, medals, the rosary, honoring holy pictures, lighting blessed candles...

Sacramentary: (*Roman Missal*) The celebrant's book to celebrate Mass. It contains: the 'General Instruction'; the 'Order of Mass', ritual texts for the Mass; Masses within the Liturgical Calendar, for Solemnities, and for Feasts of Saints; and Special Masses and Blessings. The first edition of the *Roman Missal, the Gregorian Sacramentary,* was issued by Pope Adrian 1st in 786, and was last revised in the 1500s. The second edition of the *Sacramentary* was issued in 1970, the first revision of the Latin *Roman Missal* in 400 years. The third edition[56] of the *Roman Missal* was issued in Latin on Holy Thursday of 2000 by Pope John Paul II; it is yet to be published in the various languages of Catholics of the world.

55a. Retable: see picture in Part Five, Church Norms, The Tabernacle.
55b. CCC 1677, 1678.
56. Third Edition of the *Roman Missal*: see 'Acknowledgment' at the beginning of the book.

Sacrarium: basin without faucets and with a drain leading directly into the ground; standard equipment of a sacristy. ✝*"The practice is to be kept of building a sacrarium in the sacristy, into which is poured the water from the purification of sacred vessels and linens (cf. GIRM no. [239] 280)."* [56a]

Sacred Vessels: of the vessels used for the Eucharist, the most sacred are the chalice and the paten. The other sacred vessels are the ciborium, the pix, and the monstrance. Traditionally, the sacred vessels were made of precious metal - gold and silver -, but today other fine metals and noble materials may also be used. Sacred vessels are consecrated or blessed according to the rite prescribed by the Church.[56b]

Sacrifice of the Mass: liturgical ritual at the center of the Catholic faith. The Mass continuously makes present, in an unbloody manner, the sacrifice of Jesus Christ, Who through the priest offers Himself as victim. *"...According to traditional theology, the features constituting the nature of a true sacrifice are verified in the Mass: a sense-perceptible gift is offered and in some sense destroyed by an authorized minister for the purpose of worship of God. ..."* [56c] The Sacrifice of the Mass contains all of the elements that constitute the offering of a real sacrifice; the priest (an authorized minister) consecrates the bread and wine (gifts that are perceptible to human senses), and the nature of these gifts are destroyed (the transubstantiation) as they become the Body and Blood of Jesus Christ. The Son of God is made present with the Father and the Holy Spirit, Whom we worship and adore.

Sacristan: the person who is in charge of a church, especially the sacristy and its contents: liturgical vestments, vessels, books, etc. He is considered the door keeper of a church. The sacristan usually prepares the altar and the sanctuary before the Mass, and places the liturgical articles back in the sacristy after the Mass.

Sacristy: a room often adjacent to the sanctuary where the requisites for the celebration of the Mass are kept and where the priest vests and prepares himself for his sacred function. The sacred character of this room calls for reverence and silence. The sacristy contains chests of drawers and closets for sacred vessels, liturgical books, vestments, etc. It usually contains two sinks: a regular sink to supply water for liturgical use and to wash the sacred vessels after they have been purified, and a *sacrarium* into which the water used for purification is poured. [57]

56a. GIRM [296] 334. Sacrarium: see also Part Three, Liturgy ot the Eucharist, After the Mass, The Sacristy.
56b. Sacred Vessels: see Part Three, Liturgy of the Eucharist, Procession of the Gifts.
56c. CE, Sacrifice of the Mass.
57. Cf. CE, Sacristy. Sacristy: see also Part Three, Liturgy of the Eucharist, After the Mass, The Sacristy; Part Five, Church Norms, Norms for the Sacristy.

Saint Peter of Rome: The patriarchal Basilica of St. Peter named after the first pope, St. Peter. It is the chief church of the world, but strictly speaking is second to St. John Lateran, the papal cathedral. St. Peter of Rome does not have a permanent episcopal (bishop) throne.

Sanctuary: from the Latin *sanctus,* sacred. It is the part of the church located around the altar of sacrifice, the most holy place, the place where the liturgical ceremonies take place. It is set apart from the body of the church by a distinctive structural feature such as its elevation above the main floor, and sometimes an altar rail. Traditionally, the sanctuary is set at the head of the church, as Christ is the head of the Church. A sanctuary may also be a religious building, a holy place.

Sanctuary lamp: traditionally, an oil lamp located in the sanctuary, often hanging from the ceiling, that is kept burning continuously to indicate and honor the Presence of God in the Blessed Sacrament reserved in the tabernacle, which always used to be located in the sanctuary. This tradition dates from the 13th century, and even from the time of the Old Testament (Ex 27:20). Today, the sanctuary lamp is often a large votive candle placed on a stand near the tabernacle.

Shema: fundamental Judaic truth and duty: (Deut 6:4-5)[57a] These two verses are written on small **Mezuzah** (scrolls) that are contained in small cases that Jewish people tack to their doorpost according to the prescription of the Old Testament: (Deut 6:6-9).[57a]

State of Grace: being free and/or cleansed from all sins, being at peace with God. Thus, being in a state to receive God's graces, being in a state to receive Holy Communion; only one who is holy may receive what is Holy.

Tabernacle (Eucharistic reserve):[57b] receptacle in which the Blessed Sacrament is reserved in churches, chapels and oratories. There, are kept a ciborium containing the remaining Hosts that were consecrated during the Mass, and a pix, which holds the large consecrated Host to be placed in the monstrance for Exposition or Benediction of the Blessed Sacrament. Traditionally, the tabernacle was placed in the very heart of the church, in the retable mounted on the central wall of the sanctuary. *"The tabernacle is to be situated "in churches in a most worthy place with the greatest honor.""*[57c] Tabernacle: from the Latin *Tabernaculum,* tent. In its Judaic origin, following God's instructions, Moses built the tabernacle to house the Ark of the Covenant, which contained the Tables of the Law, a pot of manna, and Aaron's rod (cf. Ex 25-27, 30-31, 35-38).

57a. Shema: Deut 6:4-5.6-9: see Part Five, Appendix 'E', The Commandments.
57b. Tabernacle: see also Part Five, Church Norms, The Tabernacle.
57c. Cf. CCC 1183, Pope Paul VI, *Mysterium Fidei*: AAS (1965) 771.

Tridentine Mass: the 'Latin Mass' as universally celebrated before Vatican II. Tridentine: related to the 'Council of Trent'.[58]

Thurible: *censor,* metal vessel with perforated cover and suspended by chains to allow swinging the thurible while incensing. It is used for ceremonial burning of incense during some Masses, Benedictions of the Blessed Sacrament and other liturgical functions.[58a]

Thurifer: the person whose function during the Mass is to prepare and carry the thurible, to assist the celebrating priest with putting incense on the coal in the thurible, and to incense the priest when required.

Transubstantiation: word indicating that through the consecration, the substance of the bread is changed into the substance of the Body of Christ, and the substance of the wine is changed into the substance of the Blood of Christ, even though the appearances or species of bread and wine remain.[58b]

Vatican II: Second Vatican Council, see *Ecumenical Council* in Glossary.

Viaticum: sacrament of the Eucharist administrated to those who are seriously ill and to the dying, as part of the 'last rites'. The Viaticum is the divine food that one receives for the passage through death to reach God. *"The Eucharist... the last sacrament of the earthly journey, the "viaticum" for "passing over" to eternal life."* [59]

Water Font: receptacle placed at the entrance of churches containing holy water. Upon entering, the faithful dips the fingertips of his hand into the font and blesses himself by making the 'sign of the cross'. This action calls to mind three important aspects of the Christian life: the Holy Trinity, the Cross and the sacrament of Baptism. The 'sign of the cross' made with holy water renews one's baptismal commitment, that is, to reject satan and all his works, and to strive to live according to the Gospel of Jesus Christ. Holy water fonts may be installed in our homes for personal use throughout the day, that is, to bless ourselves and chase away evil spirits.[59a]

Zucchetto: A skullcap worn by bishops and other prelates. The pope wears a white zucchetto; the cardinals, scarlet; and bishops, purple. The obvious similarity between the *zucchetto* and the *yarmulka* - the skullcap worn by Jewish men - is another testimony to the Judaic origins of the Catholic religion.

---

58. Council of Trent: see Part Five, Glossary, Ecumenical Council.
58a. Thurible: see Part Three, Liturgy of the Eucharist, Offertory Rites, Incensing.
58b. Transubstantiation: cf. CCC 1376.
59. CCC 1517. Viaticum: see CCC 1524-1532; Anointing of the Sick, Glossary.
59a. Holy Water: see Part Three, Liturgy of the Word, Purification Rite.

Questions
and
Answers

Questions and Answers...
About Holy Objects present in a Church

1. What is the sign that one may expect to find in a church to indicate that the Blessed Sacrament is there present?
   *To indicate the presence of the Blessed Sacrament in a church, that is, the real presence of God, the **sanctuary lamp** is kept burning near the tabernacle, in which the Blessed Sacrament is reserved.*

2. What is a **tabernacle**?
   *A **tabernacle**, or Eucharistic reserve, is a sacred receptacle where the Eucharist, or Blessed Sacrament,[60] is reserved in a church; it is intended as a worthy place to keep consecrated Hosts for the Communion of the sick and for Eucharistic worship outside of Mass.*

3. What is the name of the receptacle of water found at the entrance of a church, and how is it used?
   *This receptacle is a holy **water font.** As one enters the church, he dips his fingertips into the font and blesses himself by making the sign of the cross; this action recalls the Trinity, the Cross of Christ, and our Baptism. The sign of the cross made with holy water renews our baptismal commitment and chases away evil influences.*

4. True or False. Holy water, incense, and a monstrance are three **sacramentals**.
   False. While holy water and incense are considered to be sacramentals, the monstrance is a sacred vessel.

5. Before the Mass starts, only four objects should be found on the altar. Can you name these objects?
   *The four objects to be found on the altar before Mass starts are the **altar cloth, two candles**, and **a crucifix.***

6. In the entrance procession at the beginning of the Mass, a minister holds a book raised in front of him for everyone to see. What is this book?
   *The book that is carried in the entrance procession and then placed on or near the altar is called the **Book of the Gospels**. It contains the official compilation of readings from the Gospel to be proclaimed by the priest or deacon during the Mass.*

---

60. See Part Five, Glossary: Blessed Sacrament, Eucharist, & Tabernacle. The first tabernacle was built by Moses to house the Ark of the Covenant (cf. Ex 25-40).

7. What are the three **sacred vessels** that the servers bring to the altar during the preparation of the gifts?
   *The three sacred vessels that are brought to the altar at the time of the offertory are the **chalice**, which is used to consecrate the wine, the **paten**, which is used to consecrate the large host for the communion of the celebrating priest, and one or more **ciboria** containing small hosts to be consecrated for the communion of the faithful. At the time of communion, the priest may also bring to the altar a ciborium containing consecrated Hosts that are kept in the tabernacle.*[60a]

8. What are the **other vessels** that the servers bring to the priest at the altar during the preparation of the gifts?
   *The servers also bring the **two cruets** containing the water and wine to be used for the consecration, and then the **wash plate** for the rite of the washing of the hands of the priest.*

9. Name the three **sacred linens** that the servers bring to the altar with the sacred vessels during the preparation of the gifts, and describe how the priest uses each one of them.
   The three sacred linens that are brought to the altar with the sacred vessels are:
   - *the **corporal**, which the priest places directly on the altar stone [61] and on which he sets the sacred vessels for the consecration;*
   - *the **pall**, which the priest uses to cover the chalice once the wine and water of the sacrifice have been poured; and*
   - *the **purificator**, which the priest uses during the preparation of the chalice to wipe any drops of wine when pouring from the cruet; after his communion to wipe the Blood of Christ from the rim of the chalice; and during the purification of the vessels to wipe dry the sacred vessels. If the faithful receive communion under both species, the purificator is also used to wipe the rim of the chalice after each communicant drinks from the chalice.*

10. What is the name of the **linen** used by the priest to dry his hands during the ritual of the washing of the hands at the time of the offertory?
    *The **manuterge**, or hand towel, is the name of the linen used during the ritual of the washing of the hands.*

60a. Cf. GIRM [56h] 85: "It is most desirable that the faithful, just as the priest is bound to do, receive the Lord's Body from hosts consecrated at the same Mass."
61. Altar Stone: see Part Five, Church Norms, I- Arrangement and Furnishing of Churches, The Altar Stone.

11. What is the name of the **collection of scenes** that are mounted on the walls of churches, chapels, and sanctuaries?
*This collection is known as the 'Stations of the Cross', and the scenes, or 'Stations', represent the **Passion and the Death of Our Lord Jesus Christ**. The 'Stations' are usually found hanging on the walls of the nave of churches - chapels and sanctuaries - presented in the form of paintings or low-reliefs. They may also be found outdoors on the grounds of churches or in cemeteries in the format of large sculptures or large low-reliefs.*

12. How many **'Stations'** are there, and what scenes of the Passion and the Death of Christ are represented?
*There are **fourteen stations** (sometimes fifteen). Each station is engraved with its own number and often adorned with a small cross on top.[62] The scenes representing the Passion and the Death of Our Lord are known and disposed as follows:*
1st Station: Jesus is condemned to death.
2nd Station: Jesus takes his Cross.
3rd Station: Jesus falls for the first time.
4th Station: Jesus meets His Blessed Mother.
5th Station: Simon helps Jesus carry His Cross.
6th Station: Veronica wipes the face of Jesus.
7th Station: Jesus falls for the second time.
8th Station: Jesus speaks to the women of Jerusalem.
9th Station: Jesus falls for the third time.
10th Station: Jesus is stripped of his garments.
11th Station: Jesus is nailed to the Cross.
12th Station: Jesus dies on the Cross.
13th Station: Jesus is taken down from the Cross.
14th Station: Jesus is placed in the tomb.
15th Station: The Resurrection of Jesus Christ. (Optional station)

*Typically, the stations of the cross are placed several feet from each other in order that, while doing the 'Way of the Cross', one walks a few steps between stations, recalling our Lord walking on **His Way to the Cross**.[62a] When doing the 'Way of the Cross', one stops before each station, meditating on what it represents, and then says quietly: 'We adore You, O Christ, and we praise You, Because by Your holy cross, You have redeemed the world'. To conclude he says one 'Our Father', one 'Hail Mary' and one 'Glory be'. A **plenary indulgence** is granted to the faithful who do the stations of the Cross under the usual conditions.[63]*

62. Illustration of the 'Stations': Part Five, Appendix 'F', Essential Catholic Prayers, The Way of the Cross.
62a. The Way to the Cross in the Gospel: Mt 27:15-28:20; Mk 15:6-16:17; Lk 23:18-24:12; Jn 18:28-19:42.
63. Plenary Indulgence: see Part Five, Catholic Glossary. Conditions to obtain a Plenary Indulgence: see Part Five, Questions & Answers, Question 25.

13. Among the **minor** (secondary) **altars** present in churches, one of these altars is almost always dedicated to …….. ?
*In most churches you will find a minor altar dedicated to the **Blessed Virgin Mary**, the Mother of God, the Mother of the Church.*

14. What is the name of the colorful and decorated **vestment** worn by the priest to celebrate the Mass?
*The colorful and decorated vestment worn by the celebrating priest on top of his alb and stole is called a **chasuble**. Its color varies with the liturgical seasons and feasts (see sacred vestments p. 192).*

15. What are the **liturgical colors** for the liturgical vestments and sanctuary ornaments for the following liturgical seasons and feasts:
   a) Palm Sunday, Good Friday, celebrations of the Lord's Passion, Pentecost, feasts of the Apostles, the Evangelists and Martyrs?
   b) Ordinary Times?
   c) Lent and Advent?
   d) Christmas, Easter, feasts of Mother Mary, and God's Angels?
   e) Most of the Solemnities of Our Lord, and feasts of Saints?
   f) The 3rd Sunday of Advent and 4th Sunday of Lent?
   The liturgical colors used for the above feasts and seasons are:
   a) Red   b) Green   c) Violet   d) White   e) White   f) Rose.[64]

16. What is the name of the sacred vessel used for Exposition, Processions, and Benediction of the Blessed Sacrament?
*The sacred vessel used to expose the Blessed Sacrament is named the **Monstrance**. The cavity in its center allows the lunette (luna) to be placed therein to show the Host in an upright position.*

17. What are the two main **parts of the church**, how are they used, and whom are they reserved for?
*The two main parts of the church are the sanctuary and the nave. The sanctuary is the place where the liturgy and the sacrifice of the Mass take place. Because of the sacredness of the Mass, the **sanctuary** is reserved for the clergy - priests and deacon -, and for some lay ministers -readers and servers. In the **nave**, pews are installed for the faithful who come to attend the Mass, or who come at other times to pray and visit with God. During the Mass, extraordinary ministers of holy communion sit in the nave with the congregation, usually in the front pews. An area may be reserved for the choir in the nave, but not in the sanctuary.*

---

64. Liturgical Colors: Part Five, Church Norms, II- Requisites for the Celebration of the Mass, Liturgical Seasons & Feasts and Liturgical Seasons & Related Colors.

Questions and Answers...
... About the Faith related to the Mass,
the Sacraments & Devotions

18. How does one **show reverence** for God's real presence in the tabernacle when entering a church?
    *One shows reverence for God's real presence in the tabernacle by making a **genuflection**, or a bow, while facing the tabernacle and making the 'Sign of the Cross'. We should show this sign of reverence to God whenever entering or leaving our pew, and each time when walking before the tabernacle. By reverence for God and by respect for those who are praying, we should maintain sacred **silence** in the church at all times.*

19. Name two things that the priest does during Mass to **venerate the altar**.
    *As a sign of veneration, the priest **kisses** the altar at the beginning and at the end of the Mass. He may also **incense** the altar with the thurible (censor) at the beginning of the Mass and again during the offertory. (Mt 23:19)"For which is greater, the gift or the altar that makes the gift sacred?"*

20. What are the **two main parts of the liturgy** of the Mass, and name the high point of each part?
    *The two main parts of the liturgy of the Mass are as follows: the **liturgy of the Word** is the first part of the Mass, and its high point is the proclamation of the **Gospel** of Jesus Christ, which is why we stand to listen to this reading; the second part of the Mass is the **liturgy of the Eucharist**, and its high point is the **consecration**, which is also the high point of the Mass. All kneel during the consecration because God then becomes present on the altar.*

21. The liturgy of the Word comprises three main scripture readings. From which **parts of the bible** is each of them taken?
    *Usually, the First Reading is taken from the **Old Testament** (the Prophets); the Second Reading is taken from books of the New Testament - **Letters** /Epistles, **Acts**, or **Revelation** (the Apostles); and the Gospel Reading - with the Gospel acclamation versicle - is taken from one of the four **Gospels** in the New Testament. After the First Reading, the Responsorial Psalm is read, that is an excerpt taken from the book of **Psalms**. During weekday Mass there is usually only one reading, taken from either the Old or the New Testament; the Responsorial Psalm; the Gospel acclamation versicle; and a reading taken from the Gospel.*

22. What happens to the bread and wine during the **consecration**?
*During the consecration, the bread and wine **become the Body
and Blood of Jesus Christ**. (Mk 14:22.24)"This is my body...
This is my blood." These are Christ's own words, which allow us to
believe that we are truly receiving the Body and Blood of Christ.*

23. Besides the bread and the wine, what **kinds of offerings** do the
faithful make during the offertory, and what becomes of these
offerings?
*The faithful participate in the offertory by presenting their **spiritual
offerings**, which will be consecrated with the bread and wine.
They spiritually put their loved ones, their own humanities, and
their petitions in the chalice and on the paten on the altar, and
their offerings will be received and sanctified by the Father. Also,
during the procession of the gifts, **money offerings** are collected
from the faithful to support the material needs of the parish.*

24. What kinds of **offerings** are known to be **pleasing to God**?
*The offerings that are pleasing to God are those made with a
contrite and reconciled **heart**, and with a **cleansed soul**.*

25. What is a **plenary indulgence** and how may one obtain it?
*A plenary indulgence is the **remission** before God of the **entire
temporal punishment** - time in purgatory[65] - for reparation of
sins that have already been pardoned in sacramental confession.
The usual conditions **to obtain** a plenary indulgence are: one
must be free of all attachment to sin - even venial - and perform
the work (devotion) to which the indulgence is attached. One must
also fulfill three other conditions: sacramental confession, which
may be fulfilled several days before or after the performance of
the prescribed work; Eucharistic Communion; and prayers for the
intentions of the pope - that is, one Our Father, one Hail Mary, and
one Glory Be. Except for confession, one must fulfill these conditions
on the same day that the work is performed.[65a]
Following, are four of the many devotional practices (spiritual work)
for which a plenary indulgence is granted:
a) **Adoration** of the Blessed Sacrament for at least one-half hour;
b) devout reading of Sacred **Scriptures** for at least one-half hour;
c) doing the **Way of the Cross**;and
d) recitation of the **Rosary** in a church (or other chapel), or in
community with family, religious community or pious association.*

65. Plenary indulgence & Purgatory: see also Part Five, Catholic Glossary.
65a. One who practices monthly confession usually fulfills the confession requirements
for a plenary indulgence. Only one plenary indulgence can be gained on the same day.

26. **Can any one attend** Mass **and receive** Holy Communion?
    *Any one is welcome to **attend Mass**, but to **receive Holy Communion**, one must fulfill the following conditions:*
    - *having been **baptized** and received into the **Catholic Church**;*
    - *having received **preparation** for the sacrament of Communion;*
    - *believing in the real presence of Jesus Christ in the Eucharist;*
    - *professing the Catholic's **creed**;*
    - *having respected the one-hour **eucharistic fast**; and*
    - *being in a **state of grace**.* [66]
    *Thus, before receiving communion, we must all examine ourselves and if conscious of not being in a state of grace, we must first reconcile with God and receive absolution in the **sacrament of penance**/reconciliation. **Catholics who have been away** from the practice of the faith for some time should receive the sacrament of reconciliation (confession) before they receive Holy Communion.*

27. May one receive **communion more than once a day**?
    By reverence for the Eucharist, and by ecclesiastical law, a person who has already received the Eucharist may receive it once again during the same day, only when attending a whole second Mass, and for special occasions such as Masses for marriages, funerals, baptisms, confirmations... or Masses during catholic congresses, catholic meetings, or sacred pilgrimages.

28. What are the main effects (**spiritual fruits**) of the Eucharistic Communion?
    *The Eucharistic Communion **renews and increases the grace** of Baptism, **increases union** with Christ, **delivers from sin**, **makes the Church**, **preserves** from future mortal sins, and **strengthens** the spiritual life.* [67] *As for all sacraments, receiving the Body and Blood of Christ gradually brings **sanctification** upon those receiving the sacrament of the Eucharist.*

29. Does the reception of all sacraments require a **preparation**?
    Yes. *Before receiving any sacrament, we need spiritual preparation such as studying the **teachings of the Church**, as found in the Catechism; we also need to **pray**, to do **self-examination**, and/or go to **confession**. It applies without saying that before entering the sacraments of Matrimony and Holy Orders, one also needs to do **retreats** to **discern** and reflect on one's calling.*

---

66. Conditions for receiving Communion: see also Part Three, Liturgy of the Eucharist, Communicants, Disposed to Receive; and (1Co 11:26-31).
67. Cf. CCC 1391 - 1398.

30. What are the **sacraments** that one may usually **receive** before or during the **Mass**?
*Before the Mass, one may meet alone with a priest and receive absolution in the sacrament of **reconciliation/ penance**. During the Mass one may receive Holy Communion in the sacrament of the **Eucharist**. The **other sacraments** are usually received during a Mass especially celebrated for the event, except for the sacrament of the Anointing of the Sick, which often is given at the bedside of the sick.*

31. **How many sacraments** are there and can you name them?
*There are **seven** sacraments, three of which can be received **only once**: Baptism, Confirmation, and Holy Orders; Matrimony, which can be **renewed**; and three that can be **renewed as often as needed**: Reconciliation, Eucharist, and Anointing of the Sick. Since Baptism is the initial sacrament, one must be baptized in order to receive any of the other six sacraments.*

32. **When** were the sacraments instituted?
*By **Jesus' presence, actions, and words** at specific events during His public life, these events and actions were raised to the status of sacraments for us to receive for our sanctification. They are:*

1. *Baptism ....* *Jesus was baptized in the Jordan, and there, the Father spoke (cf. Lk 3:21-22; CCC 1212-1284).*

2. *Reconciliation... "If you forgive the sins of any, they are forgiven" (cf. Jn 20:23; CCC 1422-1498).*

3. *Eucharist........... Jesus instituted the Eucharist at the Last Supper "This is my body... this is my blood of the covenant, which is poured out for many" (cf. Mk 14:22.25; CCC 1322-1419).*

4. *Confirmation... "[Jesus] breathed on them and said...: Receive the Holy Spirit" (Jn 20:22); Descent of the Holy Spirit (cf.Acts 2:1-4; CCC 1285-1321).*

5. *Matrimony...... Jesus' first miracle was at the marriage at Cana (cf.Jn 2:1-10; CCC 1601-1666):"What God has joined together, let no one separate" (Mt 19:6).*

6. *Holy Orders ...... At The Last Supper when Jesus said: 'Do this in memory of me.'(Lk 22:19 [NAB]); (cf. CCC 1536-1600).*

7. *Anointing of the sick... "...the presbyters of the church... should pray over him and anoint [him] with oil in the name of the Lord"*^{NAB} *(Jas 5:14). Also, "...[Jesus] gave them authority over unclean spirits to drive them out and to cure every disease and every illness"*^{NAB} *(Mt 10:1);(cf.CCC 1499-1532).*[68]

33. What may one who is ill expect from the sacrament of **Anointing of the Sick**?

When illness strikes, the sacrament of Anointing of the Sick is there to bring graces such as peace and strength, and at times, even physical or spiritual healing.

34. What does the word '**Catholic**' mean and when did it first come into use?

*The word 'Catholic' means 'general' or '**universal**', and it first appeared in the **first century** in letters of St. Ignatius of Antioch.*[69]

35. What does the word '**Mass**' and the word '**Eucharist**' mean?

*In the Catholic religion, the word 'Mass' means the unbloody **sacrifice** of the Body and Blood of Jesus Christ, done at the altar by the ministry of a priest;*[70] *and the word 'Eucharist' means '**thanksgiving**'.*

36. Among the following elements that are found in the Catholic liturgy of the Mass, only **one** of them does not have its origins in the **Judaic practices** of the Old Testament. Which one is it?
   a) worshiping the One God, the Creator;
   b) scripture readings;
   c) the priesthood;
   d) the tabernacle;
   e) the sanctuary lamp;
   f) the altar;
   g) making offerings in sacrifice for purification of sins;
   h) offering unleavened bread and wine;
   i) incensing the offerings; and
   j) Eucharistic communion.

*Among the above elements, only **j)** 'Eucharistic communion' was not part of the Judaic practices of the Old Testament.*[71] *However, Jesus instituted the Eucharist in the midst of the meal of the Passover, the most important Judaic feast.*

68. Anointing of the Sick and Viaticum:see Part Five, Catholic Glossary.
69. St. Ignatius of Antioch: Bishop of Rome ca. 69, dies a martyr ca. 107.
70. Mass: see Part Five, Catholic Glossary, Eucharist, Mass and Sacrifice of the Mass.
71. Judaic heritage of the Catholic faith: see Part One, Judaic Heritage.

Questions and Answers...
... About the Holy Bible

37. What are the **two main parts** of the bible, and why is the Bible divided this way?

    *The two main parts of the Bible, also called the Holy Scriptures, are the **Old Testament** and the **New Testament**. The Old Testament contains the Holy Scriptures relating the revelation of God to His people before Jesus Christ was born, and the New Testament contains the holy scriptures relating the revelation of God proclaimed to us by His Son Jesus Christ, whose revelation is known as 'the Good News', or 'the Gospel'.*

38. What is the **Canon** of Scriptures?

    *The Canon of Scriptures is the Catholic Church's official **list of sacred books** of the Bible; they are divided between the Old Testament with its 46 books, and the New Testament with its 27 books, for a total of 73 sacred books. (Canon: from the Greek word for 'rule').*

39. What is the word for the **first five books** of the Bible?

    *The first five books of the Bible are the books of Genesis, Exodus, Leviticus, Numbers and Deuteronomy. These books of the Old Testament are known as the **Pentateuch** or Torah. They contain the history of the Jewish people and their faith, and the revelation of God to His people. At first, the people of God were exclusively the Israelites and their ancestors since Abraham, but since Christ came, the people of God extends to all Christians.*

40. True or False. The **book of Psalms** is part of the New Testament.

    *False, the book of Psalms is among the Wisdom books of the **Old Testament**. The book of Psalms is a collection of 150 religious songs or lyrics reflecting Israelite belief and piety, of which about half of them have King David as author. These poems and hymns were meant to be sung, and many are songs of praise to God.*

41. Besides the Pentateuch, name **three other collections** of books of the Old Testament, in the order they are found in the Bible.

    *The three other book collections of the Old Testament are known as the **Historical** books, the **Wisdom** books, and the **Prophetic** books. In these three collections are gathered all the books of the Old Testament that are not part of the Pentateuch.*

42. Name the **five sections** of the New Testament.
*The New Testament starts with the four **Gospels** - the Good News - followed by the book of the **Acts of the Apostles**, the **Pauline Letters** (14 of them), the **Apostolic Letters** (7 of them), and finally the book of **Revelation**, which is the last book of the New Testament, and the last book of the Bible.*

43. What are those who wrote the **Gospels** called? Can you name them in the order that their Gospels appear in the New Testament?
*Those who wrote the Gospels are called the **Evangelists**, and they are Saint Matthew, Saint Mark, Saint Luke, and Saint John.*

44. Who wrote the **Acts of the Apostles?** What events does it relate?
*The Evangelist **Saint Luke**, a disciple of Saint Paul, wrote the book of the Acts, in which he describes the origin and spread of some of the first Christian communities from right after the resurrection of Christ to about the year 60, when Saint Paul was taken into captivity.*

45. Who wrote the **Pauline Letters?** Who were they addressed to?
*These letters that represent about one-forth of the New Testament were written by **Saint Paul**—and probably by other authors who had received Saint Paul's teachings on Christ—and they are addressed to the **early Christian communities**. They depict the development of early Christian **theology**, **spirituality**, and **morals**. Saint Paul wrote many of these letters while he was in captivity.*

46. Who wrote the **Apostolic**/Catholic **Letters?** How many did each write? Name them in the order they appear in the bible?
*The Apostolic Letters were written by the **Apostles** Saint James (1 letter), Saint Peter (2 letters), Saint John (3 letters), and Saint Jude (1 letter).*

47. Can you name **the twelve Apostles** of Jesus Christ?
*(Mt 10:2-4)"These are the names of the twelve apostles: first, Simon, also known as **Peter**, and his brother **Andrew**; **James** son of Zebedee, and his brother **John**; **Philip** and **Bartholomew**; **Thomas** and **Matthew** the tax collector; **James,** the son of Alphaeus, and **Thaddeus**; **Simon** the Cananean, and **Judas** Iscariot, the one who betrayed [Jesus]. "[bfa] After the resurrection of Jesus Christ, **Matthias***

was appointed by the eleven apostles to replace Judas Iscariot, thus he is the twelfth Apostle (cf. Acts 1:23-26).

48. How are **bible references** given?
*Bible references are given as follows: first the **book**, then the **chapter**, and then the **verses.***

49. How would you **read and find** the following bible reference: **1Ch 4:10** ?
   - *This reference **reads** as follows:*
     First book of Chronicles, chapter 4, verse 10.
   - *The book of Chronicles is found in the **Old Testament**. In the **table of contents** of bibles, the books appear in the order that they are gathered, followed by the page number of the **first page** of each book. The name of the book and chapter numbers are usually written **at the top of each page** of each book, and verses are placed in sequence **in the midst of the text**, or sometimes in the margin.*

50. How would you **read** the following bible reference, and in which part of the Bible is it **found**, the Old or the New Testament? **Ep 1:1-10, 2:4.8** [72]
*This reference is read as follows: Letter to the **Ephesians**, Chapter 1, verses 1 to 10, and Chapter 2, verses 4 and 8.*
The letter to the Ephesians is part of the Pauline Letters found in the New Testament.

---

72. In another literary style, this same reference may be presented as follows: (Eph 1, 1-10; 2,4.8).

Questions and Answers...
for Lay Ministers about Liturgical Ministries

A) For Sacristans and those who prepare the Sanctuary:

51. What is **the person** called who is usually in charge of preparing the sanctuary and the requisites for the celebration of the Holy Mass? List some of his responsibilities in preparing for the Mass.
*The person who is usually in charge of preparing the requisites and the sanctuary for the celebration of the Mass is called the **sacristan**. Among his many responsibilities, the sacristan is in charge of:*
- *setting out the **vestments** for the priest;*
- *setting out the **vessels**, the **altar linens**, the **hosts** to be consecrated, and the **cruets** of **wine** and **water**;*
- *preparing the **table of the gifts**;*
- *setting out the **sacred books** used for the Mass, and in some cases, placing the **markers** at the appropriate pages;*
- ***lighting the candles** on the altar just before the Mass, or directing the altar servers to assist him;and*
- *making sure that the **sanctuary lamp** is always lit and that the **holy water fonts** are filled with holy water.*
In some churches, the sacristan supervises the development of the celebration. However, in the case of large churches, cathedrals or for solemn Masses, the development of the Mass should be supervised by a Master of Ceremony (cf. GIRM [69] 106).

52. What **vessels** and **linens** are to be **placed** on the credence table **before the Mass**?
*The sacred vessels to be placed on the credence table before the Mass are the **chalice**, the **paten**, and a **ciborium of hosts**; the liturgical vessels are the **cruets**, the **wash plate**(s), and the **Communion-plate**, if one is to be used; the sacred linens are the **corporal**, the **purificator**, and the **pall**, plus a hand towel. If the purification of the vessels is to be carried out at the credence table, a second corporal will be needed. The **quantity** of **hosts** and **wine** prepared should be sufficient for the number of communicants expected. If communion under both species is to be given to all, additional chalices and purificators need to be placed on the credence table before the Mass.[73]*

53. Where should **the little bell** be placed before the Mass?
*The little bell should be placed on the **credence** table, or in another place in the sanctuary that is convenient for the server.*

---

73. Liturgical vessels and linens: see the answers to Questions 7 through 9.

54. What is the **credence table** and where is it located in the sanctuary?
*The credence table is a little table on which are placed the sacred vessels and other requisites for the **service** at the altar during the Mass. The credence is usually located near the wall on the **left side** of the sanctuary as seen from the nave.*

55. Where should the vessels containing the **offerings/gifts** of bread and wine be placed before the Mass?
*When members of the assembly are to present the **offerings of bread and wine**, before the Mass, the offerings are to be placed on a **'table of the gifts'** usually located at the back or at the front of the nave near the central aisle. The table should be fairly small and covered with a white cloth. However, if servers are to present the gifts, then before the Mass, the vessels with the offerings of bread and wine are placed on the **credence table** in the sanctuary.*

56. Besides the vessels and requisites that are needed for all Masses, name the additional vessels that the sacristan needs to prepare for a more **solemn Mass**.
In the case of a more solemn Mass, the sacristan also needs to prepare:
 - *the **thurible** (censor) with its **incense boat** and coal, which needs to be ready for the entrance procession;and*
 - *the **vessel of water** and **sprinkler**, which are to be set before the Mass on the credence table or near the priest's chair.*
 - *The **monstrance** with an adoration booklet needs to be set out in the sacristy before the Mass if exposition of the Blessed Sacrament is to take place right after the Mass.*

57. Name the **3 sacred books** that are needed for the celebration of the Mass; where they are to be placed before the Mass; and how they are used during the Mass?
*The 3 sacred books needed for the Mass - and that are usually kept in the sacristy - are the **Sacramentary**, the **Lectionary**, and the **Book of the Gospels**. The Sacramentary (Roman Missal) is the celebrant's Mass book; it contains the 'Order of Mass' and it is to be set near the chair of the celebrating priest before the Mass. The **Lectionary** contains the Holy Scripture readings; it is to be set on the ambo before the Mass. The **Book of the Gospels** contains the Gospel readings. It is carried by the deacon, or a reader, in the **entrance procession** before it is set on a book stand on the altar or near the altar; and at the time of the proclamation of the Gospel, the priest carries it in a procession to the ambo.*

58. Describe the **Cycles for Holy Scripture readings** for the Mass as compiled in the Lectionary.[74]
    The Holy Scripture readings for the Mass are compiled in the two volumes of the Lectionary *as follows:*
    - *Volume One contains the readings for **Sundays** and **Solemnities**, which are compiled in a three-year cycle: **Years A, B, & C**.*
    - *Volume Two contains the readings for **Weekdays**, which are compiled in a two-year cycle: **Years I & II**; and the readings for the feasts of **Saints** and for **various occasions**, which are compiled in a **one-year cycle**.*
    The Lectionary *also provides the Responsorial Psalms and the Gospel Acclamation versicles. The cycles for Holy Scripture readings follow the liturgical year, which begins with the first Sunday of Advent and ends with the week after the feast of Christ the King.*

59. Why should a **liturgical calendar** be posted in the sacristy, and what information should it provide?
    *Besides posting a regular calendar, a liturgical calendar should be posted in the sacristy in order to provide the lay ministers with the liturgical information of the day as found in the 'Ordo'; information such as **solemnities**, holy days of obligation, **feasts**, memorials, liturgical **seasons**, liturgical **color** of the day,[74a] and the cycles for **Holy Scripture readings.** This liturgical information is especially useful to the sacristan in setting out the proper color of **liturgical vestments** and **sanctuary ornaments**, and for the person marking the pages of the **sacred books** for the Mass. A **detailed list with the names** of the celebrating priests and lay ministers scheduled for each Mass should also be posted in the sacristy, along with the necessary information for **visiting priests:** the **name of the parish** and of the **local bishop**, and the Mass intentions, if any are scheduled.*

60. Name a **Catholic publication** that contains practical information regarding the preparation and development of the Holy Mass, as well as specific information for the different lay ministries?
    *A Catholic publication that provides a wealth of practical information concerning the preparation and development of the Holy Mass, and information related to the pursuance of liturgical lay ministries is the **Ceremonies Of The Modern Roman Rite.** [74b]*

---

74. Lectionary: Part Five, Church Norms, II- Requisites for the Celebration of the Mass, Cycles for Holy Scripture Readings; Part Five, Catholic Glossary. NOTE: In the USA, Volume Two of the Lectionary is also published in a 3 volume format; see above reference.
74a. Liturgical calendar: Part Five, Church Norms, II- Requisites for the Celebration of the Mass, Liturgical Seasons & Feasts and Liturgical Seasons & Related Colors.
74b. Ceremonies of the Modern Roman Rite: Bibliography, Other Catholic Publications.

B) For Those attending to Sacred Vessels and Linens: [75]

61. Name the **sacred vessels** and the **sacred linens** used for the celebration of the Eucharist?
*The sacred vessels used for the celebration of the Eucharist are the **paten**, the **chalice**, and the **ciborium**; and the sacred linens are the **corporal**, the **pall**, and the **purificator**. Several chalices and purificators are often used when communion is given under both species.*

62. **After the Mass**, what does the **sacristan do** with the sacred vessels that were used for the Eucharist?
*Right after the Mass, the sacristan picks up from the **credence table**, the sacred vessels, cruets, decanter, wash plate(s), and sacred linens used for the Eucharist and takes everything **back to the sacristy.** Although the priest has already **purified** the sacred vessels after the communion, out of reverence for the Blessed Sacrament that was consecrated in these vessels, the sacristan **rinses** the chalice(s) and ciborium with water and **pours the rinse water into the sacrarium.** If needed he then **washes** the sacred vessels by hand with soapy water, before drying them and putting them back in their safe place in the sacristy.*

63. What is a **sacrarium**?
*A sacrarium is a **basin**, or sink, without faucets and **with a drain** that goes directly to the **earth**. A sacrarium is installed in every sacristy in order to dispose worthily of rinse water containing **holy remnants from the Eucharist.** This rinse water should never be poured into a regular sink which drains into the sewage.*

64. Are the **wash plates**/basins, **cruets**, and **decanter** [75a] (wine pitcher) considered to be **sacred** vessels, and what should be done with the water and wine remaining in these after the Mass?
*No, the wash plate(s), cruets, and decanter are not considered to be sacred vessels, but **liturgical vessels**. Since the priest usually blesses the water in the cruet at the offertory, if there is any **water** left in the cruet after the Mass, it should be **poured into the sacrarium** or used to water the flowers and plants that grace the sanctuary. If there is any **wine left** in the cruet or in the decanter, it is carefully poured back into the Mass wine bottle. The decanter and the wine cruet are then washed, dried, and put away.*

---

75. Sacred Vessels & Linens: see also Part Three, Liturgy of the Eucharist, The Sacristy.
75a. Since the decanter is not to be used to consecrate the Blood of Christ, it is not considered a sacred vessel. See Part Three, Liturgy of the Eucharist, p. 143.

The water in the wash plate/basin that was used for the washing of the hands of the priest comes from the cruet of water that was **blessed** at the time of the offertory. Thus, this blessed water should be poured into the **sacrarium**. Then, since the extraordinary ministers used their wash plate/basin to **purify their fingers** after distributing Communion, this water contains **remnants of Hosts** and should also be poured into the **sacrarium**. If, unfortunately, there is no sacrarium in the sacristy, the water from the wash plates should be used to water the plants in the sanctuary or poured outside directly on the earth.

65. What does the sacristan do after the Mass with the **sacred linens** that were used during the celebration of the Eucharist?
Since the sacred **linens collect remnants** of the Body and Blood of Christ during the Mass, then after the Mass, these linens first need to be 'purified' before they are 'washed'. During the Mass, particles of Hosts might have fallen on the **corporal**, for example, during the 'Breaking of the Bread', while transferring Hosts after the communion, or during the purification of the sacred vessels. Some of the Precious Blood might also have dripped on the corporal. Thus "never flick a corporal open or shake it open in the midair"[75b] until it has been purified.

Purificators are used to wipe the rim of the chalice(s) during communion, to wipe remnants of Hosts from the paten and ciboria into the chalice and the priest's fingers during the purification, and then to dry the chalice(s). Thus after the Mass, the purificators **always contain remnants** of Host and of the Blood of Christ.

Therefore after the Mass, the sacristan, or another appointed person, must **handle with great reverence** the sacred linens that were used for the Eucharist. He should also make sure that the sacred linens containing Eucharistic remnants do not sit for days in the sacristy before they are attended to, and that these linens will not be 'washed'—in a regular sink or in the washing machine—until they have been '**purified**'.

The **manuterge** (hand towel) used by the **priest** to wipe his fingers during the 'washing of the hands' usually does not contain Eucharistic remnants. Thus, it does not need to be 'purified' before it is 'washed'. As to the **pall**, which is used to cover the chalice before and after the consecration, since it usually does not come in contact with the Blood of Christ, it does not need to be purified, nor washed, and may be put back in its place in the sacristy after the Mass.

75b. CMRR, Appendix 4, The Corporal, no. 822

66. Describe the **proper manner** to perform the purification of the sacred linens that were used for the Mass.
The proper manner to purify the sacred linens is as follows:
a) **soak the purificators** *in cool water for an hour or as needed— remember that these wine stains are really Christ's Blood;*
b) **rinse the corporal** *with water in the sacrarium, or, if needed, soak the corporal with the purificators;*
c) **pour** *the soaking water* **into the sacrarium***; and*
d) **hang the linens to dry***. This completes the purification of the purificators and the corporal.*
Pouring the soaking water into the sacrarium returns to earth any and all holy remnants from the Eucharistic meal, and hanging the sacred linens to dry allows the residual water from the purification to reverently evaporate into the air.

67. How should the sacred linens be purified if there is **no sacrarium** in the sacristy, or if the purification of the linens takes place at home?
If there is no sacrarium, after soaking the linens in a basin at the sacristy, or at home, reverently pour the soaking water outside on **the ground** *(away from a path or concrete)* **or** *use it to* **water plants***.* **Do not pour this water into a regular sink** *because it drains directly into the sewage.*

68. How should sacred linens be '**washed**' **after** they have been '**purified**'?
Once the sacred linens have been 'purified', they may be 'washed' with **soap and water***, either by hand or in the washing machine —at gentle cycle and apart from regular clothes. After the purification, if some of the sacred linens are* **stained***, for example, with the Blood of Christ, you may use a stain removing agent or a little chlorine. Be careful not to burn the linens by using too much chlorine. It is more important to purify the linens with proper reverence than to wash them until they appear to be immaculate.*

69. Is there a **specific way to fold and iron** the sacred linens after they have been washed?
Yes, there is a specific and purposeful way to fold and iron the sacred linens, and keeping them damp after they have been washed will facilitate their ironing.
• *The* **purificators***, which are in the shape of a rectangle and about half the size of a corporal, should be folded as follows:*
  - *in thirds lengthwise and then in half. The length of the folded linen offers proper presentation and use. Do not use starch.*

- The **corporal**, which is in the shape of a square of about the size of a man's handkerchief, is to be folded, and ironed, as follows;
  - fold a third of the right side in (the side with the **embroidered cross**), then fold a third of the left side in (on top), then fold a third of the top in, then fold a third of the bottom in (on top); hence it is folded into **nine square** sections (you may use starch).

The way to fold the corporal is important because it is related to the way the priest **unfolds and folds the corporal** on the altar, which is as follows:

"- Unfold the corporal, first to your left, then to your right, thus revealing **three squares**.

- Unfold the section farthest from you, away from yourself, thus making **six squares** visible.

- Finally, unfold the crease that is nearest to you, towards yourself, thus making all **nine squares** visible. Adjust the corporal so that it is about 3cm [one inch] from the edge of the altar.

- If there is a cross embroidered on one of the outer center squares, move the corporal around so that the **cross is nearest to you**.

- To fold the corporal [after the communion], reverse the above steps. Therefore fold the front three squares away from you, then fold the back three squares towards you and finally bring the right square and the left square onto the remaining central square to complete the process." [76]

Due to the way that the **corporal** is unfolded on the altar, if any particles of Host should fall on the corporal during the Mass, they will safely fall towards the center of the corporal when the priest folds the corporal after communion. The same corporal may be used for several Masses before being purified and washed.

Once the **purificator and the corporal** have been purified, washed, folded and ironed, they are placed back into their drawer in the sacristy.

Altar cloths need to be changed but only a few times a year, or if there is an "accident". They are to be purified and washed with the same care as used for purificators, and after ironing, they may be carefully rolled up and put away in their drawer in the sacristy.

---

76. CMRR, Appendix 4, The Corporal, nos. 818, 819, 820, 821, 823 (bold face added).

C) FOR ALTAR SERVERS:

70. Why should the servers **arrive** at the church ten to fifteen minutes **before the Mass starts**?
*The Servers, as well as **all the lay ministers** serving at the Holy Mass, should arrive at the church early enough so that they may have the time to properly prepare. The servers need time to:*
- **wash their hands**;
- **dress with their albs**;
- *review their **actions and positions** for the service of the Mass;*
- **inform the priest** *(or a lay minister in charge) that they have arrived, and find out if there is **anything special** for them to do during the Mass of that day; and*
- **recollect** *themselves before Mass.[77]*
*Arriving early gives servers and ministers the time to **form a unity** to better serve at the liturgy of the Mass.*

71. What is **the signal** given to the cross bearer to start, **or open,** the entrance procession?
*When the **entrance hymn** or **antiphon** begins it is usually the signal to start the entrance procession, but the celebrating **priest** is usually the one who gives the signal when he is ready. Someone may also ring the bell near the sacristy door.*

71a. What is the usual **order** of ministers in the **entrance procession**?
*The procession opens with the **cross bearer** holding the crucifix high and away from his body, with the figure of the crucifix facing forward. If incense is used for the Mass, the cross bearer is preceded by the **thurifer** (censor attendant). The one who opens the procession walks **fairly slowly**, giving the pace to the procession, followed by two altar servers walking side by side, who may act as **candle bearers**; then, the **deacon** or a **reader** follows carrying the **Book of the Gospels** slightly elevated in front of him, often followed by a second reader. In some instances, **extraordinary ministers** may be following, and then **concelebrating priests**. The **celebrating priest** always closes the procession. As they enter the sanctuary, those who are not carrying anything bow in front of the altar before taking their positions, while the others put what they are carrying at the appropriate places.*

72. During the Mass, when does the priest need assistance from the thurifer for incensing?
The thurifer might be needed for incensing during the Entrance Procession, the Veneration of the altar, before the proclamation of the Gospel, after the Offertory, and after the Consecration.[77a]

---

77. Preparation of the servers: see proposed prayer after the answer to question 84.
77a. Cf. GIRM [235] 276; Part Three, Liturgy of the Eucharist, Offertory, Incensing.

73. Why is it especially important for the servers and all those present in the sanctuary to have a **recollected attitude** during the Mass?
*A recollected attitude for those present in the sanctuary is especially important because they are seen by everyone in the church, and their recollected **attitude influences the assembly** in adopting a reverent attitude during the Mass.*

74. In some parishes, one of the servers is responsible for **holding the *Missal*** for the priest. How does the server **know when** it is the time to stand and hold the *Missal* for the priest?
*Since the priest usually gives him a sign, the server should follow closely what the priest does and says. But as a general rule, whenever the **priest stands at his chair** to speak, it is often to say a liturgical prayer or to give a blessing, and in both instances, he needs the server to come and hold the* Missal *for him. When holding the* Missal, *the server should stand a little to the left side of the priest in order not to block the assembly's view of the priest.*

74a. How do the servers assist the priest when it is time for the **proclamation of the Gospel**?
The thurifer may assist the priest by preparing the thurible during the Gospel Acclamation, and opening the procession to the ambo. He is followed by the two candle bearers and by the priest carrying the Book of the Gospels. *The candle bearers come and stand on each side of the ambo, facing one another, and the thurifer assists the priest in incensing the* Book of the Gospels *at the ambo before the proclamation of the Gospel.*[77b]

75. How do the servers know when it is **time to start assisting** the priest with their service at the altar for the Sacrifice of the Mass?
*The service at the altar begins with the **procession of the gifts**. The servers will know that it is time to start their service, when **after the General Intercessions**/Prayer of the Faithful, the priest gives them the signal by leaving his chair and standing either in front of the sanctuary or at the altar to receive the gifts. Thus, the servers need to follow the priest's actions closely.*

76. What are the **steps** that the servers should follow for the **service at the altar** during the Sacrifice of the Mass?
1. *If members of the **congregation present the gifts** (offerings), the celebrating **priest** walks to the front of the sanctuary **followed by the servers**. As the priest receives the gifts, he hands them to the servers who bring them to the altar.*

77b. Incensing the Book of the Gospels: cf. GIRM [95] 134. See also Part Three, Liturgy of the Word, Gospel.

*1a. If the **servers** are to **present the gifts** of bread and wine, then these would have been set on the credence table before the Mass. **If the priest** is to **prepare the altar**, he stands at the altar while the servers bring the gifts from the credence table. An acolyte or a server may prepare the altar but, only the priest or a deacon may prepare the gifts for the offertory, and **only a priest may offer** the Sacrifice of the Mass to God.* [78]

*2. One of the servers brings the **chalice** on which sits the **purificator**, the **paten** and the **host**, the **corporal** and the **pall**, while the other server brings the **ciborium** (ciboria) containing communion breads to be consecrated for the communion of the faithful; they present these to the priest at the altar.* [79]

*3. While the **servers go back to the credence** table, the priest unfolds the corporal on the altar, raises the paten with the Host over the altar, prays in thanksgiving to the Father, and then sets the paten on the corporal.*

*4. The servers come back to the side of the altar, one carrying the **wine cruet,** and the other the **water cruet.***

*5. Always starting with the **wine**, one of the servers hands the cruet to the priest, who pours the wine in the chalice and hands the wine cruet back to the server. The **other server** hands the **water cruet** to the priest, who pours a little water into the wine in the chalice and hands the water cruet back to the server.* [80]

*6. If **incense** is used at the Offertory, the thurifer then assists the priest in incensing the offerings, the cross, the altar, the priest, and the people.* [80a]

*7. The servers then walk back together to the credence table to gather the articles needed for the **washing of the hands** of the priest.*

*7a. One of the servers puts the **hand towel** on his left forearm and takes the **water cruet** with his right hand. The other server takes the **wash plate**/basin. Together they walk back to the side of the altar.*

---

78. "The altar is prepared with corporal, purificator, Missal, and chalice... by the deacon and servers. ..." NCUBK, PART II, no. 36; cf. GIRM [100] 139.
79. Presentation of the Gifts: see illustration at Part Three, Liturgy of the Eucharist, Offertory Rite, Procession of the Gifts; Using the burse and the chalice veil: see Liturgy of the Eucharist, Offertory Rites, Preparation of the Altar.
80. When there is a large assembly or Communion under both species is offered to all, the servers usually receive assistance from a minister to bring the additional chalices, the wine decanter, and ciboria of hosts to the altar.
80a. Incensing at the Offertory: Part Three, Liturgy of the Eucharist, Offertory, Incensing.

8. *One of the servers presents the **wash plate** in a manner so that the priest may place his hands over it. The other **server pours** some water on the priest's **fingers**, and then presents the priest with the **hand towel** hanging on his left arm so that the priest may dry his fingers.*

9. *A little **bow** is then usually exchanged between the priest and the servers. It shows the priest's appreciation for the servers' assistance, and they in turn show due respect for the holiness of the priest's function. It is also an indication for the servers that this part of the altar **service is completed**. The servers go back to the credence table where they **neatly place** the wash plate, the cruet, and the hand towel, and then **take their positions** in the sanctuary, which they will hold until communion.*

10. *The **next** action of the servers is the **ringing of the bell** at the **consecration** and at each **elevation** (see Question 82).*

77. Name the **three sacred vessels** that the servers bring to the altar during the offertory.
    *The three sacred vessels that the servers bring to the altar during the offertory are the **ciborium**, the **paten**, and the **chalice**.*

78. What are the **other vessels** that the servers bring to the priest at the altar during the offertory?
    *The other vessels brought to the altar by the servers during the offertory are the **cruets** containing the offerings of water and wine, and the **wash plate** for the washing of the hands of the priest. Since these vessels do not come directly in contact with the Body and Blood of Christ, they are not considered to be sacred vessels, but rather **liturgical vessels**.*

79. Name **three sacred linens** that the servers bring to the altar during the offertory.
    *The three sacred linens that the servers bring to the altar during the offertory are the **purificator**, the **corporal**, and the **pall**.*

80. What is the name of the **linen** that the server brings to the priest so that he can dry his fingers during the ritual of the **washing of the hands**?
    *The linen used by the priest during the ritual of the washing of the hands is called a **hand towel** or manuterge.*

81. Why does the priest **wash his hands** during the offertory?
*The priest washes his hands during the offertory as a **sign of purification** before he offers the sacrifice of the Eucharist.*

82. **How many times** does the server **ring the little bell** during the Mass and at what occasions?
*The server rings the little bell **three times** during the Mass:*
- * **once** during the **consecration**; at the invocation of the Holy Spirit, when the priest lays his hands over the offerings; then*
- * **once** at the **elevation of the Host**; when the priest elevates the Host for adoration; and*
- * **once** at the **elevation of the Precious Blood**; when the priest elevates the chalice for adoration.*
Each time he rings the bell, the server makes three rings: one for the Father, one for the Son, and one for the Holy Spirit.

82a. What other action may be performed by a server during elevation?
*If **incense** is used, the thurifer stands near the altar and incenses the Body and Blood of Christ during their **elevation**. [81]*

83. Once the servers have rung the little bell during elevation and incensed the Blessed Sacrament, what will be the servers' **next action** of service, and what should the servers do until then?
*The next action of the servers generally takes place **after the communion** of the faithful. Until then they should keep their position in a recollected attitude, thus inspiring the assembly to do likewise. However, in certain cases the servers might assist the priest during the communion by placing the **Communion-plate** under the chin of the communicants who receive the Host on the tongue.*

84. What is the name of **the ritual** that takes place after the communion, and what are **the actions** of the servers during this ritual?
*The name of the ritual that takes place after the communion is the **purification of the sacred vessels**.[81a] It may take place at the altar or at the credence table. The servers proceed as follows:*
1. *Once the priest is back behind the altar after the communion, **one of the servers** comes to the side of the altar with the **water cruet**.*

---

81. Cf. GIRM [109] 150; see also Part Three, Liturgy of the Eucharist, The Eucharistic Prayer, Consecration and Elevation.
81a. The purification ritual consists in the priest drinking the remaining Blood of Christ from the chalice, wiping all the remnants of Hosts from empty ciboria into the chalice, purifying his fingers, preparing the ablution, and drinking it. See Part Three, Liturgy of the Eucharist, Communion Rite, After Communion, Purification of the Sacred Vessels.

2. *Once the priest has wiped any remnants of Hosts from the empty ciboria into the chalice, the server hands the priest the* **water cruet.** *The priest puts his fingers over the chalice and pours some water into the chalice; he hands the cruet back to the server who returns with it* **to the credence** *table. The priest then prepares and drinks the ablution.*[82]

3. **Together** *the servers come* **back to the altar.** *The priest wipes the chalice with the purificator and places the sacred vessels and sacred linens in the same manner that the servers brought them to the altar during the 'procession of the gifts'.*[83] *After* **taking all** *the* **sacred vessels, linens,** *and* **cruets back** *to the credence table, and removing the* **Sacramentary**/*Missal from the altar, the altar is as it was before the Mass started; that is, dressed with the altar cloth, on which sit only the candles and a crucifix.*

4. *If the servers' seats are next to the priest's chair, as is the case in many parishes, then as the* **priest goes back** *to his chair, the* **servers walk back with him** *to their seats. Wherever the servers' seats are, at this time they go back to their places.*

5. *Then as the priest stands to say the prayer after communion, a server might stand in front of him to hold the* **Missal.**

6. *Finally, when the time comes to* **leave the sanctuary** *after the final blessing, the* **servers stand with the priest,** *one on each side,* **and—**except for the cross bearer and the candle bearer— **bow in front of the altar** *with the priest before leaving the sanctuary in a procession. The cross bearer leads, followed by the candle bearer, all the other ministers, and the priest; following in the same order in which they came into the sanctuary at the beginning of the Mass. If there is no procession then the servers and ministers* **quietly and reverently** *go back to the sacristy.*

PRAYER FOR SERVERS TO RECITE BEFORE THE MASS
Lord who said: "I am the living bread," You are the One gathering us here today to celebrate Your love for us. Thank You for giving me the joy to serve You at the altar. Grant me to serve with reverence and to respond to Your friendship every day of my life. Amen.

---

82. This ablution is composed of the remnants of Hosts from the empty ciboria, the remnants of the Precious Blood, and the water used to rinse the sacred vessel. See Part Three, Liturgy of the Eucharist, Purification of the Sacred Vessels.
83. See illustration, Part Three, Liturgy of the Eucharist, Procession of the Gifts.

D) For readers:

85. Describe the **appropriate way to dress** for serving as a reader for the Mass?
*Since the reader does not wear an alb over his regular clothes, to show honor for the Word of God, reverence for the sanctuary, and respect for the congregation, the reader should **dress nicely yet modestly.** Men and women readers should wear a jacket or a vest over their shirt or dress, and women's skirts should reach the knee.*

86. Why should the readers arrive at the church at least **fifteen minutes before the Mass** starts?
In addition to the reasons given in the answer to question 70, the readers should arrive early enough to have the time to review their readings before the Mass.

87. When should the readers **enter** the sanctuary; **how** should they proceed; and **where** should they **sit** during the Mass?
*When the readers enter the sanctuary and where they sit during the Mass varies according to the church design and the local customs. The **readers usually enter** the sanctuary with the **entrance procession** at the beginning of the Mass; and—except for the reader carrying the Book of the Gospels—, **bow** in front of the altar before taking their place in the sanctuary, that is usually in a pew or seat lining the wall **near the ambo.**[84] In some cases the readers sit in a front pew of the nave, and only enter the sanctuary for their readings.*

88. When it is time to do his reading, describe the **appropriate procedure** for a reader to approach the ambo.
*The reader should proceed as follows: once the **priest has finished speaking**, the reader stands, and, without haste, bows to the altar—or to the tabernacle if one is present in the sanctuary—, and then takes his place at the ambo. If he is **sitting in the nave**, once the **priest has finished speaking**, the reader **reverently** comes out of his pew and walks towards the sanctuary. Then, upon entering the sanctuary, he **stops and bows to the altar**—or the tabernacle—before taking his position at the ambo. In either case, after taking his place at the ambo and before he starts reading, the reader should discreetly verify that the Lectionary is opened to the right page and determine where the text begins and ends; this should really be done before the Mass.*

---

84. Ministers entering the sanctuary: see Part Three, Liturgy of the Word, Introductory Rites, Entrance Procession. See also question 71.

89. Where in the sanctuary is the **ambo** usually located and why?
*In order for the reader to be seen and heard by all, the ambo is usually located **in the front** of the sanctuary, and traditionally on the **left side** as seen from the nave.*[84a]

90. What are the **main qualities** of a good reader?
*A good reader **proclaims** the Word of God **loudly enough**, and **slowly enough**, for everyone in the church to hear and understand the reading, while **pausing** and making **intonations** in a manner that **promotes the spirit** of the message. Since he is not making a speech, he may abstain from making eye contact with the congregation, which tends to distract people from the Word of God Itself. Readers should be **familiar with the Lectionary** and the cycle of readings, so that they may know how to find the appropriate readings for the day.*

91. What is the **book** that the deacon, or a reader, carries in the **entrance procession**? Is this the book from which the reader will read?
*The book that the deacon, or a reader, carries in the entrance procession is the **Book of the Gospels**, and no, it is **not the book** from which the reader reads, but rather it is the book from which the celebrating priest proclaims the Gospel.*

92. What is the name of the **book** from which **the reader reads** the Word of God, and where in the sanctuary is it placed before the Mass starts?
*The name of the book from which the reader reads the Word of God is called the **Lectionary**, and it is placed on the ambo before the Mass starts. (Also see answer to question 57).*

93. What is the name given to each of the **four** scripture **readings** read during the Mass, and from which **books** of the bible are they taken?
The names of the four readings and their sources are as follows:
- *the **First** Reading is usually from one of the books of the **Old Testament** [84b] (excluding the Book of Psalms);*
- *the **Responsorial Psalm** is usually from the Book of Psalms;*
- *the **Second Reading** is usually taken from the writings of one of the **Apostles** in the New Testament: the Epistles, the book of Acts, or the book of Revelation; and*
- *the **Gospel** Reading is **always** taken from the Gospel of **Jesus Christ** according to one of the four Evangelists.*
*During **weekday** Masses, there is only **one reading**— from either the Prophets (Old Testament) or the Apostles (New Testament except the Gospels)—then, the Responsorial Psalm and the Gospel Reading.*

84a. See Part Five, Church Norms, I- Arrangement and Furnishing of Churches, the Ambo & the Crucifix; Part Two, f) Liturgy Team.
84b. During Easter Season, the First Reading is taken from the Acts of the Apostles.

94. What are the **concluding words** pronounced by the reader at the end of the First and Second Reading?

*At the end of the **First** and **Second** Reading the reader says the concluding words: **The Word of the Lord**, to which the assembly responds: Thanks be to God.*

When the reader has concluded his reading(s), before leaving the ambo he turns and bows to the altar—or the tabernacle if present in the sanctuary—, and then reverently returns to his seat.

95. Does the **assembly** participate in the reading of the **Responsorial Psalm**, and if so, how?

*Yes, the assembly participates in the reading of the Responsorial Psalm by **saying the 'responsorial'** after each verse of the Psalm. Indeed, the word 'responsorial' indicates that a 'response' is to be given, and that this is a bilateral reading. Thus, the **reader shall pause** at the end of each verse, as indicated in the text, in order to allow the people to say the 'responsorial'. The **reader does not say** the 'responsorial' with the assembly. Since the psalms are hymns, it is **appropriate to sing** the Responsorial Psalm. In many parishes, at the Sunday Mass the **cantor** sings the whole Psalm and the people sing the Responsorial.*

96. Besides the four readings mentioned in the answer to question 93, what **two other texts** are usually read by **lay readers** during the Mass?

*Besides the four readings—which, except for the Gospel, are usually read by a lay reader—the two other texts that are read by a lay reader during the Mass are the verse of the **Gospel Acclamation** (Alleluia versicle) and the **General Intentions** (Prayer of the Faithful). Usually, the assembly sings the 'Alleluia' and the **reader** reads or sings the Gospel Acclamation versicle. In order for the priest, or deacon, to be able to place the Book of the Gospels on the ambo, once the reader is done reading the Acclamation versicle, he may be expected to **remove the Lectionary** from the ambo and place it on the ambo shelf, or another appropriate place.*

97. What are the names of the three **sacred books** that are used during the liturgy of the Mass?

*The names of the three sacred books that are used during the liturgy of the Mass are the **Sacramentary**, the **Lectionary**, and the **Book of the Gospels** (also see the answer to question 57).*

98. What does a reader need to know about the **cycles for Holy Scripture readings**?
See the answer to question 58; and Part Five: Church Norms, II-Requisites for the Celebration of the Mass, Cycles for Holy Scripture Readings; Catholic Glossary, Lectionary.

99. What is the name of the **sacred book** from which the priest or deacon reads the **Gospel**, and how is it introduced during the liturgy of the Mass?
*The name of the sacred book from which the priest or deacon reads the Gospel is called the '**Book of the Gospels'**. It is first introduced by being carried **elevated** in the entrance procession at the beginning of the Mass, and then it is set on a book stand in a **place of honor**, on or near the altar. Then, during the Gospel Acclamation (the Alleluia) the priest carries the Book of the Gospels in a **procession** from the altar to the ambo, preceded by the thurifer and two candle bearers. Before proclaiming the Gospel, the priest **incenses** the Book of the Gospels while the **candle bearers** stand on each side of the ambo, facing one another.*

100. Why is **a more important place** given to the **Gospel** Reading than to the other readings?
*A more important place is given to the **Gospel** Reading than to the other readings because the Gospel is the summit of the liturgy of the Word. It is the Good News of our redemption, it is the **teaching of Jesus Christ**, Who is the Word of God incarnated. The **truths that Jesus teaches** us in the Gospel **are superior** to those brought to us through the **Prophets** of the Old Testament, and through the **Apostles** of the New Testament. The Gospel is the **summit of divine revelation**.[85] The Gospel is the reading reserved for the priest, or deacon, because during the Mass the priest acts in the person of Christ. Thus it is desirable to reserve the priest for the Gospel reading, while other readings should be done by lay people.*

All who serve as lay liturgical ministers should pray before the Mass for God's assistance in order to serve Him worthily. Besides the prayer suggested in the answer to question 84, readers may also recite the following brief prayer right before they read:
Lord, may you be in my heart and on my lips,
so that I may worthily proclaim Your Word, and
may Your word give life to Your people. Amen.

---

85. Superiority of the revelation of the Gospel: see CCC 75-76, 1965-1970.

E) For Extraordinary Ministers of Holy Communion: [86]

101. Who can become an extraordinary **minister** of Holy Communion?
*To become an extraordinary minister of Holy Communion, one must first **be a communicant** himself; then, he must be in **full communion** with the Church; be able to set a **proper example** among the congregation; show great **reverence** for the Blessed Sacrament—especially when distributing Holy Communion—; and have a special **devotion** for the Eucharist. Extraordinary ministers should be in good standing with the Church, and in a **state of grace** when distributing the Eucharist.*

101a. In regards to the prior question, **how does one usually become** an extraordinary minister of Holy Communion?
*To become an extraordinary minister of Holy Communion, one must receive a **preparation**: "...Extraordinary ministers of Holy Communion should receive sufficient **spiritual, theological, and practical** preparation to fulfill their role with **knowledge and reverence**. ..."* [87] *Thereafter, one may be temporarily deputed by his bishop to act as an extraordinary minister (e.g. for one to three years). It is desirable that extraordinary ministers be provided with a mandatory **yearly retreat** to help them renew their knowledge, faith, love, and reverence for the Blessed Sacrament.*

102. What is the **difference** between an **ordinary minister** and an **extraordinary minister** of Holy Communion?
*"...the **ordinary** minister of Holy Communion is the Bishop, the Priest and the Deacon. **Extraordinary** ministers of Holy Communion are those instituted as acolytes and the faithful so deputed. ..."* [88] *Therefore, it is **ordinarily** the office of **the priest** to distribute Communion, and it is **extraordinary** to depute a **lay minister** to distribute Holy Communion.*

102a. In **what circumstances** may the extraordinary ministers be requested to assist with distributing communion?
*When the **size** of the congregation requires it, and when **no other priests**, or deacon, are available, the extraordinary ministers may be requested to assist with distributing communion; they may not distribute communion while clergy remain seated in the sanctuary.*

---

86. See Part Three, Liturgy of the Eucharist, and read all parts on the 'Communion Rite'.
87. NCUBK, Part II, No.28 (bold face added).
88. *Instruction on certain questions regarding the collaboration of the non-ordained faithful in the sacred ministry of priest*, Practical Provisions, Article 8, The extraordinary minister of Holy Communion, §1 (bfa), Congregation for the Clergy.

103. Describe the appropriate **clothing** that one should wear while **serving as** an extraordinary **minister** of Holy Communion?
*"To distinguish their duty from the "ordinary" ministries derived from ordination, institution (acolytes) or association with the clergy (servers), [the extraordinary **ministers**] normally **do not wear robes**. ..."* [89] *Their lay dress should always be* **modest and neat**. [89a]

104. Why should the extraordinary ministers **arrive** at the church at least **fifteen minutes before** the Mass starts?
Extraordinary ministers should arrive early enough so that they are better prepared to **fulfill their duty** *and* **honor** *the Holy Eucharist. Besides the fact that they need time to recollect before the Mass, they also need to find out before the Mass starts how to proceed at communion. Are they really needed, and if so what will be* **their position** *in the nave to distribute the Eucharist; will communion be distributed under* **both species**—*which is always up to the celebrating priest and not to the lay ministers—; if so, will they be ministering a* **ciborium** *of Hosts or a* **chalice** *of the Precious Blood. Extraordinary ministers should wash their hands before the Mass, and save them for the Eucharist by abstaining from shaking hands during the Mass. A minister that has a cold, the flu or something likewise contagious should* **abstain** *from distributing Holy Communion.*

105. Name the **sacred vessels** and the **sacred linens** that are used for the celebration of the sacrament of the Eucharist?
The sacred vessels used for the Eucharist are the **chalice**, *the* **ciborium** *(ciboria), and the* **paten**. *The sacred linens used for the Eucharist are the* **corporal**, *the* **purificator**, *and the* **pall**. *It is not unusual to have several chalices and several purificators for Masses with communion under both species.*

106. At what **moment** of the Holy Mass does **Jesus Christ become truly and really present** in the Eucharist?
Jesus becomes truly and really present in the Eucharist at the moment of the **Consecration.** *That is, the moment of the Mass when the priest—acting in the person of Christ—holds the bread and wine offerings while repeating the words by which Jesus instituted the Eucharist: This is my Body... This is my Blood... . At that moment, there is a transubstantiation and Jesus becomes incarnated in the Eucharistic species on the altar.* [89b]

---

89. CMRR, Appendix 1, no. 779 (bold face added).
89a. Dress code: also see the answer to question 85.
89b. The Real Presence: also see Part Five, Appendix 'B', Eucharistic Miracles.

107. What does the word **'transubstantiation'** mean?
The word 'transubstantiation' indicates that "by the consecration of the bread and the wine there takes place a change of the whole substance of the bread into the substance of the body of Christ our Lord and of the whole substance of the wine into the substance of his blood," [90] *and this, even though the appearances of the species of bread and wine remain the same.*

108. For **how long** is **Jesus Christ present** in the Holy Eucharist?
Jesus Christ is present in the Blessed Sacrament, Body and Blood, Soul and Divinity, for as long as the eucharistic species subsists in the form of the bread and wine. [91]

109. What does the word **commingling** mean?
When at the 'breaking of the bread', the priest breaks a small piece off from the large Host and puts it in the chalice that contains the Precious Blood of Christ, there is mingling of the Body and Blood of Jesus Christ in the chalice; that is called the commingling.

110. After the 'Breaking of the Bread', if extra Hosts are needed from the Eucharistic reserve, why is it more appropriate that a **priest**, rather than an extraordinary minister, **opens the tabernacle** and brings the ciboria of Hosts to the altar?
If extra Hosts are needed, it is more appropriate that a priest rather than a lay person opens the tabernacle, because the priest is the first minister of Holy Communion. Moreover, more respect and reverence for the Eucharist is generated among the assembly when a priest or a deacon, rather than a lay person, opens the tabernacle and brings the ciboria of consecrated Hosts to the altar before distributing the Hosts to the faithful at communion. Furthermore, using Hosts from the reserve for communion during the Mass should not be a standard practice, because the faithful should receive Hosts consecrated at the same Mass. [92]

111. What is a **Eucharistic reserve**?
A Eucharistic reserve is another word for tabernacle, which is a receptacle, usually beautifully ornate, in which the Blessed Sacrament is reserved (kept) in churches, chapels, and oratories. [93]

90. CCC 1376 (bold face added).
91. Cf. CCC 1377.
92. Cf. GIRM [56h] 85; also see Part Three, Liturgy of the Eucharist, Communion Rite, The Eucharistic Reserve.
93. Tabernacle: Part Five, Church Norms, I- Arrangement and Furnishing of Churches, The Tabernacle; Catholic Glossary.

112. At **what moment** of the Mass do the extraordinary ministers enter the sanctuary, and how should they proceed?

*"During the **Communion of the celebrant**, not earlier, extraordinary ministers come to the sanctuary. They first **genuflect** to the Eucharist on the altar. Then they may go to the **credence** table to **cleanse their hands**. ..."*[94] *"... [Extraordinary ministers of Holy Communion] should not approach the altar before the priest has received Communion, and they are always to receive from the hands of the priest celebrant the vessel containing either species of the Most Holy Eucharist for distribution to the faithful."* GIRM [-] 162.

113. Since the extraordinary ministers '**washed**' their hands before the Mass, why do they need to '**cleanse**' their hands at the credence table before the communion?

*There are **two reasons** for extraordinary ministers to cleanse their hands before the communion. First, since it is a **purification** ritual, as they cleanse their hands, extraordinary ministers should pray to God to be purified, and to be made worthy to distribute the Body and Blood of Christ. They could quietly say the prayer that the priest says when he cleanses his hands before the offertory: "Lord, wash away my mistakes; cleanse me from my sin". However, the cleansing of the hands of the priest has a deeper meaning, since he does so in order to be made worthy not only to touch the Eucharist, but also to offer the Eucharistic sacrifice.*

*Secondly, when the extraordinary ministers wash their hands in the sanctuary in front of all, it shows **respect** towards the assembly, as to signify to the communicants that they, who are about to distribute the Eucharist to them, have clean hands.*

*While washing our hands is about getting them **physically** clean, cleansing our hands is primarily about getting our hands and our conscience **spiritually** clean.*

114. What should the extraordinary ministers do **after cleansing** their hands for the communion?

*After cleansing their hands, "... [the extraordinary ministers] **stand to the side**, [in a common posture] not at or around the altar, because they are not concelebrants or deacons..., nor do they assist in breaking Hosts at the fraction, which is reserved for priests. The celebrant should bless them quietly before [the] "This is the Lamb of God." [After the communion of the celebrating priest], the **celebrant**, deacon or instituted acolyte **gives [the ministers] Holy Communion** before the servers, [and] preferably under both*

---

94. CMRR, Revised edition, 2005, Appendix 1, no. 781 (bfa).

kinds. [The extraordinary ministers] **do not give themselves Communion** *as if they were concelebrants, that is, simultaneously with the celebrant or by taking the Eucharist from the altar. ...[nor] take it directly ...from the tabernacle. Again the ceremonial signs truthfully define their ministry as "extraordinary" and hence dependent on the celebrant."* [95]

115. May an extraordinary minister of Holy Communion assist the priest at **the breaking of Hosts**?

No, an extraordinary minister **may not assist the priest at the breaking** *of Hosts at the time of the fraction at the 'Agnus Dei', nor at any time during or after the communion. Neither may an extraordinary minister* **transfer** *consecrated Hosts from one ciborium to another ciborium. These acts, which may only take place at the altar, are* **reserved to the priest** *or deacon. Doing otherwise can be considered a sacrilege.*

Moreover, since the Blood of Christ is to be consecrated directly in the chalices that are to be used for the communion, under no circumstances may the Blood of Christ be transferred from one sacred vessel to another: "... the **pouring of the Blood of Christ** *after the consecration from one vessel to another* **is completely to be avoided**, *lest anything should happen, that would be to the detriment of so great a mystery. ..."* [96]

116. After their communion, how should the extraordinary ministers proceed **once they have received** from the priest **a sacred vessel** containing one of the Eucharistic species?

After receiving a ciborium of Hosts or a chalice of the Blood of Christ, the extraordinary ministers **follow the priest(s)** *and deacon out of the sanctuary and into the nave, where they* **take their position**—*which should always be agreed upon before the Mass and not improvised at the time of the Communion—and then, they* **distribute the Communion** *to the faithful according to local practice.* [97] *"Extraordinary* **ministers are not to distribute** *Holy Communion while ordinary ministers, such as* **concelebrants or clergy** *in choir, remain seated. ..."* [98]

---

95. CMRR, Appendix 1, no. 781 (bold face added).
96. *Redemptionis Sacramentum*, no. 106 (bold face added).
97. How to minister Communion: extraordinary minister should study all the text found in Part Three, Liturgy of the Eucharist, Communion Rite: from 'Communion Procession' through 'Cleansing of Hands'.
98. CMRR, Appendix 1, no. 784 (bold face added), cf. *Response of the Pontifical Commission for the Authentic Interpretation of the Code of Canon Law*, February 20, 1987, ordered to be published in *L'Osservatore Romano*, by Pope John Paul II, June 1, 1988; see *L'Osservatore Romano*, English edition, July 25, 1988, p. 8.

117. How should the extraordinary **ministers proceed after** they have finished **distributing communion**?

*Once they have finished distributing communion, the extraordinary ministers go back to the altar and "...**give the vessel** to the celebrant, deacon or acolyte, or place it on the altar. Each **genuflects** [to the Eucharist on the altar, and those who distributed the Hosts] go to the credence table to **cleanse** [their] fingers before **returning** to their places among the assembly. They do not purify the sacred vessels."* [99] *Before giving back the chalice, extraordinary ministers are usually expected to **drink the Blood** of Christ remaining in the chalice that they used to minister the Eucharist.*

118. Why do the extraordinary ministers of Holy Communion need to **cleanse** their **fingers after the communion**?

As the priest cleanses his fingers during the purification of the sacred vessels after the communion, [100] *the extraordinary ministers that have **distributed the Hosts** must cleanse their fingers after communion because **remnants of Host** are more likely left **on their fingers**. Thus, they go to the credence table and use the same wash plate that they used before the communion, and dry their fingers with a purificator. Then after the Mass, the water contained in this wash plate will be poured into the **sacrarium**.* [101]

119. Do extraordinary ministers **assist the priest** in the **purification** of the sacred vessels?

*"Extraordinary **ministers do not purify** the sacred vessels."* [101a] *However, in answer to a request from the USCCB, the Holy See has issued a decree, making an exception to this rule for the U.S.A. for a period of three years, expiring in March of 2005.* [102]

120. What do the extraordinary ministers do **once they have cleansed** their hands?

*Once they have cleansed their hands, the extraordinary ministers have **completed** their duty. Thus, they **leave** the sanctuary making a **bow** to the altar, or tabernacle, and they reverently go **back to their pews** among the assembly and recollect.*

---

99. CMRR, Appendix 1, no. 782 (bfa). See answer to Q. 119 & footnote 102 here below.
100. See Part Three, Liturgy of the Eucharist, Communion Rite, After Communion, Cleansing of Hands.
101. See Part Three, Liturgy of the Eucharist, After the Mass, The Sacristy.
101a. Only a priest, deacon or instituted acolyte can purify the sacred vessels: cf. GIRM [238] 279.
102. Part Three, Liturgy of the Eucharist, Communion Rite, After Communion, p. 151, paragraph with footnote 137.

F) FOR CHOIR DIRECTOR/CANTOR AND MUSICIANS:

121. **Where in the church** should the choir and musical instruments be placed for the Mass?
*The choir should be placed in **the nave** among the assembly of the faithful. However, its special function should stand out clearly.*[103]
✝*"The organ and other lawfully approved musical instruments are to be placed in an appropriate place so that they can sustain the singing of both the choir and the congregation... ."*[103a] *However, since the **sanctuary is reserved for the sacrifice** of the altar and the proclamation of the **Word of God**, the sanctuary is not to be used by the choir nor the organ or other musical instruments.*[103b]

122. What is the **role of the choir** and the musicians?
*The role of the choir and the musicians is to **foster** the **participation** of the assembly. Their role is not to give a recital or a concert.* [104]

123. Is it **mandatory** to have singing during the Mass?
*Although not mandatory, singing is **recommended** for Masses celebrated with a congregation, especially on Sundays and on holy days of obligation.*[104a]

123a. **How many hymns** are usually sung during the Sunday Mass, and do any of them have a **special status**?
*There may be as many as **twelve** hymns **sung by all** during the Mass, plus some Eucharistic hymns sung by **the priest alone**, and the 'Amen' sung by all at the end of the great Eucharistic Prayer.*[104b] *Among these twelve hymns, **eight** have a special status because they are either integral parts of the Order of Mass—the Kyrie, Gloria, Sanctus, Memorial Acclamation, Our Father, and Lamb of God—, or of the Scripture Readings of the day—the Responsorial Psalm and Gospel Acclamation verse. Thus, the songs chosen for these **eight** hymns, must contain the exact words as found in the Missal and in the Lectionary."It is **not permitted to substitute other chants** for those found in the Order of Mass, such as the [Kyrie, Gloria, Sanctus, Anamnesis, Our Father, and the] Agnus Dei."* [104c]

---

103. Cf. GIRM [274] 312.
103a. GIRM [275] 313.
103b. Cf. GIRM [258] 295.
104. Cf. GIRM [63] 103; [64] 104. See also Part Two, p.42
104a. Cf. GIRM [77] 115.
104b. Cf. GIRM [108] 147.
104c. GIRM. [-] 366. The same rule applies to the responsorial Psalm and the Gospel Acclamation verse, cf. GIRM [36] 61, [37] 62.

123b. Can you name the **four other** hymns and describe their purpose?
The four other hymns sung by all during the Mass are as follows:
Opening song: *opens the celebration, intensifies the unity of the assembly, leads their thoughts to the liturgical theme, and accompanies the entrance procession (cf. GIRM [25] 47). It may continue during the incensing of the altar. Another hymn may be played if there is a blessing of the people with holy water (p. 53);*
Offertory song: *accompanies the procession of the gifts. It continues until the gifts have been placed on the altar and during the incensing of the gifts if such is the case (cf. GIRM [50] 74);*
Communion song: *begins during the priest's communion and may continue until all faithful have received. It "...expresses the communicant's union in spirit by means of the unity of their voices, to show joy of heart, and to highlight... the communitarian nature of the procession... ." (GIRM [56i] 86). A hymn that favors meditation may be played after communion (cf. GIRM [56j] 88);*
Recessional hymn: *should express thanksgiving for the Mass, and the joy to be sent to proclaim the Good News.*

124. What are the general **rules** and attributes **concerning the choice** of liturgical hymns?
✣ *"...Gregorian chant holds pride of place because it is proper to the Roman Liturgy. Other types of sacred music, in particular polyphony, are in no way excluded, provided that they* **correspond to the spirit** *of the liturgical action and that they* **foster the participation** *of all the faithful."*[105] *The chosen hymns should promote recollection and never be a distraction from the sacred spirit of the Mass.*

125. How can the cantor and/or musicians **promote the sacredness** of the Eucharistic prayer?
Except for the Sanctus, the Memorial Acclamation, the Our Father, and the Lamb of God, the cantor and/or musicians can promote the sacredness of the Eucharistic prayers by making sure that ✣ *"...while the priest is speaking these texts, there should be no other prayers or singing, and the organ or other musical instruments* **should be silent."** [106] *Thus, the music should end before the celebrating priest starts to recite the Eucharistic Prayer, and even before the Offertory prayer: 'Blessed are you Lord...'; so that the faithful may follow closely the holy sacrifice of the Mass. Background music tends to put into the background what should be foremost and dominant. So, whenever the priest speaks there should be no singing and/or music.*[107]

---

105. GIRM [19] 41, cf. SVEC, Constitution on the Sacred Liturgy, *Sacrosanctum Concilium*, no. 116; cf. also Sacred Congregation of Rites, Instruction *Musicam sacram*, On music in the Liturgy, 5 March 1967, no. 30.
106. GIRM [12] 32 (bold face added).
107. See also Part Three: Offertory Rites, p.90, Sacred Silence; p. 97, Eucharistic Prayer and footnote 32.

Signs & Abbreviations

The following signs are used in this book:

✠	Indicates quotes taken from the *Roman Missal,* including OM (the Order of Mass) and GIRM, (General Instruction of the Roman Missal. See 'Notes to the reader', p. iv.
✠	Used to indicate when, during the Mass, the priest makes the sign of the cross over the gift offerings, the water or salt, the deacon, the people ... as a sign of his blessing.
ΑΩ	Alpha and Omega, *(Rev 22:13)"I am the Alpha and the Omega, the first and the last, the beginning and the end."* They are the first and last letters of the Greek alphabet.

The following abbreviations are used in this book:

AAS	*Acta Apostolicae Sedis*
bfa	**bold face added**
CB	Ceremonial of Bishops
CCC	Catechism of the Catholic Church
CCEO	Corpus Canonum Ecclesiarum Orientalium
CE	Catholic Encyclopedia
CIC	Codex Iuris Canonici (The Code of Canon Law)
CMRR	Ceremonies of the Modern Roman Rite
DR	Douay-Rheims, bible
DS	Denzinger-Schönmetzer, *(1965) Enchiridion Symbolorum, definitionum et declarationum de rubus fidei et morum*
DV	*Dei Verbum*
GIRM	General Instruction of the Roman Missal
IHS	In Greek, the first three letters in the name of Jesus
LG	*Lumen gentium,* Vatican II document
MF	*Mysterium fidei,* Vatican II document
NAB	**New American Bible**
NCCB	National Conference of Catholic Bishops - U.S.A.
NCUBK	Norms for the Distribution and Reception of Holy Communion under Both Kinds, see bibliography
OM	The Order of Mass, from the *Roman Missal*
PG	J.P. Migne, ed., Patrologia Graeca (Paris, 1857-1866)
PL	J.P. Migne, ed., Patrologia Latina (Paris, 1841-1855)
PR	*Pontificale Romanum* (The Roman Pontifical)
RCIA	The Rite of Christian Initiation of Adults
RR	*Rituale Romanum* (The Roman Ritual)
SC	*Sacrosanctum Concilium* (Constitution of the Sacred Liturgy)
SCh	*Sources Chrétiennes* (Paris:1942-)
STh	*Summa Theologiae, St.Thomas of Aquinas*
SVEC	Second Vatican Ecumenical Council
USCCB	United States Conference of Catholic Bishops

296

BIBLIOGRAPHY

Church Documents

✠ *The Roman Missal (Sacramentary),* for use in the Dioceses of the U.S.A., English translation by International Committee on English in the Liturgy, Inc., the Catholic Book Publishing Co., New York, 1974.

✠ *General Instruction of the Roman Missal, Third Edition*, International Committee on English in the Liturgy, Inc., United States Conference of Catholic Bishops, Washington, D.C., 2003.

• *The Roman Ritual,* translation of *'Rituale Romanum'*, by Philip T. Weller, S.T.D., The Bruce Publishing Company, Milwaukee, 1964.

• *Catechism of the Catholic Church*, the United States Catholic Conference, Inc., 1994—Libreria Editrice Vaticana.

• *Ecclesia de Eucharistia*, Apostolic Letter on the Eucharist in its relation to the Church, Pope John Paul II, Vatican Press, April 17, 2003.

• *Redemptionis Sacramentum*, Instruction on certain matters to be observed or to be avoided regarding the Most Holy Eucharist, Congregation for Divine Worship & the Discipline of the Sacraments, Rome, March 25, 2004.

• *Norms for the Distribution and Reception of Holy Communion under Both Kinds in the Dioceses of the U.S.A.*, Congregation for Divine Worship & the Discipline of the Sacraments, and United States Conference of Catholic Bishops, Prot. 1383/ 01/ L, March 2002.

• *Directory for Sunday Celebrations in the Absence of a Priest,* Congregation for Divine Worship & the Discipline of the Sacraments, June 2, 1988, International Committee for English in the Liturgy.

• *Collaboration of the Non-Ordained Faithful in the Sacred Ministry of Priest,* Congregation for the Clergy, Libreria Editrice Vaticana, Vatican City, August 15,1997.

• *Eucharistiae Sacramentum,* promulgating the editio typica of rites for Holy Communion and worship of the Eucharist outside Mass, Congregation for Divine Worship, June 21, 1973.

• *Inaestimabile Donum,* Instruction concerning Worship of the Eucharistic Mystery, Congregation for Divine Worship & the Discipline of the Sacraments, Rome, April 17, 1980.

• *Liturgiam Authenticam*, on the use of vernacular languages in the publication of the books of the Roman Liturgy, Congregation for Divine Worship & the Discipline of the Sacraments, March 28, 2001.

• *Mane Nobiscum Domine,* Apostolic Letter for the year of the Eucharist, Pope John Paul II, Libreria Editrice Vaticana, October 7, 2004.

• *Mediator Dei*, The Sacred Liturgy Encyclical Letter, His Holiness Pope Pius XII, November 20, 1947.

• *Mysterium Fidei*, Mystery of Faith, Encyclical Letter by His Holiness Paul VI, September 3, 1965.

• *Rosarium Virginis Mariae*, Apostolic Letter for the Year of the Rosary, Pope John Paul II, Vatican Press, October 16, 2002.

• *Sacrosanctum Concilium,* Constitution on the Sacred Liturgy, His Holiness Pope Paul VI, December 4, 1963.

Bibles

- *The Catholic Edition of the Revised Standard Version*, 1965,1966; *The New Revised Standard Version of the Bible, Catholic Edition*, 1989,1993, National Council of the Churches of Christ in the U.S.A.
- *The New American Bible for Catholics*, revised by Confraternity of Christian Doctrine, approved by National Conference of Catholic Bishops of the U.S.A., World Bible Publishers, Iowa, 1991.
- *The Holy Bible, Douay-Rheims version,* revised by Bishop Richard Challoner, A.D. 1749-1752, Baronius Press, London, 2003.
- *The New Testament, Revision of Challoner-Rheims version,* The Episcopal Committee of the Confraternity of Christian Doctrine, St. Anthony Guild Press, Paterson, New Jersey, 1941.
- *La Bible de Jérusalem*, Desclee de Brouwer, Paris, 1975.

Missals / Missalets

- *New St. Joseph Sunday Missal* (perpetual missal), 1999, themes and commentaries Rev. John C. Kersten, S.V.D.; and *New St. Joseph Weekly Missal* (perpetual missal), 2002, Scriptural commentaries Most Rev. James Sullivan, Catholic Book Publishing Co. N.J.
- *Magnificat* (monthly missal), Magnificat, Spencerville, MD.
- *Living with Christ* (monthly missal), Novalis, Montreal, Canada.
- *Missel Vespéral Romain* (perpetual missal), Dom Gaspar Lefebvre et les Moines Bénédictins de l'Abbaye de Saint-André, Latin/French, Apostolat Liturgique Abbaye De Saint-André, Bruges, Belgium, 1955.
- *Nouveau Missel Quotidien,* Latin/French, by a priest of the 'Oratoire de France', 1948, Librairie de l'Action Catholique, Quebec, Que., Canada.

Other Catholic Publications

- *A Handbook of Catholic Sacramentals*, Ann Ball, Our Sunday Visitor Publishing, 1991.
- *A Scientist Researches Mary The Ark of the Covenant*, Professor Courtenay Bartholomew, M.D., 101 Foundation, Asbury, N.J. 1996.
- *Catholic Almanac*, Our Sunday Visitor Publishing, Huntington, Indiana, 1999.
- *Catholic Encyclopedia*, Revised Edition, Rev. Peter M.J. Stravinskas, Our Sunday Visitor Publishing, 1998.
- *Celebrating the Eucharist,* The Liturgical Press, Saint-John's Abbey.
- *Cenacles of the Marian Movement of Priests, Purpose/Guide*, 2002; and, *To The Priests, Our Lady's Beloved Sons*, 18th edition English Edition, locutions received by Rev. Don Stefano Gobbi, 1998, published by the Marian Movement of Priests, St. Francis, Maine.
- *Ceremonies Of The Modern Roman Rite*, The Eucharist and the Liturgy of the Hours, Msgr. Peter J. Elliott, 1995, Copyright Ignatius Press.
- *Eucharistic Miracles & Eucharistic phenomena in the lives of the Saints*, Joan C. Cruz, Tan Books & Publishers, Rockford, Il. 1987.
- *Mary's House*, Donald Carroll, Christian Classics, Allen, TX, 2002.

- *My Daily Bread*, Fr. Anthony Paone, S.J., 1954, the Confraternity of the Precious Blood.
- *Story of a Soul,* The Autobiography of St.Thérèse of Lisieux, translation John Clarke, O.C.D., 3rd edition, ICS Publications, Washington, D.C., 1996.
- *The Book of Catholic Quotations*, Sources Selected and Edited by John Chapin, Published by Roman Catholic Books, New York, N.Y., 1984, Farrar, Straus & Giroux, Inc.
- *The Gospel for the Year 2000*, Rev. Laurent Gagnon, Penseurs du XXe Siècle, St-Jean Port-Joli, Québec, Canada, 1974.
- *The Sacraments and Their Celebration*, Fr. Nicholas Halligan, O.P., 1986 by the Society of St. Paul.
- *The Sources of Catholic Dogma*, Dr. Henry Denzinger, 1957 by B. Herder Book Co. Strong, LL.D. S.T.D., Thomas Nelson Publishers, Nashville, TN., 1990.
- *The Way of the Lord Jesus,* Dr. Germain Grisez, Vol. 1, *Christian Moral Principles*, 1983; Vol. 2, *Living a Christian Life*, 1993, Franciscan Herald Press, Chicago, IL.
- *Traditional Catholic Prayers,* compiled & edited by Msgr. Charles J. Dollen, Our Sunday Visitor Publishing, Huntington, IN., 1990.

Dictionaries
- *New International Bible Dictionary*, J.D. Douglas & M.C. Tenney editors, Zondervan Publishing House, Grand Rapids, MI, 1987.
- *A Catholic Dictionary*, Donald Attwater, Tan Books and Publishers, Inc. Rockford, IL,1997.
- *Shorter Oxford English Dictionary,* Fifth Edition, Oxford University Press, New York, NY, 2002.
- *Microsoft Encarta*, College Dictionary, St. Martin's Press, New York, NY, 2001, Copyright Bloomsbury Publishing, 2001.
- *Webster's New World Dictionary*, Michael Agnes editor in chief, Simon & Schuster, Macmillan, New York, NY, 1998.
- *Le Petit Larousse Illustré*, Dictionnaire Encyclopédique, Librairie Larousse, Paris, 1976.

Some Internet Sources
- *The Untied States Conference of Catholic Bishops*, (USCCB /NCCB): www.usccb.org
- *The Holy See* and Congregations of the *Roman Curia*: www.vatican.va
- *Adoremus*, Society for the Renewal of the Sacred Liturgy: www.adoremus.org
- *Behold the Lamb of God*, Eucharistic Miracles in the Twentieth Century: http://members.aol.com/bjw1106/euchmir.htm
- *Catholic Encyclopedia:* www.newadvent.org.
- *The Real Presence Association:* www.therealpresence.org

PENCIL DRAWINGS

The pencil drawings illustrating this book were taken from the *Nouveau Missel Quotidien*, published in Canada in 1948.

PERPETUAL MISSALS

Perpetual Sunday missals and weekday missals are available in most Catholic bookstores. They contain all the prayers of the Mass and the Holy Scripture readings for the whole year. [108] Some publications such as the Saint Joseph missal offer the weekday missal in two volumes; one that covers from Advent to Pentecost and a second one that covers the rest of the year. Perpetual missals usually contain all the Masses of the Catholic liturgical calendar year.

MONTHLY MISSALS

Yearly subscriptions to monthly Missals provide you with all of the Sunday and weekday Scripture readings and prayers of the Mass one month at a time. Here are a couple of publications:

Magnificat, www.magnificat.net

In the U.S.A. : P.O. Box 91,
Spencerville,
MD. 20868-9978 USA
1-800-317-6689 or 301-853-6600

Living with Christ,
Novalis, Periodicals Dept., www.novalis.ca

In the U.S.A.: P.O. Box 553, Rouses Point,
NY, USA 12979-0553
1-800-387-7164 or 416-363-3303

In Canada: 49 Front St. East, 2nd Floor,
Toronto ON, Canada M5E 1B3
1-800-387-7164 or 416-363-3303

The calendar of liturgical seasons, Solemnities, and major Feasts is the same all over the world in the Catholic Church, as is the cycle for Scripture readings. However, bible versions and the calendar of Feasts and Memorials for Saints vary according to the country's National Conference of Bishops, and/or local dioceses.

---

108. See Part Five: Calendar of Cycles for Holy Scripture Readings; Catholic Glossary, Lectionary; and Questions & Answers, Questions for Readers.